Handbook on
Personalized
Learning
for
States, Districts, and Schools

Edited by

Marilyn Murphy
Sam Redding
Janet S. Twyman

INFORMATION AGE PUBLISHING, INC.
Charlotte, NC • www.infoagepub.com

The Center on Innovations in Learning (CIL) is one of seven national content centers established by the U.S. Department of Education to work with regional comprehensive centers and state education agencies (SEAs) to build SEAs' capacity to stimulate, select, implement, and scale up innovations in learning. CIL focuses on two priorities: culture of innovation and personalized learning. Within the topic of culture of innovation, CIL examines change leadership, the science of innovation, and change processes: improvement, innovation, and transformation. Within the topic of personalized learning, CIL addresses several components, especially (a) learning technologies, (b) competency-based education, and (c) personal competencies.

CIL is located in the College of Education at Temple University, Philadelphia, Pennsylvania, in partnership with the Academic Development Institute (ADI), Lincoln, Illinois. Funded by the U.S. Department of Education, Office of Elementary and Secondary Education (OESE), CIL operates under the comprehensive centers program, Award # S283B120052-12A. The opinions expressed herein do not necessarily reflect the position of the supporting agencies, and no official endorsement should be inferred.

Library of Congress Cataloging-in-Publication Data

A CIP record for this book is available from the Library of Congress
http://www.loc.gov

ISBN: 978-1-68123-587-5 (Paperback)
    978-1-68123-588-2 (Hardcover)
    978-1-68123-589-9 (ebook)

Cover Design: Emily Sheley.

Printed in the United States of America

Dedication

This volume is dedicated to two colleagues who did much to shape our early and evolving thinking on what children need to learn and succeed. Dr. Herbert J. Walberg, who continues to be a valued friend and innovative thinker, and Dr. Margaret C. Wang, who, prior to her passing in 2000, inspired us to "try harder, the children can't wait."

Acknowledgements

This book would not be possible without the dedication and intellectual insight of a team of highly talented and motivated individuals.

We want to thank each of the authors for their attention to detail and thoughtful approach to the evolving topic of personalized learning.

The editorial and intellectual leadership of Dr. Stephen Page was invaluable. The expertise of his talented staff, Danielle Shaw and, especially, Robert Sullivan, who carefully proofed the whole manuscript, were likewise highly appreciated.

Thanks to Pam Sheley for her astute editorial insight and formatting talent, to Lori Thomas for her meticulous final read, to Emily Sheley for designing the cover and patiently addressing the team's feedback, and to Chris Sadjian-Peacock for seamlessly expediting the paper trail.

And finally, a heartfelt thank you to my co-editors Dr. Sam Redding and Dr. Janet S. Twyman for their comprehensive knowledge of the topic and willingness to read and reread.

—*Marilyn Murphy*

Table of Contents

V. Descriptive Studies of Specific Instructional Applications

Foreword

Marilyn Murphy

> *What the best and wisest parent wants for his child,*
> *that must we want for all the children of the community.*
>
> John Dewey, *The School and Society* (1907)

The *Handbook on Personalized Learning for States, Districts, and Schools* is presented by the Center on Innovations in Learning (CIL), one of seven national content centers funded by the U.S. Department of Education (ED). In 2014, CIL published the *Handbook on Innovations in Learning* that responded to a call by ED to "leverage the innovation and ingenuity this nation is known for to create programs and projects that every school can implement to succeed" (2010, p. v). With the recent advent of the Every Student Succeeds Act (ESSA; the new federal education law replacing No Child Left Behind) new opportunities are available for flexibility for states, districts, and schools in support of student learning. The "every" in ESSA presupposes an approach to learning that allows individual student growth for every student and for new ways for educators to implement a personalized learning approach that includes students advancing at their own pace toward rigorous benchmarks on a pathway to college, career, and citizenship; implementation of online and blended learning formats; and for rethinking and redesigning assessments to allow a personalized approach to assessing student growth rather than summative assessments.

The earlier volume focused on the harnessing of innovation to improve school success, and the authors presented chapters on defining innovation in the educational context and considered a number of best practices on emerging topics. Chapters in this new *Handbook* reflect the personalized learning goals of ESSA and reflect the view of personalized learning as a learning innovation.

There is no shortage of "personalized" in the current vernacular. The term "personal" is being widely applied to a variety of activities; there are personal trainers, personal shoppers, personal chefs, and myriad other ways that current culture and marketing encourage us to feel singled out for some particular category of attention that is supposedly

Handbook on Personalized Learning for States, Districts, and Schools, pages ix–xiv
Copyright © 2016 by Information Age Publishing

unavailable to others and specifically linked to our own "personal" profile. It sometimes seems that the term "personalized" has gone the way of the much-overused "special," so often applied as to become meaningless.

Likewise in educational discourse, "personalized" is cropping up in a number of applications and discussions. As often happens, dialogue and vocabulary sometimes outpace clarification and understanding. In introducing the *Handbook on Personalized Learning for States, Districts, and Schools*, it is important to examine briefly what we mean by personalized learning and to offer a robust definition developed by CIL around this evolving topic.

A Little Background

Educational research has long supported the pivotal importance of the relationship of the teacher and the student to a successful learning cycle; this concept is generally recognized as the ideal model for effective learning. The teacher–student relationship is critical to any definition of personalized learning. In addition to recognizing the impor-tance of developing and sustaining solid relationships, personalized learning varies the time, pace, and place of instruction. A number of learning strategies used in education over the years have contributed to these aspects of personalized learning, and the term has roots in several learning theories. Some precursors include Benjamin Bloom's theory of mastery learning, promoted in the '50s and '60s as an instructional method that advances students from one topic of study to the next based on their mastery of the current topic. Using mastery learning, the student has some control over pace. Also in the '60s, Fred Keller espoused a Personalized System of Instruction (PSI) that allowed each student to work on course modules independently. PSI is an individually paced, mastery-oriented teaching method which also incorporates behavior reinforcement theory. In the '90s, Margaret Wang researched the "adaptive learning environments model" (ALEM), an edu-cational approach that targeted instructional strategies to the needs of each student and was particularly responsive to diverse student populations in classrooms. Her ALEM was a component of Community for Learning, one of the first comprehensive school reform models validated by ED.

These early approaches to personalizing the teaching and learning experience were often referenced in their time as innovative and helped set the stage for a more complex theory of teaching and learning, a theory which is defined later in this foreword. Related work addressing student learning sometimes includes the term "deeper learning," coined by the William and Flora Hewlett Foundation, to identify certain dimensions of learning. Those dimensions of student learning have some congruency with what this book refers to as personalized learning.

ED's *National Educational Technology Plan* (2010) defined personalized learning as adjusting the pace of instruction (individualization), adjusting the instructional approach (differentiation), and connecting instruction to the learner's interests and experiences (see p. 12). This definition clarifies that personalization is broader than individualization or differentiation, in that it affords the learner a degree of choice about what is learned, when it is learned, and how it is learned. ED views this concept as having broad implica-tions for educational success. Richard Culatta, formerly the director of ED's Office of Educational Technology, has noted, "Personalized learning may be the most important thing we can do to reimagine education in this country" (2013, para 3).

In the *Handbook on Personalized Learning for States, Districts, and Schools*, CIL provides a guide for the reader interested in clarifying and organizing the many aspects of this evolving topic. The chapters developed by the author experts provide a comprehensive insight into a number of subtopics of personalized learning. The chapter authors show there is room for overlap and divergence of opinion concerning personalized learning. However, the reader of this volume will walk away with an understanding of the topic that is both broad and deep. Each of the chapters includes a list of Action Principles for States, Districts, and Schools that will be a valuable resource for implementation and sustainability of the principles of personalized learning. The descriptive studies in Section V provide insight into how the principles can be applied in real-world situations and across subject disciplines.

A Definition of Personalized Learning

The portfolio of work within CIL is organized around three aspects of personalized learning: (a) learning technologies—the tools and the processes of teaching and learning; (b) competency-based education—defining and validating competencies in an environment not bounded by time, place, or pace; and (c) personal competencies—the propellants of all learning that are especially valuable in a personalized context. These three pillars provide an organizing framework for this complex topic. The following definition is used to organize the work of CIL and the contents of the *Handbook*:

Personalized learning refers to a teacher's relationships with students and their families; the use of multiple instructional modes to scaffold each student's learning; enhancing the student's motivation to learn as well as enhancing metacognitive, social, and emotional competencies to foster self-direction and achieve mastery of knowledge and skills. Personalization ensues from the relationships among teachers and learners and the teacher's orchestration, often in co-design with students, of multiple means for enhancing every aspect of each student's learning and development. Personalized learning varies the time, place, and pace of learning for each student, enlists the student in the creation of learning pathways, and utilizes technology to manage and document the learning process and access rich sources of information.

In choosing the contributors to this volume, the editors Marilyn Murphy, Sam Redding, and Janet Twyman considered how each author's expertise would map onto CIL's broad definition of personalized learning.

Section I: Personal Competencies as Propellants of Learning

This section of the *Handbook on Personalized Learning for States, Districts, and Schools* includes chapters on the topic of the personal competencies of students, their habits of learning, and the pitfalls and successes of measurement. In his opening chapter, *Competencies and Personalized Learning*, Sam Redding sets the stage for the rest of the volume with a thorough explication of what is meant by personalized learning and untangles some of the conflicting aspects of this complex theory. Joe Layng picks up the discussion with *Converging Qualities of Personal Competencies*, taking a critical look through the lens of skill hierarchies and examining some of what he sees as overlap and interdependency among the competencies. Allison Crean Davis urges us to *Proceed With Caution: Measuring That "Something Other" in Students*, and poses the question, How do we know that we are measuring what matters most for students? Before looking at the "how" and a table of some promising measures with certain features which have been shown to be valid, Crean Davis takes us through a discussion of what we are measuring and some possible reasons to measure.

Section II: Students at the Center of Personalized Learning

Acknowledging that students are the central "person" in personalized learning, the authors in this section examine a variety of scenarios and processes that give students some control over their own learning, input that is elemental to personalized learning. Melinda S. Sota discusses one of the central concepts of personalized learning—learner choice. In *Co-designing Instruction With Students*, Sota not only provides a number of lists and suggestions to guide the reader through implementation of suggested strategies, but also considers how to maximize the positive effects of learner choice while minimizing the potential risks for students who may not be able to choose in their own best interests. In her second chapter, *Flipped Learning as a Path to Personalization*, Sota looks at two popular examples of teaching aided by technology—teaching practices that hold promise for improved instruction and personalizing education. Next, in the descriptive study *Empowering Students as Partners in Learning*, Kathleen Dempsey, Andrea D. Beesley, Tedra Fazendeiro Clark, and Anne Tweed describe the results and lessons learned from an IES-funded grant using formative assessment methods in math as part of the Assessment Work Sample Method (AWSM). They show that the infusion of assessment into the AWSM helped inform a shift in thinking from teaching as something teachers do to thinking of learning as something the learner does. In the final chapter in Section II, *Homeschooling: The Ultimate Personalized Environment*, William Jeynes notes that lessons have been gleaned from the current 1.77 million homeschooled students, a number that is expected to grow, and explores some of the particulars of this personalized environment that he suggests can be generalized to virtually any schooling situation.

Section III: Teaching and Technology in Support of Personalized Learning

Technology is viewed by some as the culprit in the growing depersonalization of our social world, untethering us from simple human interaction. But technology has a significant and thriving relationship to personalized learning and provides access both to managing and documenting the learning process and to accessing rich resources that might otherwise have been unattainable. In Section III, the authors explore a number of situations where teaching and technology provide significant support for a personalized learning environment. In her chapter, *Personalizing Curriculum: Curriculum Curation and Creation*, Karen L. Mahon presents what is meant by a personalized curriculum and how to be sure the curriculum one chooses is both appropriate and that the instruction is research based. Mahon identifies some best practices to follow and some to avoid in curating (selecting) a personalized curriculum. Well-constructed games encompass many of the elements of sound teaching and learning practice. In his chapter, *Choose Your Level: Using Games and Gamification to Create Personalized Instruction*, Karl M. Kapp looks at students' use of games for learning and discusses how game-based learning enables each student to work at her own pace; the student chooses the level and works through it successfully before advancing to the next level, a scaffolding process that is intrinsic to personalized learning. Kapp poses the questions, What game elements lead to learning, and how does one make choices about the best use for a classroom? His chapter walks the reader through the decision process. In *Personalizing Learning Through Precision Measurement*, Janet S. Twyman advocates for "precision measurement aided by technology and integrated with a strong relationship between the student and a caring teacher…instrumental in achieving the goals of personalized learning" (p. 147 in this volume). Twyman argues persuasively for a methodical approach to using measurement to sustain and advance personalized learning. Section III concludes with a discussion of learning analytics and large data sets, how they are used and how they might be more fully applied in education, including personalized learning. In *Using Learning Analytics in Personalized Learning*, Ryan Baker looks at some of the difficulties and the future potential for success with learning analytics in his exploration of this rapidly evolving and sometimes controversial field.

Section IV: The Personalized Learning Community: Teachers, Students, and Families

Much like the proverbial village it takes to raise a child, so too it takes a community of teachers, students, and families to embark on a successful personalized learning effort. In Section IV, chapters focus on relationships and community-building. *Preparing Educators to Engage Parents and Families*, by Erin McNamara Horvat, discusses what constitutes a valid connection between home and school and examines the institutional and social factors that have contributed to the current divide separating the two. Horvat argues that emerging teachers need to be self-aware and prepared to be supportive communicators and collaborators, building an environment of trust and reciprocity that truly values the assets of the home. In her chapter *Relationships in Personalized Learning: Teacher, Student, and Family*, Patricia A. Edwards looks backward—often from her own experience—to examine the history of segregation, and forward to consider inclusion as the key to creating and supporting a robust, personalized experience for all children. Edwards argues that a shared understanding of commonalities and differences among people can only help educators create a more educated (and literate) population. In their chapter entitled *Teacher–Student Relationships and Personalized Learning: Implications of Person and Contextual Variables*, Ronald D. Taylor and Azeb Gebre take a close look at students' developmental needs and adjustments in creating a personalized learning environment. Their chapter argues that process variables, personal variables, context variables, and time variables must be considered in the construction of a valid personalized learning relationship and environment. The final chapter in Section IV looks at how preparation of teachers for a personalized learning classroom relationship can be more effective than the current professional learning model. In *Personalizing Professional Development for Teachers*, Catherine C. Schifter looks at professional development for teachers through the lens of personalized learning. Schifter introduces two adult-learning theories to support "the self-directed approach of personalized professional development" (p. 222 in this volume). She also provides an example of some important elements to include in preparing teachers to succeed as valued contributors to a personalized learning community.

Section V: Descriptive Studies of Specific Instructional Applications

This last section of the *Handbook* contains four chapters that apply the principles of personalized learning in various contexts. Because these chapters are descriptive studies, they do not contain Action Principles; however, they do offer valuable reflections on the experience of applying personalized learning to instruction. In *Using Universal Design for Learning to Personalize an Evidence-Based Practice for Students with Disabilities*, Sara Cothren Cook, Kavita Rao, and Brian G. Cook take lessons from special education, noting that much of personalized learning has roots in the education of special populations. Cook and team discuss two specific contemporary educational initiatives—evidence-based practices and Universal Design for Learning—arguing that their application can help promote a personalized learning experience for students with disabilities. In her chapter, *Next-Generation Teachers in Linguistically Diverse Classrooms*, Tamara Sniad discusses how valuing all language can be used as a force to develop a personalized approach to teaching and learning in a linguistically diverse environment. Sniad provides a number of thoughtful strategies to support a community within a multiple-language environment. Frank J. Sullivan, Jr., looks at the literacy requirement of the Common Core State Standards and strategies for teaching in his chapter *On Personalized Learning in the Context of the Common Core Literacy Standards: A Sociocultural Perspective*. Sullivan argues that, although the Common Core standards prioritize literacy, the actual focus of those literacy standards is narrow. By focusing on "text-dependent reading" and "close reading" for facts, the experience of the student actively and thoughtfully engaging with the text suffers. Sullivan presents a framework that he uses to guide his own evolving teaching practice. The volume concludes with a descriptive study that includes suggested classroom activities and projects to personalize the learning experience. In *Social Studies and Personalized Learning: Emerging Promising Practices From the Field*, Christine Woyshner contends that the "learning goals of social studies and the aims of personalization overlap significantly to support the learning and development of diverse students in becoming engaged citizens in a democracy" (p. 273 in this volume). Woyshner supplements her discussion with classroom scenarios from her own teaching experience.

John Dewey argued that all students deserve an education suited for the students for whom we care most—our own children. Personalized learning has the potential to provide the optimal educational experience for every child. The intention of this *Handbook* is to advance the evolving scholarship on personalized learning and to provide a resource of strategies for those engaged in promoting and implementing personalized learning. Authors were not selected because there was necessarily agreement among them on all aspects of the topic; however, each chapter contributes to what this foreword and other sources have defined as CIL's "robust" definition of personalized learning. We look forward to our readers continuing the discussion and seeing the rewards of personalized learning in classrooms, schools, districts, and states.

References

Bloom, B. S. (1971). Mastery learning. In J. H. Block (Ed.), *Mastery learning: Theory and practice* (pp. 47–63). New York, NY: Holt, Rinehart, & Winston.

Culatta, R. (2013, February 6). Reimagining learning [Video file]. Boston, MA: TEDxBeacon-Street. Retrieved from http://www.tedxbeaconstreet.com/richard-culatta/

Dewey, J. (1907). *The school and society*. Chicago, IL: University of Chicago Press.

Keller, F. S. (1968). Good–bye, teacher. *Journal of Applied Behavior Analysis, 1*(1), 79–89.

Twyman, J., & Redding, S. (2015, January). *Personal competencies/Personalized learning: Lesson plan reflection guide*. Washington, DC: Council of Chief State School Officers. Retrieved from http://www.centeril.org/ToolsTrainingModules/assets/personalizedlearninglessonplanreflection.pdf

U.S. Department of Education, Office of Educational Technology. (2010, November). *Transforming American education: Learning powered by technology* (National Educational Technology Plan, 2010). Washington, DC: Author. Retrieved from https://ia600203.us.archive.org/5/items/ERIC_ED512681/ERIC_ED512681.pdf

Wang, M. C. (2000). *Adaptive education strategies*. Philadelphia, PA: Temple University Center for Research in Human Development and Education.

I. Personal Competencies as Propellants of Learning

Competencies and Personalized Learning

Sam Redding

This chapter elaborates on a definition of personalized learning, delineates aspects of competency inherent in the definition, traces the evolution of personalized learning, and explores the complementarity of the personal and the interpersonal in personalized education. The chapter addresses and attempts to resolve tensions and tradeoffs between seemingly competing facets of personalized learning: (a) academic, career, and personal competencies; and (b) individualization, personalization, and socialization.

What Is Personalized Learning?

The term "personalized learning" sprang onto the scene in recent years as several learning technologies and repositories of information (especially via the Internet) advanced to the point of showing great promise as efficient ways to individualize instruction and enrich the curriculum. Ronald Taylor and Azeb Gebre, in their chapter in this volume, define personalized learning as "instruction that is differentiated and paced to the needs of the learner and shaped by the learning preferences and interests of the learner." This is a lean and serviceable definition.

The Center on Innovations in Learning (CIL) has considered the concept of personalized learning and constructed a more complex definition to capture elements that are not apparent in a simpler description:

> Personalization refers to a teacher's relationships with students and their families and the use of multiple instructional modes to scaffold each student's learning and enhance the student's personal competencies. Personalized learning varies the time, place, and pace of learning for each student, enlists the student in the creation of learning pathways, and utilizes technology to manage and document the learning process and access rich sources of information. (Twyman & Redding, 2015, p. 3)

The CIL definition of personalized learning contains phrases that, when further explicated, reveal the complexities and subtleties of the concept. Let's sort them out.

Handbook on Personalized Learning for States, Districts, and Schools, pages 3–18

Personalization: Understanding the Learner

The CIL definition of personalized learning goes beyond individualization—discussed in more detail below—which, in short, attends only to the learner's prior learning and readiness for new learning. For CIL, personalization does this too, but it also seeks to understand the person of the learner—his or her personal preferences, interests, and aspirations—and to make use of that understanding. In the definition, personalization, understanding the learner, is introduced into education in three ways, through relationships, engagement, and personal competencies.

Relationships. "Teacher's relationships with students and their families" adds onto the standard definition of personalization two new elements. First, it introduces the teacher as a central figure, engaging the learner in identifying what is to be learned and in the design of how it is to be learned, intentionally building students' personal competencies that propel learning, and forming relationships with students and their families to better understand the student, the student's needs, and the student's aspirations. In fact, the teacher uniquely possesses an asset for the student through "relational suasion," as described by Redding (2013):

> The teacher possesses the power of relational suasion that technology cannot match. Through the teacher's example and her instruction, the student learns to value mastery, to raise expectations, to manage learning, and to broaden interests. The teacher is singularly capable of teaching social and emotional skills and engaging families in their children's academic and personal development. (pp. 6–7)

Second, the definition implies that relationships are important in personalization. If we were to probe even deeper into the notion of relationships and consider the collaborative and peer-learning aspects of personalization, we would extend the definition further to include under its blanket the relationships among learners, the students themselves.

Student Engagement. Enlisting "the student in the creation of learning pathways" honors the student's interests and aspirations, encourages the student's sense of responsibility for learning, and exercises the student's ability to navigate the learning process.

Personal Competencies. Enhancing "the student's personal competencies" means intentionally building the student's capacity to learn by incorporating into instruction and teacher–student interactions the content and activities that enhance the student's cognitive, metacognitive, motivational, and social-emotional competencies. These four personal competencies are the propellants of learning and together form students' learning habits. Because personalized learning emphasizes the student's self-direction in learning, personal competencies are especially important to the student's success.

Personalization: Variety and Flexibility

The CIL definition of personalized learning breaks from the traditional image of school learning—that is, a student sitting at a desk listening to a teacher or completing the same assignment as the other students—substituting a view of the teacher, aided by learning management software, pivoting from a succinct, interactive presentation of a new concept to walk among her students, encouraging them as they engage with activities they have helped plan and are preparing to continue on their laptops at home that evening. Varying the mode of instruction and the time, place, and pace of learning for each student, expanding the venue of learning beyond the classroom, and detaching expected outcomes from a rigid timeline are hallmarks of personalized learning.

Modes of Instruction. "Use of multiple instructional modes" means that the teacher's lesson plan includes the right mix of different methods of instruction: whole-class, teacher-directed small group, student-directed small group (including cooperative learning and peer-to-peer), technology-assisted (blended), independent work, and homework (including the flipped classroom). Each mode serves its own purposes, and for each mode we have a body of research on how it is most effectively employed. The teacher selects the right mode for the right student at the right time.

Time, Place, and Pace. Varying the "time, place, and pace of learning" rests, in part, on mastery learning's precept that the pace of learning is the chief variable in permitting most students to arrive at the same outcome, albeit at different points in time or with different amounts of time devoted to the specific learning task (Bloom, 1971). The variation in personalized learning goes beyond mastery learning's simple manipulation of pace and time to recognize that learning can occur anywhere. Access to the Internet—at home, in school, or at the coffee shop—is obviously the factor that animates personalized learning's extension of learning's locale.

Personalization: Individualization Facilitated by Technology

This aspect of CIL's definition of personalization concerns what is typically referred to as individualization—that is, as mentioned above, placing each student on his or her own learning plan, with assignments carefully calibrated to the student's prior mastery and expected trajectory. For teachers, true individualization has been a noble but immensely time-consuming undertaking, one likely realized only in special circumstances. Now, however, learning technology has made true individualized, targeted instruction possible for all teachers.

> For teachers, true individualization has been a noble but immensely time-consuming undertaking, one likely realized only in special circumstances.

Targeted Learning. In the CIL definition of personalization, scaffolding "each student's learning" is how a teacher individualizes learning activities to match each student's readiness and finds the appropriate level of challenge. Well-designed, computer-based instructional programs apply techniques of predictive analytics (also called learning analytics; see Ryan Baker's chapter elsewhere in this book) to adjust the learning progressions in response to an individual student's progress. "Scaffold" may be a term that is becoming obsolete, as technology is now able to do what once took massive amounts of teacher time to accomplish.

Learning Technology. Utilizing "technology to manage and document the learning process and access rich sources of information" describes the centrality of technology to the efficient individualization of learning. Not only can learning software provide for learning that is targeted to the individual student, it also tracks the learning process, adapts instruction accordingly, and tests to confirm mastery. Further, the seemingly endless resources of the Internet enable a student to pursue an infinite array of topics.

What Is Competency-Based Education?

CIL's expansive definition of personalized learning includes components that overlap with a conventional definition of competency-based education (CBE). More accurately, the definition subsumes competency-based education as one of its pillars, along with the definition's emphasis on the student's interests and aspirations, engagement in the design of learning, and relationship with the teacher and other learners. Competency-based education (CBE) supports students' progression through their academic work toward mastery within defined competencies—regardless of time, method, place, or pace of learning (U.S. Department of Education, n.d.). Competency-based education stresses acquisition and demonstration of targeted knowledge and skills (Twyman, 2014). The targeting first requires the definition of the knowledge and skills, and how they are related (clustered) to form a competency. As will be later explained, the competency may be personal, academic, or related to career and occupation.

The essential components of a competency-based approach to personalized learning are (a) an identified cluster of related capabilities (the competencies); (b) variation in the time, place, and pace of learning; and (c) criteria, including demonstrated application, to determine and acknowledge mastery. The U.S. Department of Education (n.d.) says this about competency-based learning:

> Transitioning away from seat time, in favor of a structure that creates flexibility, allows students to progress as they demonstrate mastery of academic content regardless of time, place, or pace of learning. Competency-based strategies provide flexibility in the way that credit can be earned or awarded, and provide students with personalized learning opportunities. . . . This type of learning leads to better student engagement because the content is relevant to each student and tailored to [his or her] unique needs. It also leads to better student outcomes because the pace of learning is customized to each student. (para. 1)

In competency-based education, a competency is identified and its boundaries defined by specifying the specific skills and knowledge contained within it. Sounds much like a standards-based approach. Obviously, learning standards are useful in this exercise, and a standards-based system differs from a competency-based system primarily in its: (a) close alignment with in-school, curriculum objectives; (b) reliance on written assessments; and (c) conformity to a set temporal frame (grade levels and course sequences, for example). In other words, a standards-based system does not necessarily vary the time, place, and pace of learning or include a behavioral demonstration or application of the skills and knowledge to determine mastery.

What Is a Competency?

A competency is a defined cluster of related capabilities (skills and knowledge) with methods and criteria to determine the degree to which a person demonstrates mastery in them. Competencies often correspond to roles, such as student, plumber, or writer, and mastery may be benchmarked toward the ultimate demonstration of proficiency in that role. For example, communication might be a broad categorization of a competency, and it might include subparts such as reading comprehension, speaking, listening, and writing. Or writing might be the competency under a different scheme of categorization with a finer grain size. In either case, the competency would be further defined by itemizing the measurable or observable skills and knowledge that constitute it. Finally, the competency's definition would include criteria and methods for determining mastery of the competency's constituent skills and knowledge, and the assessment would include demonstration or application.

Competencies in education can be categorized as personal, academic, or career/occupational. The first, what I call the *personal competencies*, are the propellants of learning, the inputs in the learning process. Personal competencies are "an ever-evolving accumulation of related capabilities that *facilitate learning* and other forms of goal attainment" (Redding, 2014, p. 4). The four personal competencies in my framework are:

- Cognitive competency—*what we know*; prior knowledge which facilitates new learning, broad knowledge acquired in any context, accessible in memory to facilitate new learning, sufficient depth of understanding to expedite acquisition of new learning
- Metacognitive competency—*how we learn*; self-regulation of learning and use of learning strategies
- Motivational competency—*why we learn*; engagement and persistence in pursuit of learning goals
- Social/Emotional competency—*who we are*; sense of self-worth, regard for others, emotional understanding and management, ability to set positive goals and make responsible decisions

Advocates of "deeper learning" espouse an approach that includes attention to aspects of a student's development similar to those expressed here as personal competencies. The American Institutes for Research (AIR), for example, couch deeper learning within the context of 21st-century workplace (and learning) skills. Citing the dimensions of deeper learning identified by the William and Flora Hewlett Foundation (2013), AIR lists the following characteristics: (a) mastery of core academic content; (b) critical thinking and problem-solving; (c) effective communication; (d) ability to work collaboratively; (e) learning how to learn; and (f) academic mindsets (AIR, 2014, para. 6). Table 1 illustrates the approximate relationship of personal competencies and dimensions of deeper learning.

Table 1. Approximate Relationship of Personal Competencies and Dimensions of Deeper Learning

	Personal Competencies			
	Cognitive	Metacognitive	Motivational	Social/Emotional
Dimensions of Deeper Learning				
Content Mastery				
Critical Thinking				
Communication				
Collaboration				
Learning Skills				
Academic Mindset				

The second, academic competencies, include the clusters of knowledge and skill in academic areas, associated with the school curriculum and commonly measured against content standards, such as communication (with its subparts—reading, writing, listening/speaking), or even in the more traditional disciplines (e.g., mathematics) or subjects (e.g., algebra). We use the word "academic" to describe these competencies because they relate to the subject content of school and standards set by the school, even if the competencies are acquired, at least in part, outside school.

Finally, career/occupational competencies are clusters of knowledge and skill related to the world of work, even if they are acquired largely through schooling and are commonly defined and measured within the school setting. Career competencies cover knowledge and skill in selecting, preparing for, acquiring, and transitioning between jobs. Occupational competencies are specific to a job—for example, competency in computer programming or welding. The National Skill Standards Board (2000) offers a categorization of knowledge and skills into three types—academic, employability, and occupational/technical, which correspond to the academic, career, and occupational categories proposed here.

As repertoires (the behaviors that signal competency) are complex and interlocking, overlap between personal, academic, and career/occupational competencies are expected. Figure 1 illustrates the relationships among the three types of competencies described here (academic, career/occupational, and personal) within a competency-based education model in which personal competencies converge to form the learner's patterns of behavior (learning habits) when engaged in learning.

Figure 1. Competency and Mastery in a Competency-Based System

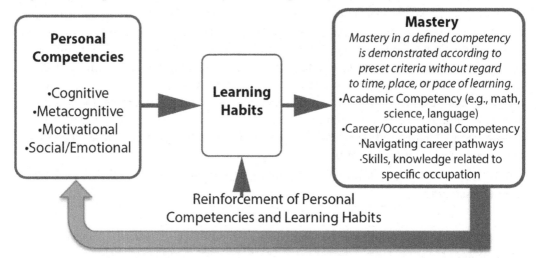

Assessing Competencies

Academic and career/occupational competencies are commonly assessed with standards-based tests, although in a true competency-based environment, evidence of application of the learning would also be required. A challenge for educators is to find ways to measure personal competencies (or deeper learning). Conley and Darling-Hammond (2013) outline directions for new assessment systems that include ways to determine students' progress toward personal competencies. Such assessments will be necessary at every level—formative assessments to guide instruction (including personalized instruction) and systems assessments to inform accountability.

A danger inherent to a competency-based approach is the fragmentation of knowledge and the shallow itemization of isolated skills. True mastery in a competency must be determined by examining the student's facility with an array of skills, understanding of overarching concepts, and ability to perform over time rather than to achieve a peak performance on a single test.

McClarty and Gaertner (2015), writing of competency-based education (CBE) in higher education but applicable to CBE at any level, stress the significance of categorical definition and valid assessment:

External validity is the central component of our recommendations:

- CBE programs should clearly define their competencies and clearly link those competencies to material covered in their assessments.
- To support valid test-score interpretations, CBE assessments should be empirically linked to external measures such as future outcomes.
- Those empirical links should also be used in the standard-setting process so providers develop cut scores that truly differentiate masters from nonmasters.
- In addition to rigorous test development and standard setting, CBE programs should continue to collect and monitor graduates' life outcomes in order to provide evidence that a CBE credential stands for a level of rigor and preparation equivalent to a traditional postsecondary degree. (pp. ii–iii)

Critical to the success of competency-based education are (a) the appropriateness of the definitional boundaries set for the competency; (b) the criteria established to determine mastery; and (c) the validity of the methods of assessment. Then the means of recognition (i.e., badges, certificates, degrees) can be established. If the student is allowed to demonstrate mastery in the competency at any time, without regard to time or place of learning, we have competency-based education. To qualify as personalized education, a few more elements are required. The student would be given a role in designing how the learning would be attained, and the content of the learning would be adapted to the student's interests and aspirations as much as the parameters of the criteria for mastery would allow. In addition, the criteria for mastery would include facility with an array of related skills, an understanding of overarching concepts, and the ability to perform over time.

The Road to Personalized Learning

The road to the modern-day version of personalized learning can be traced by examining the evolution of competency-based education, the efforts to address student diversity through differentiation, and the advent of learning technologies. Brown (1994), reviewing the substantial impact of CBE on the Australian education system, traces the origins of CBE to the scientific management movement that arose in the 19th century at the height of the industrial revolution. As jobs became more specialized, identifying competencies and their component skills enabled efficiencies in training workers for the jobs, doing the work, and evaluating performance. To this day, CBE is a strong element in the workplace and in career and technical education.

A second influence on the evolving notion of CBE developed in the 1920s and 1930s with mastery learning (popularized by Benjamin Bloom in the 1960s and 1970s), in which the time a student devoted to achieving preset learning objectives was made elastic. The emergence of mastery learning coincided with B. F. Skinner's (1954, 1968) work on behaviorism and the introduction of programmed learning. The military in the U.S., U.K., Australia, and elsewhere adopted objective-based training strategies during the World War era (WWI, WWII) to efficiently prepare unskilled soldiers for specific roles.

Mulder, Weigel, and Collins (2006) describe the behaviorist approach to competency in the business sphere, based on the research of psychologist D. C. McClelland (1973), known for his achievement motivation theory. This approach was applied by the Hay Group in behavioral-event interviews to appraise levels of competence in selecting and training corporate and governmental leaders. The behaviorist approach cleaved competency from intelligence and asserted that competency could be developed through training, can be observed and assessed in behavior, and accounts for a significant portion of the differences in the job performance of individuals.

In the 1960s, Robert Mager's (1962) writing on performance-based objectives and criterion-referenced instruction further reified school learning, reducing the curriculum to small, measurable pieces and instruction to discrete steps. Thus, measurable objectives entered the mainstream of education, paving the way for the standards movement of the 1990s that spawned curriculum content standards in every state. CBE was a perfect fit for the standards environment, and the National Skill Standards Act of 1994 created a national board to establish a voluntary set of skill standards, assessments, and certifications. The National Skill Standards Board identified 15 workforce sectors. In 2008, the National Association of State Directors of Career Technical Education Consortium (NASDCTEC) published "industry-validated expectations of what students should know and be able to do after completing instruction in a career program area" (NASDCTEC, n.d., para. 1). The statements (updated in 2011–12) are organized into career pathways for all careers in 16 career clusters. The National Occupational Competency Testing Institute (NOCTI, n.d.), a nonprofit consortium founded in the 1960s, provides assessments to determine proficiency in career and technical areas. It recognizes achievement with badges and certificates which employers and schools may choose to also recognize.

Antecedents of personalized learning can be seen in the progressive education philosophy of John Dewey, William Kilpatrick, and others in the early decades of the 20th century. A great leap forward, however, came later, as educators sought methods to address student diversity. In the wake of Congress's 1975 passage of the Education for All Handicapped Children Act (now reauthorized as the Individuals with Disabilities Education Act—IDEA), educators

> As the first decades of the twenty-first century unfolded, the time was ripe for the fabric of personalized learning to take shape...

sought methods for teaching an increasingly diverse student body. Margaret C. Wang's book, *Adaptive Education Strategies: Building on Diversity* (1992) and her related research and publications proffered an Adaptive Learning Environments Model (ALEM) with methods for individualizing instruction and managing classrooms that included students with widely divergent abilities and needs. Carol Ann Tomlinson popularized and provided research substantiation for instructional differentiation, beginning with her 1995 book, *How to Differentiate Instruction in the Mixed Ability Classroom.*

As the first decades of the twenty-first century unfolded, the time was ripe for the fabric of personalized learning to take shape from the threads of CBE, differentiation, content standards, and a national clamor for, at last, significant education reform. Technology, especially learning management software and the burgeoning resources of the Internet, catalyzed this weaving of elements and burst of enthusiasm for personalization. The technology industry, with ideas and resources from the Bill and Melinda Gates Foundation and endorsement from the U.S. Department of Education, signaled that the age of personalized learning had arrived. The Gates Foundation (2010) itemized several of the threads, as follows:

Learning models that support personalized learning pathways require some basic building blocks. These include effective assessment tools that align with college preparation standards and clear postsecondary learning objectives, engaging digital content, algorithms that match student needs with content and delivery methods, technology-enabled professional development tools, and learning management platforms that integrate and deliver these diverse components. (p. 2)

In 2012, the U.S. Department of Education funded the Center on Innovations in Learning (CIL), and among its charges was to assist state education agencies and districts with personalized learning.

The Individual, the Person, and the Group

The difference between the individual and the person, in the realm of education, is the difference between (a) a targeting of a student's learning activities based on calculations of prior learning and readiness, and (b) engaging the student in designing and navigating learning pathways based on calculations of prior learning and readiness plus personal preferences, interests, and aspirations. Individualization can be done by a machine; personalization, as CIL has defined it, requires a teacher who might employ a machine. The teacher attends to the student's subtle, behavioral idiosyncrasies. The teacher knows her subjects and the possible paths a student might take in studying them. The teacher is an indispensable component in personalized learning.

The student is at once an individual scholar and a constituent of a group of learners, and his or her relationship with the group constitutes some of what it means for a young person to become socialized. Interactions with teachers and peers sharpen a student's thinking, elicit new interests, and provide insights to the nuances of human behavior. Personhood, in fact, is acquired through social interaction, as the self is defined and understood in relationship to other people. The Internet and software that coordinates the work of co-learners across time and place provides a middle ground between isolated, individualized learning and a face-to-face classroom experience. The ideal may be a blending of group learning in the traditional classroom with individualized learning and with personalized learning that includes virtual learning cohorts.

Competency-based education and individualized education are efficient means for matching learning content and tasks with each student's readiness and for determining and recognizing the student's mastery. Personalized learning includes these pedagogical attributes—matching content and tasks to the student's readiness and assessing progress based on demonstrated mastery—and adds a deeper regard for the person of the student.

Strategies to Personalize Learning

Use of Technological Tools

Learning technology makes personalization practical, at once reducing the time required for a teacher to differentiate instruction, opening access to unlimited content, structuring content and activity into manageable pathways, assessing progress and scaffolding tasks, and facilitating individual and group work across time and place. Blended learning, a method of personalization, mixes traditional classroom instruction with online delivery of instruction and content, including learning activities outside the school, granting the student a degree of control over time, place, pace, and/or path (Bonk & Graham, 2006). In a blended learning approach, technology is not seen as a replacement for the traditional classroom, but rather as a powerful tool to enhance what is already proven to be effective pedagogy. "In this hybrid conception of personalization, educators can carry out a series of practices to make sure that technology and data enhance relationships, but do not pretend to substitute for them" (Sandler, 2012, p. 20). Personalization takes advantage of online learning, online testing for mastery, MOOCs (massive, open, online courses), and other Internet-enabled methods. Interventions in a technology-assisted personalized scheme are, in a sense, not necessary when predictive analytics are applied to continuously adjust learning tasks to demonstrated mastery, build in review spirals, and ensure each student's sufficient background of skill and knowledge before moving forward.

Competency-Based Education

Strategies to implement competency-based education in personalizing learning include:

- **Flexible credit schemes** break the ties among class time, learning time, and assessment. Flexible credit schemes include (a) dual enrollment and early college high schools, (b) credit recovery, and (c) multiple paths to graduation.
- **Service learning**, a dimension of many character and social/emotional learning programs, is easily accommodated in a personalized learning environment. Community-based learning directed at competencies (personal, academic, and career/occupational) extends the time and opportunity for learning beyond the school day and provides rich experiences beyond the classroom.
- **Internships** and **job shadowing** offer students opportunities for "real world" learning in business settings that both interest them and contribute to defined competencies.
- **Differentiated staffing**, taking advantage of teachers' different skills and interests, becomes feasible, even desirable, in a personalized learning environment in which recognition of students' progress within competencies is determined by demonstrated mastery rather than enrollment in a specific course with a specific teacher.
- **Acceleration and enrichment** flow naturally when the pace of learning is made fluid, allowing learners to move more rapidly as they demonstrate their mastery and encouraging them to pursue curricular content beyond the confines of a syllabus.
- **Recognition** of mastery may be expressed with the awarding of badges and recognition of proficiency with certificates and credits.
- **Student learning plans (SLPs)**, also known as individual learning plans, designed with a student, enable each student to take a different path, at a different pace, to reach standards. Constructing SLPs (with student input) are time-consuming for a teacher, but instructional software now makes the process more time efficient.
- **Study groups** and research teams enable students to work together to design projects aimed toward a hypothesis or outcome. The students may be members of a class or the group may be assembled across the miles via the Internet.

Personal Competencies

These strategies enhance students' personal competencies:

- **Cognitive competency** is enhanced by instruction that makes connections between what has been previously taught, what the student knows (regardless of where learned), and the new topics. Reinforcing mastered knowledge through review, questioning, and inclusion in subsequent assignments builds students' retention of knowledge in accessible memory. Vocabulary is a critical element of cognitive competency and can be built in every subject area. Writing assignments encourage the association and integration of new learning and deep understanding, especially when connected to rich reading. Student curiosity to learn, in and out of school, is enhanced when students are engaged in designing pathways to exploration and discovery.

- **Metacognitive competency** grows when students observe teachers "thinking out loud" to approach learning tasks. Specific learning strategies and techniques can be taught and learned. Also, the metacognitive processes of (a) goal setting and planning, (b) progress monitoring, and (c) revising work based on feedback can be taught and reinforced. Self-checks and peer-checks as part of assignment completion are beneficial, and student graphing of assignment completion and objective mastery reinforces attention to learning. For critical thinking, students can be taught procedures of logic, synthesis, and evaluation. For creative thinking, students can be taught methods of divergent thinking.

- **Motivational competency** accrues from a growth mindset that bolsters the student's persistence toward ultimate mastery, from differentiated instruction that targets learning activities to the student's readiness, and from connections between learning tasks and the student's personal aspirations. The goal for teachers in promoting student mastery is to encourage students to find their reward in mastery. The fun is in learning, and the reward is the celebration of mastery.

- **Social/Emotional competency** is multi-faceted, incorporating emotional management as well as personal and interpersonal skills. Skills, strategies, and techniques can be taught and learned for social interactions, goal setting, and decision making. Classroom norms model and reinforce personal responsibility, cooperation, and concern for others. Cooperative learning methods serve a dual purpose of facilitating academic learning and building social skills. Parent programs can help parents teach and reinforce personal responsibility and alert parents to signs of emotional distress. Many evidence-based programs—applied schoolwide, in individual classrooms, or with specific students—address social/emotional competency.

Caveats and Conclusions

Reservations about personalized learning, apart from the current paucity of hard evidence of its effectiveness, follow two lines of concern: (a) the potentially negative effects of over-reliance on technology, and (b) the fear that individualization (or differentiation) opens the door to lowered expectations and a fragmented or diluted curriculum. Of course, learning can be personalized without technological tools, but the tools certainly facilitate it. Sherry Turkle, a professor at MIT, set off an alarm about the ill effects of life spent with a nose (or ear) to a screen—computer, tablet, video game, or smartphone—in her 2011 book, *Alone Together: Why We Expect More From Technology and Less From Each Other*. She followed in 2015 with the publication of *Reclaiming Conversation: The Power of Talk in a Digital Age*, in which she cautions that too much reliance on social connection via technology may stunt a person's emotional development, empathy, self-reflection, and social dexterity.

In discussing the distractions (technological or otherwise) that diminish our attention, Sven Birkerts (2015) warns that "between our own inevitable adjustments to the stimulus barrage of modern life—all the editing, skimming, compartmentalizing, accelerating—and the increasing psychological assault of others using their devices, we find it ever harder to generate and then sustain a level of attention—focus—that full involvement in experience requires" (p. 7). Matthew Crawford (2015) echoes Birkert's thoughts and advocates the "point of triangulation with objects and other people who have a reality of their own" (p. x; as opposed to a virtual reality) that fosters true individuality. In essence, reservations about technology in education center around the separation of students from social interactions and the fragmentation of learning into bits of information that do not congeal into understanding.

Interestingly, personalization of learning is espoused as an "antidote to the widespread feelings of anonymity, irrelevance, and disengagement that students report, especially in large, urban high schools" (Yonezawa, McClure, & Jones, 2012, p. 1). One might read this as an indication that the group context of classrooms for some students does not provide a desirable sense of connection, belongingness, and stimulation. Rather, the individual student feels isolated within the group, perhaps alone with her or his particular interests and stymied by a pace of instruction that is too fast or too slow. Personalized learning, on the other hand, so tailors the education experience to the preferences, interests, and aspirations of the individual student that the student is enlivened and engaged.

The objections to personalization, apart from the intrusions of technology, rest on faith in the pedagogical efficacy of teacher-centered, direct, whole-class instruction and the benefits of a common or shared learning experience. A variant of this objection is the complaint that differentiation, itself, is an unproven fad. Mike Schmoker, in an *Education Week* commentary (2010), articulated the case against differentiation by arguing that: (a) no solid evidence supports the effectiveness of differentiation; (b) differentiation's emphasis on "student preference" too easily slides into a practical alliance with the much discredited "learning styles"; (c) attempts to vary instruction result in nonsense activities; and (d) a teacher's time is best devoted to constructing a single, high-quality instructional unit with frequent opportunities for student response. This critique of differentiation strikes at the heart of personalized learning.

If you think of personalization as extreme tracking (one track for each student), you run up against the standard objections to tracking. Jeannie Oakes, formerly a UCLA professor and president of the American Educational Research Association, now director of education and scholarship at the Ford Foundation, built a substantial research case against tracking and other methods of dividing students into groups based on appraisals of their ability and potential for learning. In a 1992 interview following her 1985 publication of *Keeping Track*, Oakes explained that:

> When I talk about harmful effects of tracking and ability grouping, I'm talking about all of those forms of grouping that are characterized by educators making some rather global judgment about how smart students are—either in a subject field or across a number of subject fields. Sometimes, it's defined in terms of IQ, sometimes it's defined in terms of past performance, sometimes the criteria are predictions of how well children are likely to learn. In other words, some grown-ups in the school are making a judgment about how smart the students are. (O'Neil, 1992, para. 4)

Whether the sorting of students is done by teacher or machine, into groups *or individual tracks*, some risks are involved, including especially the relegation of some students to learning opportunities well below their capacity for mastery.

Warnings about the potential abuses of personalized learning serve to moderate the enthusiasm of its proponents, put boundaries around its excesses, and encourage research to confirm its effectiveness. But the objections are likely to fall away as teachers and technology get better at personalization.

Personalized learning in schools holds the potential to engage the disengaged students and build students' academic, career/occupational, and personal competencies. Personalized learning is made practical by technology that organizes curricular content, facilitates differentiation, opens vast and diverse avenues of learning, provides ongoing checks of mastery, and ultimately confirms mastery. Personalized learning encourages and confirms learning that takes place anytime, anywhere, and is thus a companion to competency-based education.

Personalized learning steps beyond the mechanical individualization of learning by incorporating the teacher's deep understanding of each student's interests, aspirations, backgrounds, and behavioral idiosyncrasies. Personalized learning mixes the targeting of learning to the individual student with opportunities to learn with a group, one-to-one, face-to-face, or across the miles.

Action Principles for States, Districts, and Schools

Action Principles for States

a. Remove regulatory and statutory barriers to competency-based education. Course credit, grade promotion, and graduation requirements are often tied to enrollment and time spent in specific courses rather than to demonstrated mastery.

b. Define specific academic, career/occupational, and personal competencies. In order for instruction to be aimed at competencies, the competencies must first be defined, including the enumeration of their constituent skills and areas of knowledge.

c. Provide protocol and instruments for assessing competencies to determine mastery. Academic competencies may be defined as coinciding with state content standards and thus mastery may be determined through standards-based assessments. Career/occupational and personal competencies need similar means for determining mastery.

d. Ensure that all schools have technology adequate for multiple methods of personalization, and provide training for district and school personnel in the use of the technology. Indeed, personalized learning is made practical by recent advances in technology, but the technology must be available and personnel trained to use it.

e. Showcase local strategies and models that effectively employ personalized learning methods. Everywhere in the country, some teachers, schools, and districts are in the vanguard of practice in personalization. Identify them, and shine a spotlight on them in state publications and conferences.

Action Principles for Districts

a. Set district policies that encourage personalization. Be sure that course credit, grade promotion, and graduation requirements facilitate the recognition of learning wherever and whenever it occurs. Advance flexible credit schemes, such as (a) dual enrollment and early college high schools, (b) credit recovery, and (c) multiple paths to graduation.

b. Include the language of specific academic, career/occupational, and personal competencies in curriculum guides and course descriptions. In order for instruction to be aimed at competencies, the competencies must first be defined and included in curriculum guides and course descriptions.

c. Provide professional development for school leaders and teachers in methods for personalizing learning and for assessing competencies to determine mastery. Academic competencies may be defined as coinciding with state content standards, thus, mastery may be determined through standards-based assessments. Career/occupational and personal competencies need similar means for gauging mastery in formative assessments.

d. Ensure that all schools have technology adequate for multiple methods of personalization, and provide training for district and school personnel in the use of the technology. Indeed, personalized learning is made practical by recent advances in technology, but the technology must be available and personnel trained to use it.

e. Showcase schools and teachers employing strategies and models that effectively incorporate personalized learning methods. Build a vanguard of practice in personalization. Identify the leaders, and shine a spotlight on them in district publications and conferences.

Action Principles for Schools

a. Provide professional development for teachers in methods for enhancing students' personal competencies. Personal competencies are the propellants of learning, and teachers can build them in students through their intentional inclusion in instructional plans.

b. Incorporate service learning, internships, and job shadowing as means to facilitate out-of-school learning. Recognizing learning that occurs beyond the school day and outside the classroom is one thing, but enabling the learning to occur often requires intentional programming.

c. Include intentional incorporation of personalized learning methods in instructional planning, and provide teachers training and time to prepare for personalized learning. To ensure that personalized learning methods are systematically employed by teachers, make the inclusion of personalized learning strategies a routine component of instructional planning by teacher teams.

d. Ensure that school personnel are adept in the appropriate use of technology to personalize learning. Indeed, personalized learning is made practical by recent advances in technology, but the technology must be available and personnel trained to use it.

e. Enable teachers who are advanced in personalized learning strategies to share their work with other teachers. Some teachers invariably move in the direction of personalization before others; take advantage of what they are learning and doing by giving them opportunities to share with other teachers.

References

American Institutes for Research. (2014, September). *Does deeper learning improve student outcomes?* Washington, DC: Author. Retrieved from http://www.hewlett.org/sites/default/files/AIR%20Deeper%20Learning%20Summary.pdf

Baker, R. (2016). Using learning analytics in personalized learning. In M. Murphy, S. Redding, & J. Twyman (Eds.), *Handbook on personalized learning for states, districts, and schools*. Philadelphia, PA: Center on Innovations in Learning.

Bill & Melinda Gates Foundation. (2010). *Next generation learning*. Seattle, WA: Author.

Birkerts, S. (2015). *Change the subject: Art and attention in the Internet age*. Minneapolis, MN: Graywolf Press.

Bloom, B. S. (1971). Mastery learning. In J. H. Block (Ed.), *Mastery learning: Theory and practice* (pp. 47–63). New York, NY: Holt, Rinehart, & Winston.

Bonk, C. J., & Graham, C. R. (Eds.). (2006). *Handbook of blended learning: Global perspectives, local designs*. San Francisco, CA: Pfeiffer.

Brown, M. (1994). An introduction to the discourse on competency-based training (CBT). In Deakin University Course Development Centre (Ed.), *A collection of readings related to competency-based training* (pp. 1–17). Victoria, Australia: Victorian Education Foundation, Deakin University. Retrieved from http://files.eric.ed.gov/fulltext/ED384695.pdf

Conley, D. T., & Darling-Hammond, L. (2013). *Creating systems of assessment for deeper learning*. Stanford, CA: Stanford Center for Opportunity Policy in Education. Retrieved from https://edpolicy.stanford.edu/sites/default/files/publications/creating-systems-assessment-deeper-learning_0.pdf

Crawford, M. B. (2015). *The world beyond your head: On becoming an individual in an age of distraction*. New York, NY: Farrar, Straus, & Giroux.

Mager, R. (1962). *Preparing instructional objectives*. Belmont, CA: Fearon.

McClarty, K., & Gaertner, M. (2015). *Measuring mastery: Best practices for assessment in competency-based education*. Washington, DC: American Enterprise Institute. Retrieved from https://www.aei.org/publication/measuring-mastery-best-practices-for-assessment-in-competency-based-education/

McClelland, D. C. (1973). Testing for competence rather than for "intelligence." *American Psychologist, 28*(1), 1–14.

Mulder, M., Weigel, T., & Collins, K. (2006). The concept of competence in the development of vocational education and training in selected EU member states—A critical analysis. *Journal of Vocational Education and Training, 59*(1), 65–85.

National Association of State Directors of Career Technical Education Consortium. (n.d.). *Career clusters knowledge & skills statements*. Silver Spring, MD: Author. Retrieved from http://www.careertech.org/knowledge-skills-statements

National Occupational Competency Testing Institute. (n.d.). *About NOCTI*. Big Rapids, MI: Author. Retrieved from http://www.nocti.org/aboutnocti.cfm

National Skill Standards Board. (2000). *Skill scales companion guide*. Washington, DC: Author.

Oakes, J. (1985). *Keeping track: How schools structure inequality*. New Haven, CT: Yale University Press.

O'Neil, J. (1992). On tracking and individual differences: A conversation with Jeannie Oakes. *Educational Leadership, 50*(2), 18–21. Retrieved from http://www.ascd.org/publications/educational-leadership/oct92/vol50/num02/On-Tracking-and-Individual-Differences@-A-Conversation-with-Jeannie-Oakes.aspx

Redding, S. (2013). *Through the student's eyes: A perspective on personalized learning.* Philadelphia, PA: Center on Innovations in Learning. Retrieved from http://www.centeril.org/publications/2013_09_Through_the_Eyes.pdf

Redding, S. (2014). *Personal competency: A framework for building students' capacity to learn.* Philadelphia, PA: Center on Innovations in Learning. Retrieved from http://www.centeril.org/publications/Personal_Competency_Framework.pdf

Sandler, S. (2012). People v. 'personalization': Retaining the human element in the high-tech era of education. *Education Week, 31*(22), 20–22.

Schmoker, M. (2010). When pedagogic fads trump priorities. *Education Week, 30*(5), 22–23. Retrieved from http://mikeschmoker.com/pedagogic-fads.html

Skinner, B. F. (1954). The science of learning and the art of teaching. *Harvard Educational Review, 24*(2), 86–97.

Skinner, B. F. (1968). *The technology of teaching.* New York, NY: Appleton-Century Croft.

Taylor, R., & Gebre, A. (in press). Teacher–student relations and personalized learning: Implications of personal and contextual variables. In M. Murphy, S. Redding, & J. Twyman (Eds.), *Handbook on personalized learning for states, districts, and schools.* Philadelphia, PA: Center on Innovations in Learning.

Tomlinson, C. (1995). *How to differentiate instruction in the mixed ability classroom.* Alexandria, VA: Association for Supervision and Curriculum Development.

Turkle, S. (2011). *Alone together: Why we expect more from technology and less from each other.* New York, NY: Basic Books.

Turkle, S. (2015). *Reclaiming conversation: The power of talk in a digital age.* New York, NY: Penguin Press.

Twyman, J. (2014). *Competency-based education: Supporting personalized learning.* Philadelphia, PA: Center on Innovations in Learning. Retrieved from http://www.centeril.org/connect/resources/Connect_CB_Education_Twyman-2014_11.12.pdf

Twyman, J., & Redding, S. (2015). *Personal competencies/Personalized learning: Lesson plan reflection guide.* Washington, DC: Council of Chief State School Officers. Retrieved from http://www.centeril.org/ToolsTrainingModules/assets/personalizedlearninglessonplanreflection.pdf

U.S. Department of Education. (n.d.). *Competency-based learning or personalized learning.* Washington, DC: Author. Retrieved from http://www.ed.gov/oii-news/competency-based-learning-or-personalized-learning

Wang, M. C. (1992). *Adaptive education strategies: Building on diversity.* Baltimore, MD: Paul H. Brookes.

William and Flora Hewlett Foundation. (2013, April). *Deeper learning competencies.* Menlo Park, CA.

Yonezawa, S., McClure, L., & Jones, M. (2012.). *Personalization in schools.* Boston, MA: Jobs for the Future. Retrieved from http://www.studentsatthecenter.org/sites/scl.dl-dev.com/files/Personalization%20in%20Schools.pdf

Converging Qualities of Personal Competencies

T. V. Joe Layng

What is to be taught? How is learning to occur? What makes for a truly successful learner? Educators are increasingly looking to the learning and psychological sciences for help in answering these questions. Covering content is no longer considered adequate, nor is a simple emphasis on the purely academic domain sufficient. Schools are being challenged with developing competencies that extend beyond what might be called the cognitive domain. In addition to cognitive competencies, three other competencies have been identified that some have suggested are essential for learners to master (see Redding, 2014a, 2014b): metacognitive, social/emotional, and motivational competencies. Although there is an emerging consensus that these are important, there is not widespread agreement on precisely how these competencies are defined and how they may be acquired. This chapter provides a behavioral description of each competency and describes how the competencies converge, that is, how each competency may contribute an important component to another.

Cognitive Competencies

Let's begin with what many consider a familiar competency category—cognitive competencies. For most teaching activities, some form of cognitive competency on the part of the learner is required. Cognitive competencies refer to those repertoires required to gain the knowledge and skills directly related to the subject matter taught. Redding (2014a) refers to a cognitive competency as "prior learning that facilitates new learning" (p. 4). Learning scientists and education researchers have for many years tried to provide various taxonomies of cognitive competencies. Bloom (1956) and his associates focused on content-neutral cognitive competencies that could be applied across content areas. Others have approached cognitive competencies through content learning; that is, they analyze instructional content in such a way that cognitive competencies can be defined based on the type of learning required for mastery of specific content (for insightful early treatments, see Mechner, 1962, 1965). One such model was first offered by Philip Tiemann and Susan Markle (1973). They provided what they called a "remodeled model," which

Handbook on Personalized Learning for States, Districts, and Schools, pages 19–36

was based on David Merrill's (1971) revision of Robert Gagne's (1965, 1970) famous *Conditions of Learning*. Tiemann and Markle (1991) later went on to produce a comprehensive guide to applying their model to content analysis (also see Layng & Twyman, 2013). An updated version of their model was recently described by Layng (2014a). As described later in this chapter, the advantage of this approach is that precise cognitive competencies can be described and evaluated in the context of the specific subject matter that is to be mastered. I will return to Bloom in our discussion of metacognitive competencies.

To analyze cognitive competencies in the context of subject matter, Tiemann and Markle (1991) provide a matrix that describes "types of learning." The matrix provides a guide for ensuring that "prior learning that facilitates new learning" is acquired (Figure 1). The cell at the bottom left is labeled "Responses." To determine if learning in this category has taken place, we ask the question, "Can the learner actually perform the behavior requested?" An example of a response is grasping a pencil.

Figure 1. Types of Learning

Psychomotor	Simple Cognitive		Complex Cognitive
Kinesthetic Repertoires	Verbal Repertoires		Strategies
Chains	Sequences		Principles (Rule Applying)
		Algorithms	
	Serial Memory		
Responses	Paired Associates	Multiple Discriminations	Concepts
	Associations		

Note. Adapted from *Analyzing Instructional Content* (4th ed.), by P. W. Tiemann & S. M. Markle. Copyright 1991.

Just above the "Responses" cell, the "Chains" cell concerns how responses are linked to perform a sequence of behaviors in which one behavior must be successfully completed before another can occur if the entire "chain" of behaviors is to be completed successfully. Sharpening a pencil is an example of such a chain. Often these behaviors may appear simple and may be considered relatively unimportant, but, without them, more complex behaviors may be difficult to learn. These behaviors often make up what some authors have called "tool skills," the fundamental building blocks of more complex skills (Johnson & Layng, 1992). For example, clearly and quickly writing digits 0 to 9 may be essential to reach fluency in performing addition and subtraction math computations. The top cell in the psychomotor category, "Kinesthetic Repertoires," refers to linked, and often recombinant, motor patterns. They include such skills as competitive cycling, ice skating, and hockey. They are complex and require sophisticated methods of instruction (see, for example, Mechner, 1994, for a detailed description of the teaching and evaluating of complex psychomotor behavior).

The next column, labeled "Simple Cognitive," has at its basic level what psychologists have called paired–associate learning or stimulus–response relations, cognitive scientists call condition–action pairs, and behavior analysts call occasion–behavior relations. That is, a response is provided to a stimulus, for example, seeing a picture of a truck (stimulus) and saying, "Truck" (response). Often, the task is made more complicated by placing several stimuli together and providing each stimulus with its own response, such as seeing a car and saying, "Car"; seeing a truck and saying, "Truck"; and seeing a bicycle and saying, "Bicycle" when the pictures of each are all presented together. Learning scientists call this simple cognitive activity a "Multiple Discrimination" (see bottom cell in middle under "Simple Cognitive"). The next cell up in the "Simple Cognitive" column, "Sequences," includes "Algorithms." Solving a long-division problem is an example of an algorithm. Although different long-division problems may be presented, the algorithm, or the steps that are followed, is the same for solving each one. "Serial Memory" requires learners to perform a sequence that is arbitrarily defined by the outcome. An example is playing a sequence of notes on a musical instrument that results in "Twinkle Twinkle, Little Star." At the top of the "Simple Cognitive" column, the "Verbal Repertoires" cell refers to being able to speak or write knowledgeably about a topic. When one uses knowledge, one has to provide an account of some type. Although essays are often thought to tap into a more complex cognitive domain than answering multiple-choice questions, this may not always be the case. Whereas an essay can simply be the phrasing of material read or heard, a well-designed multiple-choice question may include distinguishing examples from very similar nonexamples, thus requiring a deep understanding of the subject matter.

Often principles are stated in terms of "if, then" relations: If there is an action, then there will be an equal and opposite reaction.

In the third column, labeled "Complex Cognitive," the cell at the bottom, "Concepts," is not a mental construct but instead refers to stimuli that share a set of common (*must have*) features found in each example of the concept but that also may differ from one another by including varying (*can have*) features. The *must have* features provide the defining properties that make something a concept. "The *can have* features describe the many ways examples of a concept can be different" from one another (Layng, 2012, p. 2). Teaching a concept requires the learners to respond to all examples that include the *must have* features and not to respond to "nonexamples" missing one or more of the *must have* features. To test if a learner actually has learned a concept, new examples (not presented during instruction) containing the *must have* features must be correctly identified, and close-in nonexamples, items for which often only one of the *must have* features is missing, are rejected. Furthermore, the testing examples must be drawn from examples that include the full range of *can have* features.

"Principles" (center cell) describe the relation between concepts. For example, in the physical law "For every action there is an equal and opposite reaction," four concepts—equal, opposite, action, and reaction—are related to one another in a specific way. Often principles are stated in terms of "if, then" relations: If there is an action, then there will be an equal and opposite reaction. At the top of the "Complex Cognitive" column, the "Strategies" cell describes repertoires required for solving problems of various types.

One feature that distinguishes the "Simple Cognitive" from the "Complex Cognitive" column is how the cognitive repertoires are assessed. In the "Simple Cognitive" column, what is presented in instruction is what is tested. In the "Complex Cognitive" column, new examples and nonexamples not presented in instruction must be tested. This is the case for all the cells in the "Complex Cognitive" column. For a detailed description of this topic, see Tiemann and Markle (1991).

Teaching Cognitive Competencies

Cognitive competency is built when content is described in terms of the relations found in each of these cells (see Figure 1) and those relations are taught and mastered, as evidenced by the evaluation criteria appropriate to each cell. One definition considers cognitive competency learning that assists new learning (Redding, 2014a, 2014b), but further analysis suggests something a bit more complex than that. Two aspects of cognitive competency must be considered: (a) the repertoires acquired (content), and (b) the methods used to establish and assess the various types of cognitive competency. Teachers tap the acquired repertoire of learners to teach further skills and strategies. An example of the first is provided by Markle (1982); learners may be asked to do the following: "With appropriate tools, construct a useful object out of wood." A cognitive competency that is likely required to achieve this is "measure accurately to 1/16th of an inch on any board from which a piece is to be cut." To do this likely requires learners to "read a tape measure, interpolating to 8th and 16th between the marked 4ths of an inch." Earlier cognitive competencies may also be described, such as, "Read numbers, including fractions" (Markle, 1982, p. 18). The methods (b, above) used to teach and test these competencies depend on the cognitive domain into which each numeracy competence falls. As noted earlier, algorithm following is taught and tested differently than is a concept or principle.

Metacognitive Competencies

Three discrete categories tend to define metacognitive competency. The first category is not specific to the metacognitive category, but without it, many metacognitive competencies cannot be truly acquired. This category concerns the skills learners need to be able to carry out independent work or to complete activities required by a problem or project. Archer and Gleason (2002) have identified many of these skills and strategies. They include—to name but a few of the many skills—gaining information and responding in class, completing assignments with directions, memorizing and studying information, taking notes, using a book's front and back matter, selecting the appropriate reference source, reading and interpreting graphs and tables, alphabetizing, locating and using the information in dictionary or encyclopedia entries, and effectively searching for and using online resources. None of these refers to the content to be learned; rather, they refer to how one may go about learning the content.

The second metacognitive category has to do with a range of skills that can best be characterized as making one's behavior more effective through organization, planning, and other strategies. This includes appropriate school behaviors and organizational skills such as arriving on time, having materials organized and at hand, participating meaningfully in class, preparing for and doing homework, and using strategies for studying for and taking tests (Archer & Gleason, 2002).

How does a student plan, evaluate what is required, and evaluate if he or she is on the right track if skills from these two metacognitive categories are absent? Some of these are taught directly, some are acquired by trial and error as one progresses through school, and some may never be acquired through typical school activities. For the purpose of teaching metacognitive skills, a focus on the metacognitive domain may be illusory; it is in the cognitive domain where our effort needs to be directed. To ensure full metacognitive competency, all of these skills need to be specified and directly taught. What is notable here is that no special "metacognitive instruction" is required. Accordingly, to ensure metacognitive competency, the skills in these first two categories must be treated as being part of the "cognitive domain." It is only when they are used together, when they converge and when they are applied to new situations that this constellation of skills would be called a metacognitive competency. When they are a part of the learner's repertoire, they may be called upon by learners to achieve the independent learning goals that are so valued.

The third category of metacognition involves evaluating one's own behavior. Evaluation requires a comparison with a standard or set of criteria. The answer to the question, "Am I really doing what is required?" implies that one can discriminate between what is and what is not required. Next, one must match what one has done with respect to those requirements, noting where they are met and possibly where they may not be met. The steps also involve a repertoire of self-dialogue, reasoning, and a fluent repertoire of questioning. Furthermore, the key repertoires for meeting the criteria fall into the two categories described earlier. They may also serve to provide a basis of evaluation; the answer to, "Do I have enough sources?" will likely require a broad knowledge of what sources are available and how they are accessed. Ensuring metacognitive competency is not a simple matter, nor can it be achieved by simply providing projects and encouragement. It requires the convergence of all three categories of skills that comprise metacognitive competence after all have been taught so as to be part of a learner's cognitive competency.

Teaching Metacognitive Competencies

Fortunately, there are relatively simple ways classroom teachers can ensure that these competencies are established. But directly teaching the skills described in each of the three categories is not enough; also required is a certain classroom culture—a culture that hopefully extends not only among classrooms within the same grade but across all grades. The learning of these competencies does not happen necessarily over a period of weeks or months but over a period of years. An easy-to-implement and comprehensive (and inexpensive) curriculum, *Skills for School Success* (Archer & Gleason, 2002), teaches most of the skills described in the first two categories and cumulatively builds these skills beginning in third grade. The bulk of the skills are learned in third through sixth grades, with more advanced skill instruction available to middle and high school learners. To be successful, these skills must be integrated into the fabric of classroom learning if they are to transfer from the cognitive to metacognitive domain. They need to be a part of how one learns, not simply something one learns but seldom uses.

The skills related to the third metacognitive category must also be thoroughly integrated into the classroom practices if they are to be taught successfully, and they can be difficult to teach. This category involves not only behaving but also seeing that one is behaving and evaluating that behavior in accord with the requirements of the situation. It is not enough to provide opportunities in the way of problems or projects but requires that specific learner repertoires be established. In the 1950s, Benjamin Bloom became interested in what separated some of the more successful students at the University of Chicago from some of the less successful. He was particularly interested in what the successful students actually did while mastering a subject. He began observing students as they studied. What surprised him was that many of the successful students shared a similar pattern of studying, one that was different from those who were less successful (Bloom, 1950). The successful students would today be regarded as demonstrating substantial metacognitive competency.

Later, an investigator at Purdue University, Arthur Whimbey, decided to follow up on Bloom's initial observations. He began to observe highly successful individuals across a range of disciplines and professions. Whimbey was surprised to find that these individuals not only resembled the students Bloom observed in how they solved problems, but they also resembled each other. He was able to distill the critical behaviors into a small set anyone could learn. This formed the basis for the book, *Problem Solving and Comprehension* (1985), that Whimbey coauthored with Jack Lochhead. In that book, they described both effective and ineffective strategies for solving problems. In a more than 20-year quest to improve the metacognitive problem solving of chemical engineering students, McMaster University found the only successful method was to directly teach the methods described by Whimbey and Lochhead. A similar discovery was made by educators at Xavier University in New Orleans (Carmichael et al., 1980; McMillan, 1987). Xavier was able to use the methods to greatly increase the number of African American students accepted to medical school (Carmichael, Bauer, Hunter, & Sevenair, 1988). What is most interesting is that the reasoning strategies described in the most recent edition of the book (Whimbey, Lochhead, & Narode, 2013) are relatively easy for learners to master.

After working with college students, Robbins (1996, 2011, 2015) began investigating how the Whimbey et al. (2013) strategies could be further broken down and taught to learners beginning in third grade. After years of development and testing, she produced a program that any teacher can use to teach this set of complex metacognitive skills to young learners. She defined, with simplified terminology, the critical qualities of the third metacognitive category: behaving, observing one's own behavior, and responding to it. Robbins's (2015) program is designed to develop five qualities that comprise successful problem solving and five qualities comprising successful active listening as a partner in problem solving. Each quality is learned separately in the context of a continual self-dialogue that involves breaking problems into parts and determining the requirements—that are often only implicitly specified. In a collaborative setting, one learner takes the role of the problem solver and the other the role of an active listener.

> In a collaborative setting, one learner takes the role of the problem solver and the other the role of an active listener. The qualities of each are pretaught.

The qualities of each are pretaught. After learners are well practiced in each role across a range of academic and nonacademic problems, the students can combine the problem-solving and self-observational repertoires to guide future independent work. They achieve a high level of metacognitive competency. Applying this repertoire in combination with the skills described earlier, learners can be true independent learners. They can evaluate the requirements, assess what is required, determine a plan of attack by breaking down the problem into parts, keep up continual evaluation as to whether what they are doing is reaching the goal, reflect on the soundness of their work, and continually check for accuracy of their work. Furthermore, each step is observable and measurable. Teachers can actually see the metacognitive process occurring (e.g., see the video file by Robbins,

2014). By separately teaching and then bringing together these metacognitive skills, a metacognitive repertoire can be produced that is applicable across a range of challenges (for a similar approach, see Mechner, Fredrick, & Jenkins, 2013).

All three categories of metacognitive competency are critical for what Joseph Schwab (1960) called "stable enquiry." In stable enquiry, the learners guide themselves (metacognitive competency) through the application of various heuristics, algorithms, and resources (cognitive competency) required to produce a project or solve a problem. This type of enquiry comprises the bulk of activities learners encounter in school. It can be complex and challenging. Another repertoire that Schwab identified is "fluid enquiry." In fluid enquiry, learners must step outside the bounds of the prescribed problem, asking themselves questions such as, "Is there another approach not yet tried?" "Is the question framed correctly?" and "What if a different question were asked?" The learner is asking, "What if I looked at this in a different way?" and then begins to examine all the assumptions of the problem. This is a very sophisticated repertoire. It not only requires cognitive competencies in the topic being investigated, but it also requires an advanced metacognitive repertoire that includes another element: asking meaningful questions that result in discovering new problems or challenges not before described. Although questioning is a valued skill and there are programs targeted at getting learners to ask questions, the primary point of questioning is often overlooked, that is, to create a meaningful discrepancy that will take real effort to resolve. This level of questioning goes beyond content queries and requires the full metacognitive repertoire described earlier to achieve. The question and its relation to the discrepancy created must be examined, requiring considerable reflection. A program for college students was created in the mid-1990s that was geared to this outcome and was successful with factory workers, drugstore managers, and other professionals (Robbins & Layng, 2010; Robbins, Layng, & Jackson, 1994). Recently, efforts have been directed toward adapting this program for use with children in school settings in the context of both stable and fluid enquiry (Robbins & Layng, 2015).

All the elements of metacognitive competency described here can be made explicit, readily taught, and evaluated within the context of a typical school day. Learning metacognitive competency can readily become metacognitive learning. That is, the procedures required to learn in the cognitive domain can be used to teach the critical skills required to produce a functioning metacognitive repertoire, which is the result of the convergence of the three metacognitive categories (Robbins, 2015; Robbins et al., 1994). These categories are themselves products of skills learned by using methods derived to establish cognitive competencies. Accordingly, taxonomies such as those provided by Tiemann and Markle (1991) or Bloom (1956) can be useful in teaching the components of a metacognitive repertoire. When evaluating a project, for example, the student tells whether or not a given product meets specified criteria or compares two products for some purpose, often providing reasons as he or she responds. Students can be taught a vocabulary that specifically supports such reasoning. For example, the vocabulary most likely to be used when a student says, "How do I…" "assess," "decide," "rank," "test," "measure," "convince," and so on, all speak to the evaluation level in the Bloom taxonomy. Once a course of action is identified, multiple discrimination, concept and principle applying, and perhaps strategies from Tiemann and Markle's taxonomy will likely be required. In short, linking vocabulary appropriate to metacognitive requirements posed by a problem to the type of learning required is a primary goal of teaching metacognitive competency.

Social/Emotional Competencies

After a basic metacognitive repertoire is acquired and there has been practice in acquiring both problem-solving and active-listening repertoires, a firm foundation for important social/emotional learning (SEL) is in place. SEL is increasingly being considered an important component of school curricula. The Austin Independent School District (AISD, 2015) in Texas lists behavioral skills, based on recommendations by the Collaborative for Academic, Social, and Emotional Learning (CASEL, 2015), as central to its SEL curriculum. The skills listed are representative of other districts' SEL guidelines:

- Students will develop and demonstrate self-management skills, regulate emotions, and monitor and achieve behaviors related to school and life success.
- Students will develop self-awareness skills, have knowledge of their emotions, develop an accurate and positive self-concept, and recognize individual strengths and external support systems.
- Students will develop social-awareness skills needed to establish and maintain positive relationships, including recognizing feelings and the perspectives of others, appreciating individual and group differences, and contributing to the well-being of one's school and community.
- Students will demonstrate interpersonal skills needed to establish and maintain positive relationships, including using social skills and communication skills to interact effectively with others while developing healthy relationships and demonstrating an ability to prevent, manage, and resolve interpersonal conflicts.
- Students will demonstrate decision-making skills, problem-solving skills, and responsible behaviors in school, personal, and community contexts.

On its website, AISD presents a specific breakdown of the goals and more specific objectives for each guideline by category. For example, one of the four objectives in the self-awareness category is that a student demonstrates an awareness of his or her own emotions. This outcome is to be achieved by acquiring a set of cumulatively learned skills beginning in kindergarten and continuing through Grade 12. For kindergarten through Grade 2, the skills are recognizing and accurately naming feelings, identifying and communicating an emotion, and identifying emotions related to situations or events (triggers). For Grades 11 through 12, they are differentiating between the factual and emotional content of what a person says, expressing empathy toward others, and comparing multiple perspectives on an issue. There are three or four objectives for each of the five categories, with more specific enabling objectives for each grade level under each category.

Obviously, a robust SEL program based on those of CASEL or similar recommendations is a major, time-consuming project. Furthermore, even though the objectives appear to be clear, plenty of ambiguity exits. Exactly how does a teacher help a learner recognize and accurately name feelings? This is not the same teaching task as recognizing and accurately naming letters of the alphabet. At best, naming feelings is an inference based on observing the context, the behavior in the context, and the likely consequences of the behavior in the context. An often-overlooked limitation is teachers' lack of direct access to what the child is feeling. A teacher may often rely on how he or she might feel in a similar situation, but does that guarantee that is what the learner feels, and more specifically, what a 6- or 7-year-old learner feels?

The teaching task is further complicated by considering how one knows that the emotion one thinks one feels is actually the emotion one is feeling. How does one distinguish between true emotions and emotional behavior? In other words, is the emotional behavior occurring as the result of consequences being produced, which have little to do with the circumstances with which the emotion is typically associated, or is it reflective of conditions under which the emotion is likely to occur? If a learner acts aggressively in a classroom, is it to drive away someone with whom one is angry, or is it to gain the attention of classmates? Accordingly, the objectives targeting social-emotional competency require a different approach than that which teachers may use when teaching and evaluating academic subjects.

Teaching Social/Emotional Competencies

For an individual to be socially and emotionally competent, that student needs to not only understand why he or she may be feeling a certain way under certain circumstances, but also be able to harness those emotions to help deal with those circumstances. When emotions are felt, often readily observable and assessable behavior also occurs. An observer can see how situations are handled, the interpersonal dialogue that occurs, and the consequences of those actions. If emotions reflect circumstances, then they may be harnessed to help understand those circumstances. The concept of a "triggering event" included in the AISD objectives may not be adequate to understanding emotions in context. A common stimulus–response description goes something like this: An event (triggering) occurs, feelings occur, and the feelings result in some behavior. However, another description might be that an event occurs, behavior and feelings occur, and the behaviors have consequences. The feelings serve to describe the relation among the event, the behavior, and the consequences. Emotion is not separated from the entire context, nor is it treated as causal; rather, emotion is a natural and understandable part of the context, a type of byproduct (Goldiamond, 1975; Layng, 2006). For example, fear may describe situations when putting distance between an individual and a harmful event is desirable. We want to run away. We are not running because we are afraid, nor are we running and therefore feeling afraid. Rather, we are running *and* feeling afraid because something harmful is nearby. It does not really matter that our feeling of fear matches anyone else's; it only matters that we understand that the emotion reflects (but does not cause) the need to take effective action to create distance from a harmful situation. When a learner says, "You don't understand how I feel; you never had anyone say that to you," one can say, "I do know what it's like to really want to get away from something. What can be done when you feel you really want to get away?" We can use our feelings of fear to ask, "What do I think is harmful?" "Why do I think that?" and "What do I need to do so as not to be harmed?" Each situation involves consequences important to someone. The procedures typically described as being in the cognitive competency domain can be used to teach the critical discriminations and actions required.

> Empathy is contacting the context and consequences that others may face and having that influence how one behaves toward others.

Empathy as an Example of a Complex Social Competence

Empathy is contacting the context and consequences that others may face and having that influence how one behaves toward others. In essence, learners must apply many of the metacognitive repertoires described earlier to determine what context and consequences are responsible for how they or others are feeling and what those feelings suggest about what needs to be done. Of particular importance is the application of problem solving and active listening. Here the issue involves navigating the world of others, what Sternberg (2006) calls "practical intelligence." It is not the problem-solving behaviors that differentiate SEL from other types of learning; rather, it is the subject matter to which those behaviors are applied. Accordingly, it is important to define precisely the contextual conditions and to build simulated scenarios around them, possibly using role-playing and encouraging the application of steps outlined by Robbins (2011) and Robbins and Layng (2015) in real time. By linking feelings to context, learners can be led to discover the relation of feelings to context and consequences and to build a sophisticated repertoire throughout their schooling. Learners can begin to describe other learners' contexts and infer what emotions others may be feeling or might likely feel. Furthermore, they can be taught to assess the consequences of their actions for themselves and for others. Learners can apply these skills to all social relations. Using their emotions as guides, learners can be taught to take the steps to arrange the conditions that produce the social outcomes they seek while not creating undesired outcomes for others. It is important that learners begin to recognize that there are no "bad" feelings. Even their painful feelings are telling them something about the world and helping them find what they value and the goals they want to achieve.

Teacher assessment of SEL competencies involves determining if learners apply the metacognitive competencies described earlier to the solution of problems of social and emotional importance. Correctly answering a series of multiple-choice questions about various scenarios may help, but only the real-time sampling of the application of problem solving and active listening to real-world social and emotional behavior can provide a true indication that such SEL competency actually exists. This reflects yet another convergence: metacognitive competency and a set of social-emotional cognitive skills that, combined, will produce a reliable social-emotional competency.

Insider–Outsider Considerations

So far, the discussion concerning SEL has focused on what the learner is doing. Teachers also need to be sensitive to the fact that some aspects of their students' social and emotional status may be very difficult for the "insider" to see and may require an "outsider" to understand and help. Specifically, isolation or exclusion is felt (by the learner) more often than it is seen (by the teacher). An apparently successful learner goes home feeling left out, even isolated. What the teacher or other classmates may see is a learner's success and perhaps even smiles. This apparent success masks the felt isolation. One first needs to understand what makes someone feel left out. Happiness often depends on the number of alternative ways of obtaining important consequences in comparison with the number of alternatives available to a peer group (Goldiamond, 1974, 1976a, 1976b; Layng, 2014b; Layng & Robbins, 2012; Rayo & Becker, 2007; Robbins, 1995).

Figure 2. Available Alternatives and Their Elements

Opportunity	Means		Benefits
School Dance	Dance Skills	⟶	Invited to Dance
Debate Club	Debate Skills	⟶	Invited to Debate
Lunch	Talking Skills	⟶	Invited to Sit

Consider Figure 2. To the extent that all elements—the opportunities, means, and benefits—are present and all alternatives are as available as they are to others, one feels relatively included. But what if one has no dance skills? Even if there is a school dance and the learner is present, the learner cannot participate. Or, in the school cafeteria, what if the learner is not invited to sit even though there are open seats at lunch and the learner can converse? It is not only the opportunities that matter but whether or not one has the means of taking advantage of them or whether the benefits everyone else seems to enjoy are available. If one has all three alternatives available, one can choose any of them to get valuable social interaction. One has more degrees of freedom and feels it (after Goldiamond, 1976b). No dance skills, not invited to sit—one is coerced into debate club only. The learner does not feel that a real choice is available. Feelings of exclusion describe alternatives relative to those available to peers; a learner may feel left out or lonely even if he or she is a successful debater. These relations are responsible for the feelings and any actions taken by the learner as a result. Stated differently, the feeling of isolation is not the cause of the actions; rather, the actions and the feelings are a function of the restricted alternatives in reference to the alternatives available to others. If one who is experiencing restricted degrees of freedom relative to his or her peers is now subject to even minor insults or teasing, the result can make distancing (from school and those responsible for allowing the restriction and the bullying) a potent reinforcer. When escape is not possible, the emotion that describes this situation is often anger. The SEL competence of teachers must include the ability to detect and intervene to increase the social alternatives available to learners as well as attend to insults or teasing and its direct effects. This requires very special training and is not currently a part of most SEL programs. For example, teachers must not simply assume a remark or a joke at a learner's expense is inconsequential. Nor should they regard as harmless recognizing the birthday of one student one day and overlooking the birthday of another student on another day. Schoolwide programs that encourage inclusion may also be required and may need to include school personnel beyond a classroom teacher. Inclusion is, however, a key to avoiding many of the serious conditions that may lead to school violence.

Motivational Competencies

Motivation is commonly considered some type of internal drive that may keep one at something over long periods of time or when keeping at something may create hardship. A lack of motivation is often posited when such perseverance or "grit" is not observed. One learner works diligently at something for hours; another may give up right away. This raises the question as to how motivation can be instilled in learners.

Strategies for building motivation can draw upon a strong literature that has both experimental and real-world roots. Laboratory work has shown that human persistence can be shaped (e.g., Wylie, 1986a, 1986b; Wylie & Dubanoski, 1988) with a considerable amount of work but with very little payoff. Procedures can be applied that help us forgo near-term small rewards for much more delayed larger ones (Rachlin, 2004). Learners can be helped to specify goals, assess current strengths, and proceed in small enough steps when clear movement toward the goal will motivate behavior (Goldiamond, 1974). What is really important to someone can be determined, and help can be provided to build the person's life around it through problem solving (Goldiamond, 1984; Layng, 2009; Liden, 2015) and building resilience and "grit" (e.g., Smith, 2010) in challenging conditions. This vast literature can be valuable, but for teachers, understanding motivation may not be an easy task.

The term *motivation* may be used to describe behavior under a range of circumstances that may be quite distinct (after Goldiamond, Dyrud, & Miller, 1965). Food can be a good motivator if we wait to leave some time since one has last eaten: We define by those things we may do to make a consequence effective. A high frequency of someone doing something may cause us to say he or she is really motivated to do it: We define by behavior frequency. We may conclude that someone is motivated to get something if we see that person obtaining something over and over: We define by consequence. We may attribute motivation to a certain condition or setting if we see someone repeatedly do something in these settings: We define by occasion. We see someone continue to work even though there is a distracting siren blaring and lights flashing outside a window: We define by level of distractibility. We notice one consistently choosing one activity over another: We define by preference among alternatives. We see someone continue with an activity in the face of obstacles or infrequent reward: We define by persistence. Accordingly, motivated behavior may be a product of very different variables. No single motivational state accounts for all of them. Additionally, a variety of methods are available for helping to make particular behavioral outcomes important to a person (Goldiamond, 1974; Langthorne & McGill, 2009). Furthermore, some students may show plenty of motivation but not for doing the things that they might benefit from in school.

Initial assumptions about the motivations of those who finish a task and those who do not may also be inaccurate. In developing academic support programs for community college learners (see Johnson & Layng, 1992), a research team of which I was a part, working at Malcolm X College in Chicago, was curious as to what separated the B+ and A students from the C+ and B students in a health science program. The placement test data for these students showed little difference. However, we found that the better students took more and better notes. They also tended to turn in assignments on time, particularly when the assignments required taking notes and using them to answer a question. Was there a difference in student motivation? Were the better students simply willing to work a little harder? We examined the note taking and discovered that the poorer students took notes at about 5 to 10 words per minute and that the better students could take notes at a rate of between 25 and 30 words per minute, at least triple the rate of the poorer students. Library assignments often involve extensive note taking. The better students took about an hour to complete a typical assignment; for the very same assignment, the poorer students would take nearly three hours to complete, if they completed it at all. If the poorer learners are equally as motivated as the better learners—that is, they can work continuously for an hour—they will fail to complete the assignment. The poorer learners must be about three times as motivated—to do the same thing. Was it possible that what appeared to be a motivational problem separating good from poor students might instead simply be a function of writing speed? We decided to find out by providing a special type of practice on "tool skills" (see Johnson & Layng, 1992)—hear word/write word, and see word/write word—until the writing rate of the poorer learners reliably equaled the rate of the better learners. After the practice, the difference in students' performance outcome virtually disappeared. Instead of increasing motivation, the tool skills brought the performance of the task at hand in line with the requirements one could reasonably meet. The solution to what appeared to be a lack of motivational competence was teaching a psychomotor skill, yet it was a question of motivational competence that led us to the solution.

There are other times that a lack of performance may be mistakenly attributed to a lack of internal motivation. Take an example of a youth who plays video games instead of doing homework. The student does not have the motivation to do the work; competing activities appear to be far more motivating. But perhaps the situation is not one of simply working on his motivation for schoolwork directly. If the outcome of doing homework versus the outcome of playing the video game is compared, it may be discovered that this student prefers hanging with friends, playing a little basketball, texting with others, caring for a car, and a range of other activities to playing video games. The question might then be asked, "What has happened to this learner when homework was submitted in the past?"

Figure 3. Motivational Matrix: Possible Costs and Benefits of Two Alternatives

Occasion	Behavior		Cost	Benefit
Video Game	Play Game	→	Reprimand for no work, poor grade	Kill a few Orcs, get to next level; poor academic abilities not on display
Homework Problems	Do Problems	→	Get many wrong, embarrassment; poor academic ability on display, poor grade	Chance for improvement, teacher feedback

The learner may very much want to be good at academics, and the fact that there is reluctance to show bad works suggests that looking "smart" may be important. Is this a lack of motivation or an indicator of a different type of motivation, that is, a motivation to cover up one's shortcomings? What might our learner be feeling? Conflicted emotions are likely; comments to himself might be, "I know I should do the work; I am falling further behind." It is tempting to suggest that playing video games is a way to escape these thoughts and feelings. Some may advocate saying positive things to oneself or simply accepting that one feels this way and attempting to move on. But to understand the motivation, one needs to understand the feelings in context. Conflicted feelings may reflect conflicting circumstances and consequences. It is not only the benefits of homework and the costs of failing to complete it that need to be compared. Providing our learner with an immediate academic success and slowly requiring more behavior that results in even more success may change what was historically an unmotivated student into a focused, committed learner (see, e.g., Johnson & Layng, 1992).

Teaching Motivational Competency

There is no singular motivational competency that can be taught. Instead, arranging environments that increase the likelihood of certain behaviors across a range of conditions is required. This applies to both learners and teachers. For the learner, using emotions to help uncover important consequences, needed additional skills, the right circumstances, a program of gradually increasing behavioral requirements (teaching grit), and so on requires a convergence of competencies. This convergence includes an SEL repertoire, a metacognitive repertoire, and a range of cognitive competencies. For teachers, it is important to ask, "What am I really saying when I say there is a motivational problem?" "Have I examined all the reasons for why the behavior I would like to occur is not occurring?" Different circumstances will require different programs.

Summary

In conclusion, the essential repertoires described as cognitive competencies, metacognitive competencies, social and emotional competencies, and motivational competencies consist of critical building block competencies that converge in such a way that a clear demarcation between each may not be possible. What separates them are the conditions under which often-well-defined competencies occur and are taught. As metacognitive competencies are acquired, they can be harnessed to teach SEL and motivational competencies. Accordingly, the critical repertoires in all of these competencies can be directly taught and hence measured using criteria established for teaching complex cognitive skills (after Tiemann & Markle, 1991) and can produce actions that result in meaningful differences for all learners.

Action Principles for States, Districts, and Schools

Action Principles for States

a. Do not order cognitive, metacognitive, social-emotional, and motivational competencies in some hierarchy of importance. All are equally important. Treat them as converging repertoires.

b. When setting objectives and priorities, include metacognitive, SEL, and motivational learning.

c. Provide adequate funding for professional development for all competencies.

d. Draw from a range of disciplines—including cognitive science, behavior analysis, learning science, neuroscience, and education—when developing strategies and goals.

e. Avoid vague objectives that could lead to multiple interpretations. Carefully specify the behaviors learners would be observed to perform or each accomplishment achieved for each competence.

Action Principles for Districts

a. Do not order cognitive, metacognitive, social-emotional, and motivational competencies in some hierarchy of importance. All are equally important. Treat them as converging repertoires.

b. Clarify the components of each competence and what form of teaching from the cognitive domain is required. A taxonomy such as provided by Tiemann and Markle (1991) or Bloom (1956) is helpful (see, e.g., the comprehensive identification of the minimum competencies required of applied learning scientists or instructional designers provided by Layng, 2014a).

c. Build a culture in which reflection, analysis, and problem solving are supported throughout the curriculum and throughout the day for academic and nonacademic challenges. Learners should be encouraged to continually apply their problem-solving and active-listening repertoires.

    d. Understand that interpersonal competence comes from the applications of skills that can be learned (cognitive domain) and carefully used (metacognitive domain) and continually evaluated on their effect on us and others (social and emotional domain).

    e. When setting objectives and priorities, include metacognitive, SEL, and motivational learning.

    f. Provide adequate funding for professional development for all competencies.

    g. Draw from a range of disciplines—including cognitive science, behavior analysis, learning science, neuroscience, and education—when developing strategies and goals.

Action Principles for Schools

    a. Do not order cognitive, metacognitive, social-emotional, and motivational competencies in some hierarchy of importance. All are equally important. Treat them as converging repertoires.

    b. Clarify the components of each competence and what form of teaching from the cognitive domain is required. A taxonomy such as provided by Tiemann and Markle (1991) or Bloom (1956) is helpful (see, e.g., the comprehensive identification of the minimum competencies required of applied learning scientists or instructional designers provided by Layng, 2014a).

    c. Use available programs and resources that have been developed by educators to help teachers teach the components necessary for metacognitive competence (highly recommended are *Skills for School Success* by Archer and Gleason, 2002, and *Learn to Reason with TAPS: A Talk Aloud Problem Solving Approach* by Robbins, 2015).

    d. Build a culture in which reflection, analysis, and problem solving are supported throughout the curriculum and throughout the day for academic and nonacademic challenges. Learners should be encouraged to continually apply their problem-solving and active-listening repertoires.

    e. Help learners to understand that emotions are often the sensible outcome of the situation one is in and reflect that situation.

    f. Help learners to use emotions as indicators of the conditions they are facing and to plan and execute strategies for dealing with that situation.

    g. Understand that interpersonal competence comes from the applications of skills that can be learned (cognitive domain) and carefully used (metacognitive domain) and continually evaluated on their effect on us and others (social and emotional domain).

    h. When choosing motivational strategies, first determine the possible reasons the learner may appear unmotivated or motivated to do something not in his or her best interest. Ask what the consequences are, both costs and benefits, of each alternative available to the learner. Ask what would make someone behave that way.

    i. When setting objectives and priorities, include metacognitive, SEL, and motivational learning.

References

Archer, A., & Gleason, M. (2002). *Skills for school success*. North Billerica, MA: Curriculum Associates.

Austin Independent School District. (2015). Department of social and emotional learning: Tools for learning, tools for life [Website]. Retrieved from https://www.austinisd.org/sites/default/files/dept/sel/images/A.I.S.D._SEL_Standards_-_Elementary_and_Secondary_9-11-12_0.pdf

Bloom, B. S. (1950). Problem-solving processes of college students: An exploratory investigation. *Supplementary Educational Monographs, The School Review and The Elementary School Journal, 73*, 1–109.

Bloom, B. S. (Ed.). (1956). *Taxonomy of educational objectives. Handbook l: Cognitive domain*. New York, NY: David McKay.

Carmichael, J. W., Bauer, J. D., Hunter, J. R., & Sevenair, J. P. (1988). An assessment of a premedical program in terms of its ability to serve Black Americans. *Journal of the National Medical Association, 80*(10), 1094–1104.

Carmichael, J. W., Hassel, J., Hunter, J., Jones, L., Ryan, M. S., & Vincent, H. (1980). Project SOAR (stress on analytical reasoning). *The American Biology Teacher, 42*(3), 169–173.

Collaborative for Academic, Social, and Emotional Learning. (2015). Social and emotional learning core competencies [Website]. Chicago, IL: Author. Retrieved from http://www.casel.org/social-and-emotional-learning/core-competencies

Gagne, R. M. (1965). *The conditions of learning*. New York, NY: Holt-Rinehart Winston.

Gagne, R. M. (1970). *The conditions of learning* (2nd ed.). New York, NY: Holt-Rinehart Winston.

Goldiamond, I. (1974). Toward a constructional approach to social problems: Ethical and constitutional issues raised by applied behavior analysis. *Behaviorism, 2*(1), 1–84.

Goldiamond, I. (1975). A constructional approach to self-control. In A. Schwartz & I. Goldiamond (Eds.), *Social casework: A behavioral approach* (pp. 67–130). New York, NY: Columbia University.

Goldiamond, I. (1976a). Coping and adaptive behaviors of the disabled. In G. L. Albrecht (Ed.), *The sociology of physical disability and rehabilitation* (pp. 97–138). Pittsburgh, PA: University of Pittsburgh.

Goldiamond, I. (1976b). Protection of human subjects and patients: A social contingency analysis of distinctions between research and practice, and its implications. *Behaviorism, 4*(1), 1– 41.

Goldiamond, I. (1984). Training parents and ethicists in nonlinear behavior analysis. In R. F. Dangel & R. A. Polster (Eds.), *Parent training: Foundations of research and practice* (pp. 504–546). New York, NY: Guilford.

Goldiamond, I., Dyrud, J., & Miller, M. (1965). Practice as research in professional psychology. *Canadian Psychologist, 6a*(1), 110–128.

Johnson, K. R., & Layng, T. V. J. (1992). Breaking the structuralist barrier: Literacy and numeracy with fluency. *American Psychologist, 47*(11), 1475–1490.

Langthorne, P., & McGill, P. (2009). A tutorial on the concept of the motivating operation and its importance to application. *Behavior Analysis in Practice, 2*(2), 22–31.

Layng, R. R., & Robbins, J. K. (2012, November). *Toward a new consequentialism: Nonlinear contingency analysis and the understanding of moral behavior*. Poster presented at the Theory and Philosophy Conference, Association for Behavior Analysis International, Santa Fe, NM.

Layng, T. V. J. (2006). Emotions and emotional behavior: A constructional approach to understanding some social benefits of aggression. *Brazilian Journal of Behavior Analysis, 2*(2), 155–170.

Layng, T. V. J. (2009). The search for an effective clinical behavior analysis: The nonlinear thinking of Israel Goldiamond. *The Behavior Analyst, 32*(1), 163–184.

Layng, T. V. J. (2012). *Understanding concepts: Implications for science teaching*. Boston, MA: Mimio. Retrieved from http://www.mimio.com/~/media/Files/Downloads/Partner-Resources/Whitepapers/whitepaper_science_teaching.ashx

Layng, T. V. J. (2014a). Learning science design and development requirements: An update of Hendrix and Tiemann's "designs for designers." *Mexican Journal of Behavior Analysis, 40*(2), 39–57.

Layng, T. V. J. (2014b, November). *Social policy and terrorism: Contingencies of exclusion.* Invited address presented at the 11th International Congress on Behavioral Studies, Milan, Italy.

Layng, T. V. J., & Twyman, J. S. (2013). Education + technology + innovation = learning? In M. Murphy, S. Redding, & J. Twyman (Eds.), *Handbook on innovations in learning* (pp. 133–148). Philadelphia, PA: Center on Innovations in Learning. Retrieved from http://www.centeril.org

Liden, T. A. (2015). *Parent partnership: Towards a constructional approach to improving the life of parents with children with autism* (Unpublished master's thesis). University of North Texas, Denton, TX.

Markle, S. M. (1982). *Formulating clear objectives.* Unpublished self-instructional program.

McMillan, J. H. (1987). Enhancing college students' critical thinking: A review of studies. *Research in Higher Education, 26*(1), 3–29.

Mechner, F. (1962). *Behavioral analysis for programmers.* New York, NY: Basic Systems.

Mechner, F. (1965). Science education and behavior technology. In R. Glasser (Ed.), *Teaching machines and programmed learning, II: Data and directions* (pp. 461–484). Washington, DC: National Education Association.

Mechner, F. (1994). *Learning and practicing skilled performance.* New York, NY: The Mechner Foundation.

Mechner, F., Fredrick, T., & Jenkins, T. (2013). How can one specify and teach thinking skills? *European Journal of Behavior Analysis, 14*(2), 285–293.

Merrill, M. D. (1971). Necessary psychological conditions for defining instructional outcomes. In M. D. Merrill (Ed.), *Instructional design: Readings* (pp. 173–184). Englewood Cliffs, NJ: Prentice-Hall.

Rachlin, H. (2004). *The science of self-control.* Cambridge, MA: Harvard University Press.

Rayo, L., & Becker, G. S. (2007). Evolutionary efficiency and happiness. *Journal of Political Economy, 115*(2), 302–337.

Redding, S. (2014a). *Personal competencies in personalized learning.* Retrieved from http://www.centeril.org/publications/Personalized_Learning.pdf

Redding, S. (2014b). *Personal competency: A framework for building students' capacity to learn.* Retrieved from http://www.centeril.org/publications/Personal_Compentency_Framework.pdf

Robbins, J. K. (1995, May). *Contingencies of exclusion: Why we need diversity training.* Paper presented at the 21st Annual Convention of the Association for Behavior Analysis, Chicago, IL.

Robbins, J. K. (1996). *TAPS for teachers.* Seattle, WA: Robbins/Layng & Associates.

Robbins, J. K. (2011). Problem solving, reasoning, and analytical thinking in a classroom environment. *The Behavior Analyst Today, 12*, 42–50.

Robbins, J. K. (2014). Learn to reason with TAPS: A talk aloud problem-solving approach [video file]. Seattle, WA: P.E.E.R. International. Retrieved from http://peerinternational.org/taps.html

Robbins, J. K. (2015). *Learn to reason with TAPS: A talk aloud problem solving approach.* Seattle, WA: P.E.E.R. International.

Robbins, J. K., & Layng, T. V. J. (2010). *Fluent thinking skills: A generative approach* (2nd ed.). Seattle, WA: P.E.E.R. International.

Robbins, J. K., & Layng, T. V. J. (2015, August). *Teaching children to ask meaningful questions.* Invited workshop presented at the National Autism Conference, Pennsylvania State University, University Park, PA.

Robbins, J. K., Layng, T. V. J., & Jackson, P. (1994). *Fluent thinking skills.* Seattle, WA: Robbins/ Layng & Associates.

Schwab, J. J. (1960). The teaching of science as enquiry. In J. J. Schwab & P. F. Brandwein (Eds.), *The teaching of science* (Burton Lecture; pp. 3–103). Cambridge, MA: Harvard University Press.

Smith, J. (2010). *When "it" happens in college: Lead yourself through any change.* Morgantown, WV: ChangeMatters, LLC.

Sternberg, R. J. (2006). The scientific basis for the theory of successful intelligence. In R. Subotnik & H. Walberg (Eds.), *The scientific basis of educational productivity* (pp. 161–184). Charlotte, NC: Information Age Publishing.

Tiemann, P. W., & Markle, S. M. (1973). Remodeling a model: An elaborated hierarchy of types of learning. *Educational Psychologist, 10*(3), 147–158.

Tiemann, P. W., & Markle, S. M. (1991). *Analyzing instructional content.* Seattle, WA: Morningside Press.

Whimbey, A., & Lochhead, J. (1985). *Problem solving and comprehension.* Hillsdale, NJ: Lawrence Erlbaum.

Whimbey, A., Lochhead, J., & Narode, R. (2013). *Problem solving and comprehension* (7th ed.). Hillsdale, NJ: Lawrence Erlbaum.

Wylie, A. M. (1986a). The establishment of high rate schedule control through the use of clinical transfer procedures: Historical, instructional, and imitative transfer. *Experimental Analysis of Human Behavior Bulletin, 4*(2), 26.

Wylie, A. M. (1986b). Implicit programming strategies in the development of high rate schedule control. *Experimental Analysis of Human Behavior Bulletin, 4*(2), 27.

Wylie, A. M., & Dubanoski, R. (1988). Program determinants of fixed-ratio performance by humans. *Experimental Analysis of Human Behavior Bulletin, 6*(2), 21–22.

Proceed With Caution: Measuring That "Something Other" in Students

Allison Crean Davis

Over the last several years, there has been a growing sense that we are not measuring what matters for children and their development. That is, by focusing assessment narrowly on academic growth, we may be missing the "something other" that seemingly lies below the surface of overt knowledge yet influences student results (Redding, 2014).

"Noncognitive variables" is the catch-all term often used to describe this "something other," capturing an array of constructs including "grit" (Duckworth, Peterson, Matthews, & Kelly, 2007), "mindset" (Dweck, Chiu, & Hong, 1995), "aspirations" (Quaglia, 1989), and now-classic terms such as "attitude" (Allport, 1935), "locus of control" (Rotter, 1954), "learned helplessness" (Seligman, 1972), and "self-efficacy" (Bandura, 1977). An unfortunate misnomer, the associated "noncognitive" constructs indeed represent cognitive (Borghans, Duckworth, Heckman, & ter Weel, 2008) and even metacognitive processes (Conley, 2013; Messick, 1979). The term is as inaccurate as it is vague.

Weak nomenclature aside, noncognitive variables seem to be having their day. They matter for their own sake, round out what is meant by an "educated" person, and contribute to successes we have in school, socially, and in our careers (Garcia, 2014). Philanthropists are investing millions of dollars to fund the development of measures for noncognitive variables (Blad, 2015a). The National Assessment of Educational Progress (NAEP), also known as the Nation's Report Card, is working to include measures of motivation, mindset, and grit in its background survey by 2017 (Sparks, 2015). The U.S. Department of Education's Skills for Success program awarded four 3-year grants nearing half a million dollars a year to school systems in 2015 for "implementing, evaluating, and refining tools and approaches for developing the noncognitive skills of middle-grades students in order to increase student success" (U.S. Government Printing Office, 2015, p. 32545). The recent renewal of the Elementary and Secondary Education Act (ESEA), now called the Every

> *They matter for their own sake, round out what is meant by an "educated" person, and contribute to successes we have in school, socially, and in our careers.*

Handbook on Personalized Learning for States, Districts, and Schools, pages 37–53

Student Succeeds Act (ESSA, 2015), allows states to use measures of social/emotional competency in their new accountability systems.

This growing awareness, understanding, and interest in noncognitive variables fuels motivation to make the elusive observable and transform the abstract into the concrete. Because they seem to matter in important ways to attainment and lifelong functioning, measuring these variables—and doing it well (i.e., accurately and consistently)—will provide the foundation to effectively cultivate them. So how do we do it?

A Series of Conundrums

The process of determining how to measure something involves preliminary steps that include agreeing upon what we are measuring, why we are measuring it, and for whom. Therein lies the measurement conundrum with these constructs (Dinsmore, Alexander, & Loughlin, 2008; Willingham, 2013). The challenge relates in part to the emerging discussion of just what these factors are, how they cluster and relate to each other, and how we collectively agree to define them.

Clarity in Concept: What Are We Measuring?

The idea that one must "define it before you size it" (Keohane, 2014) comes into play here. A strongly operationalized definition provides for construct validity, or "truth in labeling" (Trochim, 2006). This, in turn, can assist in the development of an array of measurement tools that, given the inherently varied assets and limitations of its parts, is, as a whole, securely tied to a consistently labeled, agreed-upon idea.

> *In education, clarity and agreement can be elusive. The concept of learning, which at face value seems basic, generates an array of uncertainty.*

In education, clarity and agreement can be elusive. The concept of learning, which at face value seems basic, generates an array of uncertainty. Are we capturing what a student knows at one point in time, or should we look at growth over time? Are we attending to the right learning standards that define what students should know and be able to do at various points in their educational journeys? Should these standards be consistent nationwide, or should states be allowed to define what is important in their own ways? Disagreement over these questions has stimulated pushback on attempts to measure learning, which relates not only to how we use assessment tools, but also what those assessments measure. Clear and agreed-upon definitions are critical to measurement, but achieving consensus is not always simple.

Redding (2014) has synthesized a range of these variables into four composite factors—cognitive, metacognitive, motivational, social/emotional—which he collectively terms the "personal competencies." These competencies represent many of the noncognitive factors as well as traditional "academic" learning and provide a categorical framework that can guide additional research, practice, and the development of metrics. Table 1 describes each of these competencies and represents some of the components within them.

Table 1. Personal Competencies Definitions and Components

Competency	Description	Components/Similar Concepts
Cognitive	Prior learning that organizes the mind and provides associations and understanding to facilitate new learning	• Cognitive content: Knowledge held in memory • Stored knowledge and understanding • Cultural knowledge • Cognitive structures (associational webs) • Curiosity: Cognition plus motivation • Vocabulary

Meta-cognitive	Self-regulation of learning and use of learning strategies	• Thinking about thinking
		• Self-regulation of learning; Self-appraisal and self-management:
		  ◊ Goal-setting and planning
		  ◊ Progress monitoring
		  ◊ Adaptation based on feedback
		• Problem-solving and analytical thinking
		• Learning strategies, such as mnemonics, distributed practice, practice testing
		• Logic, synthesis, evaluation
		• Divergent (creative) thinking

Motivational	Engagement and persistence in pursuit of learning goals	• Agency (locus of control; attribution) • Extrinsic and intrinsic • Incentives • Motivation to learn (mastery) • Self-efficacy perception • Expectancy value theory • Mindset (especially a growth mindset) • Flow • Aspiration

Social/ Emotional	Sense of self-worth, regard for others, and emotional understanding and management to set positive goals and make responsible decisions	• Character traits, such as grit, resilience, generosity, independence, courage, optimism
		• Behaviors, such as attentiveness, impulse control, context-appropriate language
		• Learned skills, especially related to:
		  ◊ Understanding and managing emotions
		  ◊ Setting and achieving positive goals
		  ◊ Feeling and showing empathy for others
		  ◊ Establishing and maintaining positive relationships
		  ◊ Making responsible decisions

Note: This table was devised by Sam Redding and provided in a personal communication, March 4, 2015. Used by permission.

The University of Chicago Consortium on Chicago School Research (Farrington et al., 2012) has an alternative framework comprised of five composite factors related to academic performance, including:

a. **Academic behaviors:** Going to class, doing homework, organizing materials, participating, studying

b. **Academic perseverance:** Grit, tenacity, delayed gratification, self-discipline, self-control

c. **Academic mindsets:** Psychosocial attitudes or beliefs one has about oneself in relation to academic work

d. **Learning strategies:** Study skills, metacognitive strategies, self-regulated learning, goal-setting

e. **Social skills:** Cooperation, assertion, responsibility, empathy

These frameworks, which conveniently and hypothetically cluster finer-grained noncognitive variables, may aid the sector by easing communication and leading to more consistent understanding and cohesive measurement approaches, particularly if a singular framework ultimately solidifies based on additional research. Currently, the nascent nature of the evidence about these frameworks precludes a decisive path forward. Frameworks can also introduce challenges by obscuring potentially valuable nuances within their factors or clusters. The degree to which overarching noncognitive constructs, such as Redding's motivational and social/emotional competencies, are interrelated or independent is unknown. Neither is it known if other components comprise these broader constructs, such as self-efficacy and mindset, and how they may overlap in practice. Finally, even with a reasonably consistent aversion to the "noncognitive" label among researchers and its portrayal in the educational media as a "big ambiguous category" (Blad, 2015b), the term continues in high rotation, necessitating its inclusion in any discussion about measuring this phenomenon.

> Socrates told us that the act of applying a common name is justified when we can account for the common nature behind that name.

Socrates told us that the act of applying a common name is justified when we can account for the common nature behind that name. With noncognitive variables, we have work to do. Getting the categories and their components right, then agreeing upon their labels, is no small nor insignificant matter for the reliable understanding of these factors and, subsequently, our ability to measure them.

Clarity in Purpose: Why We Are Measuring

Studies factoring in the application of noncognitive variables in a variety of fields suggest the value they may add to long-term outcomes of elementary and secondary education. Economists have found that cognitive and noncognitive skills are equally important to an array of labor market (e.g., schooling, employment, wages) and behavioral outcomes (e.g., teenage pregnancy, smoking, drug use, participation in illegal activities; see Heckman, Stixrud, & Urzua, 2006). The military has identified that noncognitive factors such as grit predict the success of military officer candidates (Kelly, Matthews, & Bartone, 2014). Meta-analyses have shown that measures of noncognitive variables, such as integrity and conscientiousness, improve the ability to predict training success and job performance by 20% and 16%, respectively, over use of cognitive ability measures alone (Schmidt & Hunter, 1998). Sackett, Schmitt, Ellingson, and Kabin (2001), in examining employee selection and ethnic diversity, found that persistent gaps between ethnic groups on cognitive assessment scores were reduced or eliminated on measures of noncognitive skills. Similarly, noncognitive measures have been universally predictive of employment outcomes, regardless of education level.

In higher education, concentrating on noncognitive variables has proven valuable to the admissions process and to ultimate success in higher education (Sedlacek, 2003, 2005).

Namely, students representing strengths in the following areas have had more positive outcomes in postsecondary education, including retention, grade point average, involvement in extracurricular activities, and matriculation:

a. Positive self-concept
b. Realistic self-appraisal
c. Successful leadership experience
d. Ability to understand and cope with racism or the "system"
e. Preference for long-range goals
f. Access to a strong support person
g. Participation in a community with which they can identify and from which they can receive support
h. Ability to acquire nontraditional knowledge from outside the classroom

Evidence in the K–12 sector is slim but building and suggests a strong relationship between these kinds of noncognitive competencies, academic performance, and career success (Pellegrino & Hilton, 2012). Accessible and valid measures have the potential to help educators understand the baseline noncognitive tendencies of their students and bolster them as needed to enhance their learning experience. This brings us to back to the issue of "how."

Clarity in Process: How to Measure the Obscure

In the social sciences, constructs are called "latent" when they cannot be directly observed or measured. As with other latent variables, researchers and practitioners have drawn inferences about noncognitive variables both from other indicators, or "imperfect proxies" believed to represent them, and through statistical modeling (Bollen, 2002; Heckman et al., 2006). Herein lie additional issues related to the "measurement conundrum."

The "Doesn't-Add-Something" Issue

Many policymakers and scientists do not believe noncognitive variables can be accurately and consistently measured (Kyllonen, 2005). Behaviorists, in particular, suggest that it is useless to measure hypothetical constructs at all because they do not add value to pedagogy (i.e., tell us how to teach) and, in fact, may impede progress. Too often, the behaviorists argue, the constructs are used as "explanatory fictions" that serve to make instructional goals seem even more inaccessible and tend to provide new rationalizations for inadequate instruction (Greer, 1992, p. 27). Although they may acknowledge the presence of noncognitive variables, the inability to observe them directly prevents what behaviorists would consider the most rigorous method of measurement: the frequency and accuracy of desirable responses. This kind of measurement is not always familiar or valued by educators, who generally have little training in behavioral techniques, consider them difficult to accomplish, and, importantly, may find them objectionable for philosophical reasons.

The Flawed Measure Issue

Those attempting to tap into latent noncognitive variables are constrained to measure something else that is manifest or simpler to obtain, such as the opinions of students (self-report) or other knowledgeable sources, such as teachers or parents (other-report).

Surveys allow these opinions to be gathered at a relatively low cost across large groups and provide data that can be quantified. Interviews can probe more deeply into the perceptions of students or others but may not be feasible at a large scale due to cost, time requirements, and the difficulty of analyzing qualitative data.

Both self- and other-reports, no matter the method, have constraints. They lack standard benchmarks (e.g., how much "motivation" is enough, or necessary, or right?) to help researchers/practitioners interpret results. Research, in fact, suggests standards for noncognitive variables are context-sensitive, making ratings across educational systems susceptible to reference bias due to differences in school climate and the related standards to which students are held (West, 2014). Self-report methods, in particular, are notorious for their ability to be "faked" by respondents (i.e., have responses that are, either consciously or unconsciously, skewed to present the person advantageously). Even researchers engaged in this work lament that "unbiased, unfakeable, and error-free measures are an ideal, not a reality" (Duckworth & Yeager, 2015, p. 243).

The "Why Not?" Issue

Having deployed various strategies for gathering information and researching noncognitive variables for decades, William Sedlacek adds context to what could be perpetual hand-wringing about the limitations of measurement, saying: "Why wouldn't you try this? Maybe it won't work, but if you want to be innovative at all…why wouldn't you want to experiment?...Lead the way….don't wait for others…" (Sedlacek, as quoted by Martin, 2013).

Standardized tools may add value to the integrity of measurement but could homogenize what we attend to, value, and emphasize with a set of legitimately diverse characteristics. In relation to the purposes noncognitive measures are used for in higher education (e.g., student admissions), Sedlacek contends differentiated attempts to gather this information can align to the natural diversity of educational settings.

The Unintended Consequences Issue

To the degree measures do not capture what we intend to assess (i.e., they are invalid), or cannot do so consistently (i.e., they are unreliable), we risk drawing false conclusions and potentially allocating limited resources to ultimately ill-matched, poorly designed, or unnecessary interventions. These psychometric properties form the "evidential basis" for measurement. Yet the "consequential basis" matters too. Messick (1979) points out that noncognitive variables are entangled with value judgments, yet value judgments are subjective and socially influenced. At a time when the pursuit of "not trying" has become a matter of interest (Slingerland, 2014), the thought of making that which is unconscious and spontaneous (e.g., noncognitive variables) conscious, deliberate, and intervened-upon may, paradoxically, be counterproductive. Using noncognitive variables must be done with care and attention to potential drawbacks.

Existing Resources, Developing Work

Measurement challenges are not unique to noncognitive variables, and knowing the limitations does not need to contribute to paralysis for the education sector in its aim to capture information about them. Instead, the challenges highlight the importance of a balanced portfolio of measures representing multiple indicators of various kinds, yielding data captured at different points in time, and ideally assessing an array of noncognitive factors to best understand the nuance and developmental changes of students (Dinsmore et al., 2008; West, 2014).

As with academic measures, so with multiple noncognitive measures: The inherent limitations of each individual tool or method may be mitigated and confidence in conclusions may be enhanced with findings that are consistent and/or complementary. Measurement portfolios may include tools capturing classroom climate and/or educational norms within a system that may contribute to and interact with self- and other-assessments of noncognitive variables. Ideally, a balanced portfolio would gather feedback from students and adults and about various learning settings, allowing us to consider the interaction between these factors.

Some measurement tools, both broader in noncognitive scope and more targeted to specific concepts and skills, have been developed for the K–12 sector. They are being deployed for research and practice purposes and are being enhanced over time. As more dollars have begun to flow to encourage researchers to develop valid and reliable metrics for this work, a more extensive collection of tools should begin to form.

Table 2 represents a sample of self- or teacher-report tools that show evidence of validity, are easily accessed, and are designed to be used with children, adolescents, and young adults. Not exhaustive, the list is intended to provide a sound starting point for educators and policymakers interested in investigating measurement options and has been aligned to Redding's four personal competencies. Several tools capture data across these competencies and are represented separately.

Table 2. Sample of Validated Self- and Other-Report Tools Developed for K–12 and Postsecondary Education

Personal Comp.	Instruments of Note	Examples/Sample Items
Cognitive	Existing tools within a balanced academic assessment framework.	• Large-scale, summative, standardized, annual • Formative, standardized • Diagnostic assessments • Classroom assessments • Behavioral indication of intellectual curiosity and cultural awareness

Personal Comp.	Instruments of Note	Examples/Sample Items
Metacognitive	**Self-Regulation Questionnaire (SRQ)** 63-item survey with 7 subscales related to planning behavior to reach goals. Scoring and psychometric information included (Brown, Miller, & Lawendowski, 1999). There is also an academic-specific self-regulation questionnaire (SRQ-A), including a standard version for elementary and middle school students (Ryan & Connell, 1989) and one specifically designed for students with learning disabilities (Deci, Hodges, Pierson, & Tomassone, 1992).	**SRQ** • *I usually keep track of my progress toward my goals.* • *My behavior is not that different from other people's.* • *Others tell me that I keep on with things too long.* • *I doubt I could change even if I wanted to.* • *I have trouble making up my mind about things.* • *I get easily distracted from my plans.* • *I reward myself for progress toward my goals.* **SRQ-A (Standard)** • *Why do I try to do well in school?* • *Because I enjoy doing my school work well.* • *Because I will get in trouble if I don't do well.* **SRQ-A (Learning Disabled)** • *I do my classwork because I want to learn new things.* • *I do my classwork because that's the rule.*
Motivational	**Theory of Intelligence** (Growth Mindset; Dweck, Chiu, & Hong, 1995), 16-item survey, available online with immediate feedback, with a focus on fixed vs. growth mindset in relation to intelligence and talent. **Harter Self-Perception Profile** (Harter, 2012), with versions for children, adolescents, learning disabled students, etc. The number of items on these multi-dimensional self-report questionnaires varies, but for each, the focus is on reporting self-concept domains that are sensitive to the relevant concerns at that developmental period. Each version is comprised of several scales (e.g., scholastic, social, athletic).	**Theory of Intelligence** • *You have a certain amount of intelligence and you really can't do much to change it.* • *You can learn new things, but you can't really change your basic intelligence.* **Self-Perception** • *Some kids feel that they are very good at their school work BUT* • *Other kids worry about whether they can do the school work assigned to them.* • *Some kids like the kind of person they are BUT* • *Other kids often wish they were someone else.*

Personal Comp.		Instruments of Note	Examples/Sample Items
Social/Emotional		**Grit Scale measure** (Duckworth, Peterson, Matthews, & Kelly, 2007), 12-item survey with two scales with focus on the specific concept of grit. Scoring information included. **Devereux Student Strengths Assessment (DESSA;** teacher report; LeBuffe, Shapiro, & Naglieri, 2009), 72 norm-referenced items across 8 scales assess social/emotional competencies for children in K–8th grade.	**Grit Scale** Consistency of Interest Scale: • *I often set a goal but later choose to pursue a different one.* • *New ideas and new projects sometimes distract me from previous ones.* Perseverance of Effort Scale: • *I have achieved a goal that took years of work.* • *Setbacks don't discourage me.* **DESSA (teacher report)** During the past four weeks, how often did the child… • Give an opinion when asked? • Stay calm when faced with a challenge? • Keep trying when unsuccessful? • Express concern for another person? • Handle his/her belongings with care? • Accept responsibility for what he/she did? • Say good things about herself/himself?
Multiple Competencies	K–12	**Character Report Card (KIPP)** Multiple teacher ratings pooled for students on factors such as zest, grit, self-control, optimism, gratitude, social intelligence, and curiosity.	• Actively participates • Finishes whatever he or she begins • Comes to class prepared • Keeps his/her temper in check • Gets over frustrations and setbacks quickly • Recognizes and shows appreciation for others • Is able to find solutions during conflicts with others • Is eager to explore new things
	Postsecondary	**Motivated Strategies for Learning Questionnaire** (MSLQ; Pintrich, Smith, Garcia, & McKeachie, 1991) **Noncognitive Questionnaire** (NCQ; Sedlacek, 1996) Designed to assess long-range goals, positive self-concept, realistic self-appraisal, racism, and availability of strong support. **Personal Potential Index** (PPI; Kyllonen, 2008) In 24 items, captures applicant-specific information from multiple raters on core personal attributes important for success in graduate study (knowledge and creativity, resilience, communication skills, planning and organization, teamwork, ethics, and integrity) **Taps** Motivation (31 items: goals and value beliefs); Learning strategies (31 items: cognitive & metacognitive strategies); Management of resources (19 items). Manual with scoring and psychometric data included (updated psychometric information from Rotgans & Schmidt, 2010).	**MSLQ** • *If I study in appropriate ways, then I will be able to learn the material in this course.* • *When I take a test, I think about how poorly I am doing compared with other students.* • *I think I will be able to use what I learn in this course in other courses.* • *I believe I will recieve an excellent grade in this class.* **NCQ** • *These are three things that I am proud of having done.* • *Once I start something, I finish it.* • *When I believe strongly in something, I act on it.* • *If I run into problems concerning school, I have someone who would listen to me and help me.* **PPI** • Is intensely curious about the field • Works well in group settings • Can overcome challenges and setbacks • Organizes work and time effectively • Demonstrates sincerity

Another promising measure is a survey slated for imminent release by the California Office to Reform Education (CORE) and developed in collaboration with the organization Transforming Education (2014). Designed and piloted to assess four competencies, which are described as interpersonal and intrapersonal, the measure suggests consistency in thinking, if not clear alignment, to Redding's personal competencies, as indicated in Table 3. Sample items released in 2014, provide insight into what to expect (see Table 3).

Going beyond the limitations of self-report tools, KIPP (KIPP Foundation, 2016) has deployed a Character Growth Card (Character Lab, 2016) that pools multiple teacher ratings for students on factors such as zest, grit, self-control, optimism, gratitude, social intelligence, and curiosity, hitting cross-cutting elements of the personal competencies. Some sample indicators in the Character Growth Card include:

- Actively participated
- Finished whatever s/he began
- Came to class prepared
- Kept temper in check
- Recognized what other people did for them
- Was able to find solutions during conflicts with others
- Was eager to explore new things

Table 3. CORE's Four Competencies' Alignment to Redding's Competencies and Sample Survey Questions

CORE Competency	Description	Alignment to Redding's Personal Competencies	Sample Survey Questions
Growth Mindset	Belief that one can change as a result of effort, perseverance, and practice	**Motivational**	(reverse coded) • *My intelligence is something that I can't change very much.* • *Challenging myself won't make me any smarter.* • *There are some things I am not capable of learning.* • *If I am not naturally smart in a subject, I will never do well in it.*
Self-efficacy	Belief in one's ability to succeed in achieving an outcome or reaching a goal	**Motivational**	• *I can earn an A in my classes.* • *I can do well on all my tests, even when they're difficult.* • *I can master the hardest topics in my classes.* • *I can meet all the learning goals my teachers set.*

CORE Competency	Description	Alignment to Redding's Personal Competencies	Sample Survey Questions
Self-management	Also known as "self-control" or "self-regulation," this is the ability to regulate one's emotions, thoughts, and behaviors effectively in different situations	Metacognitive and Social–Emotional	• *I came to class prepared.* • *I remembered and followed directions.* • *I allowed others to speak without interruption.* • *I worked independently with focus.*
Social Awareness	Ability to take the perspective of and empathize with others from diverse backgrounds and cultures; to understand social and ethical norms for behavior; and to recognize family, school, and community resources and supports	Social–Emotional	• *When others disagree with you, how respectful are you of their views?* • *When people are already talking together, how easy is it for you to join the group?* • *When you have problems at school, how easily can you find ways to solve them?* • *To what extent are you able to stand up for yourself without putting others down?*

On the international K–12 scale, the Programme for International Student Assessment (PISA), developed and administered by the Organisation for Economic Co-operation and Development (OECD), has complemented the data it collects related to cognitive student achievement in reading, mathematics, and science literacy with information on noncognitive outcomes (e.g., students' learning motivation), individual conditions (e.g., students' cultural, ethnic, and socioeconomic background), and characteristics of the institutional context (e.g., instructional practices, opportunities to learn, professional development). Various stakeholders, namely students and school principals, participate. Although the tool is not designed for application in practice and represents a narrow band in the developmental continuum (i.e., participants are 15-year-old students), the longitudinal data it provides lends international context to understanding how these factors play out over time, in relation to educational outcomes and contextual variables, and on a comparative basis with 65 countries and world economies. Already, PISA data suggest that student self-efficacy on cognitive tasks correlates with student achievement within and across participating countries (OECD, 2015).

In the higher education sector, Sedlacek (n.d.) has developed many freely available resources for measuring noncognitive variables that, albeit developed in the context of student selection, may suggest modified versions or methods for the K–12 sector. Richardson, Abraham, and Bond (2012), in a meta-analysis focused on 13 years of research with university students, provide an exceptionally thorough inventory of noncognitive (or nonintellective, as they call it) measures used in hundreds of studies that the researchers align to distinct research domains:

- Personality traits
- Motivation factors
- Self-regulatory learning strategies
- Students' approach to learning
- Psychosocial contextual influences

Included in this resource is a definition for each noncognitive attribute and representative items from key measures. Although compiled for research purposes, this too may provide valuable guidance to K–12 educators and researchers eager to develop ways to measure, either formally or informally, these variables. They also provide an extension to the developmental context of noncognitive factors as they suggest what is valued and applicable beyond the K–12 experience.

Emerging rapidly, due to an assist from technology, are efficient ways to capture behavioral representations of noncognitive performance (Stecher & Hamilton, 2014). By mining data behind virtual learning programs, researchers are beginning to understand learner behavior in response to challenges in those environments—mapping interactive engagement to user frustration, perseverance, persistence, motivation, or attempts to "game" the system. These data, examined for specific tasks or aggregated over many tasks, are being used to understand the relationship they have with learning outcomes and to improve the design of the systems themselves. Baker's chapter in this book explores this topic in depth.

Finally, research and development agendas related to measuring these "hard-to-measure" but important noncognitive variables are underway and are likely to bear fruit in the years ahead. RAND Education has discussed the importance of an evidence-based, rigorous, outcomes-related effort focusing on those variables that are of greatest interest and may be most likely to be used in high-stakes situations (e.g., college admissions). This lengthy process, it indicates, should be managed by independent research-coordinating boards, funded by foundations and agencies, and done in collaboration with tool developers (Stecher & Hamilton, 2014).

Onward

What we measure affects what we attend to, how we think, and what we do (Hauser & Katz, 1998). Accordingly, we must measure what we believe matters, even if it is difficult. In education, it is undeniably necessary to measure academic learning, but such measurements are arguably insufficient due to our recognition that the "something other" does matter, even if it is dicey to measure (Shechtman, DeBarger, Dornsife, Rosier, & Yarnell, 2013; West, 2014). As the evidence builds that noncognitive variables are a critical component to human development, learning, and achievement, we may need to accept (for now) the value of measuring what is "vaguely right," which is arguably better than measuring what is "precisely wrong" (Hauser & Katz, 1998).

Over time, educators must strive to emphasize these factors with students in the pursuit of greater and more holistic learning, work to refine their understanding of these variables, arrive at consensus in their definitions, then determine how they are best measured. Effective measurement legitimizes concepts, allows us a method to understand their state in both static and dynamic ways, provides the opportunity to experiment and capitalize upon them, and helps us understand their value. Better measurement will help refine our work.

Important and meaningful research and development is likely to ensue over the years, and policymakers are providing incentives to do so. Eventually, with valid, reliable, and realistically attainable feedback on noncognitive variables, traditional accountability frameworks may be supplemented with additional practical information that can be integrated into program designs, instructional methodologies, student skillsets, and differentiated interventions. Other reasons for measuring these constructs include:

- Providing practical tools to guide educators in their work with learners
- Assisting with program design and evaluation
- Aiding further research
- Providing early warnings for vulnerable students who may benefit from special services

That said, now is not the time to embed these factors into formal accountability frameworks. It required decades to ready academic assessments for this purpose, and educators must allow the scientific method to unfold to support doing so with noncognitive variables. In the meantime, educators may proceed with caution. Because the act of measuring mirrors the act of attending to a matter, that may be a reasonable starting point for educators and their relationship with these individual noncognitives and/or their related composites, such as personal competencies. In the spirit of Sedlacek (2005), we may opt not to wait and to use existing measures or create new methods. Or we may take a cautious approach, given the various issues related to the "measurement conundrum." Either way, some recommendations may be in order as educators build awareness for themselves and the field.

Action Principles for States, Districts, and Schools

Action Principles for States

a. Start by understanding the value of noncognitive variables. Read the existing literature and keep tabs on progress, as new developments, both in terminology and metrics, are occurring rapidly.

b. Remember context. Emphasize that, as we measure students, we must also reflect on teachers, the environment, and the interaction among these, or at least keep those influences in mind as we draw inferences and act.

c. Encourage healthy pedagogical exploration but avoid embedding results into formal accountability systems, as the tools are not designed for that purpose and, psychometrically, have too many limitations at this time to do so.

Action Principles for Districts

a. Frame the work as complementary to whatever standards of learning are being embraced by the district. Using the research, help teachers understand how noncognitive skills are part of a whole for child development, not a different or unrelated strand of work happening. Reflect upon the values (and limitations) of the measurement tools and interventions.

b. Encourage the use of multiple formative measures to avoid "locking" students into a noncognitive performance level. Foster a culture that can respond dynamically to the predictable developmental changes of students as well as those that are cultivated intentionally by the learning climate.

Action Principles for Schools

   a. Observe the learning process with fresh eyes. Build your awareness of how non-cognitive factors manifest themselves, not only in students, but also in yourselves and in other adults. Pay attention.

   b. Hypothesize. In terms of practice, consider whether particular students are candidates for knowing more about their current status and/or may benefit from intervention/support.

   c. Consider piloting some measures. Within a low-stakes environment, use some measures to gather evidence on targeted noncognitive variables; attempt a few complementary approaches such as self- and other-report (likely teacher). Work with perhaps a small group of interested educators to review findings and discuss how the learning environment or process may shift or adjust to help students harness or improve upon their noncognitive skills and learning performance.

References

Allport, G. W. (1935). Attitudes. In C. Murchison (Ed.), *Handbook of social psychology* (pp. 798–844). Worcester, MA: Clark University Press.

Bandura, A. (1977). Self-efficacy: Toward a unifying theory of behavioral change. *Psychological Review, 84*(2), 191–215.

Blad, E. (2015a). Measuring grit, character draw new investments. *Education Week, 35*(6), 6.

Blad, E. (2015b, November 23). New ESEA may use noncognitive traits in accountability. Is that a good idea? [Web log post]. Retrieved from http://blogs.edweek.org/edweek/rulesforengagement/2015/11/new_esea_may_use_non-cognitive_traits_in_accountability_is_that_a_good_idea.html

Bollen, K. A. (2002). Latent variables in psychology and the social sciences. *Annual Review of Psychology, 53*, 605–634.

Borghans, L., Duckworth, A. L., Heckman, J. J., & ter Weel, B. (2008). *The economics and psychology of personality traits* (Working Paper 13810). Cambridge, MA: National Bureau of Economic Research. Retrieved from http://www.nber.org/papers/w13810.pdf

Brown, J. M., Miller, W. R., & Lawendowski, L. A. (1999). The self-regulation questionnaire. In L. VandeCreek & T. L. Jackson (Eds.), *Innovations in clinical practice: A source book* (Vol. 17, pp. 281–289). Sarasota, FL: Professional Resource Press.

Character Lab. (2016). Character growth card. Philadelphia, PA: Author. Retrieved from https://characterlab.org/character-growth-card/

Conley, D. T. (2013). Rethinking the notion of "noncognitive." *Education Week, 32*(18), 20–21.

Deci, E. L., Hodges, R., Pierson, L., & Tomassone, J. (1992). Autonomy and competence as motivational factors in students with learning disabilities and emotional handicaps. *Journal of Learning Disabilities, 25*(7), 457–471. Retrieved from http://www.ravansanji.ir/?std1005SRQA

Dinsmore, D. L., Alexander, P. A., & Loughlin, S. M. (2008). Focusing the conceptual lens on metacognition, self-regulation, and self-regulated learning. *Educational Psychology Review, 20*(4), 391–409.

Duckworth, A. L., Peterson, C., Matthews, M. D., & Kelly, D. R. (2007). Grit: Perseverance and passion for long-term goals. *Journal of Personality and Social Psychology, 92*(6), 1087–1101.

Duckworth, A. L., & Yeager, D. S. (2015). Measurement matters: Assessing personal qualities other than cognitive ability for educational purposes. *Educational Researcher, 44*(4), 237–251.

Dweck, C. S., Chiu, C., & Hong, Y. (1995). Implicit theories and their role in judgment and reactions. A world from two perspectives. *Psychological Inquiry, 6*(4), 267–285.

Every Student Succeeds Act, Public Law 114-95, 114th Cong., 1st sess. (December 10, 2015). Retrieved from https://www.congress.gov/bill/114th-congress/senate-bill/1177?q=%7B%22sear ch%22%3A%5B%22every+student+succeeds+act%22%5D%7D&resultIndex=1

Farrington, C. A., Roderick, M., Allensworth, E., Nagaoka, J., Keyes, T. S., Johnson, D. W., & Beechum, N. O. (2012). T*eaching adolescents to become learners. The role of noncognitive factors in shaping school performance: A critical literature review.* Chicago, IL: University of Chicago Consortium on Chicago School Research. Retrieved from https://consortium.uchicago.edu/sites/default/files/publications/Noncognitive%20Report.pdf

Garcia, E. (2014). *The need to address noncognitive skills in the education policy agenda.* Briefing Paper No. 386. Washington, DC: Economic Policy Institute. Retrieved from http://www.epi.org/ publication/the-need-to-address-noncognitive-skills-in-the-education-policy-agenda/

Greer, R. D. (1992). The teacher as strategic scientist: A solution to our educational crisis? In R. P. West & L. A. Hamerlynck (Eds.), *Designs for excellence in education: The Legacy of B.F. Skinner* (pp. 261–279). Longmont, CO: Sopris West, Inc.

Harter, S. (2012). *Susan Harter self-report instruments.* Retrieved from https://portfolio.du.edu/SusanHarter/page/44210

Hauser, J., & Katz, G. (1998). Metrics: You are what you measure! *European Management Journal, 16*(5), 517–528.

Heckman, J., Stixrud, J., & Urzua, S. (2006). The effects of cognitive and noncognitive abilities on labor market outcomes and social behavior. *Journal of Labor Economics, 24*(3), 411–482. Retrieved from http://www.nber.org/papers/w12006.pdf

Kelly, D. R., Matthews, M. D., & Bartone, P. T. (2014). Grit and hardiness as predictors of performance among West Point cadets. *Military Psychology, 26*(4), 327–342. Retrieved from https:// www.researchgate.net/publication/256063679_Psychological_Hardiness_Predicts_Adaptability_in_Military_Leaders_A_Prospective_Study

Keohane, D. (2014, November 10). The shadow banking system, define it before you size it [Web log post]. London, England: FT Alphaville. Retrieved from http://ftalphaville. ft.com/2014/11/10/2036962/the-shadow-banking-system-define-it-before-you-size-it/

KIPP Foundation. (2016). Character counts [Webpage]. New York, NY: Author. Retrieved from http://www.kipp.org/our-approach/character

Kyllonen, P. C. (2005). *The case for noncognitive assessments.* Princeton, NJ: Educational Testing Service. Retrieved from https://www.ets.org/Media/Research/pdf/RD_Connections3.pdf

Kyllonen, P. C. (2008). *The research behind the ETS® Personal Potential Index (PPI).* Princeton, NJ: Educational Testing Service. Retrieved from http://www.ets.org/Media/Products/PPI/10411_PPI_bkgrd_report_RD4.pdf

LeBuffe, P. A., Shapiro, V. B., & Naglieri, J. A. (2009). *The Devereux Student Strengths Assessment (DESSA).* Lewisville, NC: Kaplan Press.

Martin, J. (2013, January 21). Sedlacek on assessing non-cognitive variables: From the USC Attributes that Matter Conference [Web log post]. Retrieved from http://21k12blog.net/2013/01/21/ sedlacek-on-assessing-non-cognitive-variables-from-the-usc-attributes-that-matter-conference/

Messick, S. (1979). Potential uses of noncognitive measurement in education. *Journal of Educational Psychology, 71*(3), 281–292.

Organisation for Economic Co-operation and Development. (2015). *PISA 2015: Draft questionnaire framework.* Paris, France: Author. Retrieved from http://www.oecd.org/pisa/pisaproducts/PISA-2015-draft-questionnaire-framework.pdf

Pellegrino, J. W., & Hilton, M. L. (Eds.). (2012). *Education for life and work: Developing transferable knowledge and skills in the 21st century.* Washington, DC: The National Academies Press.

Pintrich, P. R., Smith, D. A. F., Garcia, T., & McKeachie, W. J. (1991). *A manual for the use of the Motivated Strategies for Learning Questionnaire (MSLQ).* Technical Report No.91-8-04. Ann Arbor, MI: The Regents of The University of Michigan.

Quaglia, R. (1989). Student aspirations: A critical dimension in effective schools. *Research in Rural Education, 6*(2), 7–9.

Redding, S. (2014). *The something other: Personal competencies for learning and life.* Philadelphia, PA: Center on Innovations in Learning. Retrieved from http://www.centeril.org

Richardson, M., Abraham, C., & Bond, R. (2012). Psychological correlates of university students' academic performance: A systematic review and meta-analysis. *Psychological Bulletin, 138*(2), 353–387.

Rotgans, J. I., & Schmidt, H. G. (2012). The intricate relationship between motivation and achievement: Examining the mediating role of self-regulated learning and achievement-related classroom behaviors. *International Journal of Teaching and Learning in Higher Education, 24*(2), 197–208.

Rotter, J. B. (1954). *Social learning and clinical psychology.* New York, NY: Prentice-Hall

Ryan, R. M., & Connell, J. P. (1989). Perceived locus of causality and internalization: Examining reasons for acting in two domains. *Journal of Personality and Social Psychology, 57*(5), 749–761. Retrieved from http://www.ravansanji.ir/?std1005SRQA

Sackett, P. R., Schmitt, N., Ellingson, J. E., & Kabin, M. B. (2001). High-stakes testing in employment, credentialing, and higher education. *American Psychologist, 56*(4), 302–318.

Schmidt, F. L., & Hunter, J. E. (1998). The validity and utility of selection methods in personnel psychology: Practical and theoretical implications of 85 years of research findings. *Psychological Bulletin, 124*(2), 262–274.

Sedlacek, W. E. (n.d.). Publications, articles, surveys [Webpage]. Retrieved from http://williamsedlacek.info/publications.html#Surveys/Instruments

Sedlacek, W. E. (1996). An empirical method of determining nontraditional group status. *Measurement and Evaluation in Counseling and Development, 28*(4), 200–210.

Sedlacek, W. E. (2003). Alternative measures in admissions and scholarship selection. *Measurement and Evaluation in Counseling and Development, 35*(4), 263–272.

Sedlacek, W. E. (2005). The case for noncognitive measures. In W. Camara & E. Kimmel (Eds.), *Choosing students: Higher education admission tools for the 21st century* (pp. 177–193). Mahwah, NJ: Lawrence Erlbaum.

Seligman, M. E. P. (1972). Learned helplessness. *Annual Review of Medicine, 23*(2), 407–412.

Shechtman, N., DeBarger, A. H., Dornsife, C., Rosier, S., & Yarnell, L. (2013). *Promoting grit, tenacity, and perseverance: Critical factors for success in the 21st century.* Menlo Park, CA: Center for Technology in Learning, SRI International.

Slingerland, E. (2014). *Trying not to try: The art and science of spontaneity.* New York, NY: Crown Publishers.

Sparks, S. D. (2015, June 3). 'Nation's Report Card' to gather data on grit, mindset. *Education Week, 34*(32), 15. Retrieved from http://www.edweek.org/ew/articles/2015/06/03/nations-report-card-to-gather-data-on.html

Stecher, B. M., & Hamilton, L. S. (2014). *Measuring hard-to-measure student competencies: A research and development plan.* Santa Monica, CA: RAND Education. Retrieved from http://www.rand.org/pubs/research_reports/RR863.html

Transforming Education (2014). *Introduction to social emotional learning: 4 competencies.* Sacramento, CA: Author. Retrieved from http://static1.squarespace.com/static/55bb6b62e4b00dce923f1666/t/565dcdf5e4b082ff9ff5e727/1448988149417/Introduction_to_SEL_4Competencies.pdf

Trochim, W. M. K. (2006). *Research methods knowledge base* (2nd ed.). Retrieved from http://www.socialresearchmethods.net/kb/

U.S. Government Printing Office. (2015, June 9). *Applications for new awards: Skills for Success Program.* Federal Register, 80(110), 32545–32551. Retrieved from https://www.gpo.gov/fdsys/pkg/FR-2015-06-09/pdf/2015-14081.pdf

West, M. R. (2014, December 18). *The limitations of self-report measures of non-cognitive skills.* The Brown Center Chalkboard Series Archive, Number 92. Washington, DC: The Brookings Institution. Retrieved from
http://www.brookings.edu/research/papers/2014/12/18-chalkboard-non-cognitive-west

Willingham, D. (2013, January 21). Measurement of non-cognitive factors [Web log post]. Retrieved from http://www.danielwillingham.com/daniel-willingham-science-and-education-blog/measurement-of-non-cognitive-factors

II. Students at the Center of Personalized Learning

Co-Designing Instruction With Students

Melinda S. Sota

Learner choice is a defining feature of personalized learning (Patrick, Kennedy, & Powell, 2013), setting it apart from the related concepts of individualized and differentiated learning. Although these related concepts imply some change in instruction based on learner skills, knowledge, or performance, only personalization implies that the learner is an active agent in the decision-making process.

In its National Education Technology Plan, the U.S. Department of Education (USDOE, 2010) defines personalized learning as "instruction that is paced to learning needs, tailored to learning preferences, and tailored to the specific interests of different learners. In an environment that is fully personalized, the learning objectives and content as well as the method and pace may all vary" (p. 12). In this definition, personalization encompasses both differentiation and individualization but adds learner interests as a specific element of personalization.

The International Association for K–12 Online Learning (iNACOL) is more explicit in including learner choice as part of its working definition of personalized learning, defining it as "tailoring learning for each student's strengths, needs, and interests—including enabling student voice and choice in what, how, when, and where they learn—to provide flexibility and supports to ensure mastery of the highest standards possible" (Patrick et al., 2013, p. 4). Adding to these features, Redding's (2013) model of personalized learning emphasizes interpersonal relationships and explicitly includes motivation as well as metacognitive, social, and emotional competencies:

> Personalization refers to a teacher's relationships with students and their families and the use of multiple instructional modes to scaffold each student's learning and enhance the student's motivation to learn and metacognitive, social, and emotional competencies to foster self-direction and achieve mastery of knowledge and skills" (Redding, 2013, p. 6).

Although these features—varying time, pace, place, content, goals, instructional methods, and especially learner choice—define personalized learning, it is also important to note that instruction can be more or less personalized, involving different levels of choice within different aspects of an instructional episode. For the purposes of this chapter, an instructional episode will be defined as any activity undertaken to reach a learning goal. Breaking down an instructional episode into relatively standard parts can help to both define personalization as a continuum of choice and serve as a framework for thinking about how to design and implement partial or complete systems for personalizing learning.

Within instruction, what can be personalized? Any instructional episode involves key parts and aspects, including (a) types and features of learning activities; (b) where the learner engages in these activities—at home, at school, or elsewhere; (c) the pace of instruction; (d) the amount of instruction and practice; (e) the instructional goals or objectives; and (f) the standards by which learning or performance will be evaluated. In what is typically thought of as traditional, standard, teacher-directed instruction, the teacher or educational system specifies each of these factors. All learners may go through a fixed instructional sequence at a fixed pace with a fixed amount of instruction and practice in an attempt to reach standard objectives with performance evaluated against standard criteria. At the other extreme is completely self-directed learning. Here, the learner may set her own learning goals and her own criteria for meeting them. She may select her own preferred method to reach them and move at her own pace at home or at school, with an amount of instruction and practice that she deems necessary to meet her goal. In between these two extremes are variations on differentiated, individualized, and personalized learning. In an individualized program, for example, the goals, standards, and activities may be set, but the pace and amount of instruction may vary based on individual learner performance. In a personalized system, the teacher may select from a fixed set of learning goals but work with the learner to choose appropriate and preferred learning activities to reach those goals (see USDOE, 2010, for definitions that differentiate among these three concepts).

> In a personalized system, the teacher may select from a fixed set of learning goals but work with the learner to choose appropriate and preferred learning activities to reach those goals...

Why would a school want to develop a system of personalized learning? First, it can support lifelong learning when implemented with student training in developing self-regulated learning (learning-to-learn) skills such as (a) selecting goals, (b) identifying criteria to indicate when a goal is achieved, (c) selecting learning activities, and (d) monitoring learning to determine whether the selected activities are working and how much more work is required to reach mastery. Each of these skills can be taught in a well-developed personalized learning system that includes explicit, systematic instruction focused on building and using these skills as students advance across grade levels. Explicit and systematic teaching of self-regulation strategies may incorporate scaffolding and teacher models or demonstrations as well as guided and independent student practice with feedback. Activities should be carefully planned and should systematically build on prior knowledge and previously taught skills (see Zumbrunn, Tadlock, & Roberts, 2011, for an overview of self-regulated learning and teaching strategies for developing it).

A second reason for implementing a personalized learning system lies in its potential to increase motivation and learning. Some studies have shown that even very limited choice over seemingly irrelevant factors within a learning activity can increase motivation and learning (see, for example, Cordova & Lepper, 1996). When choice is implemented within a mastery-based system, motivation and learning may be further increased. In mastery-based systems, learners work at their own pace to meet learning goals and move on once they've met a specific criterion on an assessment of the learning goal. Mastery-based systems that include proactive goal selection and learner-involved formative assessment can support learners in developing growth (vs. fixed) mindsets and learning-goal (vs. performance–goal) orientations, both of which predict important outcomes, such as academic achievement, persistence, and resilience in the face of setbacks. With a growth mindset, learners believe that their effort will result in learning and performance gains (rather than believing they are either good at something or not). With a learning orientation, learners' focus is on learning and mastering challenges rather than demonstrating ability or lack thereof (Dweck, 1986; Dweck, Walton, & Cohen, 2014; Grant & Dweck, 2003). Within a well-developed personalized learning system, learners can regularly see their skills and knowledge grow as a result of their effort.

However, learner choice related to factors affecting instruction, such as the best learning method to use or the amount of instruction and practice necessary, requires that learners know what they know, what they don't know, and how to best go about gaining the necessary skills or knowledge—abilities often referred to as "metacognition" (see Redding, 2013, on metacognitive skills and how to support their development in the classroom). This is a tall order even for adults (Dunning, Heath, & Suls, 1994), and without well-developed self-regulation skills, learner choice is likely to have a detrimental effect on learning (Kirschner & van Merriënboer, 2013).

How can the positive effects of learner choice be maximized while minimizing risk that learners will not be able to choose in their best interests? By designing models in which teachers and learners co-design instruction, with learners making choices coached by a teacher and informed by knowledge of current and desired skills. In this type of model, learners not only work on the knowledge and skills related to the instructional materials but also on self-regulated learning skills—learning how to learn. Three components are important in such a system: (a) detailed maps that link learning goals to standards, specify the skills and knowledge necessary to meet learning goals, and show hierarchical relationships among goals; (b) continuous formative assessment that involves the learner in a proactive manner; and (c) a systematic, explicit focus on developing self-regulated learning skills, with learners gradually taking on more responsibility in determining what they need to learn, how they can go about learning it, and measuring their own skill mastery to determine whether their chosen method is working for them. Self-regulated learners choose challenging learning goals, select learning strategies to help them reach those goals, and continuously monitor their learning to determine whether the learning strategies and methods that they have selected are working and make changes when they are not (Zimmerman, 1990). Here, the goal is to help learners develop mastery over the process of learning as well as the products (skills and knowledge).

Implementing a fully personalized learning system is a major undertaking often requiring cultural shifts in the way students and educators view learning and school (see Berger, Rugen, & Woodfin, 2014, and Mechner, Fiallo, Fredrick, & Jenkins, 2013). However, personalization can also be implemented in differing degrees and within different parts of the learning process. The following sections describe issues related to personalized learning in each aspect of the instructional episode and how that aspect may be co-designed with the learner.

Co-design Within the Instructional Episode

Each part of an instructional episode—from setting goals to evaluating progress and achievement—can involve differing degrees of learner choice. Although learner control over all aspects of learning may not be optimal (Kirschner & van Merriënboer, 2013), co-designing instruction with learners can help to increase learning and motivation (Ames, 1992; Corbalan, Kester, & van Merriënboer, 2006, 2008, 2009), and learners at all levels can play some role in setting their learning goals, selecting activities to reach those goals, and monitoring their learning as they work to achieve mastery.

Setting Learning Goals

Learning goals are fundamental to a personalized learning system, although the degree of learner choice in selecting goals may vary. For example, whereas young learners may have very limited choice in which goals to pursue at any given time, older learners may be offered more choices. Goal choice may also be constrained by standards and learners' current skill level within a particular area. To personalize learning around learning goals while ensuring that all learners master the necessary fundamental skills, it is important to develop goals that are (a) clearly aligned with standards, (b) well-defined so that they are specific and measurable, (c) written in terms of what learners will be able to do upon mastery, and (d) depicted in a manner that makes the relations among them (e.g., prerequisites or component skills) clear. Goals with these attributes are more easily communicated and understood and can make goal setting, activity selection, and progress monitoring easier for both students and teachers. In addition to fundamental skills that all learners should master, the scope of learning goals may also include advanced goals for learners who have a particular interest in or facility for the area.

Standards, Goal Definition, Relations, and Scope

A detailed goal map can guide both teachers and learners in choosing appropriate learning goals. Beginning with standards helps to ensure alignment between standards and goals. To be most useful, however, goals should *not* be equivalent to standards. Instead, goal analyses should be conducted in order to analyze the standards (and perhaps other sources) for the purpose of creating clearly defined learning goals. Goal analysis is a process in which a larger, more general goal is analyzed to clearly outline what achievement of that goal would look like and what skills, knowledge, or attitudes it would be necessary to develop in order to achieve the goal (the process of identifying the necessary skills, knowledge, and attitudes is often called *instructional analysis*). As a simple example of the process, imagine that one of the goals for an elementary science class is that students understand the concept of *density*. An analysis of this goal would first focus on defining what exactly is meant by the term "understand." In other words, if students *understand* density, what will they be able to *do*? Will they be able to calculate the density of a material given its mass and volume? Will they be able to create a conceptual model of density? Will they be able to employ density as an explanation of a phenomenon? Will they be able to state the definition? Will they be able to do all of these things?

To conduct a goal analysis:

1. Write down the initial goal statement—for example, "understand density," "read with understanding," or a specific standard.

2. Make a list describing what someone who has reached the goal can do—for example, "calculate the density of an object," "create a conceptual model of density," "retell the main events of a story," or "answer questions that require an inference from the text."

3. Review the list to ensure that each description is clear and truly describes what the goal means. Ask yourself, "Am I sure that another teacher would be able to write an assessment of the goal based on this statement that would accurately measure everything I intend?" If not, clarify the goal further.

4. Create the final list of goals by writing the goal statements in complete sentences.

5. Ensure that your list is complete. Ask yourself, "If a student were able to do all of these things, would I agree that the student had mastered the goal?" If the answer is no, work to figure out what is implied by the initial goal statement that is not in your final list (Mager, 1997).

In addition to clarifying what a goal means, analysis of goals can be useful in deriving learning goals from statements of standards because a single standard may encompass a number of skills and an array of knowledge. Analyzing each standard into multiple, more specific goals can help to clarify the standard and make it easier to align assessment, instruction, and practice (see Mager, 1997, for a step-by-step description of the goal analysis process,).

After you've clarified your goals through goal analysis, think about what component skills and knowledge students will need to master in order to achieve the goal. Analysis of the goal in these terms is often called *instructional* analysis and portrays the component knowledge and skills in terms of their hierarchical relationships. Figure 1 illustrates a partial instructional analysis of a standard that could be used to construct a goal map based on the Next Generation Science Standards (NGSS Lead States, 2013). This analysis is based on the science practice of "supporting an argument with evidence, data, or a model," and focuses on using evidence to support a claim. Grade 5 performance expectations related to the practice across content areas are listed below it. Below those is a partial analysis of using evidence to support a claim. To read the analysis, first read one line and then read a connected line below it in the pattern: "in order to ____, students will need to be able to _____." For example, in order to "support an argument with evidence," students will need to be able to "identify evidence that supports the claim" and "evaluate evidence for the claim." In order to "identify evidence that supports the claim," students will need to be able to both "distinguish between evidence that supports the claim and evidence that refutes the claim," and "distinguish between evidence that is relevant to the claim and evidence that is irrelevant to the claim." In order to distinguish between relevant and irrelevant evidence, students will need to be able to "explain the logical connection between a claim and evidence and state scientific principles that link the claim and evidence." This analysis shows that, while basic skills related to working with evidence cut across subject areas, science practice and science content are connected in that—to identify relevant evidence for a claim—the student will need relevant subject matter knowledge and skills in making logical connections between claims and evidence in that subject area.

Figure 1. A Partial Analysis of the Next Generation Science Standards, Identifying Embedded Component Skills and Knowledge

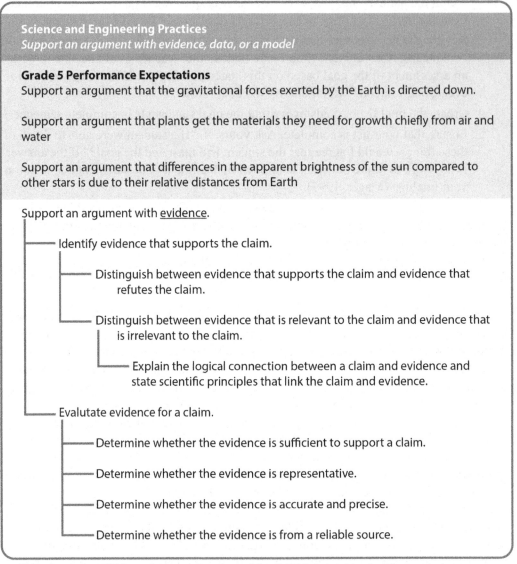

Science and Engineering Practices
Support an argument with evidence, data, or a model

Grade 5 Performance Expectations
Support an argument that the gravitational forces exerted by the Earth is directed down.

Support an argument that plants get the materials they need for growth chiefly from air and water

Support an argument that differences in the apparent brightness of the sun compared to other stars is due to their relative distances from Earth

Support an argument with <u>evidence</u>.

— Identify evidence that supports the claim.

— Distinguish between evidence that supports the claim and evidence that refutes the claim.

— Distinguish between evidence that is relevant to the claim and evidence that is irrelevant to the claim.

— Explain the logical connection between a claim and evidence and state scientific principles that link the claim and evidence.

— Evalutate evidence for a claim.

— Determine whether the evidence is sufficient to support a claim.

— Determine whether the evidence is representative.

— Determine whether the evidence is accurate and precise.

— Determine whether the evidence is from a reliable source.

Note. A portion of this analysis was conducted for Outthink, Inc. Used with permission.

The process in Figure 1 also suggests how such an analysis can support work across and within grade levels. For example, when just beginning to learn these skills, students might focus more energy on mastering each of the component skills (for example, by practicing distinguishing relevant from irrelevant evidence across a variety of relatively simple or familiar content). Once these skills have been mastered, they may be incorporated into the broader task of supporting an argument. The full skill set can also be taught across grade levels by increasing the complexity of the arguments and the level of subject matter while still employing the entire skill set at an appropriate level.

A clearly defined learning goal allows both the teacher and learner to evaluate work and determine when the learner has reached the goal. It also allows the teacher and learner to work together in identifying appropriate activities to help the learner work toward that goal. For example, although identifying learning and evaluation activities for "understanding density" might be unclear to both teacher and student, being able to state a definition, perform a calculation, or build a conceptual model are more straightforward.

It is important to note that, although a goal should be specific, it should not be trivial. A risk in writing for specificity is writing the intended meaning out of the goal. Care should be taken to write goals that are both specific *and* meaningful (see Tiemann, 1971, for a description and example of this process; see Berger et al., 2014, for descriptions of writing and using learning goals or *targets* within a personalized learning system). For example, although the three performance expectations in Figure 1 specify particular arguments to support, it is unlikely that the true goal is to support only *those* claims with evidence. Rather, educators hope that the skills involved in supporting an argument would transfer to a variety of claims in addition to those encountered in school

More specific goals also allow for project-based or problem-centered group work in which learners joining a group may have different levels of skill mastery.

(provided that the learner has the requisite content knowledge). Specifying the component skills involved in supporting a claim with evidence can help ensure that the necessary general skills are gained and applied across a variety of content areas.

More specific goals also allow for project-based or problem-centered group work in which learners joining a group may have different levels of skill mastery. By understanding where students are in terms of skill mastery, groups of students with complementary skill sets can be created for larger projects requiring a combination of skills. Learning and problem-solving activities can occur flexibly within individual, small-group, and large-group activities. For example, students who each have differing levels of skill in math, problem solving, argument, and science content knowledge could each use their respective skills to solve a problem more advanced than an individual could solve independently.

By linking goals with standards, the fundamental skills necessary for all students to master should be identified. However, extended goals—goals that build on the fundamentals but that are not required for all students to master—may also be available for advanced students to work on if they have mastered the necessary prerequisite skills and have a particular interest or aptitude in an area. Extending the scope of potential learning goals beyond those required allows for additional personalization as students have an opportunity to extend their skills as their particular interest and aptitudes allow. An extended scope may also motivate students to master lower level skills in order to attain higher level and potentially more interesting goals.

Table 1 lists a sample of performance expectations from the Next Generation Science Standards along with related goals based on the analysis shown in Figure 1. All of these goals are relevant to the standard related to supporting an argument with evidence and can be repeated across grade levels. While the topic areas and complexity of the subject matter increases across grade levels, the goals in this case would remain essentially the same. Performance expectations such as these with related goals may make up part of a goal map in order to link standards and goals within and across grade levels.

Table 1. Sample Performance Expectations from the Next Generation Science Standards and Related Goals Derived from Goal/Instructional Analyses

Next Generation Science Standards Performance Expectations	Related Goals*
2-PS1-4. Construct an argument with evidence that some changes caused by heating or cooling can be reversed and some cannot.	State what you would expect to happen if the claim was true.
3-LS2-1. Construct an argument with evidence that some animals form groups that help members survive.	Explain what would make you believe that the claim is true and why.
3-LS4-3. Construct an argument with evidence that in a particular habitat some organisms can survive well, some survive less well, and some cannot survive at all.	Given evidence, state whether it makes you believe that the claim is true or false and why.
5-PS2-1. Support an argument that the gravitational force exerted by Earth on objects is directed down.	Given data, state whether it is relevant to the claim and why or why not.

*Note: All of the related goals apply to each performance expectation.

Goal setting with students: Interim goals and learner choice

Goal setting for a particular student requires knowledge of the student's current achievement level because goals should be challenging yet achievable. In addition to selecting an appropriate goal toward which to work, goal setting may also involve further break down of a selected goal into interim goals. For example, if a defined goal is to read at a particular rate with fluency and accuracy, the specific student goal selected may not be that particular rate but an interim rate based on the student's current reading rate. For example, an interim goal might be to increase reading rate by 1.5 times the student's current rate. Interim goals such as these can help ensure that students see continuous improvement in their skills as a result of their effort (see Lindsley, 1992, for an example of continuous progress monitoring).

For younger students, goals may be set that can be achieved in shorter time frames; for example, an interim goal may be met in a single activity session. More advanced learners may work on extended goals that take significant time and effort to achieve and may contain several interconnected parts. For advanced students undertaking performance or production goals, co-creating rubrics with the student by analyzing expert or advanced-level performance can help to more fully define the goal and aid in progress monitoring and self-evaluation. After standards of final performance are agreed upon, interim goals may be created and set at challenging yet achievable levels by considering the ultimate goal (expert performance) in combination with the students' current performance level. Even young students can play a part in selecting interim goals, and as students advance, they can take on more responsibility in identifying and selecting their own interim goals.

Selecting Activities to Reach Goals

Results of studies investigating the effects of learner control on learning have been equivocal, with some studies finding benefits, some finding no effects, and others finding detrimental effects (Schnackenberg & Hilliard, 1998; Williams, 1993). One reason that learner control may result in poorer outcomes is that learners do not have the skills necessary to make informed choices regarding their own learning (Williams, 1993). First, to make informed decisions, people need to be able to accurately judge their current state of knowledge. However, in general, people are often poor at making this evaluation, often overestimating their knowledge and skill (Dunning et al., 2004; Williams, 1993). To reach a selected goal, learners will need to engage in learning activities designed to help them achieve that goal. Choice in activity selection may be informed by both learner preferences and how effective a particular activity or type of activity may be in helping the learner to reach that goal and may involve choice related to differences in simple surface features or significant differences in instructional type or strategy. Because making an informed choice about instructional type or strategy is often difficult—requiring knowledge about the content area that a novice may not have, knowledge of how a learner's current skills may influence success in an activity, and knowledge of how effective different instructional strategies are in helping learners acquire different types of skills—teacher coaching is particularly important in making an informed choice when factors other than surface features differ among possible activities.

> Results of studies investigating the effects of learner control on learning have been equivocal, with some studies finding benefits, some finding no effects, and others finding detrimental effects.

Surface versus instructional differences in activity type

Choice in activity may involve surface features (e.g., two computer-based programs that both teach the same skills in the same ways but differ in their game-like elements, characters, or similar features) or features fundamental to learning. Although choice of surface features may not have a great effect on learning progress, choice related to instructional factors may have a significant effect. For example, a learner may attempt to learn a concept by reading about it or by reading followed by a classification or analysis activity related to identifying or analyzing instances of the concept. Based on research on concept learning, classification or analysis of examples and non-examples should result in greater learning than reading only (Tennyson & Park, 1980). Thus, when choosing activities that involve instructional differences, coaching by the teacher as to what type of instructional activity may be best suited for achieving a particular learning goal can be important. However, learners may still be able to choose learning activities based on their preferences when activities differ only in surface features.

Selection versus design and resource use

Another issue in choosing activities is whether to select from activities readily available or to design new activities. More advanced students may choose to develop a unique learning sequence by selecting a number of different resources available in print, on the web, or via other sources. For example, a student might look up instructions and work examples in a textbook, watch a Khan Academy video, search for other relevant information available on the Internet, and work with the instructor and other students to discuss and solve problems. Because learning from resources is more challenging for learners with lower prior knowledge, self-directed, resource-based learning activities may best be used by more advanced students who already have acquired knowledge of the subject area and skills in resource use (Kirschner & van Merriënboer, 2013).

When selecting activities, it is important to identify those that align well with the learning goal. For example, if a student's goal is increasing fluency in recalling math facts, a suitable learning activity might involve engaging in computer-based math games that require learners to recall math facts under some time pressure or that reward fast, accurate recall. If a student's goal is solving math word problems, then different activities would be most appropriate unless the student is struggling with word problems because of a lack of prerequisite skills in math fact fluency.

Finally, when possible, information about activities should be used in determining what activity might be best for a particular student working on a particular goal. This information may come from the publisher (e.g., information on necessary prerequisites, characteristics of target learners, and results of any studies that have been done) or from information gathered from prior use (e.g., have students like this one succeeded in this activity in the past; has it helped students achieve this goal?).

If choice of activity involves more than choice of surface features, then teacher input regarding the most appropriate learning activities for that learning goal is warranted. Because students are likely to be novices both in the subject and in optimal learning activities for different learning types, the expert input of a teacher is invaluable. However, when multiple activities are appropriate for similar learning outcomes and when learners are more sophisticated in terms of prior knowledge, skills in learning from resources, and monitoring their own learning to determine whether what they are doing is working, learner preference may play a larger role in activity selection and planning.

Monitoring Learning: Formative Assessment

In formative assessment, information on student performance is gathered and used, not to evaluate the learner, but to evaluate whether learning methods and strategies are working for that learner. If learner performance indicates that specific methods or strategies are not working, a different learning method or strategy is indicated. Here, the focus is on evaluating the effectiveness of the learning activity during the learning process rather than on evaluating final learner achievement. As noted by Black and Wiliam (2009),

> Practice in a classroom is formative to the extent that evidence about student achievement is elicited, interpreted, and used by teachers, learners, or their peers, to make decisions about the next steps in instruction that are likely to be better, or better founded, than the decisions they would have taken in the absence of the evidence that was elicited. (p. 9)

There may be several reasons why a learning method or strategy is *not* working: (a) the activity itself may be poorly designed and therefore not effective, (b) the activity may be misaligned with the learning goal and therefore not teaching what the assessment is measuring, (c) the learner may be missing some prerequisite skills that the activity assumes are in place, or (d) the activity may not be effective for some other reason related to learner and activity characteristics. If a learner is not showing progress with a particular activity, then a different or modified activity should be tried and evaluated.

Studies have shown that students engaging in learner-controlled instruction who receive information on their mastery level do better than students in learner-controlled conditions who do not receive such information (see Williams, 1993). When learners take an active role in measuring their own progress and use that information to continue or change what they have been doing to reach their goal, they are practicing important skills involved in self-regulated learning (Nicol & Macfarlane-Dick, 2006). Formative assessment can also be a potentially powerful tool in helping students adopt learning (vs. performance) goals and a growth (vs. fixed) mindset, predictors of learning and perseverance (Grant & Dweck, 2003). Although formative assessment can be conducted by the teacher or program, as often occurs in individualized and differentiated instruction, a *personalized* learning system with emphasis on active student involvement in gathering and interpreting performance information can help to encourage application of self-regulated learning skills (Andrade, 2010; see also Berger et al., 2014; Lindsley, 1992, for examples of learning systems focused on progress monitoring and formative assessment systems that feature high student involvement).

Mastery Learning: Pace and Practice

When learning pace is set by the teacher or system, learner achievement must vary. When learning pace is variable and the signal to move on is mastery rather than a set period of time, time varies rather than achievement, and more students are able to reach higher achievement levels (USDOE, n.d.). Under the right instructional conditions, all students can achieve at higher levels (Bloom, 1968, 1974, 1984).

A fully personalized instructional system with a focus on continuous formative assessment and learner choice with teacher support in which students move at their own pace in meeting their selected goals is a type of mastery-based learning system. Mastery-based learning systems can result in increased student achievement (Kulik, Kulik, & Bangert-Drowns, 1990) and can support the development of positive motivational factors such as learning goal orientations and growth mindsets (Ames, 1992; Covington, 2000). In this type of system, assessments that show a lack of mastery indicate that more practice or a change in learning strategy or instructional materials is necessary to successfully reach the learning goal. The idea that learners can master learning goals with effort combined with the right learning methods illustrates the growth mindset and supports a learning goal orientation in which students persist in learning and mastering challenges.

Designing a System

A school where each student is motivated and engaged in mastering challenging learning goals matched to his or her skills and interests is one where most students would love to learn, where educators would love to teach, and that communities would love to see. People have been imagining and writing about such a system since at least the late 1800s (Keefe & Jenkins, 2002).

However, setting up such a system is a challenge—one that requires cultural shifts in school systems and that will only result from focused experimentation. The process of designing this type of system is parallel to the process of co-designing learning. First, goals for the system—criteria by which it would be evaluated as being successful—should be discussed and clearly outlined. Second, methods and strategies to reach those goals should be identified. These methods and strategies might be inspired by or borrowed from others or designed from first principles. Third, continuous progress monitoring regarding a number of measures needs to be undertaken as new things are tried. The design process is not cheap or quick, but it is invaluable for innovation and is necessarily iterative. When designs fail (and they will, again and again), that evidence is not evidence for the claim that "personalized learning systems are not effective," just as a student failing is not evidence that "the student is dumb." Rather, it is evidence only for the claim that what was tried did not work. A "mastery learning" perspective would indicate that you modify what you did and try again. Just as a student's instruction can be co-designed with the teacher, learning systems and school cultures can be co-designed with students, faculty, administrators, and state agencies (see Brown, 2009, for a description of design thinking).

Although a schoolwide personalized system might be the ideal, this analysis also illustrates that single instructional episodes can be more or less personalized in different ways. Small, informal, localized experiments with these factors within a classroom or subject area can help build personalization into the curriculum at a smaller, more manageable scale while offering the opportunity to try out different methods and strategies and assess their effects. In this way, the system can grow via a bottom-up, organic process as different practices are tried and effective practices are identified and implemented on a wider scale.

Action Principles for States, Districts, and Schools

Action Principles for States

a. Provide resources for the design, development, and testing of co-designed personalized learning systems. Resources may include funding for design research as well as for development and dissemination of key principles and processes.

b. Identify and develop evaluation measures that capture the range of criteria for judging a "successful" system. For example, student measures may focus on learning motivation and learning-to-learn skills as well as achievement in subject areas.

c. Set an expectation that districts will continually experiment in order to reach goals. Districts should report successful and unsuccessful experiments as each provides information on what worked and what did not work (see Mirabito & Layng, 2013).

d. Identify "showcase" districts that can serve as examples of design processes as well as outcomes.

e. Embrace failure as a learning mechanism. Failure in experimentation should not be punished because innovation is unlikely without failure, and failure offers important information on what did not work. To mitigate the consequences of large-scale failure, a model with multiple local, small-scale, limited-duration experiments with frequent monitoring and adjustment should be adopted.

Action Principles for Districts

a. Offer professional development in design thinking for teachers and school administrators.

b. Reward thoughtful experimentation and consistent implementation of design processes within schools.

c. Celebrate achievements without punishing failures. Failure is likely when trying something new and is important for innovation.

d. Collect and disseminate case studies from district schools that illustrate design processes, what worked, what did not work, and what unexpected outcomes may have resulted.

e. Develop clear goals for schools to reach that include process as well as product criteria for the school, classroom, and student levels.

Action Principles for Schools

a. Create detailed goal maps aligned with standards that clearly define knowledge and skills and the relationships among them. Goal analysis is a challenging but invaluable process for defining goals that are specific enough to work with yet still capture the spirit of the intended outcome.

b. Design a system for continuous formative assessment that involves the student. Continuous, proactive self-assessment can empower learners and keep them actively engaged in working toward their goals.

c. Move toward a mastery-based system. Although mastery-based systems can be challenging to implement because of their conflict with time-based instructional systems, even limited mastery-based systems can help students see their progress and achieve goals they may otherwise not have achieved.

d. Develop and implement a learning-to-learn curriculum. Learning-to-learn or self-regulation and metacognitive skills support informed student choice in personalized systems and can help students develop the skills necessary to become lifelong learners.

e. Work on developing a schoolwide culture focused on key values of mastery and autonomy.

References

Ames, C. (1992). Classrooms: Goals, structures, and student motivation. *Journal of Educational Psychology, 84*(3), 261–271.

Andrade, H. L. (2010). Students as the definitive source of formative assessment: Academic self-assessment and the self-regulation of learning. *NERA Conference Proceedings 2010*. (Paper 25). Retrieved from http://digitalcommons.uconn.edu/nera_2010/25

Berger, R., Rugen, L., & Woodfin, L. (2014). *Leaders of their own learning: Transforming schools through student-engaged assessment*. San Francisco, CA: John Wiley & Sons.

Black, P., & Wiliam, D. (2009). Developing the theory of formative assessment. *Educational Assessment, Evaluation, and Accountability, 21*(1), 5–31.

Bloom, B. S. (1968). Learning for mastery. *Evaluation Comment, 1*(2), 1–12.

Bloom, B. S. (1974). Time and learning. *American Psychologist, 29*(9), 682–688.

Bloom, B. S. (1984). The 2 sigma problem: The search for methods of group instruction as effective as one-to-one learning. *Educational Researcher, 13*(6), 4–16.

Brown, T. (2009). *Change by design: How design thinking transforms organizations and inspires innovation*. New York, NY: Harper Collins.

Corbalan, G., Kester, L., & van Merriënboer, J. J. G. (2006). Towards a personalized task selection model with shared instructional control. *Instructional Science, 34*, 399–422.

Corbalan, G., Kester, L., & van Merriënboer, J. J. G. (2008). Selecting learning tasks: Effects of adaptation and shared control on efficiency and task involvement. *Contemporary Educational Psychology, 33*(4), 733–756.

Corbalan, G., Kester, L., & van Merriënboer, J. J. G. (2009). Combining shared control with variability over surface features: Effects on transfer test performance and task involvement. *Computers in Human Behavior, 25*(2), 290–298.

Cordova, D. I., & Lepper, M. R. (1996). Intrinsic motivation and the process of learning: Beneficial effects of contextualization, personalization, and choice. *Journal of Educational Psychology, 88*(4), 715–730.

Covington, M. V. (2000). Goal theory, motivation, and school achievement: An integrative review. *Annual Review of Psychology, 51*(1), 171–200.

Dunning, D., Heath, C., & Suls, J. M. (1994). Flawed self-assessment: Implications for health, education, and the workplace. *Psychological Science in the Public Interest, 5*(3), 69–106.

Dweck, C. S. (1986). Motivational processes affecting learning. *American Psychologist, 41*(10), 1040–1048.

Dweck, C. S., Walton, G. M., & Cohen, G. L. (2014). *Academic tenacity: Mindsets and skills that promote long-term learning.* Retrieved from https://ed.stanford.edu/sites/default/files/manual/dweck-walton-cohen-2014.pdf

Grant, H., & Dweck, C. (2003). Clarifying achievement goals and their impact. *Journal of Personality and Social Psychology, 85*(3), 541–553.

Keefe, W., & Jenkins, J. (2002). Personalized instruction. *Phi Delta Kappan, 83*(6), 440–448.

Kirschner, P. A., & van Merriënboer, J. J. G. (2013). Do learners really know best? Urban legends in education. *Educational Psychologist, 48*(3), 169–183.

Kulik, C. C., Kulik, J. A., & Bangert-Drowns, R. L. (1990). Effectiveness of mastery learning programs: A meta-analysis. *Review of Educational Research, 60*(2), 265–299.

Lindsley, O. R. (1992). Precision teaching: Discoveries and effects. *Journal of Applied Behavior Analysis, 25*(1), 51–57.

Mager, R. F. (1997). *Goal analysis: How to clarify your goals so you can actually achieve them.* Atlanta, GA: Center for Effective Performance.

Mechner, F., Fiallo, V., Fredrick, T., & Jenkins, T. (2013). *The Paideia individualized education technology.* Retrieved from http://mechnerfoundation.org/wp-content/uploads/2013/11/PIE-article1-14.pdf

Mirabito, M. M., & Layng, T. V. J. (2013). Stimulating innovation (or making innovation meaningful again). In M. Murphy, S. Redding, & J. Twyman (Eds.), *Handbook on innovations in learning* (pp. 17–32). Philadelphia, PA: Center on Innovations in Learning, Temple University; Charlotte, NC: Information Age Publishing. Retrieved from https://www.centeril.org

NGSS Lead States. (2013). *Next Generation Science Standards: For states, by states.* Washington, DC: The National Academies Press.

Nicol, D. J., & Macfarlane-Dick, D. (2006). Formative assessment and self-regulated learning: A model and seven principles of good feedback practice. *Studies in Higher Education, 31*(2), 199–218.

Patrick, S., Kennedy, K., & Powell, A. (2013). *Mean what you say: Defining and integrating personalized, blended, and competency education.* Retrieved from http://www.inacol.org/wp-content/uploads/2015/02/mean-what-you-say.pdf

Redding, S. (2013). *Through the student's eyes: A perspective on personalized learning.* Philadelphia, PA: Center on Innovations in Learning. Retrieved from http://www.centeril.org/publications/2013_09_through_the_eyes.pdf

Schnackenberg, H. L., & Hilliard, A. W. (1998). Learner ability and learner control: A 10-year literature review 1987–1997. In *Proceedings of Selected Research and Development Presentations at the National Convention of the Association for Educational Communications and Technology.* Retrieved from http://files.eric.ed.gov/fulltext/ED423858.pdf

Tennyson, R. D., & Park, O. (1980). The teaching of concepts: A review of instructional design research literature. *Review of Educational Research, 50*(1), 55–70.

Tiemann, P. W. (1971). Analysis and the derivation of valid objectives. In M. B. Kapfer (Ed.), *Behavioral objectives in curriculum development: Selected readings and bibliography* (pp. 383–389). Englewood Cliffs, NJ: Educational Technology Publications. (Reprinted from *NSPI Journal, 8*(6), 16–18.)

U.S. Department of Education. (2010). *Transforming American education: Learning powered by technology.* Washington, DC. Retrieved from http://files.eric.ed.gov/fulltext/ED512681.pdf

U.S. Department of Education. (n.d.). *Competency-based learning or personalized learning.* Retrieved from
http://www.ed.gov/oii-news/competency-based-learning-or-personalized-learning

Williams, M. D. (1993). A comprehensive review of learner-control: The role of learner characteristics. In *Proceedings of Selected Research and Development Presentations at the Convention of the Association for Educational Communications and Technology.* Retrieved from http://files.eric.ed.gov/fulltext/ED362211.pdf

Zimmerman, B. J. (1990). Self-regulated learning and academic achievement: An overview. *Educational Psychologist, 25*(1), 3–17.

Zumbrunn, S., Tadlock, J., & Roberts, E. D. (2011). *Encouraging self-regulated learning in the classroom: A review of the literature.* Richmond, VA: Metropolitan Educational Research Consortium, Virginia Commonwealth University. Retrieved from http://www.merc.soe.vcu.edu/wp-content/uploads/sites/3387/2013/11/Self-Regulated-Learning-2.pdf

Flipped Learning as a Path to Personalization

Melinda S. Sota

Digital technology is rapidly becoming ubiquitous in schools. One-to-one computing and bring-your-own-device (BYOD) initiatives are helping to ensure that each student has a device with which to work. Although these technologies can support personalized learning, they haven't yet transformed our schools into 21st-century utopias where students engage in interactive, individualized learning applications and access information in order to collaboratively solve problems while teachers roam the learning space, coaching and mentoring as their engaged and self-directed students happily work.

In fact, there have been some large, public failures. Consider, for example, Los Angeles Unified School District's $1.3 billion iPad initiative in 2013. Experts suggested that part of the reason this initiative failed so spectacularly was that it put technology first. Without a clear plan in place, the district purchased iPads not to solve a problem but simply for the sake of incorporating the technology (Lapowsky, 2015).

A technology's potential for improving education lies in its usefulness as a tool for reaching particular goals, and models incorporating technology can help to focus its use for goal achievement. Blended learning models in particular incorporate technology as a key component for reaching specified goals (Horn & Staker, 2015). One blended learning model—flipped learning—has a very simple goal: to maximize the value of in-class time (Bergmann & Sams, 2014). Although fundamentally simple, this model can help to empower teachers and enable them to begin incorporating aspects of personalized learning into their classes.

Blended Learning

Blended learning "blends" online and face-to-face instruction. The Innosight Institute has defined blended learning as "a formal education program in which a student learns at least in part through online delivery of content and instruction [with] some element of student control over time, place, path, and/or pace AND at least in part at a supervised brick-and-mortar location away from home" (Staker & Horn, 2012, p. 3). Students might engage in online learning at a station within a classroom, in a computer lab at school,

Handbook on Personalized Learning for States, Districts, and Schools, pages 73–87

or at home; they might engage in online learning as part of a class or take some courses online and others in a more traditional classroom setting (see Staker & Horn, 2012, for a taxonomy of blended learning models).

The Flipped Model of Blended Learning

The Flipped Learning Network—an organization dedicated to "providing educators with the knowledge, skills, and resources to successfully implement Flipped Learning"—hosts over 25,000 educators in its online learning community. The Flipped Learning Network has defined flipped learning (see Figure 1) as "a pedagogical approach in which direct instruction moves from the group learning space to the individual learning space, and the resulting group space is transformed into a dynamic, interactive learning environment where the educator guides students as they apply concepts and engage creatively in the subject matter" (2014).[1] Started as a grassroots movement and capable of being implemented by individual teachers with minimal support (Bergmann & Sams, 2014; Horn & Staker, 2015), the flipped model has become increasingly popular in both university and K–12 settings. In a 2014 survey of 2,358 teachers conducted by Sophia Learning and the Flipped Learning Network, 78% of teachers reported flipping a lesson, and 93% of those who flipped their classroom did so on their own initiative (Sophia Learning & Flipped Learning Network, 2015).

Figure 1. Traditional and Flipped Classroom

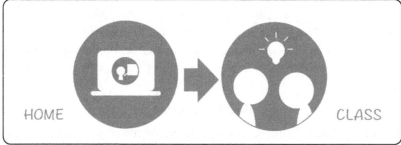

TRADITIONAL

CLASS   HOME

HOME   CLASS

FLIPPED

---

[1] Here, direct instruction refers to a general teaching method often involving lectures or demonstrations by the teacher, rather than the more specific, highly interactive teaching method by the same name (for more information on this more specific instructional method, see the National Institute for Direct Instruction at http://www.nifdi.org).

Jon Bergmann and Aaron Sams, two chemistry teachers from Woodland Park High School in Colorado, are widely credited with developing and popularizing the flipped classroom, although others have also proposed inverting the traditional classroom–homework model (e.g., Lage, Platt, & Treglia, 2000; Mazur, 2009) and the model shares similarities with other mastery-based, student-centered approaches (e.g., Bloom, 1984). Bergmann and Sams observed that, because of sports and other activities, students were often missing classes, and teachers were spending substantial class time catching students up. Sams and Bergmann reasoned that instead of spending their time reteaching material for students who missed class, they could simply record their lectures and refer students to the videos. That proved successful, and students in their classes further extended the use of the videos for reviewing before exams. Sams further observed that students most needed him when they had difficulty with homework. Instead of using class time to lecture—which students clearly could get via a posted video—Bergmann and Sams decided to use class time to offer individualized help, thus giving rise to the flipped learning model (Bergmann & Sams, 2012). Others—perhaps most notably Saul Kahn and Kahn Academy—have helped to support and popularize this model. Rather than a top-down initiative or "best practice" recommended by researchers and mandated by school districts, flipped learning began with and has spread primarily among teachers—teachers who were looking for a way to more easily connect with their students, increase the value of class time, and spend more of their time with students really *teaching* and less time talking at them in "information delivery" mode (Bergmann & Sams, 2014).

Supporting Personalized Learning With a Flipped Model

The flipped learning model has great potential for supporting personalized learning: "instruction that is paced to learning needs, tailored to learning preferences, and tailored to the specific interests of different learners" (U.S. Department of Education, 2010, p. 12). Personalized learning involves "tailoring learning for each student's strengths, needs, and interests—including enabling student voice and choice in what,

> Trying to incorporate personalization into a traditional teaching model in which teacher lecture or presentation consumes the majority of class time can be challenging.

how, when, and where they learn—to provide flexibility and supports to ensure mastery of the highest standards possible" (Patrick, Kennedy, & Powell, 2013, p. 4). In addition, "personalization refers to a teacher's relationships with students and their families and the use of multiple instructional modes to scaffold each student's learning and enhance the student's motivation to learn and metacognitive, social, and emotional competencies to foster self-direction and achieve mastery of knowledge and skills" (Redding, 2013, p. 6).

Trying to incorporate personalization into a traditional teaching model in which teacher lecture or presentation consumes the majority of class time can be challenging. Content presentation to a whole class often does not allow for flexibility in learning pace, place, or method, and when class time is used for content presentation, less time is available for building relationships and focusing on metacognitive, social, and emotional competencies. The key question to consider when implementing a flipped model is: "What is the best use of face-to-face time with students?" (Bergmann & Sams, 2014, p. 3). The benefits of the flipped model lie in its usefulness for maximizing the value of teacher–student time. By modifying how class time is spent, the flipped learning model can support personalization in several ways:

a. The pace of content delivery can be adjusted for each student's needs because content is always available to be paused, considered, and reviewed.

b. Teacher's expertise in both teaching and content—for example, assessing a student's current skills and knowledge and selecting targeted and appropriate practice opportunities based on that assessment—can be put to better use when more class time is free for individualized work.

c. With more class time available, teachers can also engage in more one-on-one interactions with students, which can help teachers and students build relationships and help teachers gain a better sense of each individual student's interests, strengths, and areas needing improvement.

d. Students have increased opportunities to actively engage in instructional content during class (Bergmann & Sams, 2012, 2014; Lage, Platt, & Treglia, 2000), and increased class time may also offer a greater opportunity for teachers to explicitly teach skills such as critical thinking, communication, and collaboration (Horn & Staker, 2015).

Fundamentally, flipping a class is a means to support student-centered learning and can help to enable individualized, differentiated, and personalized instruction as well as mastery and competency-based approaches (Bergmann & Sams, 2014).

The Teacher's Role in the Flipped Model

Much of the potential benefit of the flipped model centers on a shift in teacher roles. In a traditional model, the teacher delivers the majority of the content in class and may spend most of class time presenting information and modeling skills. In the flipped model, the teacher spends less class time delivering content and more time taking on the role of coach, tutor, and mentor. The teacher may also present content as needed and may create videos or other resources for students to engage in outside of class, but these activities are not central to the teacher's role. Instead, the teacher can spend time evaluating student work and providing feedback during class while the student is actively working (Bergmann & Sams, 2012)—activities that are often completed outside of class in a traditional model.

Flipped Models: Variations on a Theme

In flipped models, student learning activities and problem solving are central, with content playing a supporting role (Bergmann & Sams, 2012, 2014). However, there is not just one "flipped model." Several variations exist which can be implemented in ways that best meet the needs of the teachers and students in a school or individual classroom.

Flipped Classroom 101 to Flipped Learning

Any flipped model implementation will lie on a continuum. At the most basic level, a teacher can flip a lesson by recording his or her in-class presentation and having students watch the video as homework. In class, students do the homework that they would have been assigned. This is what Bergmann & Sams (2014) refer to as "flipped classroom 101." In their view, it serves as an entry point to class redesign and is where many teachers begin. However, this is just the first step in moving toward a flipped learning model that focuses on personalized learning and mastery.

In a "flipped learning" model focused on personalized learning, student projects and problem solving are central to the classroom-based learning experience. This shift in focus may also be accompanied by a shift in perspective, from projects serving as practice in applying the content covered in class, to projects serving as the driver for finding and consuming content: rather than applying content in a project as a means to learn and practice that content, students find information and learn concepts, principles, and processes in order to successfully solve a problem or complete a project. In this model, teacher-created content may no longer be the main source that students use to gain skills and knowledge. Although the teacher may provide a selection of resources, using specific resources may not be required; mastery is the goal, and students may select the best or preferred way to gain the necessary skills and knowledge (Bergmann & Sams, 2014).

> A flipped classroom may lie anywhere between the flipped classroom 101 model and a fully personalized, mastery-based, project-centered classroom.

This shift in focus and perspective—from a content-centered classroom where projects serve as practice in applying the content learned, to a project-centered classroom where projects serve as the driver for finding and consuming content—can also be viewed in terms of Bloom's taxonomy. In a content-centered classroom, students start by remembering information and understanding concepts and principles, then applying them to different situations and problems. In a problem-centered classroom, students focus on creating, evaluating, and analyzing. In doing so, they require knowledge and understanding of the fundamental concepts, principles, and procedures related to their work; students work at lower levels of Bloom's taxonomy as needed to support their work at higher levels. This is a sort of just-in-time content learning to support problem-solving and project-based work (Bergmann & Sams, 2014).

A flipped classroom may lie anywhere between the flipped classroom 101 model and a fully personalized, mastery-based, project-centered classroom. In practice, classroom redesign that starts on the more basic side of the continuum may gradually move toward a more personalized model over a period of years as components supporting personalization are added.

Mastery Versus Time-Based Progression

Variations in flipped models can accommodate both traditional time-based instructional schedules and the more flexible schedules required by mastery learning. In a traditional time-based progression, all students move at the same pace but their outcome performances differ. In a mastery-based schedule, students acquire knowledge and skills at different rates, but each student is required to meet a minimum standard before moving on (Bloom, 1968, 1974). The flipped learning model described by Bergmann and Sams (2014) is a mastery model.

Flipped Lessons Versus Flipped Classes

Implementing a flipped model is not necessarily all or none. A teacher may decide to implement a flipped model as her standard class structure, but she might also flip her classroom only a few days a week or for particular units. A survey of 2,358 teachers conducted by Sophia Learning and the Flipped Learning Network (2015) found that, while only 5.4% flip their classroom every day, 20% flip three or four times per week, and 24% flip less than once per week.

Additional Benefits of the Flipped Model

As discussed above, the flipped model supports personalized learning by allowing students to work at their own pace and by freeing up class time which can then be used more effectively by teachers and by students. Additionally:

Students who need the most help can get the most help. In a typical lecture-style class, the best students are often the ones who participate most and therefore receive the most teacher attention. In a flipped model, struggling students will more likely receive the most teacher attention as they practice and apply what they have learned in class. Students who need help can get it, and all students have a greater opportunity (and necessity) to be actively involved during class (Bergmann & Bennett, 2013; Bergmann & Sams, 2012).

Students and teachers can get immediate feedback on their work. Rather than completing homework and then waiting a day or more for feedback, student work is evaluated in class. Teachers can probe understanding on the spot, diagnose student misconceptions, and recommend additional resources. If the student shows mastery, next steps can immediately be discussed and decided upon (Bergmann & Sams, 2012). Importantly, teachers also get immediate feedback on how well their explanations were understood by the student and can elaborate or modify their instruction accordingly. This two-way feedback for both students and teachers can have a powerful effect on learning (Hattie, 2009).

> *In a typical lecture-style class, the best students are often the ones who participate most and therefore receive the most teacher attention.*

Students have more time for collaboration and interaction. With class time focused on student work, there may be more opportunity for student–student interaction and collaboration. Students who understand the content can also help those who are struggling (Bergmann & Sams, 2012).

Students can more easily predict and schedule their homework time. When homework focuses on applying what students have learned in class, that homework may require very little time and effort for some, while others may labor over it. Students (and teachers) may have difficulty predicting how much time will be required. However, when homework involves watching and taking notes on a video or interacting with instructional software, the variability in time spent should decrease and be easier to predict for both teachers and students. This predictability can be important for students who need to schedule their homework time around extracurricular activities, part-time jobs, and family obligations (Bergmann & Sams, 2014).

Students learn to take responsibility for their learning. In a flipped learning model incorporating mastery, students are required to master the content rather than simply get by. Instead of cramming for a quiz in order to get a good grade, students must work to truly understand concepts and principles in order to apply them to problems and projects. In essence, they need to take responsibility for their own learning. Taking on this responsibility can be frustrating for students who have previously focused on achieving the minimum academic requirements. However, when learning rather than getting a grade becomes the focus, it can serve students well in school and in their lives beyond school (Bergmann & Sams, 2012).

Students are required to learn time-management skills. In a flipped learning model incorporating mastery, students need to schedule their work so that they master the material in a reasonable amount of time. Time-management skills—when explicitly taught, supported, and practiced—can be an added benefit of a flipped learning model (Bergmann & Sams, 2012).

Individualization, differentiation, and personalization become possible. Individualization, differentiation, and personalization all refer to models in which instruction is modified based on the needs and/or preferences of learners. For example, in individualized instruction, the pace of learning may differ among learners. In differentiated instruction, the method of instruction might be tailored to learner preferences (for definitions of individualized, differentiated, and personalized instruction, see U.S. Department of Education, 2010). All flipped models involve some individualization (minimally, in terms of the pace of content delivery; Staker & Horn, 2012). In a flipped learning model, greater opportunities for personalization and differentiation exist. Where projects and problems are the central focus, students may have a choice of projects and how they learn the supporting content—by reading, watching presentations/demonstrations, working through interactive simulations or other educational software, or some combination of activities. Gifted students may choose advanced projects and content aligned with the learning goals and objectives (Siegle, 2014). And, because the teacher spends little class time delivering content, he has more time to respond to individual students. Students may work in collaboration with the teacher in determining how they will demonstrate mastery on an objective or set of objectives (Bergmann & Sams, 2012).

Students' repertoires are less likely to be incomplete. In a flipped learning model incorporating mastery, students must master a minimum number of skills at the designated level. This means that they should *not* have gaps in their skill sets that will make later learning more difficult—an important outcome in subjects like math, in which skills build upon one another.

At-home content delivery allows for family interaction. Where videos are used, a flipped model can increase parent participation in students' schoolwork and allow them to see what their child is learning. It even offers the opportunity to learn along with their child (Bergmann & Bennett, 2013; Bergmann & Sams, 2012, 2014). In Bergmann and Sams's (2014) *Flipped Learning*, a fifth-grade teacher tells a story about the parents of one of her students using the videos as a way to learn English.

Resource use can be optimized. The flipped model also offers the opportunity to make the most of resources. Since it is unlikely that all students will be working with the same materials at the same time, fewer materials may be needed. Additionally, because the teacher is no longer responsible for delivering all content, he can use his limited time for more frequent and more meaningful interactions with students. Given greater optimization of classroom resources and more time for the teacher's personal attention for each student, it may be tempting to increase class size under the flipped model. But larger classes may negate some of the benefits of this model; as the number of students increase, the resources and the teacher attention available to each child would necessarily decrease (Bergmann & Sams, 2012).

Some Criticisms, Drawbacks, and Challenges of the Flipped Model

Of course, just as there are benefits to the flipped model, there are criticisms, drawbacks, and challenges as well.

The flipped model relies on lecture-based teaching. One criticism of the flipped model is that it still relies on the lecture, an ineffective teaching tool (Ash, 2012). Although lectures and presentations do have a legitimate place in learning—particularly when they are short and well-structured and when students have the necessary experience, background knowledge, and motivation to learn from them (e.g., Schwartz & Bransford, 1998)—this is a valid criticism of courses based on lecture (see Freeman et al., 2014). However, this is not a fair criticism of the flipped model itself because the model does not require that students watch videos of lectures or demonstrations. The defining attribute of the flipped model is its concern for class time and how that class time is spent. Work outside of class may involve watching videos, but it may also involve reading or engaging with interactive instructional programs. In addition, while transitioning to a flipped model may involve recording lectures and having students watch them as homework, this may serve only as an initial step in modifying the class structure for flipped learning.

> *The defining attribute of the flipped model is its concern for class time and how that class time is spent.*

Content delivery doesn't occur at an optimal time. Some research has shown a benefit of hands-on exploration activities prior to reading or listening to a lecture (e.g., Schwartz, Case, Oppezzo, & Chin, 2011). The flipped model seems to do the opposite—learners first engage with content and then work on projects or problems related to it (Plotnikoff, 2013). However, there is no inherent order to the model. Especially in the flipped learning models focused on mastery and centered in projects and problems, content delivery may happen whenever the need arises. That could very well be after the learner is already heavily involved in hands-on activities related to the content.

It makes the teacher less important. This concern may stem from the belief that content presentation is a teacher's main responsibility or method of teaching. The idea that technology might replace teachers may also feed into this concern (Tucker, 2012). However, in the flipped model, the teacher is even *more* important than in a traditional model because she is assessing every student's progress and providing individualized feedback and coaching. This mode of teaching requires a great deal more expertise in both course content and effective instructional methods than does traditional lecture-based teaching (November & Mull, 2012). At any given time, individual students may be at different levels of understanding and in different places within the curriculum. Therefore, the teacher must have mastery of the content sufficient to allow him to identify student misconceptions, offer explanations, and provide targeted problems or exercises to help each student move forward. Because in a flipped learning classroom this is done on the fly, a deep mastery of the material is necessary as the teacher moves from student to student, providing the feedback, explanations, and practice that each student needs at that time. In addition to content expertise, an effective teacher will need skills in identifying student misconceptions and errors, diagnosing why they might be occurring (for example, is it an issue with the current material being learned or an issue with a prerequisite skill not having been sufficiently mastered?), knowledge of instructional strategies sufficient to choose a potentially effective method based on the reasons for the student error, and the ability to create or identify a probe to formatively assess whether what the teacher did resulted in improved student understanding.

The work to produce videos or other instructional content requires teachers to do too much work. Producing videos or other instructional content is a significant amount of work. It takes time and a certain comfort with technology to produce the content, and expertise in the pedagogical and instructional design skills to make the content interesting and effective for students. However, not every teacher needs to create all the content for her course. First, a great deal of content is already available online, so teachers can start by locating resources and building a content library. Second, teachers may team up to create content, or a few teachers who have a special interest and skill in producing content might create the majority of it. Finally, when beginning to implement a flipped model, teachers can start by flipping a few lessons or a unit and create new content over a few years rather than all at once. Students can also find and recommend sources that have helped them learn the content (November & Mull, 2012).

Not all students have Internet access. Although the majority of students (82.5% according to the 2013 American Community Survey; see Horrigan, 2015) have broadband access at home, this access varies by income. For example, almost a third of families who make less than $50,000 per year lack high-speed Internet access at home. About 40% of all families in the United States with school-aged children fall into this category (Horrigan, 2015). Although this digital divide is a significant concern that impacts some out-of-class activities that rely on Internet access, such as interactive activities and simulations, alternative access—for example, videos burned to DVD or content loaded onto a flash drive or mobile device—can increase students' access. Students may also be able to access content before or after school or during study halls (Bergmann & Sams, 2012; November & Mull, 2012).

It adds unnecessary homework. For students who do not already have homework assignments, a flipped model may mean an increase in homework time. However, the amount of time spent will likely vary less across students than it does for traditional homework and therefore be easier to predict (Bergmann & Sams, 2014).

Students cannot ask questions while interacting with content. Some may be concerned that students are not able to ask questions in real time during out-of-class content delivery (Milman, 2012). However, students can write down their questions for discussion during the next class period. If the content is being delivered via a learning management system, a discussion board or other place for students to ask questions can also be set up (Bergmann & Sams, 2012).

Students and parents don't like it. Incorporating a flipped model will not magically turn students into eager, self-directed learners. In fact, transitioning from a traditional class structure to a flipped model can be a big and unwelcome change for students. A mastery model in particular can be challenging because it will likely require more work from students—not necessarily in terms of time, but in terms of effort. For those who are used to doing just enough to get by, this transition can be especially difficult. Because the teacher's role is likely to be very different from what students and parents are used to, some may also perceive the teacher as no longer teaching. However, building in time for students to adjust, incorporating explicit instruction and support in time-management and metacognitive skills, and proactively providing parents with an explanation of and rationale for the new method can help change these perceptions and ease the transition for students (Bergmann & Sams, 2012, 2014).

Teacher Characteristics Necessary to Support a Flipped Learning Model

For teachers who are used to doing planned lectures and demonstrations during class time, implementing a flipped model will feel very different. It also may require new skills, as their classroom work is redirected from delivering content to spontaneously diagnosing and remediating student errors and misconceptions. Bergmann and Sams (2012) list four characteristics that teachers should have in order to implement a flipped mastery model: (a) content expertise that enables the teacher to quickly switch among topics and fully understand how the content is interconnected, (b) the ability to assist students at different levels of mastery and working on different learning objectives, (c) a willingness to research answers with students, and (d) a willingness to allow students to drive their own learning.

The last two characteristics—willingness to research answers with students and willingness to allow students to drive their own learning—might be summed up as "an attitude of inquiry." In other words, the act of learning is the center of the classroom and the teacher and students take part in the learning activity together. The teacher doesn't view himself or herself as a disseminator of knowledge, but rather a partner and guide in the learning process. This attitude of inquiry can be extended to the teaching practice itself: questioning, learning about, and trying out new instructional methods and evaluating the effects of those methods will help ensure that teachers are continually improving upon their teaching processes.

Effectiveness of the Flipped Model

The flipped learning model seems to have the potential to support personalization and increase student learning and motivation—but is it effective? That is a difficult question to answer. And—perhaps—not the right question to ask. Research on this model is just beginning, and much of the research done thus far has focused on university rather than K–12 settings. Although some case studies have shown promising outcomes (Bormann, 2014; Hamdan, McKnight, McKnight, & Arfstrom, 2013), many studies have failed to show significant achievement gains over a traditional model. Bormann (2014) reviewed 19 studies investigating the flipped model and found that most studies did *not* find significant differences in student achievement. However, implementations differ among studies, as do differences between the flipped and non-flipped classes being compared. Because the flipped model is not a single "thing" with a standard implementation, it is difficult to draw conclusions from the research conducted thus far.

Does this mean the model shouldn't be implemented? Not necessarily. Three considerations are important for determining whether this model is worth trying in a specific classroom or school.

First, instead of asking whether this model—in general and across all its many variations—is "effective" (however that is defined), ask whether or not it might be an effective model for meeting specific goals. What is the desired outcome? Increased student achievement? Increased student engagement? Increased teacher satisfaction? More opportunities for students to engage in higher level learning activities—problem solving, analyzing, evaluating, and creating?

Second, it is important to consider the development process used when first employing the model. It's unrealistic to expect that a first attempt at implementing a new model will be successful without planning for considerable change and fine-tuning based on what works well and what doesn't work in a particular context. Flipping a lesson or a unit in a class can serve as a useful start to examining how students respond to the model, where it should be modified and how, and whether student achievement and/or motivation is affected.

Finally, will the flipped classroom improve some fundamental aspect of teaching and learning? There is nothing magical about the flipped model itself, only what the flipped model allows teachers and students to do that they could not do in a more traditional model. For example, to what extent do current in-class activities include components that increase learning and motivation? If not at an optimal level, what could be added, changed, or removed in order to increase these components? Is the flipped model a tool that would allow teachers to more easily make some of these changes? If a teaching model already affords active and meaningful student learning and quality interactions among students and between students and the teacher, then the flipped model may not add anything new.

For example, Jensen, Kummer, and Godoy (2015) compared a flipped model to a non-flipped model. In the non-flipped model, students learned basic concepts and principles in class and did application exercises outside of class. In the flipped model, students did the reverse: They learned the concepts initially outside of class, and then worked on applying those concepts during class. The results showed no difference between the flipped and non-flipped versions on unit posttests. However, when looking at how the actual learning activities differed between the two models, one would probably not expect any difference. Both versions used a 5–E learning cycle with the following five phases:

1. **Engage:** Students are introduced to the material in a way meant to spark their interest—for example, by presenting a puzzling phenomenon.
2. **Explore:** Students can freely explore the material by looking for patterns and making hypotheses.
3. **Explain:** The instructor introduces terminology for the concepts that students have been exploring.
4. **Elaborate:** Students apply these concepts to novel situations.
5. **Evaluate:** Students' understanding of concepts is evaluated by formative and summative assessments.

In the non-flipped version, students went through the *engage* and *explore* phases in small groups using a structured guide to assist them in looking for patterns, making hypotheses, and analyzing data. Because both the instructor and teaching assistants facilitated these phases, students received immediate and individualized feedback. Rather than a lecture typical of a traditional teaching model, the *explain* phase was interspersed in the small-group work and involved brief, whole-class discussions clarifying concepts and introducing terms. The *elaborate* phase involved solving novel problems as homework.

The flipped version involved online, individual work during the *engage* and *explore* phases. Students were still encouraged to find patterns, make hypotheses, and analyze data; however, they were unable to discuss with others or work directly with materials. Instead, they watched a video of someone else working with the materials. They did receive immediate feedback online after answering questions. In class, the instructor first answered questions students had from the homework; then, the *elaborate* phase was completed in class, with students working in small groups to apply the concepts to novel situations. The instructor and teaching assistants were available to interact with students and provide immediate feedback during this time.

The only difference between the flipped and non-flipped versions in this study was whether students initially encountered the concepts outside of class or in class. Both versions seemed to be rich in opportunities for active learning and in interactions with the instructor and other students, but one could argue that the flipped version was less rich because the students lost the opportunity for initial exploration and discussion of the material. Instead of exploring it themselves and engaging in discussion, they watched others working with the material and did not have the opportunity to engage in discussion. Given the argument that the flipped model has its advantage in freeing up class time to increase active student learning and engagement, there doesn't seem to be a strong argument for flipping a classroom already rich in these elements. Further, in this case, some interaction was even lost in the flipped model, as student interaction during the engage and explore phases was transformed into student observation.

This analysis is not meant as a criticism of this study. The authors were specifically attempting to control for active learning in both versions; therefore, this design was entirely appropriate for this purpose. However, this analysis is meant to illustrate that the potential benefit does not lie in the flipped model itself, but instead in the opportunity for increasing the quality of student interactions that we know can effectively raise student learning and engagement.

The Real Value of the Flipped Model

Asking whether a flipped model is or is not superior to a non-flipped model is the wrong question. Rather, will a flipped model allow a school or a class to more easily add components that support student learning and engagement? The flipped learning model may be beneficial to the extent that it allows for an increase in these components.

Although it is often portrayed as a model in which students watch lectures outside of class and do their homework during class, this characterization is unfair and doesn't take into account the model's many variations. The fundamental goal of the flipped model is simple: to maximize the value of student–teacher time. Perhaps the real value of the model is in encouraging teachers and administrators to think deeply about this issue and begin experimenting with class structure.

Action Principles for States, Districts, and Schools

Action Principles for States

   a. Provide resources for classroom redesign, including funding for design research, research dissemination, professional development, and resource development.

   b. Provide resources for conducting evaluations that capture outcome measures related to multiple success factors, including academic achievement, time management and self-regulation/metacognitive skills, student engagement and motivation, and teacher satisfaction.

   c. Establish goals and outcomes without mandating specific resources, technologies, or methods.

    d. Encourage local experimentation by individual districts and schools in order to reach goals. Celebrate success and support problem solving without punishing failures.

    e. Assist in dissemination of successes, best practices, and lessons learned across districts and schools.

Action Principles for Districts

    a. Offer professional development, coaching, and other resources to support teachers in employing effective practices—for example, how to design more effective instructional resources and learning activities, how to explicitly teach metacognitive skills, or how to diagnose and remediate student errors.

    b. Do not mandate specific technologies or methods. Provide resources, but allow teachers to experiment with what works best in their own classrooms.

    c. Compensate teachers fairly for redesigning their classes.

    d. Support experimentation and sharing of successes and failures. If goals have not been reached, assist schools in problem solving.

    e. Plan for implementation of the model to take several years. If a school is moving from a traditional model to a mastery-based model, this shift will likely involve a cultural shift for the school and a fundamental shift in how both teachers and students approach school and learning.

Action Principles for Schools

    a. Start small. Redesigning class structure is a years-long process, but a teacher can begin the process simply by flipping a single lesson or unit.

    b. Allow plenty of time for planning, design, implementation, and collaboration. Each day of in-class work needs to be planned carefully to result in optimal learning and engagement, and activities will need revisions and fine-tuning after they've been tried. Provide additional time for teachers to collaborate in designing their lessons and solving problems together.

    c. Assign a dedicated IT person to work directly with teachers on the technology and workflows required to more easily create and post learning resources.

    d. Proactively inform parents about the flipped model in order to ease concerns.

    e. Don't punish teachers for trying things that fail. Instead, work to develop a culture that supports experimentation and the open sharing of goals, successes, and failures with both administrators and fellow teachers.

References

Ash, K. (2012). Educators evaluate 'flipped classrooms.' *Education Week, 32*(2), s6–8. Retrieved from http://www.edweek.org/ew/articles/2012/08/29/02el-flipped.h32.html

Bergmann, J., & Bennett, B. (2013). The flipped classroom for administrators [Video file]. Retrieved from https://www.youtube.com/watch?v=ggkMdVABlIw&list=PLP24P3yfORx DQK-mEkIRASwIVGecMx9bw&index=4

Bergmann, J., & Sams, A. (2012). *Flip your classroom: Reach every student in every class every day.* Eugene, OR: International Society for Technology in Education.

Bergmann, J., & Sams, A. (2014). *Flipped learning: Gateway to student engagement.* Eugene, OR: International Society for Technology in Education.

Bloom, B. S. (1968). Learning for mastery. *Evaluation Comment, 1*(2), 1–12.

Bloom, B. S. (1974). Time and learning. *American Psychologist, 29*(9), 682–688.

Bloom, B. S. (1984). The 2 sigma problem: The search for methods of group instruction as effective as one-to-one learning. *Educational Researcher, 13*(6), 4–16.

Bormann, J. (2014). *Affordances of flipped learning and its effects on student engagement and achievement* (Unpublished master's thesis). University of Northern Iowa, Cedar Falls, IA. Retrieved from http://flippedlearning.org/cms/lib07/VA01923112/Centricity/Domain/41/bormann_lit_review.pdf

Flipped Learning Network. (2014). *The four pillars of F-L-I-P.* South Bend, IN: The Flipped Learning Network. Retrieved from http://www.flippedlearning.org/definition

Freeman, S., Eddy, S. L., McDonough, M., Smith, M. K., Okoroafor, N., Jordt, H., & Wenderoth, M. P. (2014, June 10). Active learning increases student performance in science, engineering, and mathematics. *Proceeding of the National Academy of Sciences of the United States of America, 111*(23), 8410–8415. Retrieved from http://www.pnas.org/content/111/23/8410.full.pdf

Hamdan, N., McKnight, P., McKnight, K., & Arfstrom, K. M. (2013). *A review of flipped learning.* South Bend, IN: The Flipped Learning Network. Retrieved from http://www.flippedlearning.org/review

Hattie, J. (2009). *Visible learning: A synthesis of over 800 meta-analyses relating to achievement.* New York, NY: Routledge.

Horn, M. B., & Staker, H. (2015). *Blended: Using disruptive innovation to improve schools.* San Francisco, CA: Jossey-Bass.

Horrigan, J. B. (2015). *The numbers behind the broadband 'homework gap.'* Retrieved from http://www.pewresearch.org/fact-tank/2015/04/20/the-numbers-behind-the-broadband-homework-gap/

Jensen, J. L., Kummer, T. A., & Godoy, P. D. d. M. (2015). Improvements from a flipped classroom may simply be the fruits of active learning. *CBE Life Sciences Education, 14*(1), 1–12.

Lage, M. J., Platt, G. J., & Treglia, M. (2000). Inverting the classroom: A gateway to creating an inclusive learning environment. *The Journal of Economic Education, 31*(1), 30–43.

Lapowsky, I. (May 8, 2015). *What schools must learn from LA's iPad debacle.* Boone, IA: Wired. Retrieved from http://www.wired.com/2015/05/los-angeles-edtech/

Mazur, E. (2009). Farewell, lecture? *Science, 323*(5910), 50–51.

Milman, N. B. (2012). The flipped classroom strategy: What is it and how can it best be used? *Distance Learning, 9*(3), 85.

November, A., & Mull, B. (2012). *Flipped learning: A response to five common criticisms.* Marblehead, MA: November Learning. Retrieved from http://november-learning.com/educational-resources-for-educators/teaching-and-learning-articles/flipped-learning-a-response-to-five-common-criticisms-article/

Patrick, S., Kennedy, K., & Powell, A. (2013). *Mean what you say: Defining and integrating personalized, blended and competency education.* Vienna, VA: International Association for K–12 Online Learning (iNACOL).

Plotnikoff, D. (July 16, 2013). *Classes should do hands-on exercises before reading and video, Stanford researchers say.* Stanford, CA: Stanford Report. Retrieved from http://news.stanford.edu/news/2013/july/flipped-learning-model-071613.html

Redding, S. (2013). *Through the student's eyes: A perspective on personalized learning and practice guide for teachers.* Philadelphia, PA: Center on Innovations in Learning. Retrieved from http://www.centeril.org

Schwartz, D. L., & Bransford, J. D. (1998). A time for telling. *Cognition and Instruction, 16*(4), 475–522.

Schwartz, D. L., Case, C. C., Oppezzo, M. A., & Chin, D. B. (2011). Practicing versus inventing with contrasting cases: The effects of telling first on learning and transfer. *Journal of Educational Psychology, 103*(4), 759–775. Retrieved from http://www.ece.neu.edu/edsnu/mcgruer/USC/PracticingVersusInventing2011-edu-103-4-759.pdf

Siegle, D. (2014). Differentiating instruction by flipping the classroom. *Gifted Child Today, 37*(1), 51–55.

Sophia Learning & Flipped Learning Network. (2015). Growth in flipped learning: Transitioning the focus from teachers to students for education success [Infographic]. Minneapolis, MN: Sophia Learning. Retrieved from https://www.sophia.org/flipped-classroom-survey

Staker, H., & Horn, M. (2012). *Classifying K–12 blended learning.* San Mateo, CA: Innosight Institute. Retrieved from http://www.christenseninstitute.org/wp-content/uploads/2013/04/Classifying-K-12-blended-learning.pdf

Tucker, B. (2012). The flipped classroom: Online instruction at home frees class time for learning. *Education Next, 12*(1), 82–83. Retrieved from http://educationnext.org/the-flipped-classroom/

U.S. Department of Education (2010). *Transforming American education: Learning powered by technology.* Washington, DC: Author. Retrieved from http://files.eric.ed.gov/fulltext/ED512681.pdf

Empowering Students as Partners in Learning

Kathleen Dempsey, Andrea D. Beesley, Tedra Fazendeiro Clark, and Anne Tweed

Descriptive Study

In 2011, Mid-continent Research for Education and Learning (now McREL International) was awarded an Institute of Education Sciences grant to develop and study a program aimed at building middle school mathematics teachers' knowledge and skills for implementing high-quality formative assessment. The foundation for the professional development program, Learning to Use Formative Assessment in Mathematics with the Assessment Work Sample Method (AWSM), was built on authentic samples of student work, because reviewing and discussing student work helps teachers shift from thinking of teaching as something teachers do to a focus on learning as something students do (e.g., Hattie, 2009). Through our evaluation of the program's impact, we learned that the formative assessment practices supported by AWSM improved the class culture and encouraged students to take more ownership of learning, and during this process, connections between personalized learning and the formative assessment process advocated by AWSM began to materialize. In this chapter, the comprehensive definition of personalized learning described in *Through the Student's Eyes: A Perspective on Personalized Learning* (Redding, 2013) most clearly reflects the focus group statements voiced by teachers in the study. Thus the description, "personalization ensues from the relationships among teachers and learners and the teacher's orchestration of multiple means for enhancing every aspect of each student's learning and development" (Redding, 2013, p. 6) is used. This chapter discusses the challenges to mathematics teaching and learning, the AWSM professional development program, focus group feedback, and how the formative assessment process connects to personalized learning.

Challenges to Middle School Mathematics Learning

In the transition to middle school and during the middle school years, students' motivation for mathematics tends to decline from what it was during elementary school. At this age, students report less valuing of mathematics and lower effort and persistence in math problem solving than reported by students in earlier grades (Pajares & Graham, 1999; Valas, 2001; Wigfield, Eccles, & Pintrich, 1996). Middle school students also report lower

Handbook on Personalized Learning for States, Districts, and Schools, pages 89–97

confidence in their mathematics ability than before (Clarke, Roche, Cheeseman, & van der Schans, 2014; Pintrich & Schunk, 1996), influenced in part by exposure to a larger peer group with whom they begin to compare themselves. They also perceive more competition in the classroom environment and more rigorous standards for evaluation (Eccles & Midgley, 1989).

A review of national assessment results provides another perspective on mathematics learning. Mathematics results on the National Assessment of Educational Progress (NAEP) in both Grades 4 and 8 have shown significant progress since 1990, particularly for Grade 4 students. From 2000 to 2013, Grade 4 proficiency levels increased 18 percentage points, while Grade 8 proficiency levels in mathematics increased 10 points. In spite of these improvements, in 2013, NAEP results showed only 42% of Grade 4 students proficient in mathematics, with Grade 8 proficiency levels at 35%. This difference between the two grades' rates of mathematics proficiency contrasts to a near parity in proficiency levels in reading for Grade 4 and Grade 8, 35% and 36%, respectively (The Nation's Report Card, 2013).

> *The tendency to oversimplify tasks is especially true when teachers work with lower achieving students (Zohar, Degani, & Vaaknin, 2001).*

How students perceive themselves as mathematics learners can have an effect on teaching and learning at the middle school level. Students who are not confident that they can solve complex problems or who do not see the point of putting forth effort to do so try to avoid those tasks or pressure teachers to make the work simpler for them (Clarke et al., 2014). This lack of self-efficacy is a predictor of, among other things, lower math achievement outcomes (Pajares & Graham, 1999), and some middle schoolers attempt to engage in math learning only when tangible rewards are offered (Rowan-Kenyon, Swan, & Creager, 2012).

In this environment, middle school mathematics teachers can feel discouraged from giving students challenging and complex work. If they do so anyway and students encounter difficulty, some teachers oversimplify the task or tell students how to solve it (Clarke et al., 2014; Ferguson, 2009). The tendency to oversimplify tasks is especially true when teachers work with lower achieving students (Zohar, Degani, & Vaaknin, 2001). However, the common core state standards and other contemporary U.S. math standards require that students be able to solve complex problems and to explain their reasoning, so teachers need strategies to support students in these practices.

Formative Assessment Strategies

Formative assessment strategies can help students be more confident learners and can positively impact academic performance (Peterson & Siadat, 2009; Ruland, 2011; Wilson, 2009). Formative assessment is an evidence-based process of gathering information on three questions—(a) Where am I going? (b) How am I doing now? and (c) Where do I go next?—to support a learning cycle (Hattie & Timperley, 2007; Sadler, 1989). Therefore, the most important formative assessment practices involve (a) students' understanding of their learning target, (b) the criteria by which they will know how they are doing in achieving that target, and (c) the feedback they receive to help them understand next steps. Literature supports prioritizing these three dimensions of formative assessment.

The Assessment Work Sample Method Program

The Assessment Work Sample Method (AWSM) is a professional development program that builds middle school math teachers' understanding of the characteristics of high-quality formative assessment and increases their ability to use it. We were inspired to create AWSM following the results from previous research (Randel et al., 2011) on a program that did not change teacher practice in mathematics in part because it had few math examples. By contrast, AWSM provides professional development that builds formative assessment practices and skills specifically in math. The AWSM approach, adapted from a language arts study (Clare, Valdés, Pascal, & Steinberg, 2001; Matsumura et al., 2006), incorporates authentic student work samples that help ground teacher learning in daily practice. The work samples include a cover sheet that conveys the teacher's intended learning goals for the lesson, the type of student knowledge or skill to be developed, the criteria for meeting learning goals, and general information that will help reviewers understand the "what and why" of the assignment. Attached to the cover sheet are four pieces of student work, two pieces of work that met the teacher's intended learning goals and two pieces of student work that did not meet the intended learning goals. Professional development participants refine their understanding and skill for implementing formative assessment as they discuss these work samples, recommend revisions to improve the work sample, and connect the work sample to their own instructional practice.

The AWSM professional development is structured around nine face-to-face meetings, which include a two-day introductory workshop and eight sessions of about 45 minutes each. During part one of the introductory workshop, participants build their understanding of formative assessment as an instructional process. The connection of formative assessment to personalized learning begins to unfold as participants discuss why and how to create a positive classroom culture. They compare a growth-oriented mindset, the belief that intelligence can be developed (Dweck, 2006), to a fixed mindset, the belief that intelligence is static, and discuss implications for student perseverance on complex tasks. Participants also learn about the physical, social, and emotional factors that impact classroom culture. Figure 1 depicts the three AWSM dimensions with positive learning environment at the center.

Figure 1. AWSM Dimensions

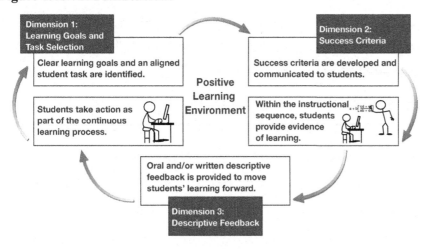

In part two of the workshop, participants plan to implement formative assessment by examining authentic student work because it is in student work that student thinking is made visible (e.g., Hattie, 2009). In collaborative groups, teachers analyze the intended learning goals, success criteria, and student tasks from anonymous work samples to determine if these lesson elements are strongly aligned, partially aligned, or weakly aligned. Mathematical content as well as the inferred cognitive demand of both the learning goal and student task are reviewed and discussed. Through this analysis, participants clarify their understanding of AWSM Dimension 1 (learning goals and aligned student task) and Dimension 2 (success criteria; see Figure 1). These dimensions are considered the foundation for the formative assessment process because without clarity about what is to be learned and clear criteria for goal attainment, the feedback process can be derailed. Figure 2 is an excerpt from a work sample used in AWSM. It shows part of the teacher's cover sheet, the formative task, and one piece of student work.

Figure 2. Work Sample Used in AWSM

Teacher Cover Sheet

5. What were your learning goals for the students for this assignment? In other words, what skills, concepts, or facts did you want students to learn, practice or demonstrate understanding of as a result of completing this assignment? (Students will know and understand that: ...)

   I wanted students to demonstrate an understanding of unit rates and be able to calculate unit rates fluently ... or be able to make comparisons when the rates were not the same.

6. Check the type of learning goal/target this assignment addresses (check all that apply):
   - ☑ Knowledge (facts/details to be memorized)
   - ☑ Skill (algorithmic procedures)
   - ☑ Conceptual Understanding (reasoning, generalizing, explaining, etc.)
   - ☑ Problem Solving within a Context (multiple procedures; solution strategy)

11. a. How was this assignment assessed? If there is a rubric, student reflection, etc., please attach it. If you are not attaching a rubric, please explain your criteria for determining if students met the learning goal of the assignment.

   The rubric is attached (on back of assignment) and shows the assignment is worth a total of 5 points (which I doubled and told the students I would do ahead of time).

11. b. Did you share these criteria with the students? ☑ Yes　[ ] No

3	2	1
Student shows an accurate comparison of costs of coffee pods at each of the three stores by calculating unit rates or other common ratios.	Student shows an accurate comparison of costs of coffee at two of the three stores by calculating unit rates or other common ratios.	Student calculates only one correct unit rate or common ratio.
	Student gives a clear written explanation for where the coffee should be purchased.	Student gives an unclear (or incorrect) written explanation for where the coffee should be purchased.

Formative Task

Mrs. H always tries to find the best deals in town before making purchases, especially when it comes to coffee (because she buys and drinks a lot of it)! She shops at several stores around Denver, including Bed, Bath, and Beyond, Safeway, and Costco. As she stops by each of these three stores this weekend, she takes note of the prices they are currently charging for pods of French Vanilla Coffee. Safeway is currently carrying her favorite brand in a box that comes with 12 pods for $9.12. Bed, Bath, and Beyond is selling the same brand, but their box is slightly larger (comes with 18 pods) and costs $14.04. Finally, she notices that Costco is also selling that brand and comes in a much larger box with 32 pods for a cost of $24.00. Where should Mrs. H buy the coffee and get the best deal in town? Please show your work and explain your thinking in the space below. You must give a mathematical and written explanation to convince Mrs. H.

Student work

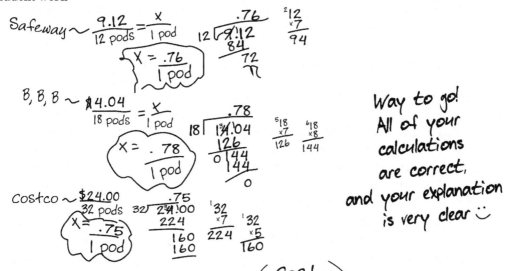

The eight short sessions are organized as teacher learning communities (TLCs) with a facilitator who has both mathematics and formative assessment expertise. The first five sessions focus on Dimension 3 (descriptive feedback), and are structured to build teacher knowledge and skill for providing effective oral and written feedback to students. Participants learn that feedback should be based on stated learning goals and success criteria established in Dimensions 1 and 2 and that general statements, such as, "Good job" or "Work harder," do little to move student learning forward. Teachers also learn to resist providing student feedback which is too specific. At times, mathematics teachers provide step-by-step notations on how to correct an inaccurate solution. Unfortunately, this practice keeps the responsibility for learning with the teacher rather than with the student, whereas providing feedback that uses cues ("Remember our work with similar figures."), questions ("How do you know the area is equivalent?"), and recommendations for next steps ("Check your notes from Tuesday.") helps students determine next-step actions and thus take more responsibility for their own learning.

In Dimension 3, teachers also learn that students should be active partners in the feedback process, and it is through this process that the self-directed aspect of personalization is incorporated. It's important to note that Dimension 3 is dependent on the clarity of criteria developed in Dimensions 1 and 2. These dimensions help teachers craft lessons that demonstrate clear alignment between the learning goal, student task, and success criteria, and this criteria is explicitly communicated to students. In Dimension 3, students gauge their own progress toward the learning goal by participating in peer- and self-assessment activities using the criteria developed in Dimension 2. Participants in AWSM implement peer- and self-assessment practices through an incremental process beginning with whole class activities, partner activities, and self-assessment activities. In the whole group activities, students compare a sample of work from an anonymous student to a set of criteria. Through discussion of the work sample, students begin to identify student work that meets or does not meet a set of criteria. As students develop skill for assessing work based on criteria, they participate in peer-assessment (feedback) activities. These activities tend to begin with identifying the presence or absence of criteria and then progress toward assessing a peer's work for solution accuracy and quality of student response. In each case, student assessors identify both strengths and recommendations for improvement based on established criteria. Teachers monitor this process and use whole group debriefing activities to make sure students receive accurate feedback from peers. This process is designed with the ultimate goal of empowering students to objectively assess their own work based on a set of criteria so that they can monitor and adjust their own learning strategies to reach intended learning goals.

During the last three short sessions, AWSM participants bring work samples from their own students to share with colleagues. These TLC sessions offer a safe environment for teachers to discuss problems of practice and refine their own implementation of formative assessment.

Connections to Personalized Learning

Although AWSM was not intended to study personalization per se, comments from teachers during focus groups revealed a connection between the strategies espoused by AWSM and aspects of personalized learning. For example, teachers noted that classroom culture, particularly teacher–student relationships and student–student interactions, were more positive as implementation of formative assessment strategies became the norm. They also made comments that align with the personal competencies (cognitive, metacognitive, motivational, and social/emotional) described in *Through the Student's Eyes: A Perspective on Personalized Learning* (Redding, 2013). In focus groups, teachers reported that students responded to formative assessment strategies with increased motivation, engagement, and persistence in math. Teachers reported that clearly communicated learning goals and success criteria helped clarify their teaching and let students know what they should expect to learn. Furthermore, having clear learning goals and success criteria facilitated communication with students and parents, thus strengthening teacher–student–family relationships. Teachers indicated that formative assessment data helped them plan activities for students at various levels of mastery.

Teachers reported that engaging students in peer- and self-assessment activities increased student awareness of success criteria and developed a heightened sense of individual accountability for learning. For example, teachers gave students tracking sheets with success criteria to use in self-assessing their level of understanding relative to the learning goal so they could monitor their progress. One teacher said, "They'll start on what they know, but then they actually take ownership of saying, 'Oh, I haven't mastered this.' And then they start testing their own learning."

At most schools, teachers said they were using peer assessment extensively. They described having students partner to discuss their approaches to homework problems or to go over in-class activities. One teacher commented that this technique made it easier for students to get help when they were reluctant to seek help from the teacher. Some teachers were initially concerned that students would be unkind to one another during peer feedback, and this turned out to be a problem when peer feedback was given in written, anonymous form.

> ...having clear learning goals and success criteria facilitated communication with students and parents, thus strengthening teacher–student–family relationships.

However, when teachers then tried structured, face-to-face peer assessment, it worked well: "I find when they verbally [provide] feedback to their peer, they're much nicer, it's more constructive, and it's actually a lot more helpful." When students gained experience with peer assessment, they participated in productive social interactions, and as student interactions progressed, teachers were more willing to reorganize classroom configurations and use flexible grouping strategies. More effective use of formative data also allowed teachers to differentiate student assignments so that students were assigned tasks specific to their learning needs, thus resulting in a more personalized learning experience for students.

Teachers in the AWSM study reported the same problems with student motivation for math (difficulty with engagement and persistence, especially with challenging problems) as reported by other teachers in the literature. Their students also were reluctant to be wrong, to show work, and to do work that was ungraded. The AWSM professional development program emphasized the role of class culture for a growth mindset and de-emphasized accurate solutions as the only measure of progress in mathematics. It helped teachers clarify learning goals and the criteria by which student progress would be measured. Additionally, it helped personalize learning through differentiated activities and empowered students to become partners in learning. At the conclusion of the study, participants shared some thoughts on the AWSM process:

- "I used to think formative assessment was about the teacher knowing where students are in the learning process. Now I know that formative assessment must include students so that they understand how to improve their own learning."
- "I used to think I had to grade everything. Now I know I can provide descriptive feedback and allow students to take action."

- "It's the dimensions of clear learning goals and success criteria that have most impacted my instruction. I think I was always clear about what was being learned, but I needed to be more explicit about sharing this information with my students."

AWSM investigators considering the next steps for this work intend to include more direct connections to the personal competencies of student cognition, motivation, and perseverance.

References

Clare, L., Valdés, R., Pascal, J., & Steinberg, J. R. (2001). *Teachers' assignments as indicators of instructional quality in elementary schools.* Los Angeles, CA: CRESST/University of California, Los Angeles.

Clarke, D., Roche, A., Cheeseman, J., & van der Schans, S. (2014). Teaching strategies for building student persistence on challenging tasks: Insights emerging from two approaches to teacher professional learning. *Mathematics Teacher Education and Development, 16*(2), 46–70.

Dweck, C. S. (2006). *Mindset: The new psychology of success.* New York, NY: Random House.

Eccles, J. S., & Midgley, C. (1989). Stage/environment fit: Developmentally appropriate classrooms for early adolescents. In R. E. Ames & C. Ames (Eds.), *Research on motivation in education* (Vol. 3, pp.139–186). New York, NY: Academic Press.

Ferguson, S. (2009). *Teachers' use of mathematics tasks: The impact on the mathematics learning and affective responses of low-attaining upper primary students.* Paper presented at the 32nd annual conference of the Mathematics Education Research Group of Australasia, Palmerston North, New Zealand.

Hattie, J. (2009). *Visible learning.* New York, NY: Routledge.

Hattie, J., & Timperley, H. (2007). The power of feedback. *Review of Educational Research, 77*(1), 81–112.

Matsumura, L. C., Slater, S. C., Junker, B., Peterson, M., Boston, M., Steele, M., & Resnick, L. (2006). *Measuring reading comprehension and mathematics instruction in urban middle schools: A pilot study of the Instructional Quality Assessment.* Los Angeles, CA: Center for the Study of Evaluation.

The Nation's Report Card. (2013). *What level of knowledge and skills have the nation's students achieved?* [Data set].
Retrieved from http://www.nationsreportcard.gov/reading_math_2013/#/what-knowledge

Pajares, F., & Graham, L. (1999). Self-efficacy, motivation constructs, and mathematics performance of entering middle school students. *Contemporary Educational Psychology, 24*(2), 124–139.

Peterson, E., & Siadat, M. V. (2009). Combination of formative and summative assessment instruments in elementary algebra classes: A prescription for success. *Journal of Applied Research in the Community College, 16*(2), 92–102.

Pintrich, P., & Schunk, D. (1996). *Motivation in education: Theory, research, and applications.* Englewood Cliffs, NJ: Prentice-Hall.

Randel, B., Beesley, A. D., Apthorp, H., Clark, T. F., Wang, X., Cicchinelli, L. F., & Williams, J. M. (2011). *Classroom assessment for student learning: The impact on elementary school mathematics in the Central Region* (NCEE 2011-4005). Washington, DC: National Center for Education Evaluation and Regional Assistance, Institute of Education Sciences, U.S. Department of Education.

Redding, S. (2013). *Through the student's eyes: A perspective on personalized learning.* Philadelphia, PA: Center on Innovations in Learning.
Retrieved from http://www.centeril.org/publications/2013_09_Through_the_Eyes.pdf

Rowan-Kenyon, H. T., Swan, A. K., & Creager, M. F. (2012). Social cognitive factors, support, and engagement: Early adolescents' math interests as precursors to choice of career. *Career Development Quarterly, 60*(1), 2–15.

Ruland, J. W. (2011). *The impact of using formative assessment attributes in daily instruction on student affect* (Doctoral dissertation). Retrieved from ProQuest. (Accession No. 3473587)

Sadler, D. R. (1989). Formative assessment and the design of instructional systems. *Instructional Science, 18*(2), 119–144.

Valas, H. (2001). Learned helplessness and psychological adjustment: Effects of age, gender, and academic achievement. *Scandinavian Journal of Educational Research, 45*(1), 71–90.

Wigfield, A., Eccles, J. S., & Pintrich, P. R. (1996). Development between the ages of 11 and 25. In D. C. Berliner, & R. C. Calfee (Eds.), *Handbook of educational psychology* (pp. 148–185). New York, NY: Simon & Schuster Macmillan.

Wilson, R. B. (2009). *The effect of a continuous quality formative-assessment program on middle school student mathematics achievement* (Doctoral dissertation). Retrieved from ProQuest. (Accession No. 3378822)

Zohar, A., Degani, A., & Vaaknin, E. (2001). Teachers' beliefs about low-achieving students and higher order thinking. *Teaching and Teacher Education, 17*(4), 469–485.

Homeschooling: The Ultimate Personalized Environment

William H. Jeynes

We are living in the Information Age—an era in which teachers appreciate the need for personalized education more than ever before (Fraser, 2007). As part of this trend, educators are inquiring about homeschooling advantages because they demonstrate the ultimate personalized schooling environment. For the purposes of this chapter, a personalized education means adapting instruction to each individual student so that it varies according to the student's needs. This individualization may affect pace, time, and/or place of learning. Homeschooling, by definition, is an environment where personalized learning can thrive (Orr, 2003). One of the reasons for homeschooling's increased popularity is that it is perceived as the ultimate personalized educational environment. In addition, unlike education in public schools, there is no negative relationship between family socioeconomic status (SES), parental education level, and the academic outcomes of their children. As Short (2010) states:

> As it turns out, in a basic battery of tests that included writing and mathematics, homeschooled children whose mothers hadn't finished high school scored at the 83rd percentile, while students whose fathers hadn't finished high school scored in the 79th percentile. (pp. 88–89)

Approximately 3.4% of students in the U.S. are homeschooled, which places the total number in excess of 1.77 million (U.S. Department of Education, 2012). This number represents about 25–30% of the school population that attends nonpublic schools (Moore & Moore, 1994; Nel, 2010). The percentage of students that are homeschooled could increase because it allows for a level of flexibility in instruction and learning that many parents and children find more personal and attractive than what is offered through public schooling (Jeynes, 2007a, 2012). For society to benefit from the growth of homeschooling, it is vital that the scholastic community realize that there is much to learn from the homeschooling environment and practice that can be applied to nearly all public schools. Admittedly, the data available on the benefits of homeschooling are rather thin. Nevertheless, when one combines the studies that have been done on homeschooling

Handbook on Personalized Learning for States, Districts, and Schools, pages 99–113
Copyright © 2016 by Information Age Publishing

and those that have been done on the specific components of this approach, there is a greater understanding of what qualities of the home's education environment can benefit public schools.

What Makes Homeschooling So Successful?

What are some key aspects of homeschooling that make it so successful and personalized that can be applied to virtually all schools? This is an important question. The answers presented here are discussed not so much to encourage homeschooling but rather to argue that public and private schooling can learn a great deal from the homeschooling rubric to make large-scale schooling more effective.

Increases Parental Involvement

Perhaps the foremost distinction of homeschooling is that it provides the ultimate expression of parental involvement (Jeynes, 2006). There is no question that the decision to homeschool is a considerable commitment. A high level of parental involvement is virtually a prerequisite in the decision to homeschool (Green & Hoover-Dempsey, 2007; Immell, 2009), and research has shown increased parental involvement improves student outcomes (Jeynes, 2003a, 2007b). Moreover, meta-analyses and the examination of nationwide data sets suggest that the most potent components of this engagement result from the family interactions and expectations that occur in the home rather than parents participating in school-based functions (Jeynes, 2005, 2007b, 2010).

> *Parenting qualities such as having high expectations, concurrently maintaining a loving and structured environment, and communicating in a constructive way with children are some of the most salient components of involvement.*

Parenting qualities such as having high expectations, concurrently maintaining a loving and structured environment, and communicating in a constructive way with children are some of the most salient components of involvement. Homeschooling provides an ideal environment for children to learn in that maximizes the time they are exposed to these qualities in their mothers or fathers (Fisher, 2003; Stevens, 2001).

Among academics, there is growing interest in homeschooling largely because of one quite amazing reality—homeschooling is the only educational approach in which youth of low SES achieve at levels that are as high scholastically as those of their high-SES counterparts (Mayberry, Knowles, Ray, & Marlow, 1995; Ray & Wartes, 1991). This parity is not only the ideal, of course, but is also a very elusive one to accomplish. Increasingly, social scientists are attributing this relationship primarily to the elevated levels of parental engagement that are present in virtually all homeschooling environments (Green & Hoover-Dempsey, 2007; Stevens, 2001). The reason they reach this conclusion is because studies suggest that a considerable percentage of SES's association with school outcomes is explained by the involvement of mothers and fathers (Gregory, 2000). Successful parents are more likely to be involved than their less successful counterparts because they are convinced that the American system works and that the investment they personally make into the schooling of their children will ultimately be worth it (Fisher, 2003; Gregory, 2000; Stevens, 2001).

The decision to homeschool almost by definition is rooted in the belief that such a sacrifice of time and effort into a child's life is worth the effort. One principle that can be learned from homeschooling is that parental involvement matters (Green & Hoover-Dempsey, 2007) and it means a great deal to the success of the student (Fisher, 2003; Green & Hoover-Dempsey, 2007). Evidence indicates that not only do homeschooled youth outperform students in public school by two years but also that they outperform those in faith-based schools by one year; these differences remain almost the same even when one adjusts for race and SES (Mayberry et al., 1995; Ray & Wartes, 1991).

To whatever extent parental engagement explains the scholastic advantage enjoyed by homeschooled children and adolescents, it befits public school instructors to do what they can do to enhance the extent to which fathers and mothers are engaged in their children's education. Public school educators need to take three specific actions to both maximize and enhance parental participation.

First, teachers should examine what traits mothers and fathers have that enable young people to thrive more from instruction at home, on average, than they do in public school even when the results are adjusted for race and SES. The answers are probably rather facile. Parents are more likely to have a deeper love for their children than educators do, and they are more likely to have a thorough knowledge of their children as individuals. Regrettably, modern society underestimates the extent to which these two qualities alone give parents a decided advantage over teachers in schooling their children.

It is ironic that the trend has been to assume that teachers, who are trained profession-als, would be better than most parents in training children. In centuries past, just the opposite was assumed. In fact, one of the founders of the public school system, Johann Pestalozzi (1746–1827), asked why it was that children learned better at home than in any alternative environment. He answered his own question by declaring the reason was because children were loved by their parents at home (Fraser, 2001; Jeynes, 2007a, Urban & Wagoner, 2009). Therefore, Pestalozzi (1901) concluded that the best teach-ers needed to be similar in the school environment to mothers in the home. He therefore argued for the maternal role of the school. Unfortunately, since the early 1900s, schooling has steered away from an emphasis on teachers supporting and loving students and has embraced more of an industrial model that emphasizes proper methodology and peda-gogy (Fisher, 2003; Fraser, 2001; Jeynes, 2007a).

A small number of academics and a myriad number of parents warned about the even-tual consequences of emphasizing the mode of teaching more than knowing and loving the children (Gatto, 2001; Horne, 1931, 1932). Horne (1931, 1932) led the academic argument in favor of loving and knowing the children. However, in a modern world that became enamored with the marvels of industrialization, those who argued that the school system needed a pragmatic approach that emphasized the teacher as a specialist within an industrial society seemed destined to win the tug of war (Dewey, 1915, 1978). Although many families opposed this new approach to education as too standardized and mecha-nized, they did not wield enough power to affect the eventual outcome (Gatto, 2001). Horne (1931, 1932) appreciated the value of efficacious pedagogy. However, he believed that if loving, supporting, and understanding the children did not make up the founda-tion of education, students would not flourish. He warned of a future educational state in which teachers were well acquainted with the best means of instructing children but whose hearts were no longer filled with love and compassion for the children. Horne was concerned that the eventual outcome would be a school system that was mechanical and overly standardized (Jeynes, 2006).

For centuries, educators, as well as those who were the foremost architects of the schooling system, recognized that parents were the primary educators, and the teacher's role was to supplement that instruction (Fisher, 2003; Gatto, 2001). However, in the past 50 years in particular, Americans, Europeans, and others have become compliant with increased government control of schooling and submission to the professional status of teachers (Fisher, 2003; Gatto, 2001, 2009; Kurtz, 2010; Whitehead, 2013). The undeniable success of homeschooling suggests that teachers need to reacquaint themselves with the salience of mothers and fathers in the schooling process (Fisher, 2003; Gatto, 2001; Rivero, 2008). The assumption that college or graduate tutelage in educational practice and theory grants teachers more instructional acumen for a given child than mothers and fathers, when parents have known their children for years and teachers have not known the children long at all, is naïve at best and blatantly presumptuous at worst (Hirsch, 2006).

When George Counts wrote his book titled *Dare We Build a New Social Order?* in 1932, it was quite controversial, especially among parents. Many Americans thought it was immensely arrogant for educators to think they could create a new social order and even more presumptuous to assume that it was desirable for them to try (Gatto, 2001). In contrast, in contemporary society, a statist philosophy in which the government is strongly involved in shaping society is often assumed or at least accepted (Welling, 2005). In the broader societal context, this statist approach may or may not be appropriate (Gatto, 2001; Welling, 2005); nevertheless, within the context of schooling, this approach, which highlights the influence of government spending for schools, public policy, and teacher professionalism, has had the effect of crowding out the primacy of the parental role (Gatto, 2001, 2009). The success of homeschooling has been a poignant reminder that research repeatedly points to family factors as being considerably more salient than school factors in predicting academic success among students (Schneider & Coleman, 1993). It is highly unlikely whether any amount of government spending increases, policy changes, or acknowledgement of teacher professionalism will outweigh the effect of family factors in influencing the scholastic outcomes of youth (Schneider & Coleman, 1993).

The second action teachers can take to enhance parental involvement is to convince parents that engagement is worth the investment. Educators need to use more than verbal communication to draw in parents. Instructors themselves need to demonstrate a love and interest in the child that makes the parents much more likely to show a commensurate level of love toward and interest in the child (Brodie, 2010). In addition, although some teachers welcome the engagement of parents, others do not (Immell, 2009). Rather, these instructors want parents to "leave the teaching to the professionals" and often want carte blanche authority to provide tutelage to the children in whatever way they see fit (Gatto, 2001, 2009). However, homeschooling is a reminder that the parental qualities of love, understanding, compassion, and patience are key if learning is to be maximized (Green & Hoover-Dempsey, 2007). Public school teachers need to realize that teachers and parents need each other (Jeynes, 2003a). Parents need the instructional knowledge that teachers possess, and teachers need the knowledge of the child that parents possess.

It is interesting that, beginning in the 1600s with the Pilgrims and Puritans until about the early 1960s, it was the general practice for elementary school teachers to visit the homes of all of their students before the commencement of the school year. The reasons for this practice were not only to build partnerships with the parents, but also to draw from the family's knowledge of the strengths and weaknesses of the child (Gangel & Benson, 1983; Jeynes, 2007a; Morgan, 1986). Ironically, when various Eastern Asian nations imitated the American paradigm of K–12 schooling in the mid-1800s until the early 1900s, they embraced this home visitation practice (Jeynes, 2007a). American schools largely jettisoned this practice just over half a century ago, concurrent with the cessation of physicians making house calls (Jeynes, 2006). In contrast, East Asians have maintained this tradition and cite these visitations as one of the key reasons why their students significantly outperform their American counterparts (Jeynes, 2006). Teachers in the U.S. need to communicate to parents that family participation in their children's schooling is worth the effort. They need to not only verbally communicate this truism to parents but also demonstrate this investment themselves by listening to and building relationships with students' families.

Third, educators need to share with parents what components of parental involvement are most helpful to children (Jeynes, 2010). What is of concern is that, although most teachers know that parental involvement in the most general sense facilitates high levels of scholastic achievement by youth, they have a dearth of knowledge about the facets of that participation that are most efficacious (Jeynes, 2010). Most educators think of parental engagement in its most traditional sense of attending school functions, checking homework, being an active member of the parent–

> ...the most vital components of parental involvement are subtle and have more to do with love, high and reasonable expectations, and positive and informative communication...

teacher association, setting household rules to make sure schoolwork gets done, and volunteering in the classroom (Jeynes, 2010). However, meta-analyses on parental involvement over the past dozen years or so have made it clear that the most vital components of parental involvement are subtle and have more to do with love, high and reasonable expectations, and positive and informative communication (Jeynes, 2003a, 2007b, 2010). Unfortunately, very few teachers are aware that the more subtle aspects of parental engagement are the most important (Jeynes, 2010). Given that numerous family members look to educators for guidance about how to best become involved, the vacuity of information is concerning.

Provides for Less Standardization and More Freedom

A second key aspect contributing to the success of homeschooling is that it generally relies considerably less on standardized testing and government mandates (Immell, 2009). Therefore, parents have greater freedom to focus on the development of the whole child, particularly when it comes to character education (Reavis & Lakriski, 2005; Ryan & Bohlin, 1999). Ironically, beginning with Plato and continuing until the early 1960s, most of the leading proponents of the Western model of education traditionally believed that teaching children to be loving, compassionate, and moral human beings was actually more important than instruction addressed solely with expanding the mind (Deresiewicz, 2011; Dupuis, 1966; Mann, 1957; Ryan & Bohlin, 1999).

The resistance of parents to the increased standardization of the curricula in No Child Left Behind and Common Core State Standards is indicative that families want more control over classroom priorities than they currently experience. Parents generally want input into how their children are instructed. Families usually place a great deal of value on character instruction which encourages youth to develop their skills, strengthen their weaknesses, and prepare for contributing to society in a meaningful and productive way. Some families believe that this translates into less standardization and more emphasis on the individual child, thus homeschooling becomes the antithesis to the current standardized environment (Immell, 2009). Under the past three presidents, Clinton, G. W. Bush, and Obama, the United States has unquestionably gone in the direction of greater standardization. Given that not all parents wish to go in this direction, perhaps it is time to learn from the strengths of homeschooling and broaden instruction to apply to the whole child. One can argue that, with the increased omnipresence of the Internet, the trend toward a more personalized education is more accessible.

Enables More Individualized Instruction

A third key beneficial aspect of homeschooling is its provision of an environment in which students receive more individualized instruction from their teachers (Green & Hoover-Dempsey, 2007; Hayes, 2002; Pyles, 2004). Nearly every type of homeschool approach yields very small class sizes, and research has shown that both smaller class size and school size are associated with higher levels of scholastic success (Feldmon, Lopez, & Simon, 2006; Jeynes, 2012). That is, students within a given nation that are in schools with very small class sizes, on average, achieve at higher levels than their counterparts that are in highly populated classrooms. Admittedly, this trend holds within nations, but does not hold across nations (Jeynes, 2007a). However, this fact should not be surprising, given that there are a multitude of complexities that reflect why average achievement is higher in certain nations than others (Jeynes, 2006). Moreover, research indicates that two reasons why students from faith-based schools outperform their counterparts in public schools are both related to receiving more individualized instruction. On average, religious schools have smaller class sizes than do public schools. In addition, their faith-based leadership generally places much more emphasis on engaging parents in their children's education than one sees in public school administrators (Jeynes, 2000, 2002). Admittedly, these factors do not totally explain the religious schools' advantage, but it is patent that they explain a significant portion of that edge. When class sizes are smaller, in practical terms, this translates into a teacher having more time with each individual student—to know the student's personality, strengths, and weaknesses. As a result, the instructor can be more adept at formulating a pedagogical strategy that is appropriate for that child (Hayes, 2002; Pyles, 2004). There is no question that small classes are appealing to students, parents, and teachers (Feldmon et al., 2006; Jeynes, 2014; O'Connell & Smith, 2000).

Another way that the homeschooling approach is more individualized is that children tend to have the same instructor for multiple years. In public schools, generally teachers have students in their class for only nine months. Often these educators bemoan the fact that, shortly after they have come to know the youth in their care, it is time for the children to progress to the next grade level (Orr, 2003; Rivero, 2008). Numerous private schools and a small percentage of public schools have concluded that a long-lasting relationship between each teacher and pupil is salient in fabricating a sensitive and individualized pedagogical plan. Although a child's parents potentially could continue to teach their children for four, eight, or twelve years, public schools cannot be expected to replicate this practice, nor would it be appropriate. Nevertheless, logic would dictate that schools should foster a longer and deeper relationship between teachers and their students than currently exists (Rivero, 2008).

The homeschool environment provides a personalized approach to instruction that makes it possible to build a curriculum that thoroughly considers the unique gifts, talents, and skills of a given student (Lesaux & Marietta, 2011; O'Connell & Smith, 2000). In a large class, a teacher often encounters the conundrum of how best to instruct the whole class and yet, in a time-efficient way, still meet the needs that emerge because of individual differences among the students (Gatto, 2001; O'Connell & Smith, 2000). A considerable amount of research indicates that certain instructional approaches may be best for particular kinds of children. Even if a given approach is better overall, there are children who thrive more when an alternative approach is used (Jeynes & Littell, 2000; Lesaux & Marietta, 2011).

Foreigners reserve their greatest praise for the American system of education by declaring that the U.S. encourages its students to develop high levels of creativity (Worek, 2008). One common testimony to American creativity is that the U.S. has, by far, won more Nobel Prizes than any other nation. In fact, the University of Chicago, the American university that has won the most Nobel Prizes, has won more awards singularly than all but a few entire nations (Worek, 2008). Many educators attribute the American edge in Nobel Prizes to fostering creativity, recognizing the value of each individual student, and urging students to develop their own unique set of skills to the fullest extent possible (O'Connell & Smith, 2000; Worek, 2008). To the degree to which this edge is typified in the academic advantage that homeschooled youth enjoy over their counterparts in public schools, contemporary school administrators and policymakers would do well to give as much personal attention to each student in their care as possible.

The research indicates that one of the major advantages of homeschooling is that the pace of learning can be adjusted to what is ideal for the individual child (Jolly, Matthews, & Nester, 2013). In a public school whole-class environment, this is harder to accomplish. In a public school, or even in a private school that may have smaller class sizes, if a student is confused about a particular concept, the teacher does not always have the freedom to stop the progress of the class simply because one student is confused (Kunzman, 2009; O'Connell & Smith, 2000).

Homeschooling offers a similar advantage when the child learns a new concept quickly. When a student easily grasps a new concept in a regular classroom, that student must wait until a large enough percentage of those in the class understand the idea for the teacher to justify moving on to the next concept. Depending on how long that delay is, it accrues into a considerable amount of wasted learning time for the student. In contrast, homeschooling allows the parent to quickly proceed to the next concept, building from what the student already understands and knows. Because of this specific advantage, some parents prefer to homeschool in the belief that there is more of an opportunity for their children to be intellectually challenged in a homeschooling environment (Jolly et al., 2013). Tsubata (2003) did a research synthesis of homeschool surveys, which indicated that 77% of homeschool parents believe that providing home-based tutelage enables them to aim higher than American school standards.

Research also indicates that homeschooling allows a personalized approach that enables children to have a broader exposure to the world than one finds in public school environments. Studies indicate that, as a result of this personalized and broad approach to schooling, homeschooled youth are more tolerant than are children from public schools (Cheng, 2014; Medlin, 2013).

Immerses Students in High Technology and the Internet

Another homeschooling advantage that public schools can emulate is immersing students in the broad use of high technology and the Internet. Many homeschool curricula use Internet- and computer-based instruction, and there is more flexibility to use technology at home (Davis, 2014; Kunzman, 2009; West, 2012). To be sure, public and private schools often require and, at times, even supply iPads, laptops, and other technological equipment. However, the teachers often utilize these tools within a narrow range. Consequently, when these students enter college, many professors report that the high school graduates are inadequately prepared to use some of the most important scholastic applications electronically available (Davis, 2014; West, 2012).

There are several reasons why the use of high technology and the Internet are popular with homeschools, including (a) it enables parents to give their children an education that is consistent with a modern Information Age model rather than the older industrial rubric practiced by public schools, (b) it enables children to explore the world more freely than in typical schools, and (c) it helps youth develop levels of technological skills that would generally not be possible in a public school environment where teachers must accommodate the pace of students who are struggling with the computer (Davis, 2014; Kunzman, 2009; West, 2012).

> *It can be said that if one falls too far behind in technological agility, acumen, and overall knowledge, it is conceivable that it could dramatically reduce that person's employment opportunities.*

Technology has brought dramatic changes to everyday life. It can be said that if one falls too far behind in technological agility, acumen, and overall knowledge, it is conceivable that it could dramatically reduce that person's employment opportunities. Moreover, it is evident that the potential for Americans to compete in the global marketplace depends substantially on the technological preparedness of its graduates for the workforce. The existence of flexible and creative school curricula that encourage students to constantly become engaged with computers and the Internet on a broad scale will produce a student population with a high level of technological sophistication. It would therefore be wise for public schools to enact more of a personalized approach to using technology. In the industrialized model of education that emerged especially during the period of 1890 to 1935, teachers replaced parents as the focal point of public school education. However, generally speaking, mothers and fathers are considerably more aware of their children's gifts than are teachers. As a result, homeschooling often encourages youth to develop their giftedness in technology considerably more than one witnesses in public schools. Public schools ought to allow more room for students to exercise technological giftedness and interest.

Currently, the primary emphasis in public education is on equality, which certainly is a worthy goal. However, this direction has resulted in an overemphasis on standardized tests and "sameness." In contrast, only about 2% of the education budget in the U.S. is spent on giftedness training (Lewis, 2008; Stevens, 2009). To most fair-minded people, this percentage suggests an imbalance. It reflects a lack of personalized education, one manifestation of which is a lack of flexibility in allowing students to pursue advanced technological skills.

Supports Students in Special Situations

An increasing amount of evidence suggests that homeschooling applied to the broader educational landscape may provide students in a variety of unique situations the best opportunity to thrive, including those with special cognitive, physical, or emotional needs, as well as those who are bullied (Hayes, 2002; Noll, 1995; Peterson, 2009; Pyles, 2004; Rafter, 2004). To be sure, there is a certain degree of irony to this. Taxation to support public schools provides a copious amount of funds with which these centers of learning can provide facilities for these youth that the majority of faith-based schools neither have the size nor the financial resources to afford (Burman & Siemrod, 2013; Sacks, 2001). The average public school in the U.S. spends about $10,658 per student, which is usually 70% higher than one finds in faith-based schools (Burman & Siemrod, 2013; Center for Education Reform, 2012; Sacks, 2001; U.S. Department of Education, 2014).

Despite this considerable financial edge that public schools enjoy, there is an increasing recognition among parents and educators that what many students with special needs require is more love, understanding, and support, more than they do sophisticated facilities (Hayes, 2002; Peterson, 2009; Pyles, 2004). There is no question that the augmenting of school grounds to include an increasing number of adaptations facilitating movement and learning for those with special needs is well intentioned and often helpful (Burman & Siemrod, 2013; Center for Education Reform, 2012; Sacks, 2001). Nevertheless, it is equally true that no amount of elaborate adjustments can replace the love, support, and understanding that these youth receive from compassionate and adoring family members (Brodie, 2010; Jeynes, 2003b; Metzel, 2004). One of the reasons why homeschooling works well for children with special needs is because the challenges these youngsters face are often truly unique and best adapted to in a personalized environment such as one finds in homeschooling (Jones, 2004; Peterson, 2009).

Allows Specialization in a Particular Discipline

Finally, homeschooling provides unique opportunities for children to specialize in a particular discipline or set of activities that inspire them. That is, homeschooling provides more opportunities for a personally chosen focus than one usually finds in the public schools. One example is that homeschoolers have developed a reputation for winning the National Spelling Bee (Smith & Campbell, 2012). This is especially impressive because homeschoolers represent just 3.4% of the school-age population (U.S. Department of Education, 2012). Another example of this ability to specialize is the debate and court teams at Patrick Henry College. The overwhelming majority of students from this institution are homeschooled. Many homeschooled children aspire to be successful debaters and prepare at home during their K–12 education because Patrick Henry's debate and court teams have had amazing success. They have often triumphed over top universities, such as Oxford University and Notre Dame University (Rosin, 2007).

Clearly, the home environment cannot be and should not be replicated. However, teachers can take a number of steps to allow for greater flexibility in the classroom experience.

First, depending on the age of the children, students can be asked about their career interests. They can then be encouraged to explore their particular career interests in terms of writing reports, taking fieldtrips with like-minded students, and conducting interviews. Second, teachers can ask students about what they would most like to learn and accomplish during their school years and explain why this is important for their lives and future. The teacher can place students with similar interests into small groups. The students can take action to improve their abilities and collectively encourage and strengthen one another in their pursuits. Third, students who are a little older can be asked what courses they intend to take in the next few years and then prepare in advance for that course in order to increase proficiency. Such an approach to education will encourage students to be better prepared for their lives ahead.

Conclusion

One should note that education, as its founders originally formulated, did not involve the degree of standardization and government intervention that it does today (Elkind, 1987; Jeynes, 2006; Perrone, 1990). Most educators believed that too much standardization and rigidity usurped the parents' and teachers' ability to personalize their instruction in a way that could best benefit the students. In contemporary society, movements such as Common Core State Standards have increasingly made schooling nationalized and standardized. As a result, there is vigorous debate in liberal, moderate, and conservative circles regarding whether the degree of this standardization and government intervention is empowering or enervating the effective practice of schooling (Jeynes, 2000, 2006).

Creativity can manifest itself in a variety of different ways along a continuum. Often creativity manifests itself in an environment with a high level of flexibility, which is why one can argue that the flexible homeschool ambience is more conducive to spawning creativity than the more standardized public school environment (Rivero, 2002, 2008). The modern-day homeschool movement appears to have started in 1969 with Herbert Kohl's book, *The Open Classroom*. In it, Kohl (1969) stated, "For most American children there is essentially one public school system in the United States, and it's authoritarian and oppressive" (p. 12). That may seem like an extreme statement, but placed in more moderating terms, Kohl's assertion reflects the attitude that the government system of schools stifles creativity. A good number of historical figures, such as Abraham Lincoln, Thomas Edison, Agatha Christie, and Jane Austen, were homeschooled (Mayberry et al., 1995). These individuals were known for their creativity while living in very unique and disparate situations. Teachers need to learn from the homeschool environment what encourages creativity. Granted, there are many creative people who have not been homeschooled. Nevertheless, homeschooling encourages a level of flexibility that fosters the development of certain talents and supports the strengthening of certain weaknesses.

It is clear that the practice of homeschooling is not merely valuable in its own right but also can provide exemplary principles that can be applied within the public school system. It offers many advantages often overlooked by those who are not directly engaged in this instructional practice. The potential benefits that can accrue from a loving and personalized environment are advantages that should not be limited to homeschooling alone but should also be considered as lessons for the practice of teaching overall.

Action Principles for States, Districts, and Schools

With the strong educational contributions that homeschooling can potentially make for children, it is wise for education agencies at various levels to consider what can be learned from the practice of homeschooling.

Action Principles for States

a. Encourage parents to become more involved in their children's education (which is inherently the case with parents who homeschool). Parental engagement at all levels is good for youth and good for society.

b. Learn from economists and recognize that monopolies are not good for society. The virtual monopoly that the public school system has is no exception. Implement policies that encourage parental- and community-level participation and choice. Ninety-one percent of K–12 students attend public schools. Public schools should encourage educational innovation in the private sector and welcome the competition.

c. Place more emphasis on individual children than on standardized testing, the overuse of which often runs antithetical to fostering an atmosphere of a personalized education. This would allow educators to decrease the percentage of time allotted to preparing for standardized tests and allow a greater flexibility in the curricula, including inviting parental suggestions.

d. Provide policy and supports to develop school leaders' and teachers' capacities to use technology to facilitate personalized learning and to support students' own skills in technologies.

e. Value character education more. When a child is homeschooled, he or she has the benefit of receiving individualized instruction to become a more virtuous and moral human being (Ryan & Bohlin, 1999). Support implementation with fidelity of research-based social/emotional learning programs and similar interventions (Durlak, Weissberg, Dymnicki, Taylor, & Schellinger, 2011).

Action Principles for Districts

a. Become more focused on the good of the overall student population in the school district rather than only those who attend public school specifically. Encourage the implementation of a variety of practices used by homeschoolers. Offer seminars on this issue and make them available to all K–12 educators, not simply those in the public schools.

b. Offer parents courses on how to be more effectively engaged in a child's schooling, even if parents are limited by workplace demands, etc.

c. Offer district facilities, when possible, so that parents can use public school equipment to enhance the homeschooling experience for their children.

d. Train teachers how to best help youngsters who either entered public school from a homeschooling environment or who are homeschooled for some classes but not for others. The training would involve the participation of teachers and families who had worked with such a transition and address what the keys are for success in these adjustments.

e. Facilitate learning from homeschooling by holding joint conferences with home-schooling advocates regarding what public school districts and homeschooling families can learn from one another to maximize educational outcomes.

Action Principles for Schools

a. Private schools should more aggressively offer homeschool options. Some schools give students the option of either attending their school or using the same text-books in a home-based environment. This benefits the school by increasing overall enrollment. It also offers advantages to the family because it makes schooling more affordable for them and more personalized.

b. Develop a more holistic approach to schooling. Leaders need to care about the edu-cation that all children receive, not merely those who attend public schools. They need to make it easier for homeschooled youth in their area to participate in extra-curricular activities and homeschool without excessive red tape from the school.

c. Contact the homeschool associations and families, encouraging them to send their children to take courses at their schools that would be difficult to teach at home (e.g., chemistry).

d. Realize that homeschooling is a very helpful and practical option for parents who encounter some rather unique situations with their children, such as children who have special needs, who have been bullied persistently, who have disabilities, or whose parents must move frequently. Be willing to encourage families in these situations to exercise these options.

e. Contact homeschool teachers and ask if they would be willing to tutor struggling public school students, given their expertise in instructing students one on one.

References

Brodie, L. F. (2010). *Love in a time of homeschooling*. New York, NY: Harper.

Burman, L., & Siemrod, J. (2013). *Taxes in America: What everyone needs to know*. London, UK: Oxford University Press.

Castaldo, J. E., & Levitt, L. P. (2010). *Uncommon wisdom: True tales of what our lives as doctors have taught us about love, faith and healing*. New York, NY: Rodale.

Center for Education Reform. (2012). *Center for education reform*. Washington, DC: Center for Education Reform [Website]. Retrieved from edreform.com/2012/04/k-12-facts/

Cheng, A. (2014). Does homeschooling or private schooling promote political intolerance? Evi-dence from a Christian university. *Journal of School Choice, 8*(1), 49–68.

Counts, G. (1932). *Dare we build a new social order?* New York, NY: John Day.

Davis, K. (2014). *The ultimate guide for using technology in homeschool*. Scotts Valley, CA: CreateSpace.

Deresiewicz, W. (2011). *A Jane Austen education*. New York, NY: Penguin Press.

Dewey, J. (1915). *The school and society*. Chicago, IL: University of Chicago Press.

Dewey, J. (1978). *John Dewey: The middle works, 1899–1924, Vol. 7*. Carbondale, IL: Southern Illinois University.

Dupuis, A. M. (1966). *Philosophy of education in historical perspective*. Chicago, IL: Rand McNally.

Durlak, J. A., Weissberg, R. P., Dymnicki, A. B., Taylor, R. D., & Schellinger, K. B. (2011). The impact of enhancing students' social and emotional learning: A meta-analysis of school-based universal interventions. *Child Development, 82*, 405–432. Retrieved from http://static1.squarespace.com/static/513f79f9e4b05ce7b70e9673/t/52e9d8e6e4b001f5c1f6c27d/1391057126694/meta-analysis-child-development.pdf

Elkind, D. (1987). *Miseducation: Preschoolers at risk.* New York, NY: Knopf.

Feldmon, J., Lopez, M. L., & Simon, K. G. (2006). *Choosing small: The successful guide.* San Francisco, CA: Jossey-Bass.

Fisher, A. L. (2003). *Fundamentals of homeschooling.* Carson, WA: Nettlepatch Press.

Fraser, J. W. (2001). *The school in the United States: A documentary history.* Boston, MA: McGraw Hill.

Fraser, J. W. (2007). *Preparing America's teachers: A history.* New York, NY: Teachers College Press.

Gangel, K. O., & Benson, W. S. (1983). *Christian education: Its history and philosophy.* Chicago, IL: Moody Press.

Gatto, J. T. (2001). *The underground history of American schooling.* New York, NY: Oxford Village Press.

Gatto, J. T. (2009). *Weapons of mass instruction.* Gabrilola Island, British Columbia, Canada: New Society Publishers.

Green, C. L., & Hoover-Dempsey, K. V. (2007). Why do parents homeschool? A systematic examination of parental involvement. *Education & Urban Society, 39*(2), 264–285.

Gregory, S. T. (2000). *The academic achievement of minority students: Perspectives, practices, and prescriptions.* Lanham, MD: University Press of America.

Hayes, L. C. (2002). *Homeschooling the child with ADD.* Roseville, CA: Prima Publishers.

Hirsch, E. D. (2006). *The knowledge deficit.* Boston, MA: Houghton Mifflin.

Horne, H. H. (1931). *This new education.* New York, NY: Abington.

Horne, H. H. (1932). *The democratic philosophy of education: Companion to Dewey's democracy and education.* New York, NY: Macmillan.

Immell, M. (2009). *Homeschooling.* Detroit, MI: Greenhaven Press.

Jeynes, W. (2000). Assessing school choice: A balanced perspective. *Cambridge Journal of Education, 30*(2), 223–241.

Jeynes, W. (2002). A meta-analysis of the effects of attending religious schools and religiosity on Black and Hispanic academic achievement. *Education & Urban Society, 35*(1), 27–49.

Jeynes, W. (2003a). A meta-analysis: The effects of parental involvement on minority children's academic achievement. *Education & Urban Society, 35*(2), 202–218.

Jeynes, W. (2003b). The effects of Black and Hispanic twelfth graders living in intact families and being religious on their academic achievement. *Urban Education, 38*(1), 35–57.

Jeynes, W. (2005). Effects of parental involvement and family structure on the academic achievement of adolescents. *Marriage and Family Review, 37*(3), 99–117.

Jeynes, W. (2006). Standardized tests and Froebel's original kindergarten model. *Teachers College Record, 108*(10), 1937–1959.

Jeynes, W. (2007a). *American educational history: School, society & the common good.* Thousand Oaks, CA: Sage.

Jeynes, W. (2007b). The relationship between parental involvement and urban secondary school student academic achievement: A meta-analysis. *Urban Education, 42*(1), 82–110.

Jeynes, W. (2010). The salience of the subtle aspects of parental involvement and encouraging that involvement: Implications for school-based programs. *Teachers College Record, 112*(3), 747–774.

Jeynes, W. (2012). A meta-analysis on the effects and contributions of public, public charter, and religious schools on student outcomes. *Peabody Journal of Education, 87*(3), 265–305.

Jeynes, W. (2014). *School choice: A balanced approach.* Santa Barbara, CA: Praeger.

Jeynes, W., & Littell, S. (2000). A meta-analysis of studies examining the effect of whole language instruction on the literacy of low-SES students. *Elementary School Journal, 101*(1), 21–33.

Jolly, J. L., Matthews, M. S., & Nester, J. (2013). Homeschooling the gifted: A parent's perspective. *Gifted Child Quarterly, 57*(2), 121–134.

Jones, K. W. (2004). Education for children with mental retardation: Parent activism, public policy, and family ideology in the 1950s. In S. Noll & J. W. Trent (Eds.), *Mental retardation in America: A historical reader* (pp. 322–350). New York, NY: New York University.

Kohl, H. (1969). *The open classroom.* New York, NY: Random House.

Kunzman, R. (2009). *Write these laws on your children.* Boston, MA: Beacon Press.

Kurtz, S. N. (2010). *Radical-in-chief: Barack Obama and the untold story of American socialism.* New York, NY: Threshold Editions.

Lesaux, N. K., & Marietta, S. H. (2011). *Making assessment matter: Using test results to differentiate reading instruction.* New York, NY: Guilford Press.

Lewis, J. D. (2008). *Advocacy for gifted children and gifted programs.* Waco, TX: Prufrock Press.

Mann, H. (1957). *The republic and the school: Horace Mann and the education of free men.* New York, NY: Teachers College, Columbia University.

Mayberry, M. J., Knowles, G., Ray, B., & Marlow, S. (1995). *Homeschooling parents as educators.* Thousand Oaks, CA: Corwin Press.

Medlin, R. G. (2013). Homeschooling and the problem of socialization revisited. *Peabody Journal of Education, 88*(3), 284–297.

Metzel, D. S. (2004). Historical and social geography. In S. Noll & J. W. Trent (Eds.), *Mental retardation in America: A historical reader* (pp. 420–444). New York, NY: New York University.

Moore, R., & Moore, D. (1994). *The successful homeschool family handbook.* Camas, WA: Thomas Nelson.

Morgan, J. (1986). *Godly learning: Puritan attitudes toward religion, learning, and education.* New York, NY: Cambridge University Press.

Nel, A. (2010). Homeschooling students score comparably to others on standardized tests. In N. Berlatsky (Ed.), *Homeschooling: Opposing viewpoints* (pp. 21–27). Detroit, MI: Greenhaven Press.

Noll, S. (1995). *Feeble minded in our midst: Institutions for the mentally retarded in the South.* Chapel Hill, NC: University of North Carolina Press.

O'Connell, J., & Smith, S. C. (2000). *Capitalizing on small class size.* Eugene, OR: University of Oregon.

Orr, T. (2003). *After homeschool.* Los Angeles, CA: Parent's Guide Press.

Perrone, V. (1990). How did we get here? Testing in the early grades: The games grown-ups play. In C. Kamii (Ed.), *Testing in the early grades* (pp. 1–13). Washington, DC: National Association for the Education of Young Children.

Pestalozzi, J. (1901). *Leonard and Gertrude.* Boston, MA: B.C. Heath & Co.

Peterson, D. (2009). You can homeschool your child with special needs. *Exceptional Parent, 39*(5), 38–39.

Pyles, L. (2004). *Homeschooling the child with Asperger syndrome.* London, UK: Jessica Kingsley Publishing.

Rafter, N. (2004). Criminalization of mental retardation. In S. Noll & J. W. Trent (Eds.), *Mental retardation in America: A historical reader* (pp. 232–257). New York, NY: New York University.

Ray, B. D., & Wartes, J. (1991). Academic achievement and affective development. In J. Van Galen & M. A. Pittman (Eds.), *Homeschooling: Political, historical, and pedagogical perspectives* (pp. 43–62). Norwood, NJ: Ablex.

Reavis, R., & Lakriski, A. (2005). Are home-schooled socially at-risk or socially protected? *Brown University Child & Adolescent Behavior Letter, 21*(9), 1–5.

Rivero, L. (2002). Progressive digressions: Homeschooling for self-actualization. *Roeper Review, 24*(4), 197–202.

Rivero, L. (2008). *The homeschooling option*. New York, NY: Palgrave Macmillan.

Rosin, H. (2007). *God's Harvard: A Christian college on a mission to save America*. Orlando, FL: Harcourt.

Ryan, K., & Bohlin, K. E. (1999). *Building character in schools: Practical ways to bring moral instruction to life*. San Francisco, CA: Jossey-Bass.

Sacks, A. (2001). *Special education: A reference handbook*. Santa Barbara, CA: ABC- CLIO.

Schneider, B. L., & Coleman, J. S. (1993). *Parents, their children, and schools*. Boulder, CO: Westview.

Short, B. N. (2010). Homeschooling should not be regulated by the government. In N. Berlatsky (Ed.), *Homeschooling: Opposing viewpoints* (pp. 84–90). Detroit, MI: Greenhaven.

Smith, L. M., & Campbell, J. (2012). *Families, education, and giftedness*. Rotterdam, Netherlands: Sense Publishers.

Stevens, M. L. (2001). *Kingdom of children*. Princeton, NJ: Princeton University Press.

Stevens, M. (2009). *Challenging the gifted child: An open approach to working with advanced young readers*. London, UK: Jessica Kingsley Publishing.

Tsubata, K. (2003). Parents share through poll results. *Washington Times*, August, 4, p. B1.

U.S. Department of Education. (2012). *National Household Education Surveys Program*. Washington, DC: Author. Retrieved from https://nces.ed.gov/programs/digest/d14/tables/dt14_206.10.asp

U.S. Department of Education. (2014). *Digest of education statistics 2013*. Washington, DC: Author.

Urban, W. J., & Wagoner, J. L. (2009). *American education: A history*. New York, NY: Routledge.

Welling, G. (2005). *From revolution to reconstruction*. Groningen, Netherlands: University of Groningen.

West, C. (2012). *Homeschooling gifted and advanced learners*. Waco, TX: Prufrock Press.

Whitehead, J. W. (2013). *A government of wolves: The emerging American police state*. New York, NY: SelectBooks.

Worek, M. (2008). *Nobel: A century of prize winners*. Richmond Hill, Ontario: Firefly Books.

III. Teaching and Technology in Support of Personalized Learning

Personalizing Curriculum: Curation and Creation

Karen L. Mahon

A personalized curriculum is one that has been crafted to provide students with individualized learning opportunities. As the use of personalization strategies has become more popular, the challenges of curating (i.e., selecting) and creating personalized curriculum resources have come to the fore. In particular, there is no systematic method by which educators learn to select and create curriculum resources that support personalized instruction. This has led to widespread confusion about what personalized instruction is and is not and has produced wide variety in what educators are applying in the name of personalized curriculum.

This chapter endeavors to provide a roadmap for educators who are selecting and creating resources for personalizing curriculum. The chapter is presented in two parts: first, descriptions of the best practices and discouraged practices for personalization are presented; second, the research base that determines whether a practice is recommended or discouraged are discussed.

Best Practices in Proven Methods of Personalization

The first section of this chapter focuses on personalization methods that have demonstrated a positive impact on student learning outcomes in the educational research literature. These practices are recommended to be included in instruction and in the resources that are selected or created in order to personalize instruction. Recommended methods include goal setting, feedback, periodic formative assessment, deliberate practice, and peer tutoring.

Goal Setting

Goal setting entails describing and defining the learning outcomes that an individual student should achieve on completion of an activity, module, or other unit of curriculum. Goals typically include not only the level of achievement to be reached but also the amount of time in which the achievement should be accomplished. According to Locke and Latham (1990), goals inform individuals "as to what type or level of performance is

Handbook on Personalized Learning for States, Districts, and Schools, pages 117–130

to be attained so that they can direct and evaluate their actions and efforts accordingly" (p. 23). Furthermore, Locke and Latham suggest that goals regulate action, explain the nature of the link between the past and the future, and assume that human goals are directed by intentions.

Performance goals should be specific, so that teacher and student have a shared understanding of the expectation, and they should be challenging relative to a student's current repertoire. Goals are likely to be very effective as a personalization strategy when cast in terms of "personal best" targets for individual learners. Personal best targets are especially positive because they give the learner the opportunity to compete only with herself, improving on her own previous performance, not with peers who may have higher skill levels. Goal setting need not be collaborative between teacher and student; effective teachers should set appropriately challenging goals that are personalized for individual learners and then arrange the learning environment to help learners achieve those goals.

> *Performance goals should be specific, so that teacher and student have a shared understanding of the expectation...*

Some digital resources evaluate performance and set a goal automatically and is a feature to look for when selecting products. When using a resource—high tech or low tech—that does not provide a goal, administering a pretest and setting a performance goal for the learner to achieve is recommended. Evaluate a student's current performance relative to mastery, then set an appropriate and achievable, yet challenging, goal that is an appropriate "personal best," given the student's current level.

Feedback

Feedback is information that a learner receives about his performance. Locke and Latham (1990) state that feedback allows learners "to set reasonable goals and to track their performance in relation to their goals so that adjustments in effort, direction, and even strategy can be made as needed" (p. 23). The rule of thumb for feedback is that it should be specific, immediate, and frequent. When feedback is specific, it includes statements such as, "You did a great job adding numbers today" instead of the more general and vague, "Great job." In the former case, the learner gets information about what, precisely, he did well. In the latter case, the lack of specificity leaves the feedback open to interpretation, thereby leaving the learner unsure of what he should be doing more of (or less of, in the case of corrective feedback) going forward.

The more immediately feedback is given following a response, the more closely the learner will associate the feedback with the task and be able to recognize clearly what she did that earned that feedback. "The way you pronounced the word 'thorough' wasn't quite right. Let's try again" immediately following the learner's speaking the word aloud is more informative than the same statement three hours after the reading aloud took place. The feedback is more easily assimilated if the recipient does not have to struggle to remember the performance that is named, particularly if the learner made a mistake. Giving immediate feedback does not mean that *every response* must be followed by immediate feedback. It just means that when feedback is given, it should follow the target response as closely in time as possible.

Finally, feedback should be delivered frequently. Frequent feedback lets learners know how successfully they are moving toward their goals as they progress. This is especially critical for learners who make errors; as they work to correct their errors, frequent feedback to shape their performance in the direction of mastery not only helps with accuracy, but it also helps keep them motivated.

When selecting digital products, test drive them to make sure that feedback for correct answers and errors is included. The higher quality instructional products will have feedback. If a digital product does not have embedded feedback or if a low-tech product has been utilized, the feedback will need to come from the teacher. Using feedback to personalize instruction for individual learners comes naturally to most teachers, without any special effort, but teachers may also build in places in the curriculum materials where students are prompted to ask for feedback. As long as the feedback is specific, it is automatically personalized for the learner because individual learners, compared with one another, do different things well and make different mistakes. As the teacher observes her students, she will likely see that the struggling learners need more frequent feedback, both to correct their errors and to help keep them motivated by pointing out what they are doing correctly. One of the keys in personalizing instruction with feedback is to be careful not to forget to give feedback to the more successful learners as well because often they are overlooked in favor of the students who require more support. In general, the goals are to keep feedback specific and immediate for all learners and to vary the frequency of the feedback depending on individual learner needs.

Periodic Formative Assessment

Periodic formative assessment includes regular and planned checks of progress toward the student performance goals set out for the curriculum. Formative assessment does not change student grades; it is not "testing." Conversely, it is intended to provide feedback to the teacher about which content the student is mastering and which content the student may be misunderstanding so that corrections can be made quickly. With formative assessment data, the teacher (or digital program) is able to make adjustments to the curriculum path, introducing remediation to clear up any difficulties the individual student may have with the content, speeding up the pace of the content or slowing it down. Thus, the student experiences personalized interventions as the curriculum path changes to meet his individual needs, whether designed by a teacher or a software algorithm.

One important benefit of ongoing formative assessment that is included in digital instruction is that it automatically adapts difficulty levels, depending on the learner's performance. This happens on the fly, without the learner or an adult needing to change settings in the program. The key to this is the automatic piece, regardless of whether it is used in online curriculum, computer-based software, or mobile apps running on a device. On a response-by-response basis, the curriculum adjusts its level of difficulty to what is most appropriate for the individual learner based on the pattern of responses produced by that learner. The algorithms that the curriculum uses to make branching and looping decisions can vary. Some curricula adjust based on a single user response. Others adjust the curriculum path based on a moving window of responses: an example is a program that is always looking at the five most recent responses and adjusting on that basis. The best algorithms look not only at correct responses (i.e., "hits") and errors (i.e., "misses") but also at "correct rejects" (i.e., what answer options a learner rejects when she makes a correct response) and "false alarms" (i.e., the answer option that a learner chooses, erroneously, when she makes a mistake). The more sophisticated the performance tracking in a program, the more sensitive that program can be in adjusting to particular student learning needs.

These adjusting levels of difficulty are, effectively, ongoing formative assessment. Adapting levels of difficulty in digital instruction provides the same tailoring opportunity that a teacher has when using feedback from formative assessment. Just as a teacher makes adjustments to a curriculum based on formative assessment data, so too does a digital program make adjustments to its curriculum based on the student performance data that it collects. The difference is that a digital program, when being used *simultaneously* by multiple students, can make different personalized adjustments for each student *simultaneously*. The decision-making algorithms allow the program to take some of the load off of teachers in personalizing instruction, and because digital programs track the history of response patterns (thus giving it a long memory), it can adjust more effectively on the fly than a person can. One can think of this process as the student and program "co-creating" a personalized curriculum path.

Formative assessment and adapting levels of difficulty allow teachers to avoid what is known to be least effective for students—a "one size fits all" approach. In the case of digital resources, every interaction the student has with the curriculum is recorded, typically, and some programs have the capability to adapt levels of difficulty automatically, as described earlier. It is recommended that instructional digital resources are selected that do have that capability. Be mindful that programs that have adapting levels of difficulty are more expensive to make; developers have to put more time and effort into designing different curriculum paths and decision-making algorithms that allow the adapting to occur. A program that can automatically personalize to an individual students' needs is more complex than a program that has a linear path through the same set of 50 questions, for example.

> *Formative assessment and adapting levels of difficulty allow teachers to avoid what is known to be least effective for students—a "one size fits all" approach.*

In the case of using low-tech approaches, teachers should consider embedding formative assessment opportunities into their lesson plans. This can be done in numerous ways, from technology-enhanced formative assessment, such as using a student response app that runs on mobile devices (e.g., Socrative, Inc., 2015), to something as low tech as giving students pieces of colored construction paper and asking them to raise the piece of paper that corresponds to the correct answer to a question presented by the teacher. Regardless of the method of data collection, the main point is for teachers to create assessment items that focus on the most critical target performances and to plan when these checks will occur during a learning session or lesson. The goal is to get insight into student progress and for the insight to occur regularly enough to make modifications to instruction and address misunderstandings and errors before they become habits. The formative assessment itself is not what is personalized; rather, the clarification and modification of the curriculum, on a student-by-student basis and in response to the formative assessment, are personalized.

Finally, graphing formative assessment data is recommended. The effectiveness of formative assessment is even greater when both the teacher and learner can see the progress displayed visually. In the case of digital solutions, look for products that include graphing and visual display. When creating curricula, teachers can include this opportunity to graph progress at regular intervals.

Deliberate Practice

Deliberate practice is the arrangement of many opportunities for active responding in a period of instruction. Unlike "time on task," which comprises all time—both active and passive—spent in the presence of a task, deliberate practice focuses intentionally on the active responding and the opportunities created to encourage active responding. Examples of active responding include "behaviors such as writing, oral reading, academic talk, asking questions, answering questions, and motor behaviors involved in participating in academic games or tasks" (Greenwood, Delquadri, & Hall, 1984, p. 65). Increasing active responding through deliberate practice also increases the likelihood that students will pay attention and stay on task.

Deliberate practice is not simply "drill and practice" but rather relies on the inclusion of feedback and established performance criteria. A student responds actively, and immediate feedback is given about the correctness of the response, which allows the student to modify her next response, if necessary. The greater the number of opportunities to respond actively in a period of academic instruction, get feedback, and respond again incorporating that feedback, the faster an individual student will achieve mastery performance.

Think of the example of a student learning to play the piano. Imagine that the student engages in deliberate practice for an hour a day, making, perhaps, hundreds of keystrokes and getting feedback from a teacher. A student in that scenario will make much more progress, much more quickly, toward playing the piano with competency than a student who may spend an hour a day *listening* to piano music but only performing a handful of active keystrokes.

Whether choosing a high- or low-tech resource, the key is to select materials that provide numerous opportunities for learners to respond actively to the materials within a fixed period of time. Many digital programs include a timed component wherein learners must not only respond actively but must also do it quickly (i.e., building fluency) but other digital programs and all low-tech activities do not. The most critical aspect in choosing resources is to select those that have many response opportunities; a teacher can easily add her own timing component to any activity with a simple stopwatch. If the teacher is adding a timing component while working with a group of learners, it is important to remember that each learner can work on a different skill simultaneously; only the timing need be shared. Do not underestimate the utility of even a simple printed worksheet that has many problems on it, each requiring an active student response. Something simple and low tech like this can be more effective than the slickest digital tool that has limited active response opportunities and consists primarily of passive presentation of material.

When you are encouraging students to make many active responses quickly and start to see mistakes in accuracy, have them slow down. This is part of the personalization piece. When students have opportunities for active responding, focus on building accuracy first and then on getting faster. Different students will progress at different rates, but a focus on deliberate practice will facilitate progress toward mastery.

Peer Tutoring

Peer tutoring is the pairing of students to work together during the course of study. Peer tutoring is often implemented with more skilled learners tutoring less skilled and struggling learners, but it is thought that one of the main reasons that peer tutoring works so well is that "it is an excellent method to teach students to become their own teachers" (Hattie, 2009, p. 186).

One type of peer tutoring implementation is classwide peer tutoring (CWPT), in which all students in a classroom are organized into tutor–learner pairs. Used to ensure that all students are actively engaged during academic instruction, CWPT increases students' opportunities for deliberate practice. Peer tutoring can be used for personalizing the experience of both students who have been paired; the challenges for and responsibilities of each student in the dyad will be different, depending on the skills and abilities of each learner. For example, if Katie is paired with a more skilled learner, the level of challenge for her will be raised, but she will have a student mentor to help her achieve progress. Conversely, if Katie is paired with a less skilled learner, then she will be the mentor; her challenge, then, is to teach skills to another student clearly and effectively. Depending on Katie's own level of skill in different topics, her teacher can personalize Katie's experience through these pairings.

Some digital products are built to allow more than one student at a time to use them. When selecting among these products for use in peer tutoring, be careful to select the collaborative products that allow individual users to *work together* to achieve a desired outcome, not products that allow users to *compete* with one another in real-time play. If you are pairing a more skilled student with a less skilled student using a collaborative digital product, make sure that the more skilled student understands how to use the product, what the learning goal of the product is, and how to monitor progress toward that goal before a session with the less skilled learner begins.

If the teacher is creating materials to be used in peer tutoring sessions, a job aid to be used by the more skilled student of the pair is recommended. This aid might entail a script to be followed, a flow chart for the desired sequence of activities, or a list of objectives that the less skilled learner must attain. In short, providing a road map for the tutor is useful in keeping the session on track, particularly when conducting a low-tech activity that is not being directed by an automated computer program.

Discouraged Methods of Personalizing Curriculum

The next section of this chapter focuses on personalization methods that have produced a neutral or negative impact on student learning outcomes in the educational research literature. These practices are not recommended to be included in instruction or in the resources selected or created in order to personalize instruction. They include self-directed learning and matching student learning styles.

Student-Directed Learning

Student-directed learning is the practice of giving students choice in or control over their learning activities or learning materials. Student-directed learning is often touted as allowing students to take responsibility for their learning (Checkley, 1995). Proponents of student-directed learning believe that this practice increases student motivation and engagement. Student-directed learning is perhaps one of the best known, most popular methods of personalizing instruction.

If teachers opt to implement student-directed learning practices in their classrooms, they should consider combining them with one or more of the proven methods of personalization described earlier. The best practices of personalizing instruction can be implemented in a student-directed learning environment because they can be applied to any subject or topic that a student may select; they are subject agnostic.

Matching Student Learning Styles

Matching learning styles is a controversial method of personalizing instruction. The philosophy behind learning styles is that different students have preferences for different ways of learning (including auditory, visual, tactile, and kinesthetic styles) and that academic achievement is improved when teaching takes these style preferences into account by matching resources to the preferred learning style. It is recommended that teachers DO NOT use products or create curricula that rely on a learning styles approach.

The Research Base of Proven Best Practices of Personalization

Some methods of personalizing curriculum have been demonstrated to be far more effective than others in the empirical educational research. The following overview discusses the research undergirding the recommended best practices discussed earlier.

Goal Setting

In goal setting, achievement is enhanced to the degree that students have challenging rather than "do your best" goals relative to their present competencies (Locke & Latham, 1990). Difficult goals are thought to be more effective because they direct students' attention to the most relevant behaviors to achieve the goals (see Chidester & Grigsby, 1984; Mento, Stell, & Karren, 1987; Tubbs, 1986; Wofford, Goodwin, & Premack, 1992; Wood, Mento, & Locke, 1987). Student commitment to the goals does not appear to be necessary for goal attainment except in the case of special education students; with these students, explicit commitment to the goals makes a large difference (see Donovan & Radosevich, 1998; Klein, Wesson, Hollenbeck, & Ange, 1999).

> In goal setting, achievement is enhanced to the degree that students have challenging rather than "do your best" goals relative to their present competencies.

Martin (2006) found that one effective method in achieving goals was to set "personal best" targets. Personal bests "primarily reflect a mastery orientation because it is self-referenced and self-improvement based and yet holds a slice of performance orientation because the student competes with his or her own previous performance" (p. 816).

Feedback

Feedback has consistently been shown to be "among the most powerful influences on achievement" (Hattie, 2009, p. 173). The most effective feedback is immediate, providing information about the response that the learner has just made, thus allowing that student to act on the feedback (see Malott & Trojan-Suarez, 2004; Miltenberger, 2008). Feedback for correct answers is known to be even more important than feedback for mistakes (see Kluger & DeNisi, 1996).

The effectiveness of feedback has been so compelling for such a long time that its use is now part of common practice in education. The research basis for using feedback goes back more than 45 years and has been demonstrated across a wide variety of settings and performances, from student academic achievement (e.g., Fink & Carnine, 1975; Martin, Pear, & Martin, 2002; Reichow & Wolery, 2011; Trap, Milner-Davis, Joseph, & Cooper,

1978; Van Houten, Morrison, Jarvis, & McDonald, 1974) and teacher behavior (e.g., Cossairt, Hall, & Hopkins, 1973; Harris, Bushell, Sherman, & Kane, 1975) to sports skills (e.g., Boyer, Miltenberger, Batsche, & Fogel, 2009; Brobst & Ward, 2002; Smith & Ward, 2006), flight training (e.g., Rantz, Dickinson, Sinclair, & Van Houten, 2009; Rantz & Van Houten, 2011), and more.

Periodic Formative Assessment

In formative assessment, the feedback to the teacher accounts for its larger effect sizes than other typical teacher effects (Hattie, 2009). According to Beatty and Gerace (2008), the efficacy of formative assessment is strongly supported by empirical results (for which they cite Bell & Cowie, 2001; Black & Wiliam, 1998b, 2005; Sadler, 1989). Black and Wiliam (1998a), in particular, point out that "innovations which include strengthening the practice of formative assessment produce significant, and often substantial, learning gains" (p. 155) across ages, school subjects, and countries—gains "among the largest ever reported for educational interventions" (p. 155). Black (1998) and Stiggins (2002) suggest that formative assessment may help narrow the achievement gap between those learners who are low achieving from low-income areas and their counterparts in more affluent socioeconomic groups.

Mazur (1997) implemented technology-enhanced formative assessment with periodic questioning during his university lectures. Multiple-choice items were presented, the students selected the correct answers via student response devices, and Mazur conducted follow-up discussions to clarify misunderstandings. The proportion of students answering questions correctly always increased after the follow-up discussion. Furthermore, Mazur (2009) elaborated: "Data obtained in my class and in classes of colleagues worldwide, in a wide range of academic settings and a wide range of disciplines, show that learning gains nearly triple with an approach that focuses on the student and on interactive learning" (p. 51) through these formative assessment practices. Beatty and Gerace (2008) point out that Mazur's assertion is supported by quantitative evidence from use in undergraduate science courses across multiple topics (e.g., Hestenes, Wells, & Swackhamer, 1992; Smith et al., 2009).

When formative assessment data are evaluated according to evidence-based models, effect sizes are higher than when the data are evaluated just by teacher judgment. Furthermore, when these data are graphed so that patterns of progress can be observed visually, the effectiveness of formative assessment is even greater (see Fuchs & Fuchs, 1986).

Deliberate Practice

Walker, Greenwood, Hart, and Carta (1994) point out that increasing the rate of correct academic responses until a mastery-based success criterion is met is critical for teachers to implement. The increasing of rates of deliberate practice is what Hattie (2009) refers to as the "common denominator" to many effective instructional methods, such as direct instruction, peer tutoring, mastery learning, and even feedback. High rates of deliberate practice provide the opportunity to improve accuracy in responding to mastery levels, but they also improve fluency, or accuracy plus speed, as in the case of precision teaching (e.g., see Lindsley, 1992). In addition, deliberate practice is likely to lead to long-term retention of learning (see Peladeau, Forget, & Gagne, 2003).

Deliberate practice requires active responding. Classrooms that emphasize active responding during more than 50% of the allocated instruction time will produce higher academic gains (Greenwood et al., 1984). A number of strategies that increase the frequency of active student responding have demonstrated improvement in academic achievement (Narayan, Heward, Gardner, Courson, & Omness, 1990). These include CWPT (Cooke, Heron, & Heward, 1983; Delquadri, Greenwood, Whorton, Carta, & Hall, 1986), computer-assisted instruction (Balajthy, 1984; Stallard, 1982; Tudor & Bostow, 1991), self-directed learning (Kosiewicz, Hallahan, Lloyd, & Graves, 1982), use of response cards (Cooke et al., 1983; Heward et al., 1996; Munro & Stephenson, 2009), choral responding (Heward, Courson, & Narayan, 1989; Sindelar, Bursuck, & Halle, 1986), timed trials (Van Houten et al., 1974; Van Houten & Thompson, 1976), and guided lecture notes (Lovitt, Rudsit, Jenkins, Pious, & Benedetti, 1985). In all cases, the strategy is the same: increase active student responding. It is only the tactic used to increase the responding that varies.

Peer Tutoring

The use of peers as co-teachers has been found to be quite powerful. The data supporting the effectiveness of peer tutoring are strong, dating back nearly 40 years. Hartley's (1977) meta-analysis of the effect of instructional method on mathematics achievement found that peer tutoring was the most effective method of those compared. Peer tutoring was most effective when used as a supplement to teacher instruction, and cross-age tutors were more effective than same-age or adult tutors. Phillips (1983) found that peer tutoring was more effective for students in the acquisition phase, rather than the maintenance phase, of learning and with clear success criteria as targets. Rohrbeck, Ginsburg-Block, Fantuzzo, and Miller (2003) found that peer tutoring that was more "student controlled," including student involvement in goal setting and monitoring performance, was more effective than when those aspects were controlled only by the teacher.

The effectiveness of CWPT has been demonstrated in studies of individual classrooms (e.g., Delquadri, Greenwood, Stretton, & Hall, 1983) and in longitudinal studies with as many as nine schools participating (e.g., Greenwood & Delquadri, 1995; Greenwood, Delquadri, & Hall, 1989). It has been shown to establish skills at a faster rate, provide better retention of what students learn, and make greater advances in student social competence "when using CWPT compared to such standard instructional methods as teacher–student discussion, lectures, seat work" and others (Greenwood, 1997, p. 55).

Discouraged Methods of Personalization

Just as some methods of personalizing curriculum have been demonstrated effective in the empirical educational research, others have been shown to be less so. The following overview discusses the research undergirding the personalization strategies discussed earlier that are not recommended.

Student Choice or Control Over Learning

Available data do not support an effect on increased student learning outcomes of student-directed learning. In a meta-analysis from Niemiec, Sikorski, and Walberg (1996), a review of 24 studies examining learner control yielded an average effect size that was small and negative, suggesting that the average student is not helped academically by student choice and might even be better off without it. A second meta-analysis of 41 studies, conducted by Patall, Cooper, and Robinson in 2008, showed that instructionally relevant student choice had no meaningful impact on task performance, intrinsic motivation, effort, or perceived self-competence.

Matching Student Learning Styles

Pashler, McDaniel, Rohrer, and Bjork (2008) report that, when asked, people will report preferences for how information is presented to them but that there is "virtually no evidence" supporting the notion that teaching according to those preferences impacts achievement. Similarly, in an extensive literature review, Coffield, Moseley, Hall, and Ecclestone (2004) point out that although learning styles has an intuitive appeal "in the idea that teachers and course designers should pay closer attention to students' learning styles," (p. 1) the available research does not support this approach in increasing achievement. In fact, Coffield et al. suggest that there is potential for the allocation of a learning style to turn into a "learning handicap" (p. 134) because learners fail to become competent with all styles of presentation. Some have proposed that matching learning styles may not help typically developing children but may be appropriate for children with learning disabilities, a hypothesis that was popular in the 1970s. Here too, however, the data do not support this notion (see Arter & Jenkins, 1979).

Action Principles for States, Districts, and Schools

The action items below recommend the building of a statewide, shared digital product repository and library and the creation of an online educator community.

Action Principles for States

a. Create an online repository in which statewide educators can list and link to the digital products they use. Resources should be tagged according to which personalization methods they include and can be categorized according to the methods used, subject, alignment to Common Core State Standards, and so on.

b. Create an online repository in which statewide educators can store and share their self-created content resources; resources should be tagged according to which personalization methods they include and can be categorized according to the methods they use; they can also be organized by district or school.

c. Create an online portal that allows teachers to communicate with each other and provide peer reviews of teacher-created content (Wiggins, 1996, 1997). Establishing this portal at the state level increases the probability of teachers finding peers who are tackling similar student personalization challenges, particularly in less commonly offered courses. This online portal should establish standardized criteria by which teachers can evaluate each other's content.

Action Principles for Districts

a. Provide training to member schools on how to evaluate digital products for personalization methods, and processes for tagging and categorizing those products according to the categories in the statewide digital repository.

b. Provide training to member schools on how to create curriculum resources that include effective personalization methods. Also train on processes for tagging and categorizing those products.

c. Train member schools in how to conduct consistent, criterion-based peer reviews, thus saving individual schools from having to reinvent the wheel by conducting these trainings themselves. Provide a floating expert to visit schools for ad hoc teacher training.

Action Principles for Schools

a. Create a folder in the statewide repository that includes a list of or links to the digital products that are owned or licensed by the individual school and available for immediate use by that school's teachers.

b. Add teachers' self-created resources to the school's folder in the statewide repository, tagging them appropriately.

c. Provide guidance for following a process to vet teacher-created resources.

References

Arter, J. A., & Jenkins, J. A. (1979). Differential diagnosis-prescriptive teaching: A critical appraisal. *Review of Educational Research, 49*(4), 517–555.

Balajthy, E. (1984). Using student-constructed questions to encourage active reading. *Journal of Reading, 27*(5), 408–411.

Beatty, I. D., & Gerace, W. J. (2008). Technology-enhanced formative assessment: A research-based pedagogy for teaching science with classroom response technology. *Journal of Science Education and Technology, 18*(2), 146–162.

Bell, B., & Cowie, B. (2001). The characteristics of formative assessment in science education. *Science Education, 85*(5), 536–553.

Black, P. (1998). Formative assessment: Raising standards inside the classroom. *School Science Review, 80*(291), 39–46.

Black, P., & Wiliam, D. (1998a). Assessment and classroom learning. *Assessment in Education: Principles, Policy, and Practice, 5*(1), 7–74.

Black, P., & Wiliam, D. (1998b). Inside the black box: Raising standards through classroom assessment. *Phi Delta Kappan, 80*(2), 139–148.

Black, P., & Wiliam, D. (2005). Developing a theory of formative assessment. In J. Gardner (Ed.), *Assessment and Learning* (pp. 81–100). London, UK: Sage.

Boyer, E., Miltenberger, R. G., Batsche, C., & Fogel, V. (2009). Video modeling by experts with video feedback to enhance gymnastics skills. *Journal of Applied Behavior Analysis, 42*(4), 855–860.

Brobst, B., & Ward, P. (2002). Effects of public posting, goal setting, and oral feedback on the skills of female soccer players. *Journal of Applied Behavior Analysis, 35*(3), 247–257.

Checkley, K. (1995). Student-directed learning: Balancing student choice and curriculum goals. *Student Directed Learning, 37*(9), 1–8.

Chidester, T. R., & Grigsby, W. C. (1984). A meta-analysis of the goal setting–performance literature. In J. A. Pearce II & R. B. Robinson, Jr. (Eds.), *Academy of Management Proceedings* (pp. 202–206). Boston, MA: Academy of Management.

Coffield, F., Moseley, D., Hall, E., & Ecclestone, K. (2004). *Learning styles and pedagogy in post-16 learning: A systematic and critical review*. London, UK: Learning and Skills Research Centre.

Cooke, N. L., Heron, T. E., & Heward, W. L. (1983). *Setting up classwide peer tutoring programs in the primary grades*. Columbus, OH: Special Press.

Cossairt, A., Hall, R. V., & Hopkins, B. L. (1973). The effects of experimenter's instructions, feedback, and praise on teacher praise and student attending behavior. *Journal of Applied Behavior Analysis, 6*(1), 89–100.

Delquadri, J., Greenwood, C. R., Stretton, K., & Hall, R. V. (1983). The peer tutoring game: A classroom procedure for increasing opportunity to respond and spelling performance. *Education and Treatment of Children, 6*, 225–239.

Delquadri, J., Greenwood, C. R., Whorton, D., Carta, J. J., & Hall, R. V. (1986). Classwide peer tutoring. *Exceptional Children, 52*(6), 532–542.

Donovan, J. J., & Radosevich, D. J. (1998). The moderating role of goal commitment on the goal difficulty–performance relationship: A meta-analytic review and critical reanalysis. *Journal of Applied Psychology, 83*(2), 308–315.

Fink, W. T., & Carnine, D. W. (1975). Control of arithmetic errors using informational feedback and graphing. *Journal of Applied Behavior Analysis, 8*(4), 461.

Fuchs, L. S., & Fuchs, D. (1986). Effects of systematic formative evaluation: A meta-analysis. *Exceptional Children, 53*(3), 199–208.

Greenwood, C. R. (1997). ClassWide Peer Tutoring. *Behavior and Social Issues, 7*(1), 53–57.

Greenwood, C. R., & Delquadri, J. C. (1995). ClassWide Peer Tutoring and the prevention of school failure. *Preventing School Failure, 39*(4), 21–25.

Greenwood, C. R., Delquadri, J. C., & Hall, R. V. (1984). Opportunity to respond and student academic performance. In W. L. Heward, T. E. Heron, D. S. Hill, & J. Trap-Porter (Eds.), *Focus on behavior analysis in education* (pp. 58–88). Columbus, OH: Charles E. Merrill.

Greenwood, C. R., Delquadri, J. C., & Hall, R. V. (1989). Longitudinal effects of ClassWide Peer Tutoring. *Journal of Educational Psychology, 81*(3), 371–383.

Harris, V. W., Bushell, D., Jr., Sherman, J. A., & Kane, J. F. (1975). Instructions, feedback, praise, bonus payments, and teacher behavior. *Journal of Applied Behavior Analysis, 8*, 462.

Hartley, S. S. (1977). *Meta-analysis of the effects of individually paced instruction in mathematics* (Unpublished doctoral dissertation). University of Colorado, Boulder, CO.

Hattie, J. A. C. (2009). *Visible learning: A synthesis of over 800 meta-analyses relating to achievement*. New York, NY: Routledge.

Hestenes, D., Wells, M., & Swackhamer, G. (1992). Force concept inventory. *Physics Teacher, 30*(3), 141–158.

Heward, W. L., Courson, F. H., & Narayan, J. S. (1989). Using choral responding to increase active student response during group instruction. *Teaching Exceptional Children, 21*(3), 72–75.

Heward, W. L., Gardener, R., Cavanaugh, R. A., Courson, F. H., Grossi, T. A., & Barbetta, P. M. (1996). Everyone participates in this class: Using response cards to increase active student response. *Teaching Exceptional Children, 28*(2), 4–10.

Klein, H. J., Wesson, M. J., Hollenbeck, J. R., & Ange, B. J. (1999). Goal commitment and the goal-setting process: Conceptual clarification and empirical synthesis. *Journal of Applied Psychology, 84*(6), 885–896.

Kluger, A. N., & DeNisi, A. (1996). The effects of feedback interventions on performance: A historical review, a meta-analysis, and a preliminary feedback intervention theory. *Psychological Bulletin, 110*(2), 254.

Kosiewicz, M. M., Hallahan, D. P., Lloyd, J., & Graves, A. W. (1982). Effects of self-instruction and self-correction procedures on handwriting performance. *Learning Disability Quarterly, 5*, 72–75.

Lindsley, O. R. (1992). Precision teaching: Discoveries and effects. *Journal of Applied Behavior Analysis, 25*(1), 51–57.

Locke, E. A., & Latham, G. P. (1990). *A theory of goal setting and task performance*. Englewood Cliffs, NJ: Prentice Hall.

Lovitt, T., Rudsit, J., Jenkins, J., Pious, C., & Benedetti, D. (1985). Two methods of adapting science material for learning disabled and regular seventh graders. *Learning Disabilities Quarterly, 8*(4), 275–285.

Malott, R., & Trojan-Suarez, E. (2004). *Principles of behaviour*. Englewood Cliffs, NJ: Pearson Prentice Hall.

Martin, A. J. (2006). Personal bests (PBs): A proposed multidimensional model and empirical analysis. *British Journal of Educational Psychology, 76*(4), 803–825.

Martin, T. L., Pear, J. J., & Martin, G. L. (2002). Feedback and its effectiveness in a computer-aided personalized system of instruction course. *Journal of Applied Behavior Analysis, 35*(4), 427–430.

Mazur, E. (1997). *Peer instruction: A user's manual*. Upper Saddle River, NJ: Prentice Hall.

Mazur, E. (2009). Farewell, lecture? *Science, 323*(5910), 50–51.

Mento, A. J., Stell, R. P., & Karren, R. J. (1987). A meta-analytic study of the effects of goal setting on task performance: 1966–1984. *Organizational Behavior and Human Decision Processes, 39*(1), 52–83.

Miltenberger, R. (2008). *Behaviour modification*. Belmont, CA: Wadsworth.

Munro, D. W., & Stephenson, J. (2009). The effects of response cards on student and teacher behavior during vocabulary instruction. *Journal of Applied Behavior Analysis, 42*(4), 795–800.

Narayan, J. S., Heward, W. L., Gardner III, R., Courson, F. H., & Omness, C. K. (1990). Using response cards to increase student participation in an elementary classroom. *Journal of Applied Behavior Analysis, 23*(4), 483–490.

Niemiec, R. P., Sikorski, C., & Walberg, H. J. (1996). Learner-control effects: A review of reviews and a meta-analysis. *Journal of Educational Computing Research, 15*(2), 157–174.

Pashler, H., McDaniel, M., Rohrer, D., & Bjork, R. (2008). Learning styles: Concepts and evidence. *Psychological Science in the Public Interest, 9*(3), 105–119.

Patall, E. A., Cooper, H. M., & Robinson, J. C. (2008). The effects of choice on intrinsic motivation and related outcomes: A meta-analysis of research findings. *Psychological Bulletin, 134*(2), 270–300.

Peladeau, N., Forget, J., & Gagne, F. (2003). Effect of paced and unpaced practice on skill application and retention: How much is enough? *American Educational Research Journal, 40*(3), 769–801.

Phillips, G. W. (1983). *Learning the conservation concept: A meta-analysis* (Unpublished doctoral dissertation). University of Kentucky, Lexington, KY.

Rantz, W. G., Dickinson, A. M., Sinclair, G. A., & Van Houten, R. (2009). The effect of feedback on the accuracy of checklist completion during instrument flight training. *Journal of Applied Behavior Analysis, 42*(3), 497–509.

Rantz, W. G., & Van Houten, R. (2011). A feedback intervention to increase digital and paper checklist performance in technically advanced aircraft simulation. *Journal of Applied Behavior Analysis, 44*(1), 145–150.

Reichow, B., & Wolery, M. (2011). Comparison of progressive prompt delay with and without instructive feedback. *Journal of Applied Behavior Analysis, 44*(2), 327–340.

Rohrbeck, C. A., Ginsburg-Block, M. D., Fantuzzo, J. W., & Miller, T. R. (2003). Peer-assisted learning interventions with elementary school studies: A meta-analytic review. *Journal of Educational Psychology, 95*(2), 240–257.

Sadler, R. (1989). Formative assessment and the design of instructional systems. *Instructional Science, 18*(2), 119–144.

Sindelar, P. T., Bursuck, W. D., & Halle, J. W. (1986). The effects of two variations of teacher questioning on student performance. *Education and Treatment of Children, 9*, 56–66.

Smith, M. K., Wood, W. B., Adams, W. K., Wieman, C., Knight, J. K., Guild, N., & Su, T. T. (2009). Why peer discussion improves student performance on in-class concept questions. *Science, 323*(5910), 122–124.

Smith S. L., & Ward, P. (2006). Behavioral interventions to improve performance in collegiate football. *Journal of Applied Behavior Analysis, 39*(3), 385–391.

Socrative, Inc. (2015). *Socrative Student* (Version 2.2.0) [Mobile Application Software]. Retrieved from https://itunes.apple.com

Stallard, C. K. (1982). Computers and education for exceptional children: Emerging applications. *Exceptional Children, 49*(2), 102–104.

Stiggins, R. J. (2002). Assessment crisis: The absence of assessment FOR learning. *Phi Delta Kappan, 83*(10), 758–765.

Trap, J. J., Milner-Davis, P., Joseph, S., & Cooper, J. O. (1978). The effects of feedback and consequences on transitional cursive letter formation. *Journal of Applied Behavior Analysis, 11*(3), 381–393.

Tubbs, M. E. (1986). Goal setting: A meta-analytic examination of the empirical evidence. *Journal of Applied Psychology, 71*(3), 474–483.

Tudor, R. M., & Bostow, D. E. (1991). Computer-programmed instruction: The relation of required interaction to practical application. *Journal of Applied Behavior Analysis, 24*(2), 361–368.

Van Houten, R., Morrison, E., Jarvis, R., & McDonald, M. (1974). The effects of explicit timing and feedback on compositional response rate in elementary school children. *Journal of Applied Behavior Analysis, 7*(4), 547–555.

Van Houten, R., & Thompson, C. (1976). The effects of explicit timing on math performance. *Journal of Applied Behavior Analysis, 9*(2), 227–230.

Walker, D., Greenwood, C., Hart, B., & Carta, J. (1994). Prediction of school outcomes based on early language production and socioeconomic factors. *Child Development, 65*(2), 606–621.

Wiggins, G. (1996). Practicing what we preach in designing authentic assessments. *Educational Leadership, 54*(4), 18–25.

Wiggins, G. (1997). Work standards: Why we need standards for instructional and assessment design. *NASSP Bulletin, 81*(590), 56–64.

Wofford, J. C., Goodwin, V. L., & Premack, S. (1992). Meta-analysis of the antecedents of personal goal level and of the antecedents and consequences of goal commitment. *Journal of Management, 18*(3), 595–615.

Wood, R. E., Mento, A. J., & Locke, E. A. (1987). Task complexity as a moderator of goal effects: A meta-analysis. *Journal of Applied Psychology, 72*(3), 416–425.

Choose Your Level: Using Games and Gamification to Create Personalized Instruction

Karl M. Kapp

Maria, an eighth-grade student, arrives to science class early, walks over to a cabinet, and chooses a tablet computer. She then sits down quietly and begins learning with the tablet. Other students slowly file in and do the same. Maria is learning about velocity as part of a unit introduced by her teacher last week. After Maria's teacher introduced the concept of velocity and how it is calculated, he assigned a learning game to reinforce what he had taught, and that is what Maria and her classmates are engaged in now.

Maria looks over and waves to her friend Juan who has just retrieved his tablet from the cabinet. Today, the first thing Maria does is choose a level. She is feeling smug but not super smart, so she decides to play Level 1 over again before proceeding to the newly unlocked and substantially more difficult Level 2. After quickly playing the first level of the game again and only having to start over once, losing only a couple of points, she proceeds to Level 2 and its terminal learning objective related to the calculation of velocity. Of course, to Maria, it's not a "terminal learning objective"; rather, it's the next level of the ROV Commander game she's been playing for the past few days (Figure 1).

Figure 1. The ROV Commander Screenshot

In the game, she is the "commander" of a remotely operated vehicle (ROV). The ROV looks like a sphere with an antenna on top. Maria's challenge is to maneuver the ROV through an obstacle course without running into anything. Her goals are to find a half dozen "hidden" waypoints and to accurately record information about distance, time, and rate and then make calculations based on the recorded information (see Figure 2). The waypoints aren't really hidden, and if she records information and performs her calculations properly, she can find them quickly. Maria maneuvers the ROV within the confines of the game's landscape and then records data for each waypoint she locates. With the recorded data, the game can "check" to see that Maria is performing the velocity calculations correctly. If she is not, the game provides corrective feedback, and Maria must recalculate the data for the waypoint. If she does hit an obstacle, the ROV loses speed and energy points. These are both undesirable outcomes to Maria, who is striving to be the first student in her class to get to Level 3 and win the game. If she loses speed, she can't get to the next level as quickly; if she sustains too much damage, her ROV will need to start over. Maria has heard that Level 3 is "cool," that the ROV uses boosters to fly. She wants to check that out, but first she will have to do some calculations. Unknown to Maria, but part of why her teacher has chosen ROV Commander as a learning game, is that each level introduces a new concept. This structure provides a scaffolded approach to content enabling Maria and her classmates to progress in both the knowledge and application of formulas for average velocity, final velocity, distance traveled, and acceleration.

Finally, Maria completes her last calculation and finds the last waypoint. She is pleased and lets out a screech. As she reflects on finding this last waypoint, it occurs to her that Juan must have missed it. Otherwise, he wouldn't be stuck driving around the ROV on Level 2, which is where he started today. Maria suspects it might be because he needs to spend some time calculating distances or travel time from one waypoint to another. Maria mentally makes a note to herself to give Juan a hint of where to look for the last waypoint. But that will have to wait, because Maria wants to make it to Level 3 and win the game before Juan does. She is feeling confident that today is the day she'll make it and win the game.

Figure 2. Calculating Speed With Distance and Time

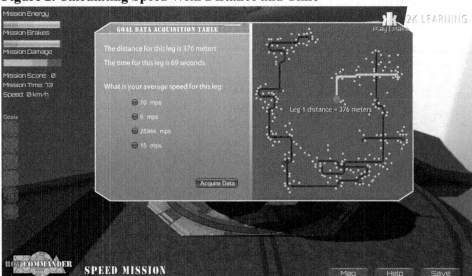

For decades, educators have been forced to choose between providing each student with personalized instruction or covering required state or locally mandated content. In many cases, the need to cover required content trumped the idea of providing personalized learning for each student. Given those requirements and typical class sizes, it has been impossible to personalize curriculum delivery, pacing, and level of difficulty for each student.

As Maria's game-playing experience indicates, game-based learning provides several advantages over traditional teacher-led instruction—that is, lecture-based instruction with uniform content delivered to all the students at the same pace, with little time for student reflection or self-direction. Game-based learning, on the other hand, enables each student to have a personalized learning experience with the same content at his or her own pace. Students can review content if they wish, speed ahead, experiment, and experience the game differently than fellow students and still reach the same learning outcomes. In addition to individualized pacing, games provide for a student to progress in different ways through the game, reviewing levels or content by replaying a level, and making new choices that impact the outcome of the game (Kapp, 2012). Games can instantly provide feedback and help when needed without the student raising his or her hand or interrupting the teacher who is helping another student.

> Game-based learning, on the other hand, enables each student to have a personalized learning experience with the same content at his or her own pace.

Well-designed game-based learning provides levels of personalization that "scaffold each student's learning and foster self-direction to help each individual achieve mastery of knowledge and skills" (Redding, 2014, p. 6) Although a similar experience could be had in many classrooms with nondigital interventions, many constraints preclude the use of those interventions in achieving personalized learning. Aspects of nondigital strategies—such as paper-based programmed instruction and personalized tutoring by the teacher providing carefully scaffolded lessons based on each student's past performance and rate of understanding—conflict with basic instructional limitations, including the available time and materials and maintaining good classroom management.

Digital games, then, offer an ideal tool for delivering what the U.S. Department of Education defines as personalized learning, which is "instruction that is paced to learning needs (i.e., individualized), tailored to learning preferences (i.e., differentiated), and tailored to the specific interests of different learners" (2010, p. 12). Games offer many of the elements of personalization as well as the ability to provide personalized instruction on a scalable level. A teacher can provide all 30 students in her classroom with a tablet, and each can then begin engaging in personalized learning (Guillén-Nieto & Aleson-Carbonell, 2012).

Although all of these features of game-based learning reflect advantages associated with personalized learning, research comparing game-based learning with traditional classroom instruction has not consistently shown one method to be superior to the other. Game-based research for education is "vast but not conclusive" (Schifter, 2013, p. 149).

Game-based research has been centered on comparison-based studies and discussions of which is better, traditional instruction or game-based learning (Kapp, 2013; Liao, 2010; Randel, Morris, Wetzel, & Whitehill, 1992; Sigurdardottir, 2012). There has not been a conclusive answer to this question. In some studies, games have proven more effective than traditional teacher-led instruction, and, in some cases, they have not. The lack of a definite winner between games and traditional instruction has led to confusion about the effective use of games in the classroom among policymakers, administrators, teachers, and parents, who have little practical or actionable advice to guide them. It has even caused some to ask, "Are games effective for teaching at all?" (Clark, 2013).

The answer to that question is a resounding "yes." Evidence strongly supports the conclusion that games are capable of being effective and efficient tools for teaching—students can and do learn from games (Hays, 2005; Ke, 2009; Randel et al., 1992; Schifter, 2013; Sitzmann, 2011; Vogel et al., 2006; Wolfe, 1997; Wouters, van Nimwegen, van Oostendorp, & van der Spek, 2013).

So the question should not be "Are games capable of teaching?" because they are. Instead, stakeholders should be asking several other questions: "What features of games lead to learning and when?" "What classroom conditions support using games?" "How should a game be integrated into the classroom to ensure positive learning outcomes?" To answer these questions, we need to delve into the rich history of game research and not look only at the comparison with other types of instruction but also review the studies which determine what elements were present in the game or classroom condition when the games led to positive learning outcomes. We need to divine what game elements lead to learning and ensure that we leverage those elements when creating, purchasing, and integrating instructional games into the classroom.

New Research Initiatives

Based on the past 40 years of games studies, a large body of research is available to draw evidence-based conclusions about when, why, and how to use games in the classroom (Hays, 2005; Ke, 2009; Randel et al., 1992; Schifter, 2013; Sitzmann, 2011; Vogel et al., 2006; Wolfe, 1997; Wouters et al., 2013). Guidelines can now be offered concerning how to successfully integrate games into K–12 curriculum to provide scalable, personalized learning opportunities for students and to engage them one-on-one with the content at their own pace and with built-in scaffolding. We can now identify the type of game elements that lead to learning. Several such guidelines are presented in this chapter.

Guidelines for Effectively Integrating Games Into the Classroom

A number of meta-analyses of studies of game-based learning have attempted to develop generalizable findings that can be used to select and create educational and instructional games (Hays, 2005; Ke, 2009; Sitzmann, 2011; Vogel et al., 2006; Wolfe, 1997; Wouters et al., 2013). Some of those findings are presented in this chapter as guidelines for using games in the classroom. The guidelines will allow state education agencies (SEAs), local education agencies (LEAs), and individual classroom instructors to make informed decisions about when and how to incorporate game-based learning into the classroom to achieve maximum learning outcomes. Recommendations based on the game-based learning literature follow.

Games should be embedded in instructional programs. The best learning outcomes from using a game in the classroom occur when a three-step embedding process is followed. The teacher should first introduce the game and explain its learning objectives to the students. Then the students play the game. Finally, after the game is played, the teacher and students should debrief one another on what was learned and how the events of the game support the instructional objectives. This process helps ensure that learning occurs from playing the game (Hays, 2005; Sitzmann, 2011).

In Maria's case, before the students began playing ROV Commander, they had several lessons outlining content, objectives, and what they would be encountering within the game. That instruction helped Maria apply new learning to the game condition. After the game was played, Maria's teacher debriefed the students and had them reflect on what they learned about rate, time, and distance—learning which included the formulas used to calculate the values of velocity and acceleration. In fact, the ROV game has a built-in feature in which students describe in a paragraph what they learned. This descriptive exercise provides the students a chance to reflect individually before sharing their reflections with the class.

Ensure game objectives align with curriculum objectives. Ke (2009) found that the learning outcomes achieved through computer games depend largely on how educators align learning (i.e., learning subject areas and learning purposes), learner characteristics, and game-based pedagogy with the design of an instructional game. In other words, if the game objectives match the curriculum objectives, disjunctions are avoided between the game design and curricular goals (Schifter, 2013). The more closely aligned curriculum goals and game goals are, the more likely the learning outcomes of the game will match the desired learning outcomes of the student.

> *Teachers do not have time to vet all games and determine the learning outcomes.*

The obligation to align the outcome of the learning games with learning objectives is ultimately the teacher's responsibility but can be aided by the creators of the games and the game vendors, who need to provide transparent explanations of the instructional goals of the games. The process should also be aided by LEAs and SEAs, who need to screen, validate, and confirm which games are aligned with the recommended or required curriculum and which games are not. Conducting a comparison of game outcomes with educational standards can be one method of helping to ensure alignment of game outcomes with desired curriculum outcomes. Teachers do not have time to vet all games and determine the learning outcomes. This information needs to be readily available from vendors or educational agencies that have undertaken a vetting process. While some vetting sites are available (for examples, see Mahon, 2014), they are not well known or circulated among teachers or administrators.

For example, in the ROV Commander game played by Maria, the vendor of the game specifically aligned the game outcomes with both the Common Core State Standards (CCSS) and Next Generation Science Standards (NGSS) and clearly spelled out what standards are being met through the game play. It may then fall on the shoulders of the teacher or the LEA or SEA to determine how the game may best support curricular outcomes reflecting CCSS and NGSS.

Games need to include instructional support. In games without instructional support such as elaborative feedback, pedagogical agents, and multimodal information presentations (Hays, 2005; Ke, 2009; Wouters et al., 2013), students tend to learn how to play the game rather than learn domain-specific knowledge embedded in the game. Instructional support that helps learners understand how to use the game increases the effectiveness of the game by enabling learners to focus on its content rather than its operational rules.

Embedded instructional support also allows personalization of learning, enabling students to explore in greater detail a game's instructional content by providing content, either remedial or supplementary deeper explanations or related topics, when a student wants to know more. Alternatively, the instructional support can be aimed toward remediation or scaffolding and can be triggered by the game itself if students suddenly encounter difficulty because they do not understand the content or some formal element of the game. Embedded instructional support provides the gamers immediate guidance when their game action triggers it.

In the ROV Commander game played by Maria and Juan, when Juan became stuck and unable to find a waypoint, the game provided hints. Juan, or any student, can choose to accept a hint and read information that will point toward solving the problem. The hint system provides progressively more revealing hints if Juan does not figure out how to solve a problem after the first hint, or Juan can ignore the hints altogether. The "hints" are actually instructional support elements presented as text-based information that explain rate, time, and distance in varying levels of detail.

Games should be highly interactive. Games are more effective for learning when they actively engage students in learning the course material as opposed to passively conveying content, such as presenting videos (Sitzmann, 2011; Wouters et al., 2013). The relationship between a student's "choice and system's response is one way to characterize the depth and quality of interaction" (Salen & Zimmerman, 2004, p. 61). In the ROV Commander module, Maria needs to make choices about what course of action to pursue. Even Maria's choice of whether or not to accept hints allows her to make decisions that directly impact her playing of the game and how the game reacts.

Games do not need to be perceived as being "entertaining" to be educationally effective. Although we may hope that Maria finds the game entertaining, research indicates that a student does not need to perceive a game as entertaining to receive learning benefits. In a meta-analysis of 65 game studies, Sitzmann (2011) found that, although "most simulation game models and review articles propose that the entertainment value of the instruction is a key feature that influences instructional effectiveness, entertainment is not a prerequisite for learning" (p. 515), and entertainment value did not impact learning (see also Garris, Ahlers, & Driskell, 2002; Tennyson & Jorczak, 2008; Wilson et al., 2009). Furthermore, what is entertaining to one student may not be entertaining to another. The fundamental criterion in selecting or creating a game should be the learner's active engagement with the content rather than simply being entertained (Dondling, 2007; Sitzmann, 2011).

Therefore, even if a student is not entertained by a game, high interactivity—an extremely important component of learning—will most likely ensure academic progress (Freeman et al., 2014). Thus, the selection process should emphasize what really counts: meaningful interactivity that promotes learning. However, as with many researched elements in the field of education, interactivity does not ensure learning; it just makes learning more likely to occur.

Provide unlimited access to the game and encourage playing the game multiple times. Sitzmann (2011) found that learners in a game group with unlimited access to the game outperformed a comparison group with limited access. Additionally, Wouters et al. (2013) found that the positive effect of multiple sessions on learning is larger for games than for conventional instruction methods. Learning benefits thus occur when students choose to freely and repeatedly engage in game play (Sitzmann, 2011; Wouters et al., 2013), a repetition that promotes mastery of the skills being taught (Sitzmann, 2011).

Wouters et al. (2013) postulate that one reason for this positive effect of multiple game sessions is the learner's growing familiarity with the game's complex learning environment. One student may want to play a game only twice, and another may want to play every chance he or she can. Such is the nature of games. Providing an electronic game or even a card or board game to students whenever they have some free time—both in and outside of the classroom—gives them an opportunity to play the game multiple times, which has the potential of improving their learning because they will tend to focus more on the features related to learning outcomes rather than the game's mechanics, structure, and rules.

Gamification for Learning

The recent emphasis, discussed previously in this chapter, on determining the most effective elements and features of games for learning has, in part, led to the concept of gamification. The term "gamification" is relatively new. The first documented print appearance of the word was in 2008, and the term did not gain widespread recognition or use until late 2010 (Deterding, Khaled, Nacke, & Dixon, 2011; Groh, 2012; Werbach & Hunter, 2012). The term "gamification" captures the idea that certain elements of games can be infused into instructional situations to provide a positive learning outcome without having to create a full-blown learning game.

Gamification has been defined as the "process of using game thinking and mechanics to engage audiences and solve problems" (Zichermann, 2010), "using game techniques to make activities more engaging and fun" (Kim, 2011), and "the use of game design elements in nongame contexts" (Deterding et al., 2011, p. 1). From an instructional context, the most relevant definition is one that combines elements from these definitions and defines gamification as "using game-based mechanics, aesthetics, and game thinking to engage people, motivate action, promote learning, and solve problems" (Kapp, 2012, p. 10). "Gamification" is a broad term that can be further refined into two types—structural gamification and content gamification.

Structural Gamification

"Structural gamification is the application of game elements to propel a learner through content with no alteration or changes to the content" (Kapp, Blair, & Mesch, 2013, p. 224). The content does not become game-like; only the structure around the content does. A common implementation of this type of gamification adopts the scoring elements of video games, such as points, levels, badges, leaderboards, and achievements and applies them to an educational context (Nicholson, 2012).

Structural gamification's continual, real-time assessment of progress provides important information to both the student and the teacher as students complete portions of content, take quizzes to gauge knowledge acquisition, and move toward the prescribed educational goals. The continual assessment of progress helps identify students' strengths and weaknesses. For example, a teacher employs structural gamification when he or she assigns students content to be learned through a daily quiz-type game for two weeks via email or a mobile app. If the students answer correctly, they earn points and progress toward earning a digital badge. If the students answer incorrectly, they are immediately presented with a short instructional piece specifically addressing the question's topic. Questions are repeated at various intervals until the student demonstrates mastery of the topic. The quiz and instruction process takes 30 to 90 seconds each day, at either the beginning or end of the day based on the choice of the student. As the students progress through the content, the number of questions they have answered correctly is indicated on a leaderboard for the entire class to view, enabling students to assess their progress relative to others, or the score can be grouped by teams to allow team-based learning. Although, as noted below, the focus should not be on comparing oneself to other students but rather on assessing one's own performance.

Content Gamification

"Content gamification is the application of game elements, game mechanics, and game thinking to alter content to make it more game-like" (Kapp et al., 2013, p. 237). A common implementation of this type of gamification adds elements—such as story, mystery, and characters—to content to engage the learner. For example, content gamification could be realized by embedding a series of math problems in a fantasy narrative or by starting a classroom dialogue with a verbal challenge instead of a list of objectives. All of these added attributes positively influence a student's emotional state and generally enhance motivation and facilitate learning and performance (American Psychological Association Work Group of the Board of Educational Affairs, 1997).

New Affordances

The fundamental elements of the two types of gamification, structural or content, are not new to instruction. For example, students commonly earn "points" for spelling words correctly on a spelling test or lose points for not showing all work on a math problem. While not traditionally called "gamification," the exchange of performance for points or an award can certainly be classified as a game-like element. Points are not a "natural" part of learning; they are added to the learning of how to spell a word as a method of motivation and assessment. Points are used to measure learner progress on tests and homework just as points are used to measure progress in games. Points are typically accumulated over a semester, and if the student has enough points, he or she earns a badge in the form of a letter grade. Students move up from one grade level to another grade level. Similarly, challenges, stories, and mysteries are routinely used by many teachers to engage students and provoke their thinking. While teachers and students many not view school as a "game," it turns out that schools appropriate many elements from games in their structure and approach to teaching.

Technology can present students with an immediate response to a question or inquiry and can provide teachers with data useful in diagnosing student progress.

What is new is technology's capability to expand and enhance gamification, especially to personalize and track individual student performance and to provide immediate, actionable feedback. Technology can present students with an immediate response to a question or inquiry and can provide teachers with data useful in diagnosing student progress. Technology also allows multiple attempts at learning without the social stigma of failure because games can be played one-on-one between the learner and the game and because the game can provide hints and eventually answers, providing appropriate scaffolding. So failure is temporary and fleeting. Games can be programmed, personalized, so that students compete against the computer or themselves rather than against fellow students. When designed properly, "gamification can shorten feedback cycles, give learners low-stakes ways to assess their own capabilities….Students, in turn, can learn to see failure as an opportunity, instead of becoming helpless, fearful, or overwhelmed" (Lee & Hammer, 2011, pp. 3–4).

Integrating Gamification Into the Classroom

Based on research into the elements of games, the following recommendations outline effective implementation guidelines for both structural and content gamification.

De-emphasize winning in learning environments. For our purposes, competition is when students are "constrained from impeding each other and instead devote the entirety of their attentions to optimizing their own performance" (Crawford, 2003, p. 8). When learners impede each other or employ defensive strategies that subvert the goal of the opponent, that can be referred to as "conflict." The goal of competition must be clearly set into the process instead of into the results, making it clear that winning or losing is very low in importance compared with learning and improving while competing (Cantador & Conde, 2010).

Create team-based games. Consider breaking students into small teams and consider using cooperative games. In a team-based environment, students believe they are contributing to a larger purpose than just competing for themselves. While not the case with all students, in any team environment some won't participate or take control, which does limit engagement. However, team-based games can minimize students' competing directly against one another; the emphasis becomes one of cooperating to make their team better rather than defeating another individual (Garcia & Tor, 2009). Team-based games also allow for a combination of both personalization and group learning as well as socialization. This combination provides learners with a safe environment in which they can learn at a comfortable pace but still feel as though their learning efforts are contributing to a larger group.

Create a challenge for the student. A challenge is a call to engage in a difficult but achievable task, suggesting uncertain outcomes resulting from one's actions, multiple goals, hidden information, and randomness (Wilson et al., 2009). Challenges have also been shown to be strong motivators in learning (Jones, Valdez, Norakowski, & Rasmussen, 1994; Malone, 1981; Schlechty, 1997). They are correlated with both intrinsic motivation and motivation related to fostering competence and student efficacy (White, 1959). Challenges should be used in gamification to initially engage students to start learning a task. Often students who are reluctant to learn content can be persuaded to begin the process by being challenged through the goals they are to achieve in the gamified context.

Of course, what one student views as an enjoyable challenge another may view as too difficult. Well-designed gamification offers multiple levels of difficulty and points of entry into the content. Such options allow learners with different knowledge levels to access the content and work toward the challenge, to personalize their learning experience from the beginning, and to change how they approach the content as their learning increases.

Make the experience goal oriented as opposed to time or duration oriented. In gamification, there are two types of goal orientation: performance orientation and mastery orientation (Blair, 2012). Each type of goal orientation impacts how achievements awarded to students should be constructed. Students who favor a performance orientation are concerned with other people's assessment of their competence. Students who have a mastery orientation are concerned more with improving their proficiency. Students have a predisposition toward performance orientation, and poor gamification tends to push students in that direction. To balance this predisposition, effective gamification should instill a mastery orientation in the goals and feedback and seek to balance both orientations. Developing students' mastery orientation means that they will more readily accept errors and seek challenging tasks, providing them with the opportunity to develop their competencies (Blair, 2012). Furthermore, when given mastery goals, students will have a higher sense of self-efficacy and use more effective strategies. Students given mastery-oriented goals perform better on complex tasks (Winters & Latham, 1996). In short, mastery orientation promotes students' accomplishing their personalized learning goals. To foster mastery orientation, educators should support students as they require them to earn achievements. Errors and mistakes should be treated as opportunities to provide feedback and encouragement.

Conclusion

Traditional schooling is often perceived as ineffective and boring by students (Dicheva, Dichev, Agre, & Angelova, 2015). The use of educational games and the gamification of instruction are promising approaches because of their abilities to engage students and teach and reinforce knowledge and to personalize instruction for each student.

Demonstrating to the student that he or she is making progress toward the content or skills to be learned is a key element in games and gamification. The act of moving through content on the way to a clear end point—such as mastery of a particular terminal, perhaps personal, objective—motivates students. Games and gamification can be used to personalize instruction so students know where they are in the instructional process, where they are going, and how much further they have to go (Kapp et al., 2013). A successful learner is typically active, goal directed, and self-regulating and assumes personal responsibility for contributing to his or her own learning. Gamification is learner centered in that it can be customized to accommodate student differences, can motivate students to put more effort into learning, and can help students take responsibility for directing and personalizing their own learning.

Action Principles for States, Districts, and Schools

Action Principles for States

a. Align game and gamification products, methods, and content with curriculum content objectives, including the Common Core State Standards and Next Generation Science Standards. Seek partnerships with organizations creating gamified curriculum and not just technology-based tools with no connection to curriculum. Curriculum first; game and gamification second.

b. Remove statutory and regulatory barriers that constrict a district's or school's ability to modify the time–pace–place structure of learning. Games and gamified instruction can be used anywhere at any time.

   c. Provide information to districts and schools on promising gamification implementations in classrooms so they can witness best practices.

   d. In teachers' and leaders' preparation and licensure requirements, include gamified learning concepts and methods.

Action Principles for Districts

   a. Be cautious of programs described as "gamified"; the term is used in various ways, so be sure the program fits your purposes. Examine the gamified intervention to ensure the emphasis is on learning and not simply on winning.

   b. Educate parents and the school board on the educational value of games and gamification. Often parents and school board members react negatively to children "playing games" instead of "serious study," so stakeholders must be educated on the value of games and gamification for learning and personalization of instruction.

   c. Provide professional development for school leaders and teachers to successfully integrate games and gamification into their instruction. Professional development needs to include instruction on software platforms that enable gamification and on the curricular elements of gamification.

   d. Create a catalog of games and gamified curricula that have been shown to enhance learning and make it widely available so schools and teachers do not have to search for effective solutions. One place to start is Mahon's (2014) *Creating a Content Strategy for Mobile Devices in the Classroom.*

Action Principles for Schools

   a. Use the data captured through games and gamified instruction to provide personalized interventions and instruction. Games and gamified systems can provide rich data on learner performance but must be monitored and leveraged properly to provide the desired learning.

   b. De-emphasize winning. Focus on the learning aspects and not on winning; keep the stakes low. Include group, cooperative gamification as much as possible as opposed to one-on-one competitions.

   c. Provide both time and required technology tools for the students to partake in the game or gamified instruction. Ensure that all students can access the game platform and know how to properly use it.

   d. Keep in mind that games and gamification are tools available to teachers but are not a panacea. Games and gamification must be appropriately integrated into the larger curriculum to achieve learner success.

   e. Integrate games and gamification into the curriculum. Do not view games and gamification as extra or something apart from what is being taught. The best results from games are gained when the instructor introduces the students to what they will learn in the game, has them play the game, and then debriefs the students on what they learned playing the game.

References

American Psychological Association Work Group of the Board of Educational Affairs. (1997). *Learner-centered psychological principles: A framework for school reform and redesign.* Washington, DC: American Psychological Association.

Blair, L. (2012). Congratulations! Selecting the right in-game achievements. In K. M. Kapp (Ed.), *The gamification of learning and instruction: Game-based methods and strategies for training and education* (pp. 219–238). New York, NY: Pfeiffer.

Cantador, I., & Conde, J. M. (2010, July). *Effects of competition in education: A case study in an e-learning environment.* Proceedings of the IADIS International Conference e-Learning 2010 (E-Learning 2010), Freiburg, Germany.

Crawford, C. (2003). *Chris Crawford on game design.* Indianapolis, IN: New Riders Publishing.

Clark, R. (2013). Why games don't teach. *Learning Solutions Magazine.* Retrieved from http://www.learningsolutionsmag.com/articles/1106/why-games-dont-teach

Deterding, S., Khaled, R., Nacke, L. E., & Dixon, D. (2011, May). Gamification: Toward a definition. *Proceedings of CHI 2011 Gamification Workshop* (pp. 1–4). Vancouver, BC, Canada.

Dicheva, D., Dichev, C., Agre, G., & Angelova, G. (2015). Gamification in education: A systematic mapping structure. *Journal of Educational Technology & Society, 18*(3), 75–88.

Dondling, M. J. (2007). Educational video game design: A review of the literature. *Journal of Applied Educational Technology, 4*(1), 21–31.

Freeman, S., Eddy, S. L., McDonough, M., Smith, M. K., Okoroafor, N., Jordt, H., & Wenderoth, M. P. (2014). Active learning increases student performance in science, engineering, and mathematics. *Proceedings of the National Academy of Sciences, 111*(23), 8410–8415.

Garcia, S. M., & Tor, A. (2009). The N-effect: More competitors, less competition. *Psychological Science, 20*(7), 871–877.

Garris, R., Ahlers, R., & Driskell, J. E. (2002). Games, motivation, and learning: A research and practice model. *Simulation & Gaming, 33*, 441–467.

Groh, F. (2012). Gamification: State of the art definition and utilization. In N. Asaj, B. Konings, M. Poguntke, F. Schaub, B. Wiedersheim, & M. Weber (Eds.), *Proceedings of the 4th Seminar on Research Trends in Media Informatics, Institute of Media Informatics* (pp. 39–46). Ulm, Germany.

Guillén-Nieto, V., & Aleson-Carbonell, M. (2012). Serious games and learning effectiveness: The case of *It's a Deal! Computers & Higher Education, 58*(1) 435–448.

Hays, R. T. (2005). *The effectiveness of instructional games: A literature review and discussion.* (No 2005-004). Patuxent River, MD: Naval Air Warfare Center Training Systems Division.

Jones, B., Valdez, G., Norakowski, J., & Rasmussen, C. (1994). *Designing learning and technology for educational reform.* North Central Regional Educational Laboratory.

Kapp, K. M. (2012). *The gamification of learning and instruction: Case-based methods and strategies for training and education.* New York, NY: Pfeiffer.

Kapp, K. M. (2013). Once again, games can and do teach! *Learning Solutions Magazine.* Retrieved from http://www.learningsolutionsmag.com/articles/1113/once-again-games-can-and-do-teach

Kapp, K. M., Blair, L., & Mesch, R. (2013). *The gamification of learning and instruction fieldbook: Theory into practice.* New York, NY: John Wiley & Sons.

Ke, F. (2009). A qualitative meta-analysis of computer games as learning tools. In R. E. Ferdig (Ed.), *Effective electronic gaming in education* (Vol. 1, pp. 1–32). Hershey, PA: Information Science Reference.

Kim, A. J. (2011, March 23). *Smart gamification: Designing the player journey* [Video file]. Retrieved from http://youtu.be/B0H3ASbnZmc

Lee, J. J., & Hammer, J. (2011). Gamification in education: What, how, why bother? *Academic Exchange Quarterly, 15*(2), 1.

Liao, Y. K. (2010). Game-based learning vs. traditional instruction: A meta-analysis of thirty-eight studies from Taiwan. In D. Gibson & B. Dodge (Eds.), *Proceedings of Society for Information Technology & Teacher Education International Conference 2010* (pp. 1491–1498). Chesapeake, VA: Association for the Advancement of Computing in Education. Retrieved from http://www.editlib.org/p/33570

Mahon, K. (2014). *Creating a content strategy for mobile devices in the classroom*. Philadelphia, PA: Center on Innovations, Temple University.
Retrieved from http://www.centeril.org/publications/MobileAppsInTheClassroom.pdf

Malone, T. (1981). Toward a theory of intrinsically motivating instruction. *Cognitive Science, 4*, 333–369.

Nicholson, S. (2012, June). *A user-centered theoretical framework for meaningful gamification*. Paper presented at Games+Learning+Society 8.0, Madison, WI.

Randel, J. M., Morris, B. A., Wetzel, C. D., & Whitehill, B. V. (1992). The effectiveness of games for educational purposes: A review of recent research. *Simulation and Gaming, 23*(3), 261–276.

Redding, S. (2014). *Personal competencies in personalized learning*. Philadelphia, PA: Center on Innovations in Learning, Temple University; Charlotte, NC: Information Age Publishing.
Retrieved from http://www.centeril.org/publications/Personalized_Learning.pdf

Salen, K., & Zimmerman, E. (2004). *Rules of play: Game design fundamentals*. Cambridge, MA: The MIT Press.

Schifter, C. C. (2013). Games in learning, design, and motivation. In M. Murphy, S. Redding, & J. Twyman (Eds.), *Handbook on innovations in learning* (pp. 149–164). Philadelphia, PA: Center on Innovations in Learning, Temple University & Charlotte, NC: Information Age Publishing.
Retrieved from http://www.centeril.org/

Schlechty, P. C. (1997). *Inventing better schools: An action plan for educational reform*. San Francisco, CA: Jossey-Bass.

Sigurdardottir, H. H. (2012). *Debating matters in digital game-based learning*. Proceedings of the European Conference On Games-Based Learning (pp. 471–477). Cork, Ireland.

Sitzmann, T. (2011). A meta-analytic examination of the instructional effectiveness of computer-based simulation games. *Personnel Psychology, 64*(2), 489–528.

Tennyson, R. D., & Jorczak, R. L. (2008). A conceptual framework for the empirical study of instructional games. In H. F. O'Neil & R. S. Perez (Eds.), *Computer games and team and individual learning* (pp. 39–54). Oxford, UK: Elsevier.

U.S. Department of Education. (2010). *Transforming American education: Learning powered by technology*. Washington, DC: Author.
Retrieved from http://files.eric.ed.gov/fulltext/ED512681.pdf

Vogel, J. J., Vogel, D. S., Cannon-Bowers, J., Bowers, C. A., Muse, K., & Wright, M. (2006). Computer gaming and interactive simulations for learning: A meta-analysis. *Journal of Educational Computing Research, 34*(3), 229–243.

Werbach, K., & Hunter, D. (2012). *For the win: How game thinking can revolutionize your business*. Philadelphia, PA: Wharton Digital Press.

White, R. W. (1959). Motivation reconsidered: The concept of competence. *Psychological Review, 66*(5), 297–333.

Wilson, K. A., Bedwell, W. L., Lazzara, E. H., Salas, E., Burke, C. S., Estock, J., . . . Conkey, C. (2009). Relationships between game attributes and learning outcomes: Review and research proposals. *Simulation & Gaming, 40*(2), 217–266.

Winters, D., & Latham, G. P. (1996). The effect of learning versus outcome goals on a simple versus a complex task. *Group & Organization Management, 21*(2), 213–238.

Wolfe, J. (1997). The effectiveness of business games in strategic management course work. *Simulation & Gaming, 28*(4), 360–376.

Wouters, P., van Nimwegen, C., van Oostendorp, H., & van der Spek, E. D. (2013). A meta-analysis of the cognitive and motivational effects of serious games. *Journal of Educational Psychology, 105*(2), 249–265.

Zichermann, G. (2010, October 26). *Fun is the future: Mastering gamification* [Video file].
Retrieved from http://www.youtube.com/watch?v=6O1gNVeaE4g

Inspect the
expected so that
it becomes the
accepted & respected
practice

Personalizing Learning Through Precision Measurement

Janet S. Twyman

> *Personalized learning may be the most important thing we can do*
> *to reimagine education in this country.*

Richard Culatta

U.S. Dept. of Education Office of Educational Technology (2013)

Promising to "meet each child where she is and help her achieve her potential" (Wolf, 2010, p. 6), personalized learning has become extremely popular in K–12 education (Cavanagh, 2014). The U.S. Department of Education emphasizes personalized learning as fundamental for student-centered, future-ready, 21st-century learning (U.S. Department of Education, 2010). State and local departments of education in Tennessee, Wisconsin, South Carolina, Michigan, Oregon, Texas, and others have created offices of personalized learning or launched personalized learning initiatives (Ventura, 2014). Several major foundations and national organizations are funding personalized learning programs, supporting personalized learning networks, or creating a myriad of resources and software programs. Personalized learning also seems to have some empirical support. A recent RAND study examining the use of personalized learning strategies across 11,000 students indicates promising results: While levels of implementation varied, in general, reading and math scores for students in schools using personalized learning strategies were substantially higher relative to national averages (Pane, Steiner, Baird, & Hamilton, 2015).

The mission underlying personalized learning and efforts to carry it out have a long history in public schools (Ventura, 2014). District-level policy suggesting educators adjust what, when, and how a student learns can be traced back to the late 1800s when Pueblo, Colorado's superintendent introduced a plan to enable students to move at their own pace. Not long after, in 1912, the San Francisco Normal School began promoting students based on demonstrations of mastery in a given subject. In *Democracy and Education*, John Dewey (1916) advocated placing the child (not the curriculum) at the center of schooling, which influenced the Dalton Plan and its encouragement of each

Handbook on Personalized Learning for States, Districts, and Schools, pages 145–164
Copyright © 2016 by Information Age Publishing
All rights of reproduction in any form reserved.

student to program his or her curriculum in order to meet his or her needs, interests, and abilities (Dewey, 1922). Within higher education, Fred Keller (1968) introduced the Personal System of Instruction (PSI) and its emphasis on student-paced mastery of content, digestible units of instruction, small-group tutoring, and formative assessments, garnering considerable credibility from empirical research (see Fox, 2004). National support for individualization and personalization for students with special needs appeared in 1990, with the Individuals with Disabilities Education Act (IDEA) and the requirement that an Individual Education Plan (IEP) consider each student's unique learning needs to determine learning goals and support needed. The 2010 National Education Technology Plan called for:

> engaging and empowering *personalized learning* [emphasis added] experiences for learners of all ages. The model stipulates that we focus what and how we teach to match what people need to know and how they learn. It calls for using state-of-the-art technology and Universal Design for Learning (UDL) concepts to enable, motivate, and inspire all students to achieve, regardless of background, languages, or disabilities. It calls for ensuring that our professional educators are well connected to the content and resources, data and information, and peers and experts they need to be highly effective. And it calls for leveraging the power of technology to support continuous and lifelong learning. (A. Duncan, in U.S. Department of Education, 2010, p. v)

Yet exactly what is personalized learning? Various organizations have similar, yet unique, definitions. The International Association for K–12 Online Learning (INACOL) states that personalized learning "is tailoring learning for each student's strengths, needs and interests—including enabling student voice and choice in what, how, when, and where they learn—to provide flexibility and supports to ensure mastery of the highest standards possible" (Patrick, Kennedy, & Powell, 2013, p. 4). The

> *Yet exactly what is personalized learning? Various organizations have similar, yet unique, definitions.*

Glossary of Educational Reform (2015) refers to personalized learning as "a diverse variety of educational programs, learning experiences, instructional approaches, and academic-support strategies that are intended to address the distinct learning needs, interests, aspirations, or cultural backgrounds of individual students" (para. 1). Next Generation Learning Challenges (n.d.) characterizes personalized learning as "an education model where students are truly at the center, learning is tailored to individual students' strengths, needs, and personal interests. Learning opportunities take into account existing knowledge, skills, and abilities, set high expectations, and push students in supportive ways to reach their personal goals" (para. 1). Wikipedia (n.d.) tells us that personalized learning is the tailoring of pedagogy, curriculum, and learning environments by learners or for learners in order to meet their different learning needs and aspirations with technology—used to facilitate personalized learning environments.

While these definitions all seem to refer to desirable goals in education, what does personalized learning really mean for the classroom? What do the different descriptions and terms entail? If we deconstruct Wikipedia's definition: *Pedagogy* is the method and practice of teaching and involves how the teacher delivers instruction, manages classrooms, motivates students, encourages learning-to-learn skills, and the like. *Curriculum* refers to the specific lessons and content to be taught. *Learning environments* are "the diverse physical locations, contexts, and cultures in which students learn" (Glossary of Educational Reform, 2013a, para. 1). A *learning need* is defined as an identified gap between the required or desired knowledge or capability and the actual knowledge or capability of the learner (Glossary of Educational Reform, 2013b), which is made more complex by differing types of context-driven learning needs. Finally, Merriam-Webster (n.d.) defines *aspirations* as "a strong desire to achieve something high or great" (para. 3).

Each of these components is highly complex on its own, requiring expertise, resources, and support to understand and implement. How does a teacher gain such pedagogical expertise? What is an effective curriculum, how do we know, and when and how do we use it? How can supportive learning environments be created and maintained? How does one determine learning needs, especially when needs may be of different types and context driven? And of course, aspirations can be very hard to discern; often one is not fully aware of one's own desires, let alone those of others. Creating a milieu that accomplishes all these things would be challenging for a teacher of a single student, exponentially more so for a class, a school, or an entire system. So how do we personalize learning, for each individual student, across subject matter and grade level, for all students? This chapter proposes that **precision measurement aided by technology and integrated with a strong relationship between the student and a caring teacher is instrumental in achieving the goals of personalized learning**.

Let us consider one more perspective on personalized learning. As defined by the Center on Innovations in Learning, personalized learning involves

> the use of multiple instructional modes to scaffold each student's learning and enhance the student's motivation to learn and metacognitive, social, and emotional competencies to foster self-direction and achieve mastery of knowledge and skills. Personalization ensues from the relationships among teachers and learners and the teacher's orchestration, often in co-design with students, of multiple means for enhancing every aspect of each student's learning and development (see Murphy, p. iii, in this volume).

It is the centralizing of the relationship between teacher and student and the deep understanding of instruction, in what and how to teach and learn, that ultimately personalizes instruction. Refining the popular personalized learning phrase "variation in time, pace, and place," this chapter proposes that, with the competent guidance of a caring teacher armed with astute technology, *true personalized learning varies the time, place, path, pace, practice, and trace of learning for each and every student* (Twyman, 2015). After briefly describing time, place, path, pace, practice, and trace, this chapter's primary focus will be on how precision measurement makes truly personalized learning possible.

Time. *Time,* or "seat time," refers to the amount of time students are required to be in a course or grade and historically has been tied to funding and student progression. Traditionally, time has been held constant (i.e., quarters, semesters, grade-level year) while individual student outcomes during that time varied widely. Personalized learning, especially in a competency-based form (see Twyman, 2014a), does away with time-based requirements in favor of individual student advancement upon mastery. It also supports the notion of "anywhere, anytime" learning, which occurs outside the traditional classroom at any time of the day.

Pace. *Pace* is the rate at which something progresses; in education it is the speed at which progress is made through a particular curriculum or instructional program, such as the number of days a student takes to master one unit on the Civil War. Instructional pacing is the speed at which a teacher presents a lesson, with most scholars advocating a brisk pace to enhance student attention, increase responding, and decrease off-task behavior (Lignugaris-Kraft & Rousseau, 1982). Historically, educational progression has been lock-stepped, with an entire class moving through a unit in the same amount of time, often dictated by the organization of the textbook or some other structural concern. Within personalized learning, pace is determined by individual progression and is not a reflection of ability (i.e., fast = smart; slow = less smart) but rather a dimension of how a particular student may cover particular material at a particular time.

Path. *Path* refers to the route a student takes to move towards his or her learning objectives. A learning pathway indicates the specific course of study and experiences a student has on the way toward his or her specific goal, such as graduation. In a personalized learning system, schools offer many pathways, including different courses, programs, and learning opportunities in and out of school so that each student may create his or her own goal path (Glossary of Educational Reform, 2013c). Learning pathways incorporate diverse educational options both outside of typical school settings (e.g., work-study, community service, internships, apprenticeships, online instruction, or even travel), as well as from more traditional learning experiences, all under the assumption that relevant learning accomplishments are to be recognized and valued equally wherever students achieve them. Personalized learning adds further refinement to learning pathways, moving from choices that are offered by the school to opportunities that are created by the student, supporting greater flexibility and customized learning experiences based on specific interests or needs (Glossary of Educational Reform, 2013c) and supporting student ownership of learning (Secondary School Consortium, n.d.).

> In personalized learning, teachers vary their practice based on the needs, interests, performance, and goals of each of their students...

Place. No longer is schooling required to happen inside the classroom. The *place* of learning can vary widely, including within or outside the bricks-and-mortar school building, students' homes, the community, places of business, and so on. As part of "anywhere, anytime" learning, the advent of digital technologies makes anyplace learning truly possible.

Practice. *Practice* refers to what the educators do to facilitate learning—in other words, the actual application or execution of teaching. On a larger scale it may also refer to the implementation of policies at the school, district, or state level and the tools and systems to support them (such as schoolwide data systems or a state waiver of the Carnegie unit). For better or worse, K–12 education proffers a myriad of educational interventions—practices to be implemented by educators—but offers little specific guidance on what practices to use, when, with whom, under what conditions. The growing field of educational data mining and predictive analytics (see Baker, 2013; Baker & Yacef, 2009) may soon change that; however, educators should always avail themselves of an array of evidence-based strategies and tactics (teaching practices) to have at the ready for use with each of their unique and diverse students. In personalized learning, teachers vary their practice based on the needs, interests, performance, and goals of each of their students, making the interactions between teacher and student one of the ultimate ways to personalize learning. The practice of personalizing learning can be complex, with the responsibility both on the teacher and on the student. Initially the student may help inform which best teaching practices might be needed based on his or her current level, goals, and interests. Once implementation of that practice has begun (the act of teaching), the student provides information on the effects of that practice based on his or her learning gains and motivation.

Trace. The effects of practice lead us to *trace*, or what remains as and after teaching occurs. How do we know when a student has learned something or, perhaps more importantly, if a student is learning? Trace is the objective, notable change that comes from teaching and learning and requires some form of detection (i.e., perceivability, recognition). Detection may be in the form of direct or indirect observation, formative assessment (see Andrade & Cizek, 2010), alternative assessments (see Herman, 1992), or in the multitude of ways learning can be validated in competency-based education (see McClarty & Gaertner, 2015). Trace may be uniformly measured (as in standardized assessments); however, its measures are probably best determined by individual context. It should be observed frequently and in real time (as found in formative assessments). Trace may be represented as a permanent product (as found in student portfolios or project-based learning), recorded automatically (as found in some computer-based instruction), represented by other means (such as grades or badges), and detected by either the teacher or student (preferably both) using some form of measurement. In other words, trace is not one thing, but represents the numerous empirical, actionable methods to indicate a learner's current status and progression, in context.

Measurement in Education

Trace relies heavily on measurement. In education, few terms evoke more emotion and opinion than measurement. Critics equate it with rather unpopular items like accountability, standardized testing, or narrowing the curriculum (i.e., teaching to test, blind memorization, or rote learning) and tie it to policies often perceived as punitive, such as adequate yearly progress, value-added tea or student tracking (see Popham, 2000). Measurement has been accused o getting at what really matters in education. Howe measurement is essential to any earnest teaching truly or well personalize instruction for any stude well and for the right reasons, measurement is on teachers can do.

Known instances of formal assessment (a form America's public education system in 1642 with School Law requiring children to know the princ the commonwealth. Given the overall purpose o surement is inevitable (Ross, 1941). Edward Th psychology, recommended collecting qualitative practical educational problems (Beatty, 1998). 1 towards greater accountability for student learn dence" within schools (Shavelson, 2007). In a c student performance (i.e., graduation rates), sch directly, with both specificity (at the level of standards or learning objectives) and broadness (across curriculum domains and subject matter). Measurement now focuses on "the common aims of (a) arriving at defensible conclusions regarding students' standing with respect to educational outcomes deemed important, (b) documenting student achievement, (c) gauging student progress, and (d) improving teaching and learning" (Agger & Cizek, 2013, para. 1). It is in the last two categories that personalization comes into play. While evidence of student learning is important, even more so is knowing what that evidence means and how to act on it. These are the core questions regarding a student's educational experience and the personalization of learning.

It may be useful to consider the difference between measurement, evaluation, assessment, and evidence, as understanding the differences is most beneficial and may be instrumental in teaching effectively (Kizlik, 2015). Most commonly, measurement involves the process by which the attributes or dimensions of something are determined, usually using some standard instrument or scale. Measurement involves collecting information using some sort of standard metric and implies some level of knowledge in how to use the scale and understand the results (an example provided by Kizlik, 2015, involves a person with no knowledge of Ohm meters applying one to an electrical circuit and unable to understand the results). Measurement provides us with evidence, which is a clear, objective indication often used to inform (or support) a conclusion. Relevant to education, Slavin (2015) asks quite succinctly: "How can we use evidence to make sure that students get the best possible outcomes from their education?" (para. 9).

Considering evidence from what has been measured moves us into the realm of assessment, or the systematic collection, analysis, and interpretation of information relevant to a particular outcome (Suskie, 2004). Various types of assessments are specifically designed to yield information relative to the question being asked (e.g., standardized assessments are administered and scored in a predetermined, standard manner, often to answer larger scale comparative questions; summative assessments are used to evaluate student learning at the end of an instructional unit or period of time and answer post hoc effectiveness questions; formative assessments are used while the learning activities are in progress and answer questions about current teaching effectiveness; see Layng, Stikeleather, & Twyman, 2006). It is when we assign some value to assessment that we arrive at evaluation or the process of making judgments based on assessment and evidence (Levine, 2005).

For example, let's consider a third-grade spelling lesson of 10 words, taught in the more traditional manner of repeated writings of the words, writing sentences containing the words, and an end-of-the-week quiz. Let's also consider the same 10 words taught using interactive digital media where the students solve games using the words, use them in an animated story, and test out on each word individually when ready. We **measure** the number of words spelled correctly by students across both conditions. This is **evidence** gleaned from the two conditions. When we look at the number correct compared to our goal of 10 words, we are making an **assessment**. When we compare those results, either to what students knew previously or between the two conditions, and make a statement about which is better, we are **evaluating** the evidence. Thus, measurement, in and of itself, does not involve judgment of the results. Additionally, although assessments are used to evaluate educational progression and inform decision making, their administration often involves contrived circumstances, necessitating inference about the results in relation to what a learner actually knows (Kizlik, 2015). Understandably, this injects skepticism into the picture. In a survey of five teaching cohorts, Miller (1998, cited in Mehrens, 1998) found that only 11.3% to 54.7% of public school teachers believed the state-mandated standardized assessments have had a positive effect on student learning, with even fewer, 13.1% to 28.7%, viewing the results as an accurate reflection of student performance.

Assessment results are often morphed into some form of statistics or average to inform our understanding of student ability. In determining what works best for which students, when, and where, the use of statistical averages poses an often-unrecognized yet persistent problem: There is no such thing as the average learner. Averages tell us nothing about an individual child, nor do they give us any indication of what worked or didn't work for that, or any, individual. As noted by Rose (2016) in *The End of Average*, it is not possible to draw any meaningful conclusions about a particular human being when using statistical averages, yet schools are designed to evaluate and recognize learning based on comparisons to the average learner, a mythical notion of a one-size-fits-most model that ignores individuality. Rose (2016) provides a useful example:

> In determining what works best for which students, when, and where, the use of statistical averages poses an often-unrecognized yet persistent problem: There is no such thing as the average learner.

In the 1950's the U.S. Air Force was investigating why pilots were struggling to control their planes. They determined it had nothing to do with training or pilot error, but instead the way the cockpits had been designed since the 1920s—to fit the 'average' pilot. In the 1920s, when military aviation was under the command of the U.S. Army Air Service, over 4,000 pilots were measured across 10 dimensions, assuming most would be within the average for most dimensions and expecting many would fit all 10. In actuality, none of the pilots fit the average size profile. Designing cockpits for the average man resulted in jets designed for no one. This discovery brought the Air Force to an adaptable design, leading to the invention of the adjustable seat (an innovation that is now commonplace). Likewise, in our efforts to support personalized learning, we must change our emphasis from the average learner and standardized assessment to that of individual learners and precision measurement.

Precision Measurement

What is meant by precision measurement? Precision yields consistent results when repeated and represents a high level of correspondence between the measured value and the "true value" based on the reproducibility of results. When "precise," one is exact, accurate, and careful about the details, and it conveys a sense of quality. We need that level of exactness, detail, and quality when caring and doing something about the learning of our students. Precision measurement done in real time, as teaching and learning are occurring, can empower both teachers and students by moving away from the rather inefficient (with regard to effecting learning) practices of statistical averages of learning, post hoc testing, and instructional decision making after the teaching is done. Precision measurement is the rational outcome of the combination of recent guidelines, such as evidence-based practice and data-based decision making; of known strategies, such as formative assessment and curriculum-based measurement; of lesser known areas, such as precision teaching and behavioral education; and of new possibilities that arise from educational data mining and learning analytics.

If, as suggested, precision measurement—aided by technology and supported by a strong relationship between the student and teacher—is instrumental in achieving the goals of personalized learning, then it is important to know exactly what precision measurement is. This chapter posits **precision measurement as the real-time, in situ collection of relevant evidence regarding the current state and progression of a student's knowledge, abilities, and attitudes—evidence to be used in making meaningful, moment-to-moment, individualized decisions about what and how to teach and learn.** It is based on these premises:

  a. The **learner** knows best;

  b. **Teacher** relationships with students are critical;

  c. **Measurement** imparts understanding; and

  d. The best **technology** is indentured to the service of decision making.

Consider this example: "Juan" was in a middle school science class learning about states of matter and applying various forces to demonstrate how molecules change matter into different states (solid, liquid, gas). Juan was interested in chemistry and liked working in the lab. Out of a variety of resources curated by his teacher and class, Juan chose to do a web-based interactive simulation,[1] adding and removing heat to watch different types of molecules form a solid, liquid, or gas and monitoring the relationship of the temperature and volume of a container to its internal pressure in real time. His goal was to relate the interaction potential to the forces between molecules. The program provided detailed information on the variables at work; peppered Juan with just-in-time "big picture" and specific questions about what he was learning; provided him with timely, real-world feedback on his experimentation; and kept a log of all his efforts, including what he tried and what did and didn't work, the types of errors he made, how quickly he worked through things, his chosen sequence of tasks, and so on. Juan had access to a steady flow of information about his learning, which he used to revisit some experiments. He and his teacher reviewed the log often, and considered its reflection of his metacognitive skills and how it fit in with his other learning. Juan soon saw that he didn't always attempt all experimental variations and that he was struggling relating a pressure–temperature diagram to the behavior of molecules. He wanted help interpreting the graphs of interatomic potential. His teacher, knowing of Juan's shyness, suggested a project with a classmate who was also interested in chemistry. They jointly created a video using materials available in the school and community that demonstrated how forces on atoms relate to interaction potential and embedded questions and answers about the graphs from their experiments to show their understanding. Juan realized that he wanted to do more field-based work in chemistry and science. We'll return to this example as we consider the premises of precision measurement.

The Learner Knows Best

All too often, students are relegated to a passive role in their own learning, plied with information that will be "on the test" (DeWitt, 2014). Two key tenets of personalized learning involve giving students "voice and choice" in their learning (Ripp, 2015), thus increasing their decision making and personal responsibility within the instructional process. "Voice" acknowledges a student's interests, values, opinions, perspectives, or ambitions; "choice" often refers to curriculum methods, time and place of learning, and

---

[1]This lesson is adapted from http://phet.colorado.edu/en/simulation/states-of-matter (log in required).

even what to learn. While each of these are important to personalized learning, a perspective incorporating precision measurement would arm students with the knowledge and tools to speak coherently about their learning and make informed choices.

In our example with Juan, he "knew best" with regard to his personal interests and aspirations and expressed his preference about what to learn and how to learn that new information and even how to demonstrate that knowledge. He was supported by precision measurement, not only by the data provided within his web-based experiments, but also by the data showing which concepts he knew well and where he needed further understanding. He used those data to choose which concepts to review or when to conduct additional experiments and saw his understanding improve immediately and over time.

Precision measurement is a vehicle for students to use their own data to make decisions, determine what they should do next, and challenge themselves to do better. Feedback on progression towards a chosen goal is highly motivating to students (Hanover Research, 2012). Students who track their own progress forward are more likely to make greater gains toward reaching their goals than students who do not, as indicated by a 32% gain in achievement found in a recent meta-analysis of research by Marzano (2010). Research indicates that individuals are motivated by success and competence, thus precision measurement and continuous assessment can enhance motivation in these ways:

- Emphasizes progress and achievement rather than failure;
- Provides feedback to move learning forward;
- Reinforces the idea that students have control over, and responsibility for, their own learning;
- Builds confidence in students so they can and need to take risks;
- Maintains relevance and appeal to students' imaginations; and
- Provides the scaffolding students need to excel (Hanover Research, 2012, p. 13).

Many believe a measurement and technology approach to personalization involves gathering data on what the student knows and can do, using algorithms to validate the information and set goals for learning, and determining a unique set of learning experiences from those analyses (Wiley, 2015), all of which result in an individualized, yet prescribed, learning path for the student. While likely effective, such systems run the risk of diminishing the rich opportunity to learn for oneself what to do next, perhaps even eliminating the learner's active role in this "personalized" method. A better model continues to involve data on what the student knows, yet also presents a comprehensible view of that information and requires students to consider and make decisions for themselves. Because precision measurement highlights ongoing performance relative to identified goals and other variables, it becomes the basis on which the student and teacher may decide what to do next—a critical form of voice and choice that is linked to higher order self-management skills (Lindsley, 1990). It has been shown that when students have access to their data, they play a larger role in choosing their own learning paths (Darling-Hammond, 2010).

Student voice and choice has roots in the concept that "the learner knows best" (Lindsley, 1972), with a difference in that "knowing best" is connected to data and analysis and not a general sense of "voice and choice." The data indicate what is working and what is not. If a student is progressing well as demonstrated by the charted data and other observed and measured variables, then the program is appropriate for the student;

conversely, if there is little or no progress or other observed variables are less than ideal (e.g., affect, attendance, alternative behaviors), then the instructional program or other variables must be changed (Binder & Watkins, 1990). The learning experience must "work" for the student. However, it takes a thoughtful and informed analysis of this information to improve the experience, best done by the teacher and student in concert. It is the role of the teacher to which we will turn next.

The Teacher–Student Relationship

Teacher relationships with students are critical. While evidence-based practice is based upon research on effectiveness, it becomes actionable and powerful when integrated with teacher expertise and a thorough understanding of a student. This understanding comes not only from multiple sources of information, but also is built upon a history of interaction, caring, interest, and support (Redding, 2013).

Precision measurement supports this relationship. In our example with Juan, his teacher could have simply identified the standard to learn and the myriad of "educational" resources available in school or online and left it to Juan to determine exactly what and how he was to learn. Instead, his teacher served as a guide through not only his study of states of matter, but in how to focus on his strengths and interests, what resources were available for concept learning and practice, which student might serve as a good partner for the project, and how to interpret and respond to data about his own learning. In this world of fingertip-ready information, learners need an advisor to help them learn to understand and organize information, comprehend complexity, write coherently, solve problems, work well on their own and with others, contextualize their own thoughts, reason productively, manage their own behavior, maintain positive motivation, and even persist in the face of difficulties (Slavin, 2016).

While noting the importance of warm and caring relationships, White (1986) further contends that "in order to be responsive to the pupil's needs the teacher must be a student of the pupil's behavior, carefully analyzing how that behavior changes from day to day and adjusting the instructional plan as necessary to facilitate continued learning" (p. 1). Precision measurement enhances this aspect of the teacher's role and perhaps changes it from that of an encyclopedia of transferable knowledge and deliverer of evidence-based procedures to that of an aware, motivating, and engaging learning guide who uses objective, in-the-moment information to ensure students become eager, competent, and self-reliant learners (see also Slavin, 2016). Before we can transform classrooms into places where students determine their own learning paths and take responsibility for their progress, teachers must understand how to plan, lead, and manage personalized learning (Grant & Basye, 2014), including knowing "academic strengths and weakness as part of a complete learner profile that gives a holistic view of each student" within an assessment process that is "embedded within each lesson and used as a tool for immediate and consistent feedback" (Mead, 2015, para. 2).

These practices are related to data-based decision making; personalization relies heavily on teacher ability to conduct formative assessments and ongoing progress checks so that they may adapt instruction to student needs (Hamilton et al., 2009). However "as data systems become more readily available to teachers, the ability to pose questions that generate useful data will become increasingly important" (Means, Chen, DeBarger, & Padilla, 2011, pp. 13–14). It is in this vein that precision measurement enhances and extends the critical practice of formative assessment and using data to personalize instruction to using empirical information to better understand and serve the "whole learner," not just the instructional problem at hand. Teachers (and learners) who pose questions that generate useful data will not simply be asking how many answers are correct, but deep, humanizing questions that support individual learning and growing. Those types of precision measurement questions will be described next.

Measurement Imparts Understanding

The premise is simple: The more a teacher knows about a student, the better he or she is able to personalize instruction and help that student. The more current and relevant that information is, the better the help is likely to be. In our example with Juan, precision measurement facilitated his teacher's (as well as his own) specific awareness and deeper understanding of his needs. This instantiation of measurement is not about compliance or punitive accountability, but is about using empirical evidence to better understand a student. We do this

> *Effective collection of, analysis of, and responsiveness to student data is central to the development of personalized learning environments at all grade levels.*
> *(Hanover Research, 2012)*

by measuring what matters. As noted by Shavelson (2007), cultures of evidence "will not automatically lead to educational improvement, if what counts as evidence does not count as education" (p. 1). We need to tie our measures to improved outcomes for all learners. It is widely acknowledged that technology enables personalized learning, involving sophisticated measurement systems that dynamically track, analyze, translate, and illustrate data to not only inform the student and teacher but also to help determine the instruction, tools, content, and other learning variables best suited for each student—all working together seamlessly (Hanover Research, 2012).

In practically all aspects of life, data support our decisions and increasingly help us personalize our experiences (e.g., when music streaming services suggest particular songs based on listening history or when shopping sites make purchase recommendations based on data from purchases, browsing, and other sources). The same is becoming true for education. The forms of precision measurement may be different depending on context (e.g., who and what is being taught, where learning is occurring, what technology resources are available), yet each form shares these common features:

- supports decision making and choice
- informs knowledge and understanding of the student or situation
- is used to understand and alter teaching practices or other variables
- aids a "bigger picture" perspective
- provides immediate, actionable information to teachers and students
- occurs frequently (continuous or ongoing)
- may be embedded or additive
- is empirical, based on direct or indirect observation, real-time or permanent product
- is reliable and valid

We know better evidence of learning is important, and even more so is knowing what to make of and how to act upon that evidence (Shavelson, 2007). Obviously precision measurement isn't simply measuring how well a student is doing the variables related to content knowledge, but repertoires related to the ability to problem-solve and extrapolate, work fluently and with generativity (a form of creativity, see Johnson & Layng, 1992), persevere under difficulty, and the many other interpersonal or "soft skills" currently referred to as grit (Duckworth, 2007), growth mindset (Dweck, 2007), or personal competencies (Redding, in this volume). Each involves potentially measurable variables that affect learning (many are still being identified), which can be strengthened to improve student learning and well-being. Aided by technology, this type of measurement supports the building of interactive programs that recognize, match, and support critical factors that influence how individuals learn (such as psychological factors, the impact of emotion on learning, or relationships between humans and the learning environment; Martinez, 2001). With this type of information, teachers can predict and alter key instructional variables, such as the type, timing, and sequencing of instructions; stimulus discrimination and generalization procedures; fluency and resistance to distraction or forgetting; or the effects of temporary, automatic, or natural social consequences. (See both Crean-Davis and Layng in this volume for further discussion on the measurement and teaching of these variables and Baker for the use of predictive analytics in personalized learning.) If we consider personalized learning to be more than a reflection of a student's interests, goals, and motivations, then measurement of the dimensions presented above *is vital for truly personalized learning.*

Technology in Service to Decisions

The best technology is indentured to the service of decision making. While the concept of personalized learning has been around for some time, advances in digital content and delivery have placed personalized learning within reach for an increasing number of students, teachers, and schools. The flexibility inherent in digital technologies supports student-directed learning, improves interest and engagement, and provides multiple learning opportunities to maximize understanding (Hanover, 2012). As noted by Greaves (cited in Demski, 2012, p. 2), "if the students are leading their personalization via technology, then their instruction can be personalized based on a hundred variables instead of one or two." Technology supports personalized learning in a number of ways: students can use interactive, innovative teaching software and applications to learn at their own pace; assessment and monitoring of student progress can occur in real time; and students can interact with course material at any time, from anywhere (Hanover Research, 2012). These features, while beneficial, refer mainly to the technology of tools (i.e., digital devices and their capabilities) and not necessarily to the process of teaching and learning (i.e., software and algorithms; for more information on the distinction between technology tools and process, see Layng & Twyman, 2013, or Twyman, 2014b). While the capabilities of digital tools to conduct and support precision measurement are essential, it's their ability to enhance decision making that ultimately helps personalize learning. In our example with Juan, technology tools supported his access to a wide range of curriculum content which he could use anywhere and measured both his experimentation and his own progress. The technologies that supported the process of teaching and learning guided him using high-quality, adaptive instruction, vetted by his teacher, matched to his interest, and tuned to his current knowledge level. It also provided him with information on his own learning that allowed him to stretch his cognitive and creative boundaries, engage in problem solving, and make meaningful decisions.

Much attention is paid to educational software's ability to prescribe learning paths, differentiate and individualize instruction, and hone in on and extrapolate from patterns in responding (Horn & Staker, 2011). Often called adaptive learning or intelligent software (e.g., Knewton, Cognitive Tutor, Lumen, etc.), these programs respond to a student's interactions in real time by automatically providing individualized support (Blair, 2016). Early research has shown that an automated personalized curriculum sequence (based on pretest scores) providing a concise learning path and modifying instruction based on course difficulty was superior to conditions in which students freely browsed learning content (Chen, 2008). In a blog posting, Feldstein (2013) discusses adaptive learning software; here are a few examples drawn from that posting:

- A student using a physics program answers quiz questions about angular momentum incorrectly, so the program offers supplemental materials and more practice problems on that topic.

- A history student answers questions about the War of the Roses correctly the first time, so the program waits an interval of time and then requizzes the student to make sure that she is able to remember the information.

- A math student makes a mistake with the specific step of factoring polynomials while attempting to solve a polynomial equation, so the program provides the student with extra hints and supplemental practice problems on that step.

- An ESL writing student provides incorrect subject/verb agreement in several places within her essay, so the program provides a lesson on that topic and asks the student to find and correct her mistakes.

Intelligently designed software that automatically adapts to each learner may be an instructional game changer; however, precision measurement embedded into technology does not mean that the technology makes all the decisions for the teacher or student. Even instructional decisions, such as the examples listed above, should be left only to software that has been tested and validated and whose educators understand the underlying decision-making pedagogy. Technology to support personalized learning should not be solely focused on automatically selecting, sequencing, and presenting just the right information for the learner at just the right time, a situation which may result in a learner simply sitting back and clicking with no judgment or thinking required (Wiley, 2015); it must, at a very minimum, provide the basic information upon which its users can make informed choices.

> "Technology alone isn't going to improve student achievement. The best combination is great teachers working with technology to... engage students in the pursuit of the learning they need."
> U.S. Secretary of Education Arne Duncan (2010)

With the guidance of an informed teacher, technology that enables precision measurement should provide the conditions learners need to develop the skills required to successfully navigate their learning pathways and the information-rich world around them. As noted by Wiley (2016):

Rather than making complicated decisions on behalf of students in a black box, these systems should surface their data and support students in evaluating them and making their own decisions about what and how to study….In the long run, the true power of adaptive and personalized systems will only be realized when they are designed to simultaneously support student learning in the discipline and increase human agency, giving students and faculty the chance to develop their metacognitive and pedagogical skills rather than contributing to their slow demise.

Hence the true power of precision measurement in the education technology process is its potential to help us make better decisions and thus become better decision makers, in education and in life.

Caveats, Considerations, and Conclusions

Like the promise of personalized learning, the potential of precision measurement to enhance learning and student outcomes is great. However, as a whole, K–12 education is not quite there yet. A first hurdle is concern and fear around data and measurement. Before considering precision measurement, the reasons for measurement should be addressed. Measurement should never be used as the lever to punish or discredit anyone or anything, including the school or the curriculum, as is too often feared (Levine, 2005). It should not be a form of educational accountability (Browder, 1971). Using precision measurement as an essential tool to make decisions about instruction may go a long way to alleviating these concerns.

This better understanding and use of measurement should be a part of professional development, another hurdle in our quest. Even teachers who regularly use performance or formative assessments, including informal observation or paper-and-pencil responses, in making day-to-day classroom decisions, believe that more training is needed in the competent use of data and making educational decisions (Kershaw & McCaslin, 1995). Related are concerns about how to share data with parents and involve both them and the student in the decision-making process, highlighting the importance of clear, meaningful data and the need to foster a culture of support for precision measurement and its use in enhancing learning and student outcomes. Directly teaching data-based decision-making skills to educators, students, and parents is essential.

Lack of common data standards and concerns about data ownership and privacy pose other hurdles. Educational data systems do not always employ interoperability standards (i.e., a system's ability to work with other systems without special effort by the user) that would support secure, easy sharing of information between educators, schools, districts, states, students, and their families. This means educators are missing significant opportunities to use data to improve and personalize learning (U.S. Department of Education, 2016); however, national interoperability standards are being proposed and tested to improve the quality and effectiveness of technology-enabled tools and resources. Additionally, educators and policymakers around the country are rightfully concerned about the protection of students and their families. At least 46 states have introduced bills addressing student data privacy, and 15 states have passed new student data privacy laws (Data Quality Campaign, 2015). For example, California's Student Online Personal Information Protection Act requires developers to meet cyber-security standards, prevents the selling of student data for advertising purposes, restricts student profiles for non-educational purposes, and requires deletion of student data at school or district requests. Questions of who owns the data, how to use it to do the most good, and how to protect the individuals and systems on which the data are based are questions facing us now, and in the coming years.

The time to act is now. Educators are acutely aware of their responsibility to ensure that all students master critical content, and they strive to do this with specific and evolving plans that incorporate the varied abilities, needs, interests, and performance of each student. Effective, caring educators don't enter a classroom simply "hoping" their students will learn—they avail themselves of everything they have to ensure student learning; "[t]he possibility of student learning needs to rely on something sturdier than 'hope'" (Meyer, 2016). Precision measurement underpins a teacher's ability to answer the question, "What does *this* student need at *this* moment in order to be able to progress with *this* key content, and what do I need to do to make that happen?" (Tomlinson & Imbeau, 2010, p. 14). If we do believe in the promise of personalized learning, then we must realize that personalized learning is something educators DO, and precision measurement supports that doing. Precision measurement aided by technology and integrated with a strong relationship between the student and a caring teacher is instrumental in achieving the goals of personalized learning. Variation in the time, place, path, pace, practice, and trace of learning is essential for each and every student. It is the trace of learning, in the form of precision measurement, that provides educators with real-time, relevant evidence regarding a student's progression of knowledge, abilities, and attitudes, so that together they can make meaningful, moment-to-moment, individualized decisions about what and how to teach and learn.

Action Principles for States, Districts, and Schools

	SEAs	LEAs	Schools
General			
Create and maintain a portfolio of personalized learning/precision measurement exemplars (at the district, school, teacher, and student level) to inspire and serve as a model and mentor for others.	◆	◆	◆
Foster a culture of support for precision measurement and its use in enhancing learning and student outcomes.	◆	◆	◆
Support small or rural communities with the development of district consortia to foster personalized learning grounded in precision measurement and enhanced by technology.	◆		
The Learner Knows Best			
Focus on students and learning; use that focus to determine what each learner needs to succeed, develop the systems of support for that need, measure and evaluate the success of that support.	◆	◆	◆
Encourage, teach, and support students to examine their own data, using it to set, modify, and reach learning goals.	◆	◆	◆
Provide supports for precision measurement and continuous assessment to enhance student motivation.		◆	◆
Teacher Relationships With Students Are Critical			
Make precision measurement an essential part of an ongoing cycle of improvement.			◆
Provide supports for precision measurement and continuous assessment to enhance educator motivation.		◆	◆
Provide job-embedded professional development focused on using data for instructional improvement and student achievement.	◆	◆	◆
Build and embed teacher evaluation frameworks that support evidence-based decision making and foster personalized learning.	◆	◆	◆

	SEAs	LEAs	Schools
Measurement Imparts Understanding			
Establish a clear vision for data use; develop and maintain a location-wide data system.	◆	◆	◆
Provide supports that foster a data-driven culture.	◆	◆	◆
Make data part of an ongoing cycle of instructional improvement.	◆	◆	◆
Teach students to examine their own data and set of learning goals.			◆
Provide ongoing and regular feedback, including, at a minimum, frequently updated individual student data that can be used to determine progress toward mastery.			◆
Ensure that LEAs and schools use interoperable data systems (e.g., student information, instructional improvement system, human resources, and budget data).	◆	◆	◆
Collect relevant, actionable data on enrollment, participation, progress, completion, and learning outcomes.	◆	◆	◆
Ensure data are accessible, discoverable, and usable (i.e., open data format to promote understanding, innovation, and personal and system responsibility. See Burwell, VanRoekel, Park, & Mancini, 2013.).	◆	◆	◆
Enable third-party providers access to data to support personalized learning, while also protecting students' privacy and FERPA rights.	◆		
The Best Technology Is Indentured to the Service of Decision Making			
Incorporate, but do not rely solely upon, comprehensive learner profiles and predictive analytics to provide adaptive learning and power customized learning paths for each student.		◆	◆
Ensure educators (and students when appropriate) understand the pedagogy, data, and decision-making opportunities in educational software.		◆	◆
Create funding mechanisms for districts and schools to encourage innovative uses of technology to support decision making at all levels.	◆		
Publish annual evidence-based digital "updates" on innovative personalized learning models, focusing on strengths and essential criteria.	◆	◆	

References

Agger, C., & Cizek, G. (2013). *Measurement in education in the United States*. Oxford, England: Oxford Bibliographies in Education. Retrieved from http://www.oxfordbibliographies.com/view/document/obo-9780199756810/obo-9780199756810-0060.xml

Andrade, H., & Cizek, G. J. (Eds.). (2010). *Handbook of formative assessment.* New York, NY: Routledge.

Baker, R. S. J. d. (2013). Learning, schooling, and data analytics. In M. Murphy, S. Redding, & J. Twyman (Eds.), *Handbook on innovations in learning* (pp. 179–190). Charlotte, NC: Information Age Publishing. Retrieved from http://www.centeril.org/handbook/resources/fullchapter/Handbook_on_Innovations_in_Learning.pdf

Baker, R. S. J. d., & Yacef, K. (2009). The state of educational data mining in 2009: A review and future visions. *Journal of Educational Data Mining, 1*(1), 3–17.

Beatty, B. (1998). From laws of learning to a science of values: Efficiency and morality in Thorndyke's educational psychology. *American Psychologist, 53*(10): 1145–1152.

Binder, C., & Watkins, C. L. (1990). Precision teaching and direct instruction: Measurably superior instructional technology in schools. *Performance Improvement Quarterly, 3*(4), 74–96.

Blair, K. (2016). *What's happening inside the adaptive learning black box?* Burlingame, CA: EdSurge. Retrieved from https://www.edsurge.com/research/special-reports/adaptive-learning/definition

Browder, L. H., Jr. (Ed). (1971). *Emerging patterns of administrative accountability.* Berkeley, CA: McCutchan.

Burwell, S. M., VanRoekel, S., Park, T., & Mancini, D. J. (2013, May 9). Open data policy—Managing information as an asset [Memorandum for the heads of executive departments and agencies]. Washington, DC: Executive Office of the President, Office of Management and Budget. Retrieved from https://www.whitehouse.gov/sites/default/files/omb/memoranda/2013/m-13-13.pdf

Cavanagh, S. (2014). What is 'personalized learning'? Educators seek clarity. *Education Week, 34*(9), s2–S4. Retrieved from http://www.edweek.org/ew/articles/2014/10/22/09pl-overview.h34.html

Chen, C. M. (2008). Intelligent web-based learning system with personalized learning path guidance. *Computers & Education, 51*(2), 787–814. Retrieved from http://dx.doi.org/10.1016/j.compedu.2007.08.004

Culatta, R. (2013). Reimagining learning [Video file]. Brookline, MA: TEDxBeaconStreet. Retrieved from http://www.tedxbeaconstreet.com/richard-culatta/

Darling-Hammond, L. (2010). Teacher education and the American future. *Journal of Teacher Education, 61*(1–2), 35–47.

Data Quality Campaign. (2015). *Student data privacy legislation: What happened in 2015, and what is next.* Washington, DC: Data Quality Campaign. Retrieved from http://dataqualitycampaign.org/wp-content/uploads/2015/09/Student-Data-Privacy-Legislation-2015.pdf

Demski, J. (2012). *This time it's personal.* Chatsworth, CA: THE Journal. Retrieved from https://thejournal.com/Articles/2012/01/04/Personalized-learning.aspx?Page=2

Dewey, E. (1922). *The Dalton Laboratory Plan.* New York, NY: E. P. Dutton.

Dewey, J. (1916). *Democracy and education.* New York, NY: Free Press. Retrieved from http://www.gutenberg.org/files/852/852-h/852-h.htm

DeWitt, P. (2014, April 6). Creating assessment-capable learners [Web log post]. Bethesda, MD: Education Week. Retrieved from http://blogs.edweek.org/edweek/finding_common_ground/2014/04/creating_assessment_capable_learners.html

Duckworth, A. (2007). Grit: Perseverance and passion for long-term goals. *Journal of Personality & Social Psychology, 92*(6), 1087–1101.

Duncan, A. (2010, November 9). The digital transformation in education: U.S. Secretary of Education Arne Duncan's remarks at the State Educational Technology Directors Association Education Forum. Retrieved from https://www.ed.gov/news/speeches/digital-transformation-education-us-secretary-education-arne-duncans-remarks-state-edu

Dweck, C. S. (2007, January 12). *The growth mindset.* Walnut, CA: Mindset Works. Retrieved from http://www.mindsetworks.com/webnav/whatismindset.aspx

Feldstein, M. (2013, December 17). What faculty should know about adaptive learning [Web log post]. Los Gatos, CA: e-Literate. Retrieved from http://mfeldstein.com/faculty-know-adaptive-learning/

Fox, E. J. (2004). The personalized system of instruction: A flexible and effective approach to mastery learning. In D. J. Moran & R. W. Malott (Eds.), *Evidence-based educational methods* (pp. 201–221). San Diego, CA: Academic Press.

Glossary of Educational Reform. (2013a). *Learning environment.* Portland, ME: Great Schools Partnership. Retrieved from http://edglossary.org/learning-environment/

Glossary of Educational Reform. (2013b). *Learning gap.* Portland, ME: Great Schools Partnership. Retrieved from http://edglossary.org/learning-gap/

Glossary of Educational Reform. (2013c). *Learning pathway.* Portland, ME: Great Schools Partnership. Retrieved from http://edglossary.org/learning-pathway/

Glossary of Educational Reform. (2015). *Personalized learning.* Portland, ME: Great Schools Partnership. Retrieved from http://edglossary.org/personalized-learning/

Grant, P., & Basye, D. (2014). *Personalized learning: A guide to engaging students with technology.* Arlington, VA: International Society for Technology in Education.

Hamilton, L., Halverson, R., Jackson, S., Mandinach, E., Supovitz, J., & Wayman, J. (2009). *Using student achievement data to support instructional decision making* (NCEE 2009-4067). Washington, DC: National Center for Education Evaluation and Regional Assistance, Institute of Education Sciences, U.S. Department of Education. Retrieved from http://ies.ed.gov/ncee/wwc/pdf/practice_guides/dddm_pg_092909.pdf

Hanover Research. (2012). *Best practices in personalized learning environments (Grades 4–9).* Washington, DC: Author. Retrieved from http://www.hanoverresearch.com/media/Best-Practices-in-Personalized-Learning-Environments.pdf

Herman, J. L. (1992). *A practical guide to alternative assessment.* Alexandria, VA: Association for Supervision and Curriculum Development.

Horn, M. B., & Staker, H. (2011, January). *The rise of K–12 blended learning.* San Mateo, CA: Innosight Institute. Retrieved from http://www.leadcommission.org/sites/default/files/The%20 Rise%20of%20K-12%20Blended%20Learning_0.pdf

Johnson, K. R., & Layng, T. J. (1992). Breaking the structuralist barrier: Literacy and numeracy with fluency. *American Psychologist, 47*(11), 1475–1490.

Keller, F. S. (1968). "Goodbye, teacher…". *Journal of Applied Behavior Analysis*, 1(1), 79–89.

Kershaw, I., & McCaslin, N. L. (1995, December). *Using assessment information in educational decision making: A study of Ohio vocational teachers' assessment practices.* Paper presented at the American Vocational Association Convention, Denver, CO. Retrieved from http://files.eric.ed.gov/fulltext/ED391059.pdf

Kizlik, B. (2015). *Measurement, assessment, and evaluation in education.* Boca Raton, FL: ADPRIMA. Retrieved from http://drjj.uitm.edu.my/DRJJ/OBE%20FSG%20Dec07/OBE-Jan2010/DrJJ-Measure-assess-evaluate-ADPRIMA-n-more-17052012.pdf

Layng, T. V. J., Stikeleather, G., & Twyman, J. S. (2006). Scientific formative evaluation: The role of individual learners in generating and predicting successful educational outcomes. In R. F. Subotnik & H. Walberg (Eds.), *The scientific basis of educational productivity* (pp. 29–44). Greenwich, CT: Information Age Publishing.

Layng, T. V. J., & Twyman, J. S. (2013). Education + technology + innovation = learning? In M. Murphy, S. Redding, & J. Twyman (Eds.), *Handbook on innovations in learning* (pp. 133–148). Charlotte, NC: Information Age Publishing. Retrieved from http://www.centeril.org/handbook/resources/fullchapter/Handbook_on_Innovations_in_Learning.pdf

Levine, A. (2005). *Educating school leaders.* New York, NY: Education Schools Project.

Lignugaris-Kraft, B., & Rousseau, M. K. (1982). Instructional pacing: Definition and research needs. *Journal of Special Education Technology, 5*(3), 5–10.

Lindsley, O. R. (1972). From Skinner to precision teaching: The child knows best. In J. B. Jordan & L. S. Robbins (Eds.), *Let's try doing something else kind of thing: Behavior principles and the exceptional child* (pp. 13–19). Reston, VA: The Council for Exceptional Children.

Lindsley, O. R. (1990). Precision teaching: By teachers for children. *Teaching Exceptional Children, 22*(3), 10–15.

Martinez, M. (2001). Key design considerations for personalized learning on the web. *Educational Technology & Society, 4*(1), 26–40. Retrieved from http://www.ifets.info/journals/4_1/martinez.html

Marzano, R. (2010). The art and science of teaching/When students track their progress. *Educational Leadership, 67*(4), 86–87. Retrieved from http://www.ascd.org/publications/educational-leadership/dec09/vol67/num04/When-Students-Track-Their-Progress.aspx

McClarty, K. L., & Gaertner, M. N. (2015, April). *Measuring mastery: Best practices for assessment in competency-based education.* Washington, DC: American Enterprise Institute. Retrieved from https://www.luminafoundation.org/files/resources/measuring-mastery.pdf

Mead, M. (2015, July 8). Formative assessment to initiate personalized learning [Web log post]. Retrieved from http://gettingsmart.com/2015/07/formative-assessment-to-initiate-personalized-learning/

Means, B., Chen, E., DeBarger, A., & Padilla, C. (2011, February). *Teachers' ability to use data to inform instruction: Challenges and supports.* Washington, DC: U.S. Department of Education, Office of Planning, Evaluation and Policy Development. Retrieved from http://www2.ed.gov/rschstat/eval/data-to-inform-instruction/report.pdf

Mehrens, W. A. (1998). Consequences of assessment: What is the evidence? *Education Policy Analysis Archives, 6*(13), 1–30. Retrieved from http://epaa.asu.edu/ojs/index.php/epaa/article/viewFile/580/703

Merriam-Webster. (n.d.). *Aspiration.* Springfield, MA: Author. Retrieved from http://www.merriam-webster.com/dictionary/aspiration

Meyer, D. (2016, January 12). Problem-based learning needs a different crux [Web log post]. Retrieved from http://blog.mrmeyer.com/2016/problem-based-learning-needs-a-different-crux/?utm_source=feedburner&utm_medium=email&utm_campaign=Feed%3A+dydan1+%28dy%2Fdan+posts+%2B+lessons%29

Miller, M. D. (1998). *Teacher uses and perceptions of the impact of statewide performance-based assessments.* Washington, DC: Council on Chief State School Officers. State Education Assessment Center.

New England Secondary School Consortium. (n.d.). *What are personalized learning pathways?* Portland, ME: Author. Retrieved from http://education.vermont.gov/documents/EDU-nessc_briefing_no6.pdf

Next Generation Learning Challenges. (n.d.). *Personalized learning.* Washington, DC: Author. Retrieved from http://nextgenlearning.org/topics/personalized-learning

Pane, J. F., Steiner, E. D., Baird, M. D., & Hamilton, L. S. (2015). *Continued progress: Promising evidence on personalized learning.* Santa Monica, CA: RAND Corporation. Retrieved from http://www.rand.org/content/dam/rand/pubs/research_reports/RR1300/RR1365/RAND_RR1365.pdf

Patrick, S., Kennedy, K., & Powell, A. (2013). *Mean what you say: Defining and integrating personalized, blended and competency education.* New York, NY: International Association for K–12 Online Learning.

Popham, W. J. (2000). *Testing! Testing! What every parent should know about school tests.* Needham Heights, MA: Allyn & Bacon.

Redding, S. (2013). *Through the student's eyes: A perspective on personalized learning and practice guide for teachers.* Philadelphia, PA: Center on Innovations in Learning. Retrieved from http://www.centeril.org/publications/2013_09_Through_the_Eyes.pdf

Ripp, P. (2015, December 29). The five tenets of personalized learning [Web log post]. Retrieved from http://pernillesripp.com/2015/12/29/the-five-tenets-of-personalized-learning

Rose, T. (2016). *The end of average: How we succeed in a world that values sameness.* New York, NY: HarperCollins.

Ross, C. C. (1941). The historical development of measurement in education. In C. C. Ross (Ed.), *Measurement in today's schools* (pp. 32–71). New York, NY: Prentice-Hall.

Shavelson, R. (2007). *A brief history of student learning assessment: How we got where we are and a proposal for where to go next.* Washington, DC: Association of American Colleges and Universities. Retrieved from http://cae.org/images/uploads/pdf/19_A_Brief_History_of_Student_Learning_How_we_Got_Where_We_Are_and_a_Proposal_for_Where_to_Go_Next.PDF

Slavin, R. E. (2015, August 13). Who opposes evidence-based reform? [Web log post]. New York, NY: HuffPost Education. Retrieved from http://www.huffingtonpost.com/robert-e-slavin/who-opposes-evidence-base_b_7982282.html

Slavin, R. E. (2016, January 28). Farewell to the walking encyclopedia [Web log post]. New York, NY: HuffPost Education. Retrieved from http://www.huffingtonpost.com/robert-e-slavin/farewell-to-the-walking-e_b_9100144.html

Suskie, L. (2004). *Assessing student learning: A common sense guide.* Bolton, MA: Anker Publishing Company.

Tomlinson, C. A., & Imbeau, M. B. (2010). *Leading and managing a differentiated classroom.* Alexandria, VA: ASCD.

Twyman, J. S. (2014a). *Competency-based education: Supporting personalized learning. Connect: Making Learning Personal.* Philadelphia, PA: Center on Innovations in Learning. Retrieved from http://www.centeril.org/connect/resources/Connect_CB_Education_Twyman-2014_11.12.pdf

Twyman, J. S. (2014b). Envisioning Education 3.0: The fusion of behavior analysis, learning science, and technology. *Mexican Journal of Behavior Analysis, 40,* 20–38.

Twyman, J. S. (2015, June). *Varying time, place, pace, path, and trace in personalized learning.* Discussant at the Center for Innovations in Learning's second annual Conversations with Innovators discussion series, Philadelphia, PA.

U.S. Department of Education. (2010). *Transforming American education: Learning powered by technology.* Washington, DC: Office of Educational Technology.

U.S. Department of Education. (2016). *Future ready learning: Reimagining the role of technology in education.* Washington, DC: U.S. Department of Education Office of Educational Technology. Retrieved from http://tech.ed.gov/files/2015/12/NETP16.pdf

Ventura, J. (2014, December 15). The history of personalized learning: Milestones on the pathway to personalize learning [Web log post]. Retrieved from http://blog.newclassrooms.org/the-history-of-personalized-learning

White, O. R. (1986). Precision teaching—Precision learning. *Exceptional Children, 52*(6), 522–534. Retrieved from https://education.uw.edu/sites/default/files/areas/edspe/white/docs/White_PT_PL(small).pdf

Wikipedia. (n.d.). *Personalized learning.* Retrieved from https://en.wikipedia.org/wiki/Personalized_learning

Wiley, D. (2015, August 19). Personalization in Lumen's "Next Gen" OER courseware pilot [Web log post]. Retrieved from http://opencontent.org/blog/archives/3965

Wiley, D. (2016). *Opinion: What WALL-E teaches us about adaptive and personalized learning.* Burlingame, CA: EdSurge. Retrieved from https://www.edsurge.com/news/2016-02-17-what-wall-e-teaches-us-about-adaptive-and-personalized-learning

Wolf, M. A. (2010, November). *Innovate to educate: System [re]design for personalized learning.* A report from the 2010 symposium. Washington, DC: Software and Information Industry Association. Retrieved from http://www.slideshare.net/TomMcDonald/per-learn-paper

Using Learning Analytics in Personalized Learning

Ryan Baker

Traditional statistical methods for data analysis involved top-down and hypothesis-driven analysis of relatively small data sets. Although more exploratory, bottom-up approaches to working with data have been around for several decades (Tukey, 1977), the past few years have seen an explosion in the use of analytics and data mining, methods for making discoveries and extracting information from larger data sets, in a more bottom-up fashion (Han, Kamber, & Pei, 2011). Analytics and data mining methods specialized for use with educational data sets—and to answer educational questions—are referred to as *learning analytics* (Siemens & Long, 2011) and *educational data mining* (Baker & Yacef, 2009).

Learning analytics (LA) and educational data mining (EDM) have been used for a range of applications. For example, these methods have been used to determine when learners are disengaged within online learning (Baker, Corbett, & Koedinger, 2004; Pardos, Baker, San Pedro, Gowda, & Gowda, 2013), to make early predictions about long-term outcomes (Bowers, 2010; Jayaprakash, Moody, Lauría, Regan, & Baron, 2014; San Pedro, Baker, Bowers, & Heffernan, 2013), to understand how different students choose to use learning resources (Amershi & Conati, 2009; Beck & Mostow, 2008; Kizilcec, Piech, & Schneider, 2013), and for many other applications. Models (automated measurements produced using EDM/LA) of student cognition, engagement, and learning can predict not just student achievement within a specific school year (Pardos et al., 2013) but also can predict outcomes several years later, including college attendance (San Pedro et al., 2013) and college major (San Pedro, Baker, Heffernan, & Ocumpaugh, 2015).

This chapter discusses LA in the context of personalized learning, discussing both past successful examples and potential future opportunities, as well as action principles for how state education agencies (SEAs), local education agencies (LEAs), and schools can best put LA into practice.

Handbook on Personalized Learning for States, Districts, and Schools, pages 165–174
Copyright © 2016 by Information Age Publishing

Learning Analytics and Personalized Learning: State of the Art

The goal of individualizing learning to each student's needs is not a wholly new goal (e.g., Parkhurst, 1922), yet education is still a long way from achieving this goal. Indeed, despite attempts to introduce demonstrably effective practices such as mastery learning as early as the 1960s (see review in Airasian, Bloom, & Carroll, 1971), much learning remains focused on whole-group activities, such as lectures, that do not offer much scope for personalization. Even as we move to an era of greater usage of online learning resources, many contemporary resources such as xMOOCs (Breslow et al., 2013) and Khan Academy (Dijksman & Khan, 2011) still emphasize "one-size-fits-all" lectures and activities with limited scope for tailoring content or presentation to individual needs.

However, an increasing number of online and blended interactive learning systems are moving toward being more personalized. A blended or online learning environment can be, in general, personalized in two ways. First, students can be given options to personalize the environment themselves.

> The goal of individualizing learning to each student's needs is not a wholly new goal (e.g., Parkhurst, 1922), yet education is still a long way from achieving this goal.

Some environments do offer students a considerable amount of choice about their learning experiences. For example, intelligent tutoring systems such as SQL-Tutor (used by hundreds of thousands of undergraduates to learn database programming) offer students choice about what topic to work on next (Mathews & Mitrovic, 2007). This type of personalization extends even to elementary school students, with systems such as the Project LISTEN Reading Tutor (for elementary school students). In Project LISTEN, students are allowed to choose what story they read next (Mostow et al., 2002). Other systems, such as gStudy, engage students in planning their learning experiences (Perry & Winne, 2006).

However, it is more common to see systems in which learning is made adaptive and personalized to the learner's needs by the teacher or by the learning system itself. This type of practice developed before the widespread use of computers in classrooms, with teachers using formative assessments to drive mastery learning practices in which students work through material on a given topic until they can demonstrate the skills relevant to that topic (Airasian et al., 1971). Indeed, some of the first individualizing of blended and online learning at scale involved replicating mastery learning practices through a computer. For example, Cognitive Tutors for Algebra, now used by hundreds of thousands of students a year, assessed student knowledge as students worked through mathematics problems (Corbett & Anderson, 1995) and used that information to implement mastery learning. Cognitive Tutors for Algebra has been effective at promoting positive learning outcomes (Pane, Griffin, McCaffrey, & Karam, 2014); its algorithms to assess student knowledge arguably represent the first widespread use of EDM/LA.

The systems that have followed the Cognitive Tutor use models developed based on learning analytics to adapt to students in many more ways than simply implementing mastery learning. For example, the ALEKS system for algebra and chemistry, used by more than 100,000 students a year and shown to be effective (Craig et al., 2013), also uses EDM/LA to determine what prerequisite skills the student is lacking in order to shift the student's work to prerequisite skills when necessary (Doignon & Falmagne, 1999). This type of practice helps to avoid situations in which a student "wheel spins" (Beck &

Gong, 2013), working continuously on material with no success and little potential of success due to not knowing the prerequisites for the current material—or worse, when the student continually advances to harder material, failing topic after topic.

Learning analytics about student knowledge is used for more than just automated adaptation. Many online learning providers use it to support instructor practice as well. For example, automated data on student success in mathematics is presented to elementary school classroom teachers by the Reasoning Mind system, used by more than 100,000 students a year and shown to be effective (Waxman & Houston, 2008, 2012). This system also provides teachers with professional development that shows them how to use the system's analytics to inform proactive remediation, in which the instructor selects students or groups of students for one-on-one or small-group tutoring during class (Miller et al., 2015). A similar approach is taken at the undergraduate level by the Course Signals system, which tracks student course participation and performance on early assignments and integrates these data sources into systems that predict eventual student course failure and dropout in order to provide instructors with reports on which students are at risk and why (Arnold & Pistilli, 2012). The reports in Course Signals are combined with recommendations for instructors on how to use them, including templates for emails that automatically fill in the student's name and performance factors that indicate risk. The use of Course Signals was shown in a study at Purdue University to lead to significantly lower dropout rates (Arnold & Pistilli, 2012).

Learning Analytics and Personalized Learning: Future Potentials

Modern LA for personalization extends further than simply assessing and supporting learning and performance to attempting to enhance engagement and affect. Although the evidence for effectiveness is still preliminary, involving small studies rather than national-level randomized controlled trials, some pilot projects have shown evidence that these approaches can be beneficial.

For example, some of the first work using EDM involved systems that could automatically infer when a student was "gaming the system," misusing a learning system in order to succeed without learning, for instance, by clicking through hints at high speed or systematically guessing (Baker et al., 2004). Automated measurements (often termed "models") of gaming the system have been used to trigger automated intervention, reducing gaming behavior and improving learning (Baker et al., 2006). They have also been used in interventions that teach students why gaming is ineffective and reduces their learning, also reducing gaming behavior and improving learning (Arroyo et al., 2007). Similarly, models that can automatically infer student emotion have been used in systems at the undergraduate level, responding in supportive ways to struggling students and in sarcastic ways to students who are generally successful but are not putting in enough effort (D'Mello et al., 2010). Further work has developed approaches that not only attempt to support students but also actually attempt to *increase* student confusion in some situations, increasing challenge and improving learning outcomes (D'Mello, Lehman, Pekrun, & Graesser, 2014).

The potential for enhancing self-regulated learning (SRL) is somewhat less certain. For example, LA was used to study which hint-use strategies led to better learning in Cognitive Tutors (Aleven, McLaren, Roll, & Koedinger, 2004). Teaching students more effective SRL strategies and providing immediate feedback on ineffective or inappropriate hint use led to lasting changes in student behavior but no difference in learning outcomes for the mathematics material students were expected to learn (Roll, McLaren, Aleven, & Koedinger, 2011). This result has been replicated in another study conducted by Albert Corbett at Carnegie Mellon University. Overall, there has been insufficient research to know whether the relative lack of success of this approach is indicative of the general difficulty of improving learning through using analytics-based SRL interventions or whether some aspect of the design of this intervention led to a lower impact on learning outcomes.

Determining the eventual impact of EDM/LA is difficult. In general, LA and EDM are still advancing relatively rapidly. The past decade has seen construct after construct that seemed difficult to measure turn out to be feasible to measure effectively using EDM/LA. However, work to use EDM/LA for personalization is still ongoing and lags a few years behind the work on measuring constructs, such as gaming the system and emotion, for the simple reason that it is not possible to use an automated measure of a learning-related construct to enhance learning before that measure exists. In addition, the individuals who are skilled in interaction and educational design—in developing interventions that use EDM/LA to improve outcomes—are not the same individuals who are good at using LA and EDM to build the measurements on which those interventions depend. As a result, readers of this chapter may find, scant years from now, that the personalization technologies that are available at the time they are reading this chapter far surpass the technologies reported today (or, alternatively, the technologies may be very similar; see some of the action principles discussed below).

> *While the methods of learning analytics have considerable potential to enable high-quality adaptive personalization to learning, there are several challenges ...*

Some Considerations on Using Learning Analytics in Personalized Learning

While the methods of learning analytics have considerable potential to enable high-quality adaptive personalization to learning, there are several challenges that must be taken into consideration for these methods to reach their full potential to enhance student outcomes. The following sections of this chapter discuss the role played by issues such as privacy and model validity and how these challenges can be appropriately addressed. The chapter also discusses the essential role played by stakeholders such as teachers, school leaders, and parents and how LA-based personalization can effectively support these stakeholders.

Privacy

In recent years, there has been considerable concern about student privacy in this emerging era of analytics (Slade & Prinsloo, 2013). There are reasons for concern when student data may be used for marketing or may be disclosed unnecessarily. Regrettably, some of this concern has led to suggesting policies that are very likely to hinder the use of educational data for educational improvement. For example, as of this writing, the U.S. Department of Education has recommended terms of use for online learning that forbid "data mining" (Privacy Technical Assistance Center, 2015) based on the apparent misconception that "data mining" is equivalent to advertising. Recent legislation has also proposed policies for handling educational data that require that no personally identifiable information be available or indeed that require that all data be discarded at the end of each school year. Discarding all data essentially destroys the potential for using analytics and data mining to enhance education, for little reduction in risk. Even the seemingly reasonable compromise of removing all personally identifiable information from data has the potential to reduce the degree to which we can improve education through personalization driven by LA. Data that do not include personally identifiable information cannot be used to conduct longitudinal research in which performance and behavior are linked to eventual learner outcomes. If it is impossible to verify long-term outcomes, technologies may be selected that enhance learning in the short term but do not produce positive outcomes in the long term.

Several possible solutions remove the drawbacks of full anonymization while protecting student privacy and maintaining compliance with the Family Educational Rights and Privacy Act (FERPA), the federal law that protects the privacy of student education records. For example, SEAs and LEAs can store personally identifying information in trust, with an individual within the LEA or SEA holding a strictly guarded key to the data sets and the links between them, allowing access only for legitimate educational research and enhancement purposes. Alternatively, a trusted broker can be selected to protect this information, as the National Student Clearinghouse does for undergraduate enrollment data. Modern technologies for data mining and analytics can support analysis by remote researchers in which analyses can be conducted using sensitive data but in which the sensitive data itself are never exposed to the remote researcher. All data would be retained by organizations entrusted to protect students, and thus it would be possible to use LA to its full potential. Modern systems for educational data, such as the MARi platform and OpenLAP, limit access to data, keep control over data in the hands of students and their parents, and do not inhibit educational improvement. SEAs, LEAs, and schools have a role to play in realizing the potential of LA by partnering with reliable commercial and nonprofit entities to insist on systems that protect privacy but do not prevent students from having access to high-quality personalized education.

Model Validity

When using LA to impact educational practice, it is important to ensure that the LA models are valid. Although a great deal of high-quality software is available, there is also considerable software that is low quality. Schools should be prepared to ask good questions of developers. Traditionally, school purchasing decisions have been based on relatively light evidence, such as testimonial evidence provided by developers. The What Works Clearinghouse (http://ies.ed.gov/ncee/wwc/) encourages schools to ask, "Does it work?" and to insist on evidence from randomized controlled trials. In a randomized controlled trial, a system is compared with some existing pedagogical practice in a study with random assignment. As schools increasingly work with vendors that provide personalized learning systems and analytics, the schools should ask to see evidence on how the personalization and analytics were developed. Scientific papers in reputable, peer-reviewed journals and conferences can provide evidence that the system under consideration was developed according to valid principles. For example, schools and school districts should examine these publications for evidence on whether models were tested on the same students they were developed for or whether the models are shown to function appropriately for students other than those for which the models were developed.

However, even this type of validation is sometimes not enough. Ideally, models should also be validated for accuracy in contexts similar to the schools where they will be used.

A rural school should be wary of using software developed for suburban students; there is evidence that the same behaviors do not always predict emotion or engagement in different populations (Ocumpaugh et al., 2014). It is increasingly considered best practice at the higher education level to validate models for individual universities, a practice adopted, for instance, by the company ZogoTech. Although it may not be feasible at the current time to validate models for each and every school in the United States, it is feasible to ask whether a model being used was validated on students similar to those in the school considering adoption. There are even metrics for the similarity between schools that can be used to inform consideration of the relevance of study evidence for a given school (Tipton, 2014).

Leveraging All the Relevant Stakeholders

Often, schools rely solely on teachers to personalize students' education beyond what online and blended learning can provide. Teachers have a key role to play in making learning effective for students, and most LA reports are targeted toward them. However, many other stakeholders also have roles to play. Guidance counselors can access LA reports and use automated predictions to identify students who are engaged by the subject they are studying but who might not be considering careers in this area, due, for instance, to demographic factors. These students can be encouraged to participate in summer or afterschool enrichment programs that give them experience in the area of study. So, too, students who are engaged by a subject but struggling with it and are not on track to be able to go into the careers they are interested in are ideal candidates for afterschool tutoring or other support. By contrast, a student who is performing well at a subject but who does not seem to be particularly engaged with it should probably be encouraged to place his or her efforts into other subjects. As such, guidance counseling can be made more personal and potentially more effective.

Similarly, school leaders—particularly those whose task it is to deal with disciplinary problems—also may benefit from LA from the systems students are using. Although a considerable proportion of disciplinary incidents involves factors outside the direct control of schools (e.g., Bachman & Schulenberg, 1993; Murray, Farrington, & Sekol, 2012), it may be beneficial for a school leader to see evidence that a student who is getting into trouble is nonetheless remaining engaged in learning one or more subjects. This may suggest positive behavior supports (Bambara, Nonnemacher, & Kern, 2009) that the school leader can consider applying, including activities to reengage the student with schooling through his or her preferred subjects.

Finally, parents can be empowered to help support their children's learning. Currently, efforts to incorporate parents in their children's learning are often very limited, with report cards only provided at occasional intervals and reports containing relatively limited information about how to help their specific child. If anything, the move to online learning has disempowered parents further because many parents cannot help students with their homework as easily as before (because it occurs within an unfamiliar online system rather than on paper). When resources are given to parents, they are often provided to every parent in a class, ignoring whether that student needs the resource or how to individualize it for that child. By contrast, reports from personalized learning systems that collect considerable data about each child can be provided to parents. For example, the ASSISTments system sends text messages and emails to parents, telling them what their children are currently struggling with (Broderick, 2011). Even simple systems that notify parents about missed assignments can lead to positive impacts on student academic outcomes (Bergman, under review).

Action Principles for States, Districts, and Schools

a. Develop data policies that make learning analytics possible. Schools, LEAs, and SEAs have an important role to play in making it possible for LA to be used to benefit students. By partnering with organizations that handle student data responsibly and by adopting policies that protect privacy but preserve data and ways to link student learning data to future data on their success, schools, LEAs, and SEAs can increase the potential for personalized learning to benefit their students.

b. Mitigate the data loss stemming from student mobility. School mobility is a fact of 21st century education; because American society is highly mobile, students are likely to change schools repeatedly during their education. Although school mobility may not be problematic for students of high socioeconomic status (SES), it is associated with poorer outcomes among lower SES and minority students, especially if a student changes schools several times (Xu, Hannaway, & D'Souza, 2009). Districts and SEAs need to work with technology providers so that a student's data in one school can follow him or her to another school. A student who is halfway through the school year and has used a high-quality system such as ALEKS all year should not start from square one if his or her new school also uses ALEKS. By coordinating between schools and technology providers, a student's account can be transferred between schools, and the student can pick up in Paterson (NJ) where he or she left off in Orange (NJ).

Action Principles for States and Districts

a. Ask for raw data and student models from providers. The data being collected by personalized learning systems is useful, not just within that specific learning system but more broadly as well. Models of constructs such as engagement can be processed by states or school districts into reports for guidance counselors that predict student long-term outcomes and help the guidance counselors advise students how to stay on track.

b. Incorporate these models into state or city early-warning systems, complementing traditional data sources, such as grade data, disciplinary incidents, standardized examination scores, and demographic data. Data from personalized learning systems are a treasure trove for SEAs and LEAs wanting to improve student outcomes.

Action Principles for Districts and Schools

a. Seek appropriate professional development for teachers working with analytics. Teaching with blended learning and online homework differs from traditional pedagogical approaches, and different teacher practices are relevant (Ronau, Rakes, & Niess, 2012). There is considerable evidence that these new approaches to teaching are more effective in the hands of teachers who have received appropriate professional development (see review in Lawless & Pellegrino, 2007). Also, instructors who have received sufficient professional development are more likely to adopt effective practices, such as viewing reports on student knowledge and success and using proactive remediation strategies to help struggling students (Miller et al., 2015). Professional development for working with modern personalized learning technologies is available from technology and curriculum providers and from universities ranging from Teachers College Columbia University to Framingham State University. Students will benefit considerably if schools make resources available for teachers to partake in these programs.

b. Leverage multiple stakeholders to participate in personalization. Personalization is not something that an online learning or blended learning system does alone. It works most effectively when it leverages—and empowers—what teachers, guidance counselors, school leaders, and parents have to offer. Extending analytics reports to all these individuals—and when appropriate, providing them with training on how to use reports—has the potential to considerably improve student outcomes.

Action Principles for Schools

a. Be an educated consumer of personalized learning software. School officials should insist on seeing evidence in appropriate peer-reviewed conferences and journals that the systems under consideration have been validated to work for students similar to the ones in their school. Failing to check this risks that students will receive ineffective learning support.

References

Airasian, P. W., Bloom, B. S., & Carroll, J. B. (1971). *Mastery learning: Theory and practice.* J. H. Block (Ed.). New York, NY: Holt, Rinehart, & Winston.

Aleven, V., McLaren, B., Roll, I., & Koedinger, K. (2004). Toward tutoring help seeking. *Proceedings of the International Conference on Intelligent Tutoring Systems* (pp. 227–239). Maceió, Alagoas, Brazil.

Amershi, S., & Conati, C. (2009). Combining unsupervised and supervised classification to build user models for exploratory learning environments. *Journal of Educational Data Mining, 1*(1), 18–71.

Arnold, K. E., & Pistilli, M. D. (2012). Course signals at Purdue: Using learning analytics to increase student success. *Proceedings of the 2nd International Conference on Learning Analytics and Knowledge* (pp. 267–270). Washington, DC: Association for Computing Machinery.

Arroyo, I., Ferguson, K., Johns, J., Dragon, T., Meheranian, H., Fisher, D., & Woolf, B. P. (2007). Repairing disengagement with non-invasive interventions. *Proceedings of the International Conference on Artificial Intelligence in Education* (pp. 195–202). Los Angeles, CA.

Bachman, J. G., & Schulenberg, J. (1993). How part-time work intensity relates to drug use, problem behavior, time use, and satisfaction among high school seniors: Are these consequences or merely correlates? *Developmental Psychology, 29*(2), 220.

Baker, R. S., Corbett, A. T., & Koedinger, K. R. (2004). Detecting student misuse of intelligent tutoring systems. *Proceedings of the 7th International Conference on Intelligent Tutoring Systems* (pp. 531–540). Maceió, Alagoas, Brazil.

Baker, R. S. J. D., Corbett, A. T., Koedinger, K. R., Evenson, S. E., Roll, I., Wagner, A. Z.,...Beck, J. (2006). Adapting to when students game an intelligent tutoring system. *Proceedings of the 8th International Conference on Intelligent Tutoring Systems* (pp. 392–401). Jhongli, Taiwan.

Baker, R .S. J. D., & Yacef, K. (2009). The state of educational data mining in 2009: A review and future visions. *Journal of Educational Data Mining, 1*(1), 3–17.

Bambara, L. M., Nonnemacher, S., & Kern, L. (2009). Sustaining school-based individualized positive behavior support: Perceived barriers and enablers. *Journal of Positive Behavior Interventions, 11*(3), 161–176.

Beck, J. E., & Gong, Y. (2013). Wheel-spinning: Students who fail to master a skill. *Artificial Intelligence in Education, 7926,* 431–440.

Beck, J. E., & Mostow, J. (2008). How who should practice: Using learning decomposition to evaluate the efficacy of different types of practice for different types of students. *Proceedings of the International Conference on Intelligent Tutoring Systems* (pp. 353–362). Montreal, Canada.

Bergman, P. (under review). *Parent-child information frictions and human capital investment: Evidence from a field experiment.* Prepublication draft retrieved from http://www.columbia.edu/~psb2101/BergmanSubmission.pdf

Bowers, A. J. (2010). Grades and graduation: A longitudinal risk perspective to identify student dropouts. *Journal of Educational Research, 103*(3), 191–207.

Breslow, L., Pritchard, D. E., DeBoer, J., Stump, G. S., Ho, A. D., & Seaton, D. T. (2013). Studying learning in the worldwide classroom: Research into edX's first MOOC. *Research & Practice in Assessment, 8*(1), 13–25.

Broderick, Z. (2011). *Increasing parent engagement in student learning using an Intelligent Tutoring System with automated messages.* Unpublished master's thesis, Worcester Polytechnic Institute, Worcester, MA, USA.

Corbett, A. T., & Anderson, J. R. (1995). Knowledge tracing: Modeling the acquisition of procedural knowledge. *User Modeling and User-Adapted Interaction, 4*(4), 253–278.

Craig, S. D., Hu, X., Graesser, A. C., Bargagliotti, A. E., Sterbinsky, A., Cheney, K. R., & Okwumabua, T. (2013). The impact of a technology-based mathematics after-school program using ALEKS on student's knowledge and behaviors. *Computers & Education, 68,* 495–504.

Dijksman, J. A., & Khan, S. (2011, March). Khan Academy: The world's free virtual school. In *APS Meeting Abstracts, 1,* 14006.

D'Mello, S., Lehman, B., Pekrun, R., & Graesser, A. (2014). Confusion can be beneficial for learning. *Learning and Instruction, 29,* 153–170.

D'Mello, S., Lehman, B., Sullins, J., Daigle, R., Combs, R., Vogt, K., & Graesser, A. (2010). A time for emoting: When affect-sensitivity is and isn't effective at promoting deep learning. *Proceedings of the International Conference on Intelligent Tutoring Systems* (pp. 245–254). Pittsburg, PA.

Doignon, J. P., & Falmagne, J. C. (1999). *Knowledge spaces.* Berlin, Germany: Springer.

Han, J., Kamber, M., & Pei, J. (2011). *Data mining: Concepts and techniques.* Waltham, MA: Morgan Kaufmann.

Jayaprakash, S. M., Moody, E. W., Lauría, E. J., Regan, J. R., & Baron, J. D. (2014). Early alert of academically at-risk students: An open source analytics initiative. *Journal of Learning Analytics, 1*(1), 6–47.

Kizilcec, R. F., Piech, C., & Schneider, E. (2013, April). Deconstructing disengagement: Analyzing learner subpopulations in massive open online courses. *Proceedings of the Third International Conference on Learning Analytics and Knowledge* (pp. 170–179). Washington, DC: Association for Computing Machinery.

Lawless, K. A., & Pellegrino, J. W. (2007). Professional development in integrating technology into teaching and learning: Knowns, unknowns, and ways to pursue better questions and answers. *Review of Educational Research, 77*(4), 575–614.

Mathews, M., & Mitrovic, A. (2007). Investigating the effectiveness of problem templates on learning in ITSs. In R. Luckin, K. Koedinger, & J. Greer (Eds.), *Proceedings of Artificial Intelligence in Education* (pp. 611–613). Los Angeles, CA.

Miller, W. L., Baker, R. S., Labrum, M. J., Petsche, K., Liu, Y. H., & Wagner, A. Z. (2015, March). Automated detection of proactive remediation by teachers in reasoning mind classrooms. *Proceedings of the Fifth International Conference on Learning Analytics and Knowledge* (pp. 290–294). Washington, DC: Association for Computing Machinery.

Mostow, J., Beck, J., Chalasani, R., Cuneo, A., Jia, P., & Kadaru, K. (2002). A la recherche du temps perdu, or as time goes by: Where does the time go in a reading tutor that listens? *Proceedings of Intelligent Tutoring Systems* (pp. 320–329). Biarritz, France.

Murray, J., Farrington, D. P., & Sekol, I. (2012). Children's antisocial behavior, mental health, drug use, and educational performance after parental incarceration: A systematic review and meta-analysis. *Psychological Bulletin, 138*(2), 175.

Ocumpaugh, J., Baker, R., Gowda, S., Heffernan, N., & Heffernan, C. (2014). Population validity for educational data mining models: A case study in affect detection. *British Journal of Educational Technology, 45*(3), 487–501.

Pane, J. F., Griffin, B. A., McCaffrey, D. F., & Karam, R. (2014). Effectiveness of Cognitive Tutor Algebra I at scale. *Educational Evaluation and Policy Analysis, 36*(2), 127–144.

Pardos, Z. A., Baker, R. S. J. D., San Pedro, M. O. C. Z., Gowda, S. M., & Gowda, S. M. (2013). Affective states and state tests: Investigating how affect throughout the school year predicts end of year learning outcomes. *Proceedings of the 3rd International Conference on Learning Analytics and Knowledge* (pp. 117–124). Indianapolis, IN.

Parkhurst, H. (1922). *A plan for individualized instruction: Education on the Dalton Plan.* New York, NY: E. P. Hutton & Co.

Perry, N. E., & Winne, P. H. (2006). Learning from learning kits: gStudy traces of students' self-regulated engagements with computerized content. *Educational Psychology Review, 18*(3), 211–228.

Privacy Technical Assistance Center. (2015). *Protecting student privacy while using online educational services: Model terms of service.* Washington, DC: U.S. Department of Education.

Roll, I., Aleven, V., McLaren, B. M., & Koedinger, K. R. (2011). Improving students' help-seeking skills using metacognitive feedback in an intelligent tutoring system. *Learning and Instruction, 21*(2), 267–280.

Ronau, R. N., Rakes, C. R., & Niess, M. (2012). *Educational technology, teacher knowledge, and classroom impact: A research handbook on frameworks and approaches.* Hershey, PA: IGI-Global.

San Pedro, M. O. Z., Baker, R. S. J. D., Bowers, A. J., & Heffernan, N. T. (2013). Predicting college enrollment from student interaction with an intelligent tutoring system in middle school. *Proceedings of the 6th International Conference on Educational Data Mining* (pp. 177–184). Memphis, TN.

San Pedro, M. O., Baker, R., Heffernan, N., & Ocumpaugh, J. (2015). Exploring college major choice and middle school student behavior, affect, and learning: What happens to students who game the system? *Proceedings of the 5th International Learning Analytics and Knowledge Conference* (pp. 36–40). Poughkeepsie, NY.

Siemens, G., & Long, P. (2011). Penetrating the fog: Analytics in learning and education. *EDUCAUSE Review, 46*(5), 30.

Slade, S., & Prinsloo, P. (2013). Learning analytics: Ethical issues and dilemmas. *American Behavioral Scientist, 57*(10), 1510–1529.

Tipton, E. (2014). How generalizable is your experiment? An index for comparing experimental samples and populations. *Journal of Educational and Behavioral Statistics, 39*(6), 478–501.

Tukey, J. W. (1977). *Exploratory data analysis.* London, England: Pearson.

Waxman, H. C., & Houston, W. R. (2008). *An evaluation of the 2006–2007 Reasoning Mind program* (Technical Report). Arlington, TX: University of Texas.

Waxman, H. C., & Houston, W. R. (2012). *Evaluation of the 2010–2011 Reasoning Mind program in Beaumont ISD* (Technical Report). University of Texas Arlington.

Xu, Z., Hannaway, J., & D'Souza, S. (2009). *Student transience in North Carolina: The effect of school mobility on student outcomes using longitudinal data* (Working Paper 22). Washington, DC: National Center for Analysis of Longitudinal Data in Education Research.

IV. The Personalized Learning Community: Teachers, Students, and Families

Preparing Educators to Engage Parents and Families

Erin McNamara Horvat

Although the relationship between parents and educators has often been characterized as oppositional and political (Cutler, 2000; Horvat, Weininger, & Lareau, 2003; Lareau, 2000; Lightfoot, 2004), significant evidence points to the importance of this relationship in creating strong school communities and improving learning outcomes for students. Although barriers to strong home–school relationships have always existed, recent developments—such as technology's use in learning, the changing curriculum, and increased pressures for parents—have created new barriers to effective parent–educator relationships that support student learning. In addition, class, race, and language barriers present special challenges to creating and sustaining these relationships. It is increasingly important for educators to have the knowledge and skill to engage parents.

Teacher preparation programs have typically not systematically addressed home–school relationships despite the importance of this topic in improving student outcomes. The advent and expansion of personalized learning—that is, efforts to attend to the pacing, preferences, and interests of the learner—bring both challenges and opportunities to efforts to improve home–school relationships. Personalized learning can, at times, contribute to the barriers between educators and parents. However, a personalized learning approach that puts the learning preferences and interests of the learner first may also provide a path forward toward the reduction of barriers and the creation of effective home–school relationships. This chapter explores the intersection of home–school relationships and personalized learning. It explores the power of personalized learning to better meet all students' needs and the challenges to equitably implementing personalized learning given the vast differences among students and the capacity of educators to meaningfully connect with students and families.

Definitional and Conceptual Differences

Ample evidence (Epstein, 2001/2011; Fan & Chen, 2001; Henderson & Mapp, 2002; Wilder, 2014) suggests that students of all ages benefit from strong relationships between the school and the family. Yet educators, researchers, and parents may have very different

Handbook on Personalized Learning for States, Districts, and Schools, pages 177–187
Copyright © 2016 by Information Age Publishing

definitions of what is meant by a home–school connection (Smith, Wohlstetter, Kuzin, & De Pedro, 2011; Wilder, 2014). Sorting out this definitional confusion is a critical first step in efforts to promote the creation of effective home–school relationships.

The literature is rife with a variety of terms that refer to home–school connections or some aspect of this relationship. The terms include *parent involvement, family involvement, teacher–family partnerships, parent–school relationship, parental engagement,* and *school–family partnerships*. These terms are often used interchangeably, yet they may mean very different things to the stakeholders involved.

Although some may intend *parent* to denote any adult who supports the student's school experience but who is not associated with the school community, the use of the terms *parent involvement* or *parent engagement* does not signal an understanding of the wider community influences that can support or impede student success. Indeed, the use of *parent* instead of *home* or *family* may reveal a lack of understanding of the important role that the extended

> Although involvement signals that family members may be involved with the school when needed, engagement implies deeper, more reciprocal relationships.

family plays in students' lives and may signal a preference for the traditional nuclear family. So, although it may seem to be an insignificant distinction, a person's selection of terms used to describe the actors involved in creating and sustaining a relationship that supports student learning in home and school contexts is critical. Using the more inclusive *family* or *home* indicates an inclusive approach to creating and sustaining relationships that support student achievement.

Likewise, the choice between using *engagement* or *involvement* may appear to be inconsequential on the surface. Yet these two terms can signal vastly different approaches to the home–school relationship. Although involvement signals that family members may be involved with the school when needed, *engagement* implies deeper, more reciprocal relationships (Smith et al., 2011). Likewise, use of the term *partnership* signals a particular orientation to the work of engaging families with the educational process.

Effective Family Engagement With Schools: Possibilities and Barriers

As noted at the outset of this chapter, historically, relations between home and school have been contentious. Although schools have for many years now understood the need to create and develop strong ties to the home—whether they are aimed at engaging parents, building partnerships, or seeking involvement—educators generally prefer to be the experts in control of these relationships. As Henderson, Mapp, Johnson, and Davies (2007) observe, schools vary in how they construct their relationships with parents. Some schools, typically those with weaker ties to parents and the community, simply want parents to come if called—to remain available to respond to the needs of the school when they are voiced, but other schools endeavor to engage in a true reciprocal partnership that provides opportunities for authentic family engagement (Auerbach, 2010). These varying approaches to the home–school relationship are often reflected in the different terminology used.

Research points to the effectiveness of reciprocal relationships between home and school (Epstein, 2001/2011; Hiatt-Michael, 2006; Horvat, 2011; Weiss, Bouffard, Bridglall, & Gordon, 2009). Whereas Epstein (2001/2011) describes the ideal approach as one that recognizes the "overlapping spheres of influence," Weiss and colleagues advocate "co-constructed shared responsibility." Also, research highlights the importance of school agents (teachers, counselors, nurses, administrators, and aides) taking the lead in developing and maintaining these relationships and holding themselves accountable for doing so (Lopez, Scribner, & Mahitivanichcha, 2001). This notion of reciprocity and the trust that is developed in reciprocal relationships are critical ideas for educators seeking to enhance their relationships with students and their families.

Myriad barriers exist for the development and maintenance of strong home–school ties. Ample research has provided insight into the ways that race, ethnicity, and social class can influence relationships between home and school. It is clear that some families are more well-positioned than others to connect with schools and have a positive influence on students' careers.

Social class has been implicated in influencing home–school relationships. Schools are middle-class places that value specific kinds of class-appropriate involvement from parents (Lareau & Horvat, 1999). Middle-class parents are better able to understand and meet the often implicit expectations for involvement held by teachers and school administrators. Working-class parents are more likely to view the school as separate from their own world and are more inclined to defer to the expertise of teachers (Crozier, 1999; Horvat et al., 2003; Lareau, 2000). They are also less well-prepared to meet the demands of educators for involvement. These fundamental class differences between parents' orientation towards schools influence both the ways that parents engage with the school and the ways that they respond to implicit and explicit expectations for involvement from schools. These differences in how parents of varying social class backgrounds are oriented towards their children's schools and the differing ways that they interact with schools represent a significant barrier for schools to overcome. While middle-class parents are generally more highly attuned to the requests of educators for involvement and in a better position to support their children in school, it can be challenging for educators to effectively engage or partner with working-class parents. Finding ways to bridge the distance between the school and working-class and poor parents and effectively engage all parents continues to be a struggle for teachers and administrators.

Likewise, race and ethnicity create differences and distance that must be bridged in order to create strong home–school connections. One of the challenges facing public schools is an increasingly homogeneous work force that is primarily White and increasingly conservative. Attracting quality candidates of color to the educational workforce has proved challenging. As our society becomes increasingly diverse, this mismatch between the cultural and racial/ethnic backgrounds of teachers and students must be addressed. Although linguistic differences create an obvious communication challenge, different cultural expectations regarding schooling and the appropriate role for families, students, and teachers create a different set of barriers that are equally challenging to overcome (Crozier & Davies, 2007; Delgado-Gaitan, 1991; Lopez et al., 2001). Overcoming these barriers is critical to effective home–school relationships.

Some recent developments have exacerbated these preexisting barriers to effective home–school relationships (Horvat & Baugh, 2015). As schools have embedded technology into every aspect of what they do, the digital divide that runs along class and race lines has influenced the capacity of some families to effectively support student learning. Although the capacity for technology to overcome barriers to access is significant—including, for instance, the use of student information systems, email, chat, teleconferencing, and classroom blogs—challenges to effective use of technology exist both in the school as well as in the home. In the home, low-income parents often have trouble acquiring the necessary resources to effectively use technology and support their children in school. For instance, access to a reliable and sufficiently powerful Internet connection paired with appropriate technology is critical to student learning at home and parent capacity to connect with the school, yet 31% of families making below $50,000 a year do not have broadband access (Horrigan, 2015). In addition, many schools have yet to adopt systematic, culturally relevant training for teachers and parents that would enable them to effectively use technology to track student progress and communicate (Children's Partnership, 2010). To close the technology gap, schools need to integrate technology and train teachers. Families need to have appropriate resources such as high-speed Internet access and computers/mobile devices as well as relevant training on their use that takes into account linguistic and cultural barriers. When these basic prerequisites are met, technology can be used to effectively enhance the student experience and better connect families with schools (Children's Partnership, 2010).

In addition to the escalating demands on schools and parents introduced by expanding technology use in schools, other recent changes have increased pressure also. As the Common Core State Standards and other high-stakes assessments have brought increased pressure to bear on educators, parents have been confronted with supporting the new ways schools deliver content and supporting educators and students in meeting new accountability demands. Additionally, school choice has raised the stakes for parents and further complicated the home–school relationship. The relationship between home and school has become strained by the twin pressures of choice and accountability. As pressure has increased on parents to choose a "good" school for their children and schools are being held accountable for showing increases on high-stakes assessments, the differences between parents who can respond to these new demands and those who cannot become visible and significant, further exacerbating the class differences among parents and complicating the home–school relationship.

Research Synthesis: The Promise of Personalized Learning for Home–School Connections

Dewey (1938/1997) long ago argued that educators must take account of their students' past experiences. Extending this argument to encompass present day realities, it is reasonable to suggest that educators who desire to be successful in personalizing learning for students ought to consider the context of their students' learning, including the influences from the home. The idea that teachers should understand their students' home environments is not new. Teachers have been doing home visits for years. However, as teaching becomes more of a commuting profession, in which the teacher does not reside in the community where he or she teaches but commutes to his or her job, taking time to know and understand the students and the context in which the students live takes on added importance, especially when trying to personalize student learning. This is especially important in low-income and urban areas, where teachers are far less likely to live in the community where they teach, situations in which teachers' day-to-day lived experiences in their own neighborhoods are markedly different from those of their students.

As educators strive to take into account their students' lived realities, developing an understanding of the home environment is a critical first step. As is warranted by the tenets of personalized learning, an educator should strive to understand a student's learning preferences and interests, which can often be best understood by understanding the home environment.

In thinking about how teachers can come to understand their students' lives, the work of Luis Moll and the concept of *funds of knowledge* is especially helpful. Moll and colleagues (Gonzales et al., 1995; Moll & Arnot-Hoppfer 2005; Rios-Aguilar, Kiyama, Gravitt, & Moll, 2011) built an approach to family involvement in schools that goes beyond a simple awareness of difference and provides educators with both the motivation and tools to understand their students more deeply and incorporate this understanding into instructional practices. Although a critical first step for teachers is to recognize and move away from a deficit-based approach to understating their students, the funds of knowledge approach is based on the notions of *confianza, reciprocity*, and *assets*. *Confianza*, the concept of mutual trust, is especially useful. Moll and colleagues argue that this trust is "reestablished or confirmed with each exchange" and leads to the development of long-term relationships (Gonzales et al., 1995, p. 447). Furthermore, these exchanges provide places and moments where and when learning can take place.

> Teachers need not, nor is it possible to, be conversant with all possible cultural backgrounds.

Moll and colleagues argued that educators must develop sociocultural competence in order to work effectively with diverse populations. This sociocultural competence is based on the understanding that all students have "historically accumulated and culturally developed bodies of knowledge and skills" (Moll, Amanti, Neff, & Gonzales, 1992, p. 133) that support their households and individual well-being—or funds of knowledge. This notion that students come to school with culture and funds of knowledge that spring from their lived experience is a critical part of developing cultural competence for teachers (Yosso, 2005). Teachers need not, nor is it possible to, be conversant with all possible cultural backgrounds. However, in order to work well with students from diverse backgrounds, teachers must "develop a critical awareness" (Saathoff, 2015, p. 36) of the ways that culture can be used to distance students from school or, conversely, the ways teachers can tap into students' cultural backgrounds and use them as resources for connecting and understanding one another. Developing this "critical awareness" of the important role culture plays is a key first step.

Once a teacher has developed sociocultural competence—a critical awareness of the role of culture in classrooms and schools generally—it is then possible to implement practices that enable that teacher to develop relationships with students that go beyond the confines of the classroom. When a teacher develops a reciprocal relationship with the student and family that extends beyond the boundaries of the classroom and values the context in which the student lives, a sense of "serious obligations based on the assumption of *confianza* (mutual trust)" (Gonzales et al., 1995, p. 447) can be established. Moll and colleagues (1992) argue that in this environment of trust and reciprocity, the teacher is able to see the student as a whole person, from an asset perspective, rather than as simply a student in the classroom. Such knowledge is critical to crafting a personalized learning agenda with the student and having the capacity to enlist the family in support of this learning.

It is widely recognized that "no 'one size fits all' when it comes to shaping effective family involvement plans" (Knopf & Swick, 2008, p. 421). Effective approaches to improving connections with families include a consideration of accessibility, supports for involvement, and multiple opportunities for families to use their talents and strengths in support of their students (Knopf & Swick, 2008). Thus, the research provides a strong basis for building the capacity of educators to effectively engage families in an environment of trust and reciprocity that values the assets in the home.

Following Wolf (2010), Redding (2014) observes that personalized learning requires the role of the teacher to be redefined. In personalized learning, the teacher is responsible for co-constructing the learning with the student and traveling with the student to understand the pacing, learning preferences, and interests of the student. Moreover, the learning is authentic and project-based—both aspects that are enhanced by an in-depth working knowledge of the student's lived reality.

The role of technology is critical in personalized learning and connecting with parents. Although technology is crucial to the anytime, everywhere nature of personalized learning, the heavy reliance on technology to deliver a personalized education can also prove to be a barrier. In addition to the problematic access imposed by low income, discussed above, the adults in students' lives may have differential experience and comfort with technology. This means that some students will have adults capable of helping them with the technology or with learning that is powered by technology, but other students will be the technology expert in their homes and will not have the support of knowledgeable adults. Thus, although technology is a critical component to the power of personalized learning and is the key driver in building the capacity of educators to engage parents and personalize learning, not all students and their families are equally equipped to benefit.

Preparing Teachers to Engage Families in the Era of Personalized Learning

Although research in the field affirms that creating strong connections between home and school benefits students and that educators must take the lead in building reciprocal trusting relationships with families, current models of teacher training devote little attention to these topics. Despite this lack of attention to the home–family connection in general and to the importance of strong sociocultural competence and home–school connection as they relate to personalized learning in particular, some practices are in place at schools and colleges of education that may improve the capacity of educators to effectively engage parents and other family members.

Internationally recognized authority on home–school–community engagement, J. L. Epstein (2013) notes, "Everyone knows *that* family and community engagement is important" (p. 115), but we have yet to systematically teach future educators *how* to effectively engage families. Teacher education candidates receive precious little training on how to effectively communicate with and engage families. Indeed, teacher education candidates want more training in this area (Ferrera & Ferrar, 2005; Hiatt-Michael, 2008). This training is especially critical for new teachers in high-poverty areas that are culturally dissimilar from their own backgrounds.

A recent study of current teacher education programs (Miller, Lines, Sullivan, & Hermanutz, 2013) found that, by and large, training on family–school partnering issues are infused into other coursework. Although students and faculty believe that developing sociocultural competence is important and believe more training in effectively engaging family members with school is critical, there is a "belief to practice gap" (Miller et al., 2013). That is, while students and faculty believe that engaging parents and other adults is critical, training for teachers in how to actually implement this into their pedagogical practice is insufficient. This is complicated by the demands of state licensure and new curricular demands, such as the Common Core State Standards, that do not recognize the need to actively teach these skills and sensibilities to new teachers. Despite this "belief to practice gap," some practices have proven effective.

Although some programs are attempting to infuse the requisite skills and training into existing curricula, other programs are meeting the issue head on. Rutgers University's Urban Teacher Fellows program expands the traditional one-semester teaching internship into a three-semester teaching residency. In addition, the program offers specialized course offerings focusing specifically on urban teaching. The program culminates with fellows returning to their schools to "run Youth in Action, an after-school enrichment program that trains youth to conduct civic action research in their schools and communities" (Rutgers University, Graduate School of Education, 2015). This program places preservice teachers in schools early in their training and sustains that involvement over time. In addition, it actively supports the conceptualization of students as active participants in their own learning and values the contributions they bring. Rather than tacking on family–school engagement, the concept is embedded in the program and enacts best principles by taking an asset-based reciprocal approach that values the skills and talents of members of the community.

Other programs have adopted less intensive practices that appear to help preservice teachers connect with families. Mehlig and Shumow (2013) found that preservice teachers who participated in teacher–parent role-playing scenarios gained more knowledge about how to connect with parents than students who did not participate. Another curricular approach that holds promise is service learning, which provides opportunities for preservice students to engage with the community surrounding them (Baker & Murray, 2011). Although these student teachers may not ultimately teach in these schools, they gain valuable knowledge about how to connect with parents and others and practice how to do so.

As educational anthropologist Gloria Ladson-Billings (2006) suggests, teacher education programs need to teach preservice teachers how to build critical cultural competence that begins with their awareness of their own culture and the recognition of the important role culture plays in the lives of their students. Further, Ladson-Billings argues that teachers need to develop opportunities to relate to students in non-classroom settings, such as community centers, sports teams, arts organizations, and so forth. Lastly, Ladson-Billings argues that teachers need to be exposed to a global perspective and become aware of the differences among schools around the world. Further research is warranted to determine how best to prepare and support teachers through ongoing professional development for the important work of engaging parents. However, it is clear that the development of a cultural awareness is key to preparing teachers to engage diverse populations.

Conclusion

Personalized learning presents both vast possibilities and significant challenges for educators. As a result of technological advances, the capacity for educators to tailor learning to best match and maximize each student's learning has never been greater. Yet this potential also highlights the inequalities inherent in our current system. One of the most important and glaring of these inequalities is the varying capacity of parents and others in the home to support students in school. This is matched only by the varying degree to which educators are prepared to meet parents and others on their own terms and engage them in their student's learning. Although there is a clear consensus as to the importance of the home–school connection in supporting learning and achievement, the field has yet to systematically address the home–school connection in teacher training or regular, mandated professional development for teachers and other school staff—counselors, nurses, administrators, and aides. Effectively addressing the home–school connection in the years ahead in an environment where personalized learning is taking hold will require attention to the training and development of educators and an expanding capacity to effectively engage parents and others in the home as partners.

Action Principles for States, Districts, and Schools

Action Principles for States

a. Ensure technology is not a barrier to personalized learning for all students. Develop the capacity to advance a technology access agenda in schools with laptop programs and broker Internet access for families.

b. Ensure public spaces (e.g. libraries, community centers, after-school programs) have access to adequate technology. As technology becomes more important, it is critical that our public spaces that serve low-income families provide sufficient access to these resources.

c. Broker partnerships with the private sector to provide adequate connectivity to low-income families. Private sector companies in some areas provide low- or no-cost Internet access to low-income families.

d. Showcase districts and schools that display high levels of sociocultural competence and connection with students' families. There are some excellent examples in the field that should be highlighted and that could provide useful examples to struggling districts.

e. Work with teacher training programs to ensure that family–school engagement competencies are included in curricula. Through targeted policies, state agencies can require the development of curricula to address this important issue.

Action Principles for Districts

a. Work with feeder teacher training programs to build sociocultural competence into the curriculum. The importance of working collaboratively with teacher training programs is greater in an environment with greater differentiation, such as personalized learning.

b. Work with feeder teacher training programs to build in training aimed at developing strong communication and connection skills with families and homes of the students. Identify the essential components of high-quality communication and connection strategies for family outreach.

c. Develop a set of core competencies concerning teacher sociocultural competence and clearly delineate the activities school staff members need to perform to connect effectively with families, such as home visits, attending community events, and working with children and youth outside of school settings.

d. Work with leadership and administration training programs to ensure attention to families is a part of the curricula. Attention to the family–school connection needs to start at the top and be integrated into all levels of schools' staff training.

e. Provide ongoing training and professional development aimed at administrators to assist them in developing their own competence in home–school relations (cultural awareness, sociocultural competence) and develop capacity among their staff. Providing effective training to school leaders will improve their capacity to implement similar training for staff.

Action Principles for Schools

a. Provide induction training for teachers that addresses sociocultural competence. Starting new teachers off on the right foot with background on sociocultural competence is critically important.

b. Provide induction training that targets teachers' capacity to effectively engage parents and families. Starting new teachers off on the right foot with background on parent and family engagement is critically important.

c. Provide ongoing professional development training for teachers on the home–school connection. Continued attention to the home–school connection will improve the capacity of school staff to effectively engage families.

d. Provide relevant, ongoing professional development for nonteaching school staff on the home–school connection. All levels of school staff need to understand the critical importance of the family–school connection.

References

Auerbach, S. (2010). *Beyond coffee with the principal: Toward leadership for authentic school–family partnerships.* Paper presented at the 15th International Roundtable on School, Family and Community Partnerships, Denver, CO.

Baker, P. H., & Murray, M. M. (2011). Building Community Partnerships: Learning to Serve While Learning to Teach. *School Community Journal, 21*(1), 113–129. Retrieved from http://www.schoolcommunitynetwork.org/SCJ.aspx

Children's Partnership. (2010). Empowering parents through technology to improve the odds for children. *Digital Opportunity for Youth Issue Brief, 7,* 1–15.

Crozier, G. (1999). Is it a case of "We know when we're not wanted"? The parents' perspective on parent–teacher roles and relationships. *Educational Research, 41*(3), 315–328.

Crozier, G., & Davies, J. (2007). Hard to reach parents or hard to reach schools? A discussion of home–school relations, with particular reference to Bangladeshi and Pakistani parents. *British Educational Journal, 33*(3), 295–313.

Cutler, W. (2000). *Parents and schools.* Chicago. IL: University of Chicago Press.

Delgado-Gaitan, C. (1991). Involving parents in the schools: A process of empowerment. *American Journal of Education, 100*(1), 20–46.

Dewey, J. (1938/1997). *Experience and education.* New York, NY: The Free Press.

Epstein, J. L. (2001/2011). *School, family and community partnerships: Preparing educators and improving schools.* Boulder, CO: Westview Press.

Epstein, J. L. (2013). Ready or not? Preparing future educators for school, family, and community partnerships. *Teaching Education, 24*(2), 115–118.

Fan, X., & Chen, M. (2001). Parental involvement and students' academic achievement: A meta-analysis. *Educational Psychology Review, 13*(1), 1–22.

Ferrera, M. M., & Ferrar, P. J. (2005). Parents as partners: Raising awareness as a teacher preparation program. *The Clearing House, A Journal of Educational Strategies, Issues, and Ideas, 79*(2), 77–81.

Gonzales, N., Moll, L. C., Tenery, M. T., Rivera, A., Rendon, P., Gonzales, R., & Amanti, C. (1995). Funds of knowledge for teaching in Latino households. *Urban Education, 29*(4), 443–470.

Henderson, A., & Mapp, K. (2002). *A new wave of evidence: The impact of school, family, and community connections on student achievement.* Austin, TX: Southwest Educational Development Laboratory.

Henderson, A. T., Mapp, K. L., Johnson, V. R., & Davies, D. (2007). *Beyond the bake sale.* New York, NY: The New Press.

Hiatt-Michael, D. (2006). Reflections and directions on research related to family–community involvement in schooling. *School Community Journal, 16*(1), 7–30.

Hiatt-Michael, D. B. (2008). Families, their children's education and the public school: An historical review. *Marriage and Family Review, 43*(1), 39–66.

Horrigan, J. B. (2015). *The numbers behind the broadband "homework gap."* Retrieved from http://www.pewresearch.org/fact-tank/2015/04/20/the-numbers-behind-the-broadband-homework-gap/

Horvat, E. M. (2011). Pioneer parents and creating pathways for involvement: A historical case study of school change and collective parental involvement. In C. Hands & L. Hubbard (Eds.), *Including families and communities in urban education* (pp. 161–185). New York, NY: Information Age Publishing.

Horvat, E. M., & Baugh, D. E. (2015). Not all parents make the grade in today's schools: Education reforms have added choice, raised standards, and made schools safer places, but parents haven't acquired the necessary skills to navigate this new education landscape. *Phi Delta Kappan, 96*(7), 8–13.

Horvat, E. M., Weininger, E. B., & Lareau, A. (2003). From social ties to social capital: Class differences in the relationships between schools and parent networks. *American Education Research Journal, 40*(2), 319–351.

Knopf, H. T., & Swick, K. (2008). Using our understanding of families to strengthen family involvement. *Early Childhood Education Journal, 35*(5), 419–427.

Ladson-Billings, G. (2006). It's not the culture of poverty, it's the poverty of culture: The problem with teacher education. *Anthropology and Education Quarterly, 37*(2), 104–109.

Lareau, A. (2000). *Home advantage.* New York, NY: Rowman and Littlefield.

Lareau, A., & Horvat, E. M. (1999) Moments of social inclusion and exclusion: Race, class, and cultural capital in family–school relationships. *Sociology of Education, 72*(1), 37–53.

Lightfoot, S. L. (2004). *The essential conversation.* New York, NY: Ballantine Books.

Lopez, G. R., Scriber, J. D., & Mahitivanichcha, K. (2001). Redefining parental involvement: Lessons from high-performing migrant-impacted schools. *American Educational Research Journal, 38*(2), 253–288.

Mehlig, L., & Shumow, L. (2013). How is my child doing?: Preparing pre-service teachers to engage parents through assessment. *Teaching Education, 24*(2), 181–194.

Miller, G. E., Lines, C., Sullivan, E., & Hermanutz, K. (2013). Preparing educators to partner with families. *Teaching Education, 24*(2), 150–163.

Moll, L. C., & Arnot-Hoppfer, E. (2005). Sociocultural competence in teacher education. *Journal of Teacher Education, 56*(3), 242–247.

Moll, L. C., Amanti, C., Neff, D., & Gonzales, N. (1992). Funds of knowledge for teaching: Using a qualitative approach to connect homes and classrooms. *Theory Into Practice, 31*(2), 132–141.

Redding, S. (2014). Getting personal: The promise of personalized learning. In M. Murphy, S. Redding, & J. Twyman (Eds.), *The handbook on innovations in learning* (pp. 113–130). Charlotte, NC: Information Age Publishing. Retrieved from http://www.centeril.org/handbook/Getting_Personal_SA.pdf

Rios-Aguilar, C., Kiyama, J. M., Gravitt, M., & Moll, L. C. (2011). Funds of knowledge for the poor and forms of capital for the rich? A capital approach to examining funds of knowledge. *Theory and Research in Education, 9*(2), 163–184.

Rutgers University, Graduate School of Education. (2015). *GSE's Urban Teaching Fellows Program* [webpage]. New Brunswick, NJ. Retrieved from http://gse.rutgers.edu/content/gses-urban-teaching-fellows-program

Saathoff, S. D. (2015). Funds of knowledge and community cultural wealth: Exploring how preservice teachers can work effectively with Mexican and Mexican-American students. *Critical Questions in Education, 6*(2), 30–40.

Smith, J., Wohlstetter, P., Kuzin, C. A., & DePedro, K. (2011). Parent involvement in urban charter schools: New strategies for increasing participation. *School Community Journal, 21*(1), 71–94. Retrieved from http://www.schoolcommunitynetwork.org/SCJ.aspx

Waller, W. (1932/1965). *The sociology of teaching.* New York, NY: Wiley.

Weiss, H. B., Bouffard, S. M., Bridglall, B. L., & Gordon, E. W. (2009). Reframing family involvement in education: Supporting families to support educational equity. *Equity Matters: Research Review, No. 5.* New York, NY: Teachers College, Columbia University.

Wilder, S. (2014). Effects of parental involvement on academic achievement: A meta-synthesis. *Educational Review, 66*(3), 377–397.

Wolf, M. (2010). *Innovate to educate: System [re]design for personalized learning.* A report from the 2010 symposium. Washington, DC: Software & Information Industry Association.

Yosso, T. J. (2005). Whose culture has capital? A critical race theory discussion of community cultural wealth. *Race, Ethnicity, and Education, 81*(1), 69–91.

Relationships in Personalized Learning:
Teacher, Student, and Family

Patricia A. Edwards

Rich, personalized relationships thrived among the teacher, student, and family in the segregated South, and several researchers have provided in-depth and insightful accounts into this historical phenomenon (Edwards, 1993a; Irvine & Irvine, 1983; Lightfoot, 1978; Siddle-Walker, 1996). By documenting African American teachers' voices at the Caswell County Training School, Siddle-Walker (1996) paints a vivid picture of traits, policies, and support that allowed the personal, intellectual, and social development of students. For example, teachers were active community members as well as powerful and positive role models. Teachers taught, but this activity involved much more than instructing students in a given subject. Faculty members served as advisers to extracurricular clubs, spent funds for transporting students to after-school competitions, and opened their homes to students. Teachers also transcended the boundaries of their profession by visiting their pupils' homes and churches, and many taught Sunday school at churches where their students attended. These visits blurred the lines of authority between teacher, parent, and preacher and functioned as a community-sanctioned safety net. Billingsley (1968) and Belt-Beyan (2004) reiterated this point. According to Billingsley (1968), before desegregation, the African American community was an institution to which parents and children specifically looked for strength, hope, and security:

> In every aspect of the child's life a trusted elder, neighbor, Sunday school teacher, school teacher, or other community member might instruct, discipline, assist, or otherwise guide the young of a given family. Second, as role models, community members show an example to and interest in the young people. Third, as advocates, they actively intercede with major segments of society (a responsibility assumed by professional educators) to help young members of particular families find opportunities that might otherwise be closed to them. Fourth, as supportive figures, they simply inquire about the progress of the young, take special interest in them. Fifth, in the formal roles of teacher, leader, elder, they serve youth generally as part of the general role or occupation. (p. 99).

Handbook on Personalized Learning for States, Districts, and Schools, pages 189–204
189

Through these varied roles, community members set the stage for personalized learning. Belt-Beyan (2004) revealed that, through local organizations such as the church and the school, the African American community represented, enacted, and inscribed uniquely stylized characteristics and values. The core values of intellectualism, freedom, collective success, and hard work were essential to the African American community. Belt-Beyan also noted that "children, as well as adults [in the African American community] were expected to be resourceful and ever watchful for opportunities to meet any of their life's goals" (Belt-Beyan, 2004, p. 162).

The rallying call in segregated communities was that education would do much to uplift the race and help establish a necessary and viable separate social and cultural existence. For example, Belt-Beyan (2004) revealed that "many [African American] parents expressed the beliefs that even if they did not learn to read and write themselves, they would have considered themselves successful if their children did" (p. 163). Gadsden (1993) noted: "Literacy and education are valued and valuable possessions that African American families have respected, revered, and sought as a means to personal freedom and communal hope, from enslavement to the present" (p. 352). Literacy, as Harris (1990) found, has been attached historically to the uplifting of Black people—uplifting steeped in understanding the traditions and beliefs of literacy and education as communal knowledge and hence group strength.

Through the years, these community-oriented values, beliefs, and dispositions have been encoded in long-standing cultural sayings such as "each one, teach one" and "we lift as we climb." Moreover, the standards of community success were transmitted through the African American literacy traditions, which were built on narratives by slaves or former slaves such as Phyllis Wheatley and Frederick Douglas (Belt-Beyan, 2004). Some of today's researchers draw on three frameworks to describe the personalized relationships that existed among teachers, students, and families in the segregated South: (a) community of possibility (Belt-Beyan, 2004; Billingsley, 1968), community of cultural wealth (Oliver & Shapiro, 1995; Yosso, 2005), and funds of knowledge (Gonzales, Moll, & Amanti, 2005; Moll, Amanti, Neff, & Gonzales, 1992).[1]

I was born and raised in a midsized southwestern Georgia community. I entered school a few years after the 1954 U.S. Supreme Court landmark decision *Brown v. Topeka Board of Education*, which declared segregation in education unconstitutional. I grew up in a stable, close-knit neighborhood where I knew many eyes watched me and that neighbors would tell my mama when I misbehaved. My elementary school principal and most of

---

[1]**Community of possibility** can be characterized as a place where everyone feels at home, where people care about community life and want to contribute, where people in the community serve as role models and encourage their youth that they can become what they want to become and that the sky is the limit.

Yosso's six-part **cultural wealth model** includes six types of capital that educational leaders may use to frame their interactions with students. The six forms of cultural capital are aspirational, linguistic, familial, social, navigational, and resistance. Yosso argues that all forms of capital can be used to empower individuals. Yosso designed this model to capture the talents, strengths, and experiences that students of color bring with them to their college environment.

Funds of knowledge is defined by researchers Moll, Amanti, Neff, and Gonzalez (2001) "to refer to the historically accumulated and culturally developed bodies of knowledge and skills essential for household or individual functioning and well-being" (p. 133).

my teachers lived in my neighborhood. Consequently, there were many opportunities outside of school for my principal and teachers to talk with my parents about my progress and behavior in school. My principal, teachers, and neighbors, as well as my parents, all shared and reinforced similar school and family values.

Before school desegregation, African American parents had a place in the school. They felt comfortable coming and going to the school at their leisure. The faces of teachers and administrators were familiar to them because, in many instances, the teachers and administrators were their friends, neighbors, and fellow church members. Parents could voice their concerns, opinions, and fears about their children's educational achievement, and teachers and administrators listened and responded.

For many African American parents whose children attended segregated schools, parent involvement connoted active participation, collaboration, and co-generative discussions with teachers and administrators. It meant African American parents had some control of the school and school systems that helped shape the character and minds of their children. For example, teaching personnel were accountable to the community and therefore had to teach effectively if they wanted to retain their jobs. School

> "distribution of power among schools, families, and communities is a crucial piece of the complex puzzle leading toward educational success for all children" (Lightfoot, 1980).

performance was relevant to the life experiences and needs of African American children and provided motivation to learn. African American children developed self-worth and dignity through knowledge of their history and culture and through the images provided by community leaders and teachers. African American parents had control through coalition. The schools maintained continuous communication with African American parents and developed with these parents a structure that included them in the governing of the schools. African American parents could exert influence to protect their most precious resources, their children. This involvement assisted schools in providing a more relevant education for students.

In a 1993 article published in *Educational Policy* titled "Before and After School Desegregation: African-American Parents' Involvement in Schools" (see Edwards, 1993a), I had the opportunity to interview three people: my mother, a first-grade teacher, and an elementary school principal, Mr. Eramus Dent. My mother was president of the parent–teacher association (PTA) throughout my entire six years of elementary school. When my mother was asked by Mr. Dent, the teachers, and the parents to run for PTA president, she was honored to do so. My mother knew my elementary school principal—Mr. Dent—before I entered school, and she knew what was expected of me at each grade level.

The interviews with my mother, first-grade teacher, and elementary school principal provided an insightful look into the personal relationships that existed among parents, teachers, and the principal in this segregated Southern community. These interviews also demonstrated that the close relationships in my elementary school community allowed for power and responsibility to be shared among home, school, and community. As Lightfoot (1980) revealed, the "distribution of power among schools, families, and communities is a crucial piece of the complex puzzle leading toward educational success for all children" (p. 17). In segregated settings, there was the recognition that most parents were eager for their children to learn, grow, succeed, and feel accepted in school. Also, there was consensus that schools, parents, and the community should work together to promote the health, well-being, and learning of all students. When schools actively involve parents and engage community resources, they are able to respond more effectively to the needs of children and families (for further information, see Edwards, 1993a).

Pleas for Home–School Collaboration

After school desegregation, researchers began to plead for educators to develop a closer working relationship with the home. Fletcher (1966) was quick to build the case that "Education is simply not something which is provided either by teachers in schools or by parents and family members in the home. It must be a continuing cultivation of the child's experiences in which both schools and families jointly take part" (p. 66). Potter (1989) continued this line of thought by candidly stating, "Teachers have the important responsibility of working with and relating to families, not just children" (p. 21). Seeley (1989) argues that "the crucial issue in successful learning is not home or school—teacher or student—but the relationship between them. Learning takes place where there is a productive learning relationship" (p. 11). In Gordon's (1979) plea to educators to develop a closer working relationship with the families, he stated:

> Parent involvement holds the greatest promise for meeting the needs of the child—it can be a reality rather than a professional dream. Of course, the bottom line is not only that involving parents holds the most realistic hope for individual children but also it serves as a hope for renewing the public's faith in education. This faith is needed if public schools are to continue as a strong institution in our democratic form of government, which, ironically, can only survive with a strong educational program. (pp. 2–3)

"Teachers have the important responsibility of working with and relating to families, not just children" (Potter, 1989).

Berger (1991) made a very realistic and logical appeal to educators regarding the need to make a commitment to "parent education" or "parent involvement." She stated: "Schools have more contact with families than any other public agency [and the] school and home...have a natural opportunity to work together" (p. 118). I believe that learning about students' home literacy environments and learning how to interact with diverse families are the lifelines for creating better family–school partnerships. These lifelines will improve the academic achievement of all children regardless of race or economic status. Furthermore, today's teachers must make a concerted effort to reach out to diverse family groups even if they do not share the same heritage (Edwards, 2004). However, it should be noted that collaboration may not seem very natural to teachers today, who are more likely than ever in our nation's history to live in communities different and distant from where they work, speak a different language, represent different cultural backgrounds from their students, and may not have many natural, everyday encounters with parents.

Recognizing Parent Differences

In thinking about parent involvement and developing family–school partnerships, educators must understand that parents are not all the same. Parents bring their own strengths and weaknesses, complexities, problems, and questions; because of this, teachers must work with them and see them as more than "just parents." In my work with parents, I coined two terms, *differentiated parenting* and *parentally appropriate*, to help teachers find new ways to think about parents (Edwards, 2004, 2009). I proposed the concept of *differentiated parenting* "as a way to urge schools not to place all parents into one basket" (Edwards, 2011, p. 113).

Although parents might have the same goals for their children (i.e., to read, write, and spell well), they might have different ideas about how they can help their children accomplish these goals (Edwards, 2004, 2009). *Parentally appropriate* means that, because parents are different, tasks and activities must be compatible with their capabilities. For example, parents who do not read well might be very intimidated and frustrated by teachers who expect them to read to their children every night, and teachers might need to select other activities parents can do to support their children in developing reading fluency (Edwards, 2004, 2009). Parents who work multiple jobs or who are raising their children by themselves might not be able to attend parent conferences after school or in the early evenings, and teachers might need to make other arrangements to accommodate them. When teachers plan activities and tasks designed to engage parents in collaboration and support of their child's learning, most parents will want to successfully accomplish them. Teachers might work to provide as much support as possible to assist parents in completing these activities and tasks.

Creating a Personalized Learning Environment in a Professional Development School

In the fall of 1989, I joined the Michigan State University faculty, where I continued to expand my research agenda on creating a structure for families to be involved in the literacy development of their children. This agenda includes as well the pursuit of a professional mission involving locating and testing ways to communicate with urban families. At Morton Professional Development School (PDS)[2] (a pseudonym) located in Lansing, Michigan, I conceptualized and served as principal investigator of the Home Literacy Project from 1990 until its conclusion in 1993. Many of the concepts implemented then are still integral to the school. The goals of the project were to (a) respect the multiple literacy environments the families represented; (b) become knowledgeable of the family's capability, responsibility, and willingness to be involved in the school; (c) help educators recognize that not all families are the same; (d) help schools reach out to diverse families in new and different ways; (e) help educators create a personalized learning environment among the teacher, student, and families that many expressed they had witnessed in years past; and (f) develop a scope and sequence of family involvement activities coordinated around the grade level literacy curriculum. As part of that project, I created what I called a *scope and sequence of family involvement*. At each grade level, I developed family involvement activities coordinated around the grade level literacy curriculum. Family participation in these literacy activities was critical to their child's success. I learned that families were composed of busy people and that I needed to consider their work schedules and other personal and professional commitments in order to develop approaches to and expectations for parent involvement.

---

[2]Professional development schools (PDSs) are formed through partnerships between professional education programs and P–12 schools. PDS partnerships have a four-fold mission: the preparation of new teachers, faculty development, inquiry directed at the improvement of practice, and enhanced student achievement. PDSs are often compared to teaching hospitals.

Before the Home Literacy Project began, the existing parent involvement activities at Morton PDS varied in substance and duration, much like the conventional activities described in the literature (Delgado-Gaitan, 1991; Epstein, 1987; Hess & Shipman, 1965; Lareau, 1989, 2000). At Morton PDS, when teachers solicited parent participation in classrooms, they often wanted parents to perform mechanical tasks, such as typing, editing, or binding children's stories. Such tasks offered little opportunity for significant involvement in the curriculum, required the availability of parents during working hours, and involved no opportunity or expectation for reciprocity (i.e., seeking information or feedback from parents as "experts" on their children). Annual open houses and semiannual parent–teacher conferences provided time for parents to see their child's classroom and get a brief overview of subject matter covered in a specific grade level. Teachers and administrators had set up PTA or parent–teacher organization meetings, held parent–teacher conferences, made home visits, and encouraged parents to attend field trips and student performances. Although these events brought families and teachers together, they did not necessarily bring them together around specific literacy events or involve families in ways that would enable them to support children's literacy learning (Edwards, 1991).

New Parent Involvement Structures Emerge

Much has been written about the benefits of involving families in their children's literacy development (Edwards, 1991, 2004, 2009; Epstein, 2001; France & Hager, 1993; Handel, 1992). A major focus of this work has centered around the question of how educators and families can better understand, cooperate, and communicate with each other in order to more effectively work together to support children's acquisition of literacy. One of the most important themes that has surfaced in the literature is the need for improving current structures for family involvement in schools (Edwards, 1996; Fear & Edwards, 1995). A second important theme is that families need to be heard; they need to be given time as well as opportunities to share their ideas, questions, and insights with teachers and administrators (Lynch, 1992). Simply put, teachers, administrators, and parents should become communicating allies in the education of all children.

At Morton PDS, the home literacy project can be defined as a curriculum-centered parent involvement project. Pizzo (1990) reports that parents should sustain strong attachments to their young children and advocate for them in the face of exceptionally adverse circumstances. Supporting families provides a boost to the overall development of children. It seems reasonable to conclude then that parents should be involved in their children's school curriculum. Thirty years ago, Seefeldt (1985) stated that schools should communicate with parents through the curriculum. She noted that educators should do the following:

> Capitalize on the curriculum as a means of communicating with parents. It is an ongoing way to keep parents totally informed of their child's day, the school's goals and objectives, and the meaning of early childhood education. It's one way to begin to establish close, meaningful communication with busy parents...remember—informed, involved parents, those who are aware of what their children do in an early childhood program, are also supportive parents. (p. 25)

Researchers such as Keenan, Willett, and Solsken (1993) also believe that schools should communicate through the curriculum. The aims of their curriculum project were to strengthen the children's academic learning, foster school–home collaboration, and construct a multicultural community strong enough to nurture the diverse children of the urban elementary classrooms where they worked. Keenan and colleagues (1993) believed that the project's focus on communication and meaning in the language arts provided a rich context for children's learning, but they also saw opportunities for further enriching their learning through new forms of parent participation in the curriculum.

Cummins (1986) argues that efforts to improve the education of children from dominated societal groups have been largely unsuccessful because the relationship between teachers and students and between schools and communities have remained unchanged. In his view, "The required changes involve personal redefinitions of the way classroom teachers interact with the children and communities they serve" (Cummins, 1986, p. 18). He posits that school programs will be more successful at empowering minority children if (a) students' language and culture are incorporated into the school program, (b) community participation is encouraged as an integral component of children's education, (c) the pedagogy promotes intrinsic motivation on the part of students to use language actively to generate their own knowledge, and (d) professionals involved in assessment become advocates for students

> Unlike other approaches that focus on changes that families must make to support schools, I begin with ways that schools must change to support families.

rather than legitimizing the location of the "problem" in the students. Although, like Cummins, I am particularly concerned with the success of children from dominated societal groups, I believe that his work speaks to school–home collaboration more generally and provides directions for raising all children in our increasingly diverse and complex villages. Unlike other approaches that focus on changes that families must make to support schools, I begin with ways that schools must change to support families.

Teachers and the whole school "family" have the responsibility for encouraging and facilitating parents' exposure to and integration into their children's classroom curriculum (Beane, 1990, p. 362). According to Knapp, Turnbull, and Shields (1990), all students must learn the culture of the school while they are attempting to master academic tasks. This is especially so for disadvantaged learners. Lyn Corno (1989) summarizes well why the home and school should communicate around curricular issues, noting:

> With some shared understanding of their commonalities and differences, schools and homes should be able to work together to support each other in the development of a literate populace. There is, indeed, evidence that this is already occurring in certain enlightened contemporary homes and classrooms. It seems that the polarization of these subcultures may be transformed in important ways, and that families and classrooms wishing to move in this direction can benefit by a better understanding of the other's special traditions. Becoming literate about classrooms, then, is also in part becoming literate about the home; for this view suggests that effective classrooms are a blend of classroom and home—of family and knowledge workplace. (p. 41)

At Morton PDS, in our move toward a personalized learning environment, I assisted the teachers with developing a scope and sequence of parent involvement activities grade by grade around curriculum issues. I shared with the teachers that, even though school begins in August, very few schools provided a detailed schedule of literacy activities for parents throughout the school year in August (see Edwards, 2004). As a result, parent involvement did not become for families a set of structured activities that they could expect to participate in throughout the year (see Edwards, 2004). Advice to teachers included "to note that when children enter school not only are they affected by the new school environment, but their parents are as well" (Edwards, 1993b, p. 1). Also, I reminded them of a statement by Fletcher (1966), which I referenced earlier in this chapter: "Education is simply not something which is provided either by teachers in schools or by parents and family members in the home. It must be a *continuing* cultivation of the child's experiences in which *both* schools and families jointly take part" (p. 189).

I informed teachers that I believe that a good relationship between parents, child, and teacher should be a priority. Potter (1989) echoed my position by arguing that "the teacher should strive to develop an environment where there is a *participatory role* for the family, which facilitates the parent–teacher–child relationship and so enables the teaching and evaluation of the child to be appropriate and just" (p. 21).

Based on our initial conversations about parents' struggles to support their children's learning, I helped the teachers organize grade-level parent informant literacy group meetings, in which teachers and parents collaborated on a grade-level literacy project. The purpose of the face-to-face monthly group grade-level meetings was to provide an opportunity for teachers, parents, and me to participate in conversations that would facilitate parent understanding of how their children were developing as readers and writers. The parent informant meetings established a predictable structure for parents to communicate information about how their children responded to instruction in school. Parents not only became more knowledgeable about the school curriculum, but they also contributed information about their children's struggles, concerns, and progress. They began to inform other parents and teachers about their children's desires, and they made sense of the topics, audiences, and kernel issues in children's lives. Many parents gave each other ideas about how they wrote with their children and what ideas had stirred their children's curiosity. Parents became more than recipients and overseers of assignments. Their creative responses also changed the dynamics of the informant group. There was a mutual sense of pride and enjoyment shared by parents and professional educators alike. It should be noted that, in addition to meeting with the grade-level groups monthly, we communicated with specific parents within the grade-level group individually by email, telephone, or other means. This was another way we tried to develop a personalized learning relationship with parents centered on their children's literacy development.

In addition, I encouraged the teachers to collect parent stories so they could get an in-depth understanding of how parents constructed literacy learning for their children at home.[3] From the information the teachers and I accrued from the grade-level parent informant literacy group meetings and from the collection of parent stories, we then organized a scope and sequence of parent involvement built around the school's curriculum (see Table 1).[4] To begin the discussion on a scope and sequence of curriculum-based parent involvement with an emphasis on personalized learning, I asked the teachers a series of questions: (a) What does an elementary teacher need to know at each grade level (K–5)

[3]**Parent stories**—Narratives gained from open-ended interviews. In these interviews, parents respond to questions designed to provide information about traditional and nontraditional early literacy activities and experiences that have happened in the home.

[4]**Scope and sequence**—Grade-level family involvement activities that are developmentally based on shared decision making and built around the elementary literacy curriculum.

about how to involve parents in the literacy support of their children? (b) What should be the "scope and sequence of parent involvement" around literacy from kindergarten to fifth grade? and (c) What specific literacy activities should teachers ask parents to participate in at home or school with their children? In the next section, I provide a more detailed account of what occurred in three of these grade-level parent informant meetings (i.e., kindergarten, first, and second grade).

Table 1. Scope and Sequence of Curriculum-Based Parent Involvement at Morton Professional Development School

Grade	Parent Involvement Activity
Kindergarten	Sharing time
First	Emergent literacy
Second	Reading and writing connections
Third	Writing process
Fourth	Content area reading
Fifth	Content area reading

Kindergarten Project

I asked the two kindergarten teachers, Mrs. Bowker and Mrs. Dozier (pseudonyms), where they found dissatisfaction with their programs. Both immediately said they were dissatisfied with sharing time. After thinking about the teachers' comments, I recommended we work together on involving parents in helping their children construct sharing time conversations. They agreed.

The teachers wanted the children to stay on the topic so they could follow what the children were saying and so that they could ask the children questions. These kindergarten teachers highlighted an issue that Michaels (1981, 1986) raised in her research. She reported that when the children's discourse style matched the teacher's own literate style and expectations, collaboration was rhythmically synchronized and allowed for informal practice and instruction in the development of a literate discourse style. For these children, sharing time could be seen as a kind of oral preparation for literacy. In contrast, she noted that when the child's narrative style was in variance with the teacher's expectations, collaboration was often unsuccessful. Michaels (1981) also observed:

> The discourse of the white children tended to be tightly organized, centering on a single, clearly identifiable topic, a discourse style..."topic-centered." This style closely matched the teacher's own discourse style as well as her notions about what constituted good sharing....In contrast to a topic-centered style, the black children and particularly the black girls, were far more likely to use a "topic-associating" style, that is, discourse consisting of a series of implicitly associated personal anecdotes. (pp. 428–429)

In their experiences, Mrs. Bowker and Mrs. Dozier observed that White children as well as Black children failed to use a topic-centered style during sharing time. Based on this observation, Mrs. Bowker and Mrs. Dozier recognized the need to make changes in their sharing time program. The teachers organized the sharing time topics within units in the following categories: Self-Awareness (This Is Me, My Neighborhood, My Favorite Color, All About Me, and My Year), Books and Writing (My Favorite Book, A Story by Me, The Public Library, Finger Puppets, and Making a List), Holidays (My Favorite

Thanksgiving, My Favorite Holiday Season, Art Project, and A Valentine for Someone), Measuring (World's Greatest Cook), Senses (Mystery Tastes, Mystery Smells, Things to Feel and Guess, and What Is It?), Environment (Nature Hunt, The Weather, Plants, and I Found a Leaf), Families (This Is My Family and All About My Family), and Animals (Bears, Dogs, Cats, Snakes, and so on). To monitor parent–child sharing time conversations, I recommended that the teachers send a tape recorder home and to record the children's sharing time presentations at school. This information allowed teachers to assist both children and parents with oral language development.

With my assistance, Mrs. Bowker and Mrs. Dozier organized parent forums to explain their ideas about sharing time and address the differences between sharing time and homework. These forums became a place for informal conversation and the exchange of ideas. The teachers asked several parents to talk about how they made time each week for sharing time preparation. The conversation proved helpful for parents. Many commented that they learned strategies for assisting their young children with sharing time.

In the past, Mrs. Bowker and Mrs. Dozier assumed that low-income parents did not take the time to prepare their children for sharing time. They further noted:

> The sharing time topics that we included in our new approach are topics that middle-class parents normally talk to children about. And these conversations help them to grow into good readers and good writers because they have this kind of information. We have many young and teenage parents that didn't have examples of good parenting, so we've tried to create a structure that makes conversation in the home a natural part of what we do. (Edwards, 1996, p. 348)

What Mrs. Bowker and Mrs. Dozier did by creating a structure for sharing time is supported by Epstein (1988) in her warning that "unless we examine both family and school structures and practices, we will continue to receive contradictory and often false messages about the capabilities of unconventional, minority, and hard to reach families" (p. 58). In the beginning, the teachers made assumptions about low-income parents but did not create a structure that would help these parents understand the school structures and practices (for further information on the sharing time project, see Edwards, 1996).

First-Grade Project

I asked first-grade teachers at Morton PDS to describe their perceptions of parent involvement. The teachers responded by voicing frustration because they said that parents lacked respect for their children's gradual movement toward becoming readers and writers. After several discussions with the three first-grade teachers, I was able to help them understand the importance of closely examining their conversations with parents about reading and writing. I was also able to help teachers see that they needed to develop specific ways to help parents understand what was happening in first grade. I reminded the teachers that the children were trying to construct an understanding of reading and writing, but that it was important to help their parents construct an understanding of how their children were developing as readers and writers (for more information, see Edwards, Fear, & Harris, 1994).

The purpose of the first-grade parent informant literacy group was to provide an opportunity for teachers, parents, and me to participate in conversations that would facilitate parents' understanding of how their children were developing as readers and writers. We used Marie M. Clay's books, *What Did I Write? Beginning Writing Behaviour* (1975) and *Reading: The Patterning of Complex Behaviour* (1979) as guides for helping parents understand how their children were developing as readers and writers.

Second-Grade Project

Similar to the first-grade teachers, second-grade teachers at Morton PDS were unsure of how they wanted to involve parents in the literacy support of their children. Teachers struggled to find ways to connect parent involvement activities to the curricula in their classrooms. After multiple discussions with the second-grade group, we decided to help parents understand the connections between reading and writing curriculum. The parents and teachers discussed children's interests, successes, struggles, and uses of writing at school. Some parents joined in to affirm their children's growth and to describe their children's writing initiatives at home; others raised concerns about their children's reticence and lack of initiative. Teachers shared their work, plans, questions, and uncertainties about differences in students' development as writers.

Parents were truly involved in the group and the group process. The curriculum was not simply handed out, and parents were not just told about how their children were learning reading, writing, English grammar, and spelling. Instead, the informant meetings—in conjunction with the audiotapes, videotapes, invitations to the classroom, and journals— created an organizational structure for parent interpretation and expression. Parents could listen in on how their child's interests and problems were addressed during in-school writing conferences. More important, the videotaped instruction help parents visualize and consequently discuss the community of readers and writers that teachers were attempting to build within the classroom. By changing the organizational structure of parent meetings and allocating resources to help parents gain access to information about the school, parents participated in more meaningful ways. They contributed and developed an interpretation of their children's reactions to school assignments, classmates, and their teacher as they developed strong parent–teacher and parent–parent relationships.

Parents began to raise questions about how they might respond to their children's writing, topic selections, and mechanical errors. These questions added a new level of complexity in the writing instruction taking place in the classroom. These children in the second-grade classroom had developed as very different writers and gained expertise in several different writing genres. For example, one student wrote a fantasy story that included a dialogue between a fork and a spoon, another student wrote about his goals as a Cub Scout, and another wrote about how he cared for his "pet slug." In response to parents' questions, the team designed a method to show parents how teachers responded in school to children, depending on the child's development and writing purposes.

The teachers began to audiotape conferences with individual students during their regular classroom writing conferences. These tapes were sent home in the "traveler's briefcase" with a brief message to the parent at the end of the tape. Each child took a tape recorder and tape home for three days on a rotating basis. Parents could hear examples of how teachers were responding to their children, as well as the contents and mechanics in their children's writing. A parent journal was also sent home with the tape, and parents were encouraged to respond to the child's writing and also to the teacher's conference either orally or in writing or both, depending on their preferences.

The impact of these changes reached the parent community and the teachers and had an effect on the entire Morton PDS staff. In response to the information and questions shared in the informant journals and meetings, additional times were scheduled, attendance increased, and parents began to ask more questions. Parents asked the team to continue the project with their children during the next year in third grade.

Concluding Comments

The personalized relationships that existed among the teacher, student, and family in the segregated South described at the beginning of this chapter highlighted the crucial roles that teachers, community members, and parents played in children's learning. In these communities, teachers taught students, but their teaching and interactions did not stop at the classroom door. Teachers' involvement in the local community and close relationships with parents helped children to grow as students and as individuals.

During the Home Literacy Project at Morton PDS described in the middle of this chapter, teachers worked to build closer relationships with the families of the children in the classrooms. They put structures into place that encouraged parents, caregivers, and community members to become communicating allies in the education of all children. The personalized relationships that emerged in many of the teachers' classrooms supported students' academic success. Just as in the segregated South, teachers' relationships with families and communities led to personalized learning environments that extended beyond the walls of the school and fostered students' personal and academic development.

Action Principles for States, Districts, and Schools

Action Principles for States

a. Require teacher preparation programs to have pre- and in-service teachers participate in cross-cultural conversations and interactions.

b. Require teacher preparation programs to provide training for pre- and in-service teachers to effectively work with parents.

c. Develop guidelines for helping schools to create family-friendly schools.

d. Require teacher preparation programs to integrate community action projects in their educational programs in order to connect with and support community agencies (i.e., service-learning opportunities).

e. Develop guidelines for prioritizing issues of equity, diversity, and language differences in funding opportunities.

Action Principles for Districts

a. Encourage parents and students to create a vision statement with schools about family involvement.

b. Support and use parent focus groups to make important decisions at the schools.

c. Encourage family events and invite parent stories.

d. Determine parent capabilities, interests, willingness, and responsibility in order to make home-to-school connections.

e. Conduct a school climate assessment survey to understand family perceptions and open dialogue about family involvement.

Action Principles for Schools

Although state and local education agencies have an important role to play in supporting parent involvement, it is ultimately the schools that provide the front line contact with parents. The following action principles will help schools to proactively engage families in their children's education:

a. Define parent involvement so that everyone understands what it means in your school. For instance, you need to ensure that the teachers' and school's definition of family involvement do not conflict. In a broad sense, parent involvement includes home-based activities that relate to children's education in school. It can also include school-based activities in which the parents actively participate, either during the school day or in the evening.

b. Assess parent involvement climate. Many of the parents at your school may not become involved if they do not feel that the school climate—the social and educational atmosphere of the school—is one that makes them feel welcomed, respected, trusted, heard, and needed.

c. Consider the needs of parents. Before launching any program, first consult with a group of parents to identify the needs of the children and their families. Remember that all programs your school offers to benefit adult family members also will have positive effects on the children in the school. When the parents or guardians receive support, they become empowered and develop self-esteem. This affects the way they interact with their children.

d. Ask questions. As J. L. Epstein (1988) noted in *Education Horizons*, "Schools of the same type serve different histories of involving parents and have teachers and administrators with different philosophies" (p. 59). Epstein's observations should encourage teachers and schools to consider several questions:

   • What is our school's history of involving parents and families?
   • What is our school's philosophy regarding parents' involvement in school activities?
   • What training and skills do we need for involving parents in school affairs?

e. Create a demographic profile. This is a short questionnaire that compiles information about the school's families. There are two different types of demographic profiles—one is conducted at the school level and the other at the classroom level (Edwards, 2009). Gathering this information has several benefits. It allows you to:

   • **Set your scope and sequence**. It is vital to help teachers and parents "get on the same page" by organizing and coordinating parent informant literacy groups, which will make school-based literacy practices and skills more accessible to parents. In essence, the goal is to make the school's "culture of power" (Delpit, 1995) explicit to parents so that they can familiarize themselves with school-based literacy knowledge (McGill-Franzen & Allington, 1991). You need to have a clear plan and a set of goals that you would like to achieve at each grade level and decide how parents can assist.
   • **Raise awareness**. After you have identified the needs of your school's families, make community members aware that they can help. Make announcements on local radio stations and cable TV channels. Have ads printed in local

newspapers. Meet with the "movers and shakers" of the community—political leaders, religious leaders, business owners, or influential parents.

f. Create a learning management system (LMS) that manages and documents the learning process while permitting access to rich resources of information. LMSs house all of the curricular learning modules in one centralized location that can easily be differentiated for personalized learning. By empowering students to participate in the design of their learning experiences, learning suddenly becomes more meaningful to them. Parents can also monitor their students' academic growth and maintain consistent communication with their children's educators by way of the LMS. LMSs allow for:

- continuous, meaningful feedback;
- real-time decisions based on student assessment data;
- a personalized dashboard for the students, parents, and teachers;
- development of student personalized learning goals; and
- student voice and choice.

References

Beane, D. B. (1990). Say YES to a youngster's future: A model for home, school, and community partnership. *The Journal of Negro Education, 59*(3), 360–374.

Belt-Beyan, P. M. (2004). *The emergence of African American literacy traditions: Family and community efforts in the nineteenth century*. Santa Barbara, CA: Greenwood Press.

Berger, E. H. (1991). *Parents as partners in education: The school and home working together* (3rd ed.). Columbus, OH: Charles E. Merrill.

Billingsley, A. (1968). *Black families in White America*. Englewood Cliffs, NJ: Prentice-Hall.

Clay, M. M. (1975). *What did I write? Beginning writing behavior.* Auckland, New Zealand: Heinemann.

Clay, M. M. (1979). *Reading: The patterning of complex behaviour.* Portsmouth, NH: Heinemann.

Corno, L. (1989). What it means to be literate about classrooms. In D. Bloome (Ed.), *Classroom and literacy* (pp. 29–52). Norwood, NJ: Ablex Publishing Corporation.

Cummins, J. (1986). Empowering minority students: A framework for intervention. *Harvard Educational Review, 56*(1), 18–36.

Delgado-Gaitan, C. (1991). Involving parents in the schools: A process of empowerment. *American Journal of Education, 100*(1), 2–46.

Delpit, L. (1995). *Other people's children: Cultural conflict in the classroom*. New York, NY: The New Press.

Edwards, P. A. (1991). Fostering early literacy through parent coaching. In E. Hiebert (Ed.), *Literacy for a diverse society: Perspectives, programs, and policies* (pp. 199–213). New York, NY: Teachers College Press.

Edwards, P. A. (1993a). Before and after school desegregation: African-American parent involvement in schools. *Educational Policy, 7*(3), 340–369.

Edwards, P. A. (1993b). *Parents as partners in reading: A family literacy training program* (2nd ed.). Chicago, IL: Children's Press

Edwards, P. A. (1996). Creating sharing time conversations: Parent and teachers work together. *Language Arts, 73*(5), 344–349.

Edwards, P. A. (2004). *Children's literacy development: Making it happen through school, family, and community involvement*. Boston, MA: Allyn & Bacon.

Edwards, P. A. (2009). *Tapping the potential of parents: A strategic guide to boosting student achievement through family involvement*. New York, NY: Scholastic.

Edwards, P. A. (2011). Differentiating family supports. In S. Redding, M. Murphy, & P. Sheley (Eds.), *Handbook on family and community engagement* (pp. 113–116). Charlotte, NC: Information Age Publishing.

Edwards, P. A., Fear, K. L., & Harris, D. L. (1994). Designing a collaborative model of family involvement in literacy: Researchers, teachers, and parents working together. In D. F. Lancy (Ed.), *Children's emergent literacy: Social and cognitive processes* (pp. 325–340). Westport , CT: Greenwood Publishing Group.

Edwards, P. A., & Young, L. S. (1992). Beyond parents: Family, community, and school involvement. *Phi Delta Kappan, 74*(1), 72–80.

Epstein, J. L. (1987). Parent involvement: State education agencies should lead the way. *Community Education Journal, 14*(4), 4–10.

Epstein, J. L. (1988). How do we improve programs for parent involvement? *Educational Horizons, 66*(2), 58–59.

Epstein, J. L. (2001). *School, family, and community partnerships: Preparing educators and improving schools.* Boulder, CO: Westview Press.

Fear, K. L., & Edwards, P. A. (1995). Building a democratic learning community within a PDS. *Teaching Education, 7*(2), 12–24.

Fletcher, R. (1966). *The family and marriage in Britain.* Harmondsworth, UK: Penguin.

France, M. G., & Hager, J. M. (1993). Recruit, respect, respond: A model for working with low-income families and their preschoolers. *The Reading Teacher, 46*(7), 568–572.

Gadsden, V. L. (1993). Literacy, education, and identity among African-Americans: The communal nature of learning. *Urban Education, 27*(4), 352–369.

Gonzales, N., Moll, L. C., & Amanti, C. (2005). *Funds of knowledge: Theorizing practices in households, communities, and classrooms.* New York, NY: Routledge.

Gordon, I. J. (1979). Parent education: A position paper. In W. G. Hill, P. Fox, & C. D. Jones (Eds.), *Families and schools: Implementing parent education* (Report No. 121; pp. 1–5). Denver, CO: Education Commission of the States.

Handel, R. E. (1992). The partnership for family reading: Benefits for families and schools. *The Reading Teacher, 46*(2), 117–126.

Harris, V. J. (1990). African-American children's literature: The first one hundred years. *Journal of Negro Education, 59*(4), 539–555.

Hess, R. D., & Shipman, V. (1965). Early experience and the socialization of cognitive modes in children. *Child Development, 36*(4), 869–886.

Irvine, R. W., & Irvine, J. J. (1983). The impact of the desegregation process on the education of Black students: Key variables. *The Journal of Negro Education, 52*(4), 410–422.

Jenkins, G. (1969). Understanding differences in parents. In N. Headley, H. Merhill, E. Mirbaha, & M. Rasmussen (Eds.), *Parents–children–teachers: Communication* (pp. 35–40). Washington, DC: Association for Childhood Education International.

Keenan, J. W., Willett, J., & Solsken, J. (1993). Focus on research: Constructing an urban village: School/home collaboration in a multicultural classroom. *Language Arts, 70*(3), 204–214.

Knapp, J. S., Turnbull, B. J., & Shields, P. M. (1990, September). New directions for educating the children of poverty. *Educational Leadership, 48*(1), 4–8.

Lareau, A. (1989). *Home advantage: Social class and parental intervention in elementary education.* New York, NY: Falmer Press.

Lareau, A. (2000). *Home advantage: Social class and parental intervention in elementary education* (2nd ed.). Lanham, MD: Rowman, & Littlefield Publishers.

Lightfoot, S. L. (1978). *Worlds apart: Relationships between families and schools.* New York, NY: Basic Books.

Lightfoot, S. L. (1980). Families as educators: The forgotten people of Brown. In D. Bell (Ed.), *Shades of Brown: New perspectives on school desegregation.* New York, NY: Teachers College Press.

Lynch, A. (1992). The importance of parent involvement. In L. Kaplan (Ed.), *Education and the family*. Boston, MA: Allyn & Bacon.

McGill-Franzen, A., & Allington, R. L. (1991). Every child's right: Literacy. *The Reading Teacher, 45*(2), 86–90.

Michaels, S. (1981). Sharing time: Children's narrative styles and differential access to literacy. *Language and Society, 10*(3), 423–442.

Michaels, S. (1986). Narrative presentations: An oral preparation for literacy with first graders. In J. Cook-Gumperz (Ed.), *The social construction of literacy* (pp. 94–116). Cambridge, England: Cambridge University Press.

Moll, L. C., Amanti, C., Neff, D., & Gonzalez, N. (1992). Funds of knowledge for teaching: Using a qualitative approach to connect home and classrooms. *Theory Into Practice, 31*(2), 132–141.

Oliver, M., & Shapiro, T. (1995) *Black wealth/White wealth: A new perspective on racial inequality.* New York, NY: Routledge.

Pizzo, P. D. (1990, September). Family-centered Head Start for infants and toddlers: A renewed direction for the project Head Start. *Young Children, 45*(6), 30–39.

Potter, G. (1989). Parent participation in the language arts program. *Language Arts, 66*(1), 21–28.

Seefeldt, C. (1985). Communicate with curriculum. *Day Care and Early Education, 13*(2), 22–25.

Seeley, D. S. (1989). A new paradigm for parent involvement. *Educational Leadership, 47*(2), 46–48.

Siddle-Walker, V. (1996). *Their highest potential: An African-American school community in the segregated south.* Chapel Hill, NC: The University of North Carolina Press.

Yosso, T. J. (2005). Whose culture has capital? A critical race theory discussion of community cultural wealth. *Race Ethnicity and Education, 8*(1), 69–91.

Teacher–Student Relationships and Personalized Learning: Implications of Person and Contextual Variables

Ronald D. Taylor and Azeb Gebre

Personalized learning involves instruction that is differentiated and paced to the needs of the learner and shaped by the learning preferences and interests of the learner. In personalized learning environments, "the learning objectives and content as well as the method and pace may all vary" (U.S. Department of Education, 2010, para. 13). Important in constructing personalized learning environments is an understanding of the developmental needs and functioning of the learner and the environments and social forces that help shape the learners' experiences and adjustment.

In personalized learning, competency aims are held constant across learners, and learning needs, pacing, instructional practice, and teaching strategies may vary as a function of the learner. Personalized learning is meant to enhance students' motivation and engagement by increasing their autonomy and self-direction. Redding (2013) suggests that personalized learning also involves the teacher's relationship with students and their parents and the awareness of their needs and resources. Personalized learning includes teachers' awareness of students' needs and attributes in order to scaffold their learning to foster their self-direction and self-efficacy and enhance their social and emotional competencies.

Bronfenbrenner's Model of Human Development

Urie Bronfenbrenner's theory of child development (Bronfenbrenner & Morris, 2006) informs our conceptualization of personalized learning by identifying important attributes in students, key social relationships, and primary social contexts that influence their social, emotional, and physical well-being. Bronfenbrenner's theory has had a profound influence on research and practice in the U.S. and around the world. Bronfenbrenner's work (Bronfenbrenner, 1979; Bronfenbrenner & Morris, 2006) has provided a comprehensive conceptual rationale of how central social contexts in a child's life interact and influence key outcomes, including social and emotional adjustment and school performance and engagement. Bronfenbrenner maintains that human development takes place through complex interactions between an active and evolving human organism and the

Handbook on Personalized Learning for States, Districts, and Schools, pages 205–220
Copyright © 2016 by Information Age Publishing

persons and objects in the surrounding environment. The nature of the interactions (e.g., their form, power, content, direction) that influence development may vary based on attributes of the developing person, the environment, and the areas of development that are evolving at the time. The model may help inform creation of the personalized learning environment because it helps identify (a) the central social interactions important to development and learning called *process variables* (e.g., parent–child, teacher–child interactions), (b) the role students' characteristics play in their development called *person variables* (e.g., gender, age, health, intelligence, temperament), (c) the importance of the environments the child inhabits called *context variables* (e.g., home, school, culture), and (d) the influence of time and developmental change called *time variables* (e.g., significant historical events, pubertal development). The present chapter is guided by Bronfenbrenner's conceptual model and addresses important knowledge and information that agents such as teachers and administrators should have in creating personalized learning experiences for their students.

Students' Developmental Needs and Adjustments

According to Redding (2013), an important feature of personalized learning is teachers' awareness of the attributes, needs, and resources of their students. Bronfenbrenner's bioecological model (Bronfenbrenner & Morris, 2006) is useful in application to personalized learning because it explains the interactions that students experience that help direct and shape their development and learning. Bronfenbrenner suggests that students learn and develop through their person-to-person interactions with parents, teachers, and peers, and through the influence of their personal characteristics (e.g., personality, intelligence, gender). Students' behavior and development are also influenced by the social environments they inhabit (family, neighborhood, school) and the particular historical time when they live. Students' development and learning are then shaped by the factors in Bronfenbrenner's model, including process, person, context, and time variables. These components of Bronfenbrenner's model help explain how children learn and develop, the importance of their individual traits and attributes, and the role of the social environments they inhabit in shaping their learning and adjustment.

Process

Bronfenbrenner argues that development takes place as a result of *processes* consisting of complex, reciprocal interactions among the persons, objects, and symbols in the immediate environment. These interactions are also embedded in a larger context that plays a significant role in development. Effective interactions are those that take place regularly and over an extended period of time. The interactions are labeled *proximal processes*. Examples of proximal processes include parent–child activities, teacher–child interactions, and instruction and participation in educational activities. In teacher–student relations, proximal processes may involve instructional time and the creation of relations that promote student discovery and competence. Proximal processes are crucial experiences and represent the space where teachers and student interact to move learning forward. Bronfenbrenner also maintains that the "form, power, content, and direction of the proximal processes effecting development" are influenced by the characteristics of the developing *person*, the environmental *context*—both immediate and more distal—and the *time* (e.g., developmental period, amount of time, historical time; Bronfenbrenner & Morris, 2006, p. 798). From the standpoint of personalized learning, the model suggests that the degree to which personalized learning can take place depends on the quality of teacher–student interactions and on whether a student's characteristics, living situation, and stage of development (e.g., person, context, and time as variables) are part of his or her personalized learning plan.

Person

In line with the aims of personalized learning to accommodate the differentiated needs and preferences of the learner, the bioecological model suggests that understanding significant person or dispositional variables that individuals possess can help shape and inform the creation of effective environments for students. From the perspective of key aspects of the person, gender and temperament represent two salient characteristics that may have important implications for producing contexts that are individualized to enhance students' competence and adjustment.

Gender

Bronfenbrenner and Morris (2006) note that expectations and perceptions regarding a child's gender may affect important developmental processes and experiences. Among school-aged children, parents expect sons to find science easier and more interesting than daughters despite no differences in performance (Tenenbaum & Leaper, 2003). Parents' stereotyped views of differences in boys' and girls' abilities in English, math, and sports are linked to both children's performance and self-perceptions of ability (Fredricks & Eccles, 2002). Children's genders also influence their interactions in school. Throughout the school years, teachers interact and attend more to boys than girls (Ruble, Martin, & Berenbaum, 2006). Teachers also believe that elementary school boys are better at math and science than girls (Tiedemann, 2000). In elementary school, teachers tend to call on boys more than girls but call on boys and girls equally when they volunteer answers (Altermatt, Jovanovic, & Perry, 1998). Teacher's sex-differentiated responses are most pronounced in elementary school and less evident in high school.

Clearly, in line with the bioecological model, gender as a person variable helps shape children's experiences in the classroom and represents an important attribute in the teacher–student relationship to consider in creating individualized learning experiences. It may be important to consider gender in the nature of how lesson plans are constructed and where teachers' instruction and attention are directed in the classroom.

Temperament

Temperament represents an additional person variable that may influence students' adjustment and experiences in the classroom. Temperament represents individual differences in reactivity and self-regulation and is determined by inborn physiological mechanisms (Rothbart & Bates, 2006). Reactivity includes a range of responses including but not limited to fear, anger, positive affect, and orienting or negative emotionality. Self-regulation includes processes such as effortful control and modulation aimed at monitoring or controlling reactivity. Studies of temperament have examined direct effects in which temperament traits are linked to adjustment behavior. Research has also examined indirect effects in which the effects of temperament on adjustment are moderated by their association with some additional variable. Findings of direct effects revealed that a difficult temperament (negative emotionality) was associated with externalizing and internalizing problems. For instance, whereas anger, impulsiveness, and low self-regulation were linked to externalizing problems, sadness and low impulsivity were associated with internalizing problems in middle childhood (Eisenberg et al., 2000). The need to address students' problem behavior may be detrimental to instructional time and class climate. Negative emotionality has also been linked to aggression, guilt, help seeking, and negativity (Rothbart, Ahadi, & Hershey, 1994). Although much of the work has focused on temperament and the links to negative adjustment, links to positive adjustment have shown that effortful control at ages 2 and 3 years predicted more advanced moral development at age 6 years (Kochanska & Knaack, 2003). Also, teacher and parent ratings of higher emotional and behavioral self-regulation were associated with lower acting-out behavior (Eisenberg et al., 1996).

Evidence of the indirect effects of temperament is especially noteworthy because it illustrates how a child's temperament and social context may act together to produce important outcomes. For example, a theme across investigations indicates that the links between difficult temperament and poor adjustment are less evident in more effective contexts. For instance, the association of children's dysregulation with externalizing problems in the classroom was less apparent for children whose mothers were more skilled at administering discipline (Stoolmiller, 2001). Similarly, the positive association of children's resistance to control with externalizing problems was more evident for children whose parents were low in control in the home (Bates, Pettit, Dodge, & Ridge, 1998). Among elementary school children, the negative association of externalizing behavior with children's agreeableness was less likely among parents who administered angry discipline (Prinzie et al., 2003). Morris et al. (2002) found that the association of children's irritability with externalizing problems was stronger for children whose mothers were overtly hostile. More irritable children displayed an increase in internalizing problems when mothers displayed covert hostility and intrusive control over their children's feelings. An important implication of these findings is that effective social environments that teachers create may moderate behavior in students that would otherwise be disruptive to their learning. These findings also suggest that, in the creation of personalized learning, it may be important for teachers to convey to parents the link between children's temperament, their family relations and parenting practices, and children's conduct in the classroom. Effective parenting in the home may increase the likelihood of better behavior in the classroom. Also, findings have shown that instruction on implementing effective parenting practices is fairly easy to incorporate into services offered to communities through schools (Brody, Yu, Chen, & Miller, 2014). Socialization behaviors known to be effective in the home (e.g., skilled discipline, firm and direct control) may be transferred and incorporated into the classroom.

The implications of the research for personalized learning experiences suggest that effective teacher–student relations and productive classroom climates may depend on the degree to which teachers understand the role and operation of key person variables. Teachers might consider beginning the school year with a survey of the students, assessing areas such as their self-concept (self-esteem, self-efficacy), resources in the homes, work habits, and parents' involvement in their school activities. By understanding how children's characteristic behaviors may be evident in the classroom and the role of students' experiences at home, teachers may be able to create classroom environments that increase the likelihood of effective behaviors.

Contexts

According to the bioecological model, students' behavior is strongly influenced by forces in the social environments they inhabit. In the creation of personalized learning, understanding the links between students' formative social experiences and their behavior appears essential. In the bioecological model, contexts consist of important environments that students and teachers inhabit and are organized and conceptualized into separate systems, including the microsystem, mesosystem, exosystem, and macrosystem (Bronfenbrenner & Morris, 2006).

Microsystems

Microsystems consist of the most immediate contexts in which a child may reside, such as the family, peers, school, or neighborhood. In managing teacher–student relations, teachers may be able to capitalize on student's experiences in other contexts by incorporating relevant behaviors, interactions, or experiences in some manner in the classroom. The nature and quality of relations that children have at home or among their peers have been shown to carry over and influence their behavior in school.

Home environment. One way that families influence children's behavior is through the parenting style present in the home. Parenting style reflects parent's goals and strategies in child-rearing. There is a preponderance of evidence showing a strong link between parenting style and academic performance (Amato & Fowler, 2002; Boon, 2007; Steinberg, Lamborn, Dornbusch, & Darling, 1992; Steinberg, Mounts, Lamborn, & Dornbusch, 1991; Turner, Chandler, & Heffer, 2009). Children and adolescents who live in authoritative parenting households, characterized by high levels of warmth and responsiveness and demandingness and firm control, fare better academically than those from authoritarian or permissive parenting homes. For example, Steinberg and colleagues (1991) found that, compared with their nonauthoritatively reared peers, adolescents from authoritative homes earned higher grades in school, were more self-reliant, and reported less psychological distress. Adolescents exhibit healthier psychosocial development and higher academic competence when they perceive that their parents grant more psychological autonomy, stay actively engaged in their lives, and establish firm standards for behavior (Gray & Steinberg, 1999).

Parents and schools. Parents can also exert an impact on their children's school performance through their direct involvement with school activities, such as supervising and helping with schoolwork, attending parent–teacher conferences, offering encouragement for success, and establishing high expectations for achievement (Astone & McLanahan, 1991; Hill et al., 2004; Hill & Tyson, 2009; Steinberg et al., 1992). Parental involvement at school has been associated with higher academic achievement (Lee & Bowen, 2006). Studies of young children have shown that parent–child educational interaction at the home significantly contributes to children's cognitive development. Englund, Luckner, Whaley, and Egeland (2004) found that the quality of instruction parents provided for their children in problem-solving situations before school entry explained a significant amount of the variance in child's IQ and indirectly affected achievement in the first and third grade. Similarly, parenting behaviors that stimulate reading and constructive play and provide emotional support have been shown to promote academic achievement in young children (Davis-Kean, 2005).

For teachers, the home environment and parenting practices have important implications for creating personalized learning environments for students. Students' school performance is in part a reflection of their experiences in the home. Knowing more about children's home lives and experiences may provide teachers direction in shaping learning contexts that fit the particular needs of their students. For example, students from authoritative and authoritarian homes may approach their schoolwork differently and perform best in the context of separate kinds of instructional strategies. For example, teachers might capitalize in the classroom on the autonomy and initiative students from authoritative homes are encouraged to display. Students from authoritative homes might serve as models of self-directed behavior and initiative for students from authoritarian homes where autonomy and independence are discouraged.

Peer relationships. Peer interactions provide another important context for intellectual and socioemotional development. Researchers have long suggested that close and harmonious relationships with peers can enhance children and adolescents' social and academic adjustment. The development and maintenance of friendships have been shown to influence perceived competence (Buhrmester, 1990), self-esteem (Keefe & Berndt, 1996), and academic performance (Liem & Martin, 2011; Wentzel & Caldwell, 1997). In early education, whereas children with the most number of friends in the classroom report gains in school performance over time, those who are rejected by their peers show less favorable attitudes, avoidance, and lower levels of performance (Ladd, 1990). The relationship between academic achievement and peer popularity has also been documented among elementary school students. For example, Austin and Draper (1984) reported that children in Grades 3 through 6 who were most accepted by their peers were also those who performed at the highest levels in their schoolwork. Academic goals and motivations are affected by interactions with peers. One study of grade school children revealed that friends are more similar on dimensions of self-efficacy, motivation, academic standards, and preference for challenging work than nonfriends (Altermatt & Pomerantz, 2003). Activities in the classroom that integrate skill-building activities with those that support students' interpersonal skills (e.g., effective communication skills, conflict resolution strategies) may benefit peer relations and school performance. Providing students with opportunities to take on leadership roles may also be one way teachers could build students' self-confidence and social skills and enhance peer relations. Teachers with a clearer understanding of peer relations in their classroom may be in a better position to influence the social dynamics in ways to create effective, personalized learning environments for their students.

Mesosystem

The mesosystem consists of processes and linkages taking place between or among two or more of the settings in which children interact (e.g., family–school, peers–family, neighborhood–peers). Understanding how mesosystems operate may be the most important application of the bioecological model to the creation of personalized learning environments for students. The mesosystem is essentially a system of microsystems and illuminates the ways in which these contexts typically are integrated and act together to influence children's behavior.

School and home. Evidence has revealed clear linkages between the home and school. In a study of parents' involvement in inner-city elementary and middle schools, Dauber and Epstein (1993) found that parents were more likely to be involved in their children's education if they perceived that schools had strong practices to involve parents at school and at home on homework and reading activities. When parents perceived that the schools were doing little to involve them, they reported doing little at home. Parents who were more involved tended to have children who performed well in school. Sheldon, Epstein, and Galindo (2010) assessed the effects of activities designed to promote family involvement and the links to school levels of math achievement. They found that better implementation of math-related practices to enhance family involvement predicted stronger support from parents for schools' partnership programs. Strong support, in turn, predicted students' performance on math achievement tests. The most effective activities implemented by schools to promote parents' involvement included family math nights, volunteer math aides, and math projects involving family partners. Schools that reported more positive partnership climates had higher levels of math achievement. Evidence also suggests that, by fostering a strong partnership with families, schools can also lower student absenteeism (Epstein & Sheldon, 2002). In creating personalized learning for students, this work suggests that there are reciprocal relations between teachers' practices and other key environments such as the home. Thus, teachers can expect that effective, personalized learning may positively affect parents' involvement with their students' schooling. As the research has shown, increased parental involvement may support teachers' practices in school, including creating personalized learning environments. It may be helpful for teachers to obtain information directly from students and their parents on family relations and parental support and involvement in students' academic development (e.g., help with schoolwork, trips to museums, use of tutors). Short surveys in the classroom and during back-to-school nights may help teachers understand students' strengths and weaknesses and needs in the classroom. Teachers might also consider organizing activities (e.g., potluck dinner, picnics, fundraising activities, school repair projects) designed to help get to know their students and involve and inform parents regarding students' schooling. Through frequent contact with parents, via phone or email, teachers can foster supportive parent–teacher relations.

Also, emerging research suggests that supportive school environments may buffer against the negative effects of adverse home experiences. O'Malley, Voight, Renshaw, and Eklund (2015) examined the moderating effects of school climate on the relation between family structure and academic performance. The authors found that, regardless of family structure (i.e., two-parent, one-parent, foster-care, homeless households), students with more positive school climate perceptions reported higher GPAs. It has also been documented that children at risk for school failure who experience more caring and supportive relationships with teachers express greater satisfaction with school than children at risk for school failure who do not have such support (Baker, 1999). Students who are most academically and socially competent are those who experience an authoritative teaching style with consistent classroom management, support for students' autonomy, and personal interest in students (Walker, 2008). Mesosystem influences provide some of the clearest examples of the potential of how teacher–student relations may intersect with other social contexts (home) in ways that are relevant to students' personalized learning. Findings on mesosystem influences highlight the importance of understanding how key social environments (home, school, peers) and social relationships have implications for students' personalized learning and behavior in the classroom.

Exosystem

Beyond the proximal contexts of the microsystems and mesosystem, the exosystem consists of the linkages and processes between settings in which the child does not directly interact but that nonetheless may play a significant role in the child's adjustment. These contexts include the parent's workplace, neighborhood or community contexts, and family social network. In the same manner that relations at home may be reflected in the classroom, events and interactions in social contexts students do not inhabit may have implications for their schooling.

Working mothers. Evidence from a large number of studies has shown that maternal employment early in a child's life is linked to children's cognitive and socioemotional well-being later. For example, maternal employment before a child's ninth month was linked to negative cognitive outcomes at age 36 months and poor cognitive and behavioral outcomes at first grade (Brooks-Gunn, Han, & Waldfogel, 2010). In contrast, positive links between maternal employment during the first year and children's later functioning have been obtained for low-income families (Coley & Lombardi, 2013). Recent findings suggest that the discrepancy in the effects of maternal employment may have to do with the quality of the mother's work and the implications for family life. Thus, maternal employment in high-quality, stable work during early childhood was linked to enhanced cognitive and behavioral skills at 9 years (Lombardi & Coley, 2013). Other research suggests that the processes at work may include that stable employment enhanced the mother's psychological well-being, which in turn supports children's functioning over time (Conger et al., 1992). Parents in unstable or stressful work conditions may be less actively involved in their children's educational activities because of strain and difficult work schedules. These findings are important for teachers in that the impact of mothers' poor work experiences appear to be manifest in children's conduct in the classroom. Stressful work experiences appear to negatively impact family life, and children's experiences at home may transfer to the classroom. It is important for teachers to be aware of the diverse family backgrounds students come from. Parents may become disengaged from their children's education because of external stressors or merely lack of time. If teachers are aware of these challenges, they may be able to make accommodations in scheduling events and the use of time and resources. For instance, events might be scheduled at times when these parents are more readily available. Also, strategies and resources for time management (tutoring and after-school programs on weekends) to increase parental involvement in schooling might be discussed at parent–teacher conferences.

Neighborhoods. Studies of the links between neighborhoods and children's functioning have considered the effects of safety and resources, among others. Research has shown that caregivers who perceive their neighborhoods as unsafe may display lower positive parenting, including lower warmth and control and monitoring of children (Chung & Steinberg, 2006; Gayles, Coatsworth, Pantin, & Szapocznik, 2009). Evidence suggests that parents in dangerous neighborhoods may be chronically stressed, and their stress may in turn affect their parenting and children's adjustment (McLoyd, 1990). In contrast, other studies revealed positive links between safety concerns and positive parenting behavior (Jones, Forehand, O'Connell, Armistead, & Brody, 2005). This work suggests that parents may increase their positive parenting to offset and protect their children from danger in the neighborhood. Research has also assessed the link between neighborhood resources and family functioning. Findings have shown that the more parents perceived their neighborhood was devoid of economic and institutional resources, the less they engaged in positive parenting (Taylor, 2000). One explanation for this finding may be that the lack of access to economic and institutional resources may expose parents to increased stress and health problems, which may in turn compromise parenting practices and negatively affect students' adjustment and school performance (Cuellar, Jones, & Sterrett, 2015). Anxieties that parents and children feel about dangerous living conditions may make their way into the classroom. Schools in high-risk neighborhoods often have relationships with important social agents, including neighborhood and parent associations, businesses, and police, to enhance children's safety both inside and outside school (Taylor, 2000). Personalized learning in some circumstances may include understanding children's experiences and reactions to the challenges of their living conditions and the development of effective coping strategies for students and their school.

Family social network. An additional context in the exosystem that has been linked to children's adjustment is family social network. A key social context for families is the extended family. Across ethnic groups, families rely on kin for a variety of forms of support, including social and financial assistance and help with child care (Sarkisian & Gerstel, 2004). For example, Sarkisian and Gerstel (2004) found that African American and White families were both involved with kin but engaged extended family in different areas. Blacks tended to be more involved with kin in practical support (e.g., help with transportation, child care, housework), and Whites were more involved in financial and emotional support. Support from kin is especially important for low-income African American families that may rely on kin extensively. Evidence has shown that more than half of poor African American women living in urban areas interact with kin regularly as primary members of their social networks and rely on extended family for important functions, including child care, household tasks, and financial assistance (Jarrett, Jefferson, & Kelly, 2010). Kin support has also been linked to African American parents' emotional well-being (Budescu, Taylor, & McGill, 2011; Ceballo & McLoyd, 2002; Taylor, 2011; Taylor & Roberts, 1995), adolescents' adjustment (Lamborn & Nguyen, 2004; Taylor, 1996), and parents' child-rearing practices (Ceballo & McLoyd, 2002; Taylor, 1996; Taylor, Seaton, & Dominguez, 2008).

The findings on kin relations and other exosystem variables have direct implications for personalized learning and teacher–student relations. Findings have shown that kin social support may promote parenting practices that include family routine and parental involvement in schooling. Family routine and parental involvement in schooling in turn appear to promote effective attitudes and behavior in the classroom, including higher engagement and improved performance (Taylor, 1996; Taylor & Lopez, 2005). Among some segments of their students and communities, teachers and administrators may find it particularly helpful to engage extended family in school functions as a means of promoting family involvement and student achievement. For teachers in particular, it may be important to understand the family relations of their students. Among some students, extended family may play a primary role in students' socialization, and for others, the absence of support from kin may be at the root of dysfunctional behavior.

For teachers, understanding the social contexts in which their students live and the social resources and challenges they face may help shape teachers' personalized learning strategies. For example, for a teacher in a school serving an economically disadvantaged community with a majority of working mothers and extensive family social networks, personalized learning may address known challenges to student functioning (e.g., mothers' poor-quality, stressful employment) and capitalize on available positive resources (e.g., access to kin social support). It may also be helpful for teachers in at-risk communities to incorporate into the curriculum topics including effective stress management, conflict resolution, and effective communication and interpersonal skills.

Macrosystems

Additional contextual variables in the bioecological model relevant to constructing personalized learning for students are the macrosystems, which represent the broader cultural and subcultural systems that help shape relations in microsystems, mesosystems, and exosystems. Macrosystems comprise the belief systems, customs, lifestyles, material resources, and opportunities that help shape interactions across social contexts. The macrosystem may be characterized as the societal blueprint (Bronfenbrenner, 1994).

Socioeconomic status. A primary context in the macrosystem for families consists of their socioeconomic status and financial resources. To the degree that families have significant financial and material resources, they tend to function well. However, family economic pressure from having unmet material needs, having unpaid debts, or having to make difficult economic cutbacks is linked to poorer functioning in families. Conger and associates (Conger & Donnellan, 2007; Conger et al., 1992; Conger, Ge, Elder, Lorenz, & Simons, 1994) have shown that economic pressure in the home has a detrimental effect on family relations and children's adjustment. Parents in economically distressed homes tend to be psychologically distressed, and distressed parents are more likely to interact poorly with one another and display harsh and inconsistent parenting with their children. Harsh and inconsistent parenting in turn is linked to emotional and behavioral problems and lower competence in children and adolescents. The applied implications of this work to students' personalized learning and teacher–student relations are important. As the U.S. economy recovers from the latest recession, there is concern that restructuring in the labor market may take place with a permanent loss of some jobs (Rothstein, 2014). Changes in the labor market may create economic insecurity and pressure on families. The fallout for schools in many communities may be the need to cope with fewer resources because of a shrinking tax base and the need to accommodate students from a growing number of economically insecure homes. It may be increasingly important for teacher–student relations to be informed by an understanding of the economic and social forces operating on students and their families. Schools facing both short-term and more chronic economic crises in their communities may need to adopt practices aimed at addressing the needs of students and families, including school-based health services; emergency food pantries; school materials and clothes; and after-school, extended day, and summer programs. It may also be important to consider whether school curricula are best structured to help students address the future.

Time

An additional contextual parameter with implications for teacher–student relations and personalized learning is the variable of time. Bronfenbrenner suggests that an important feature of relationships is the amount of unbroken time spent in interaction. Longitudinal studies have shown that stability and steadiness in children's living conditions—including responsive adults, family routine, and stable child care and school arrangements—were related to greater cognitive and social competence in adolescence and adulthood (Pulk-kinen & Saastamoinen, 1986; Wachs, 1979). Similarly, family routine, organization, and structure were linked to students' school engagement and achievement (Taylor, 1996; Taylor & Lopez, 2005).

Historical time also represents a dimension of time relevant to student's adjustment in school. Elder (1998) notes that individuals are "shaped by the historical times and places they experience over their lifetime (p. 3). Findings have shown that the historical events experienced at particular developmental periods may have a profound impact on an individual's functioning. For example, Elder (1974) found that adolescents whose fami-lies experienced severe income loss during the Great Depression fared better than their nondeprived peers in terms of later life satisfaction. Boys and girls from economically deprived families who committed themselves to helping their families through difficult times also developed practices, goals, and aspirations benefitting them in the future. For teachers and the creation of personalized learning for students, these findings suggest the importance of how students occupy their time. Students appear to do best in structured, stable environments both at home and school. These findings also suggest that in teacher–student relations, important goals may be to help students understand the meaning and implications of historical events of their time and to help them develop the drive and capacity to adapt to the challenges they may experience.

Summary and Conclusions

The creation of personalized learning environments involves understanding the needs, preferences, and experiences of individual learners. From the perspective of teacher–student relationships, the bioecological model provides a conceptual framework from which to organize and rationalize information to structure personalized learning for students. The model suggests that at the most basic level, the *process* of learning and development takes place through teacher–student interactions in the classroom. Personalized relations and interactions in the course of instruction and the climate of the classroom are the means through which progress moves forward. The teacher–student relationship within personalized learning also requires understanding features of the *person* (e.g., gender, race, temperament). Differences based on gender or temperament may shape how students function in the classroom and may benefit from the input and attention of teachers. The model also highlights the diverse ways in which the various *contexts* in which students reside should be considered in creating personalized learning. Families, peers, schools, or neighborhoods may be resources or impediments to students' learning, and none of the contexts operates in isolation. Teacher–student relations are invariably influenced by how families, peers, and neighborhoods interact and operate together. It is also crucial to recognize that students' functioning is significantly affected by events and activities in the contexts in which they do not directly interact (e.g., parents' work or social networks) and the world that surrounds them (e.g., global and national economies). Finally, *time* is an element in students' learning in complex ways. Students need time to learn, and thus basic instructional time is an important element to consider. Historical time is also a crucial force operating on teachers and students and their relations. Historical events and technological innovations taking place at a particular point in time represent challenges which teachers are uniquely positioned to help students address.

Action Principles for States, Districts, and Schools

Action Principles for States

a. Ensure that there is equity (e.g., gender, racial, economic) in access to best policies and practices to enhance student engagement and achievement.

b. Invest resources to enhance access to technological innovation in schools and communities.

c. Partner with local governments and school districts to establish context-driven ordinances to promote and enhance school and community safety.

d. Locate comprehensive family resource centers in at-risk communities for the administration of services (adult education and literacy, employment training, mental and physical health, parent training).

e. Establish regular assessment of the evolving needs of communities (e.g., social, economic, technological) and the effectiveness of the services provided.

Action Principles for Districts

a. Assess and match the curricular needs and preferences of local communities and school districts with the appropriate available options.

b. Partner with local stakeholders and universities to increase student access to educational innovation.

c. Identify unique and common needs across schools and communities (crime prevention, safety, access to services) and develop integrated strategies.

d. Coordinate the services of stakeholders and agencies (e.g., employers, schools, police, social services) in the communities to meet the broader needs of schools and communities.

e. Consult with parents, schools, districts, and prevailing scientific evidence on the effective organization of time in school (e.g., start time, length of day, length of school year).

Action Principles for Schools

a. Devote regular in-service educational opportunities to understanding the role of students' attributes (e.g., gender, ethnicity, class) and ecological systems in students' education.

b. Develop opportunities to enhance parental involvement and engagement with school and teacher's awareness of the links between children's experiences at home and performance in school (e.g., fundraising, mentoring, advisory boards).

c. Partner with relevant stakeholders, including parents, employers, police, and social service agencies, to identify the community's resources (e.g., sports teams, recreational activities, open space) and challenges (e.g., crime, safety, health care, nutrition) and increase awareness that each social agent has a role in teacher–student experiences and relations.

d. Assess and monitor how issues of equity (gender, racial, economic) are manifest in school in student engagement and achievement.

e. Host regular events aimed at developing information on prevailing social forces at work in students' communities (e.g., parenting practices, family structure, economic opportunities, unemployment, homelessness, gentrification) and how they may impact student adjustment and behavior in the classroom.

References

Altermatt, E. R., Jovanovic, J., & Perry, M. (1998). Bias or responsivity? Sex and achievement-level effects on teachers' classroom questioning practices. *Journal of Educational Psychology, 90*(3), 516–527.

Altermatt, E. R., & Pomerantz, E. M. (2003). The development of competence-related and motivational beliefs: An investigation of similarity and influence among friends. *Journal of Educational Psychology, 95*(1), 111.

Amato, P. R., & Fowler, F. (2002). Parenting practices, child adjustment, and family diversity. *Journal of Marriage and Family, 64*(3), 703–716.

Astone, N. M., & McLanahan, S. S. (1991). Family structure, parental practices, and high school completion. *American Sociological Review, 56*(3), 309–320.

Austin, A. M. B., & Draper, D. C. (1984). The relationship among peer acceptance, social impact, and academic achievement in middle childhood. *American Educational Research Journal, 21*(3), 597–604.

Baker, J. A. (1999). Teacher–student interaction in urban at-risk classrooms: Differential behavior, relationship quality, and student satisfaction with school. *The Elementary School Journal, 100*(1), 57–70.

Bates, J. E., Pettit, G. S., Dodge, K. A., & Ridge, B. (1998). The interaction of temperamental resistance to control and restrictive parenting in the development of externalizing behavior. *Developmental Psychology, 34*(5), 982–995.

Boon, H. J. (2007). Low- and high-achieving Australian secondary school students: Their parenting, motivations, and academic achievement. *Australian Psychologist, 42*(3), 212–225.

Brody, G. H., Yu, T., Chen, E., & Miller, G. E. (2014). Prevention moderates association between family risks and youth catecholamine levels. *Health Psychology, 33*(11), 1435–1439.

Bronfenbrenner, U. (1979). *The ecology of human development: Experiments in nature and design.* Cambridge, MA: Harvard University Press.

Bronfenbrenner, U. (1994). Ecological models of human development. In T. Husen & T. N. Postlethwaite (Eds.), *International encyclopedia of education* (2nd ed., Vol. 3, pp. 1643–1647). Oxford, England: Pergamon Press/Elsevier Science.

Bronfenbrenner, U., & Morris, P. A. (2006). The bioecological model of human development. In W. Damon & R. M. Lerner (Eds.), *Handbook of child psychology, Vol. 1: Theoretical models of human development* (6th ed., pp. 793–828). New York, NY: John Wiley.

Brooks-Gunn, J., Han, W., & Waldfogel, J. (2010). First-year maternal employment and child development in the first 7 years. *Monographs of the Society for Research in Child Development, 75*(2), 144–145.

Budescu, M., Taylor, R. D., & McGill, R. K. (2011). Stress and African American women's smoking/drinking to cope: Moderating effects of kin social support. *Journal of Black Psychology, 37*(4), 452–484.

Buhrmester, D. (1990). Intimacy of friendship, interpersonal competence, and adjustment during preadolescence and adolescence. *Child Development, 61*(4), 1101–1111.

Ceballo, R., & McLoyd, V. C. (2002). Social support and parenting in poor, dangerous neighborhoods. *Child Development, 73*(4), 1310–1321.

Chung, H. L., & Steinberg, L. (2006). Relations between neighborhood factors, parenting behaviors, peer deviance, and delinquency among serious juvenile offenders. *Developmental Psychology, 42*(2), 319–331.

Coley, R. L., & Lombardi, C. M. (2013). Does maternal employment following childbirth support or inhibit low-income children's long-term development? *Child Development, 84*(1), 178–197.

Conger, R. D., Conger, K. J., Elder, G. H., Jr., Lorenz, F. O., Simons, R. L., & Whitbeck, L. B. (1992). A family process model of economic hardship and adjustment of early adolescent boys. *Child Development, 63*(3), 526–541.

Conger, R. D., & Donnellan, M. B. (2007). An interactionist perspective on the socioeconomic context of human development. *Annual Review of Psychology, 58*, 175–199.

Conger, R. D., Ge, X., Elder, G. H., Lorenz, F. O., & Simons, L. (1994). Economic stress, coercive family process, and developmental problems of adolescents. *Child Development, 65*(2), 541–561.

Cuellar, J., Jones, D. J., & Sterrett, E. (2015). Examining parenting in the neighborhood context: A review. *Journal of Child and Family Psychology, 24*(1), 195–219.

Dauber, S. L., & Epstein, J. L. (1993). Parents' attitudes and practices of involvement in inner-city elementary and middle schools. In N. F. Chavkin (Ed.), *Families and schools in a pluralistic society* (pp. 53–71). Albany, NY: State University of New York Press.

Davis-Kean, P. E. (2005). The influence of parent education and family income on child achievement: The indirect role of parental expectations and the home environment. *Journal of Family Psychology, 19*(2), 294.

Eisenberg, N., Fabes, R. A., Guthrie, I. K., Murphy, B. C., Poulin, R., & Shepard, S. (1996). The relations of regulation and emotionality to problem behavior in elementary school children. *Development and Psychopathology, 8*(1), 141–162.

Eisenberg, N., Guthrie, I. K., Fabes, R. A., Shepard, S., Losoya, S., Murphy, B. C.,...Reiser, M. (2000). Prediction of elementary school children's externalizing problem behaviors from attentional and behavioral regulation and negative emotionality. *Child Development, 71*(5), 1367–1382.

Elder, G. H., Jr. (1974). *Children of the great depression.* Chicago, IL: University of Chicago Press.

Elder, G. H., Jr. (1998). The life course as developmental theory. *Child Development, 69*(1), 1–12.

Englund, M. M., Luckner, A. E., Whaley, G. J., & Egeland, B. (2004). Children's achievement in early elementary school: Longitudinal effects of parental involvement, expectations, and quality of assistance. *Journal of Educational Psychology, 96*(4), 723.

Epstein, J. L., & Sheldon, S. B. (2002). Present and accounted for: Improving student attendance through family and community involvement. *The Journal of Educational Research, 95*(5), 308–318.

Fredricks, J. A., & Eccles, J. S. (2002). Children's competence and value beliefs from childhood through adolescence: Growth trajectories in two male-sex-typed domains. *Developmental Psychology, 38*(4), 519–533.

Gayles, J., Coatsworth, J., Pantin, H., & Szapocznik, J. (2009). Parenting and neighborhood predictors of youth problem behaviors within Hispanic families: The moderating role of family structure. *Hispanic Journal of Behavioral Sciences, 31*(3), 277–296.

Gray, M. R., & Steinberg, L. (1999). Unpacking authoritative parenting: Reassessing a multidimensional construct. *Journal of Marriage and the Family, 61*(3), 574–587.

Hill, N. E., Castellino, D. R., Lansford, J. E., Nowlin, P., Dodge, K. A., Bates, J. E., & Pettit, G. S. (2004). Parent academic involvement as related to school behavior, achievement, and aspirations: Demographic variations across adolescence. *Child Development, 75*(5), 1491–1509.

Hill, N. E., & Tyson, D. F. (2009). Parental involvement in middle school: A meta-analytic assessment of the strategies that promote achievement. *Developmental Psychology, 45*(3), 740.

Jarrett, R. L., Jefferson, S. R., & Kelly, J. N. (2010). Finding community in family: Neighborhood effects and African American kin networks. *Journal of Comparative Family Studies, 41*(3), 299–328.

Jones, D. J., Forehand, R., O'Connell, C., Armistead, L., & Brody, G. (2005). Mothers' perceptions of neighborhood violence and mother-reported monitoring of African American children: An examination of the moderating role of perceived support. *Behavior Therapy, 36*(1), 25–34.

Keefe, K., & Berndt, T. J. (1996). Relations of friendship quality to self-esteem in early adolescence. *The Journal of Early Adolescence, 16*(1), 110–129.

Kochanska, G., & Knaack, A. (2003). Effortful control as a personality characteristic of young children: Antecedents, correlates, and consequences. *Journal of Personality, 71*(6), 1087–1112.

Ladd, G. W. (1990). Having friends, keeping friends, making friends, and being liked by peers in the classroom: Predictors of children's early school adjustment? *Child Development, 61*(4), 1081–1100.

Lamborn, S. D., & Nguyen, D. G. T. (2004). African American adolescents' perceptions of family interactions: Kinship support, parent-child relationships, and teen adjustment. *Journal of Youth and Adolescence, 33*(6), 547–558.

Lee, J. S., & Bowen, N. K. (2006). Parent involvement, cultural capital, and the achievement gap among elementary school children. *American Educational Research Journal, 43*(2), 193–218.

Liem, G. A. D., & Martin, A. J. (2011). Peer relationships and adolescents' academic and non-academic outcomes: Same-sex and opposite-sex peer effects and the mediating role of school engagement. *British Journal of Educational Psychology, 81*(2), 183–206.

Lombardi, C. M., & Coley, R. L. (2013). Low-income mothers' employment experiences: Prospective links with young children's development. *Family Relations, 62*(3), 514–528.

McLoyd, V. (1990). The impact of economic hardship on Black families and children: Psychological distress, parenting, and socioemotional development. *Child Development, 61*(2), 311–346.

Morris, A. S., Silk, J. S., Steinberg, L., Sessa, F. M., Avenevoli, S., & Essex, M. J. (2002). Temperamental vulnerability and negative parenting as interacting predictors of child adjustment. *Journal of Marriage and Family, 64*(2), 461–471.

O'Malley, M., Voight, A., Renshaw, T. L., & Eklund, K. (2015). School climate, family structure, and academic achievement: A study of moderation effects. *School Psychology Quarterly, 30*(1), 142–157.

Prinzie, P., Onghena, P., Hellinckx, W., Grietens, H., Ghesquiere, P., & Colpin, H. (2003). The additive and interactive effects of parenting and children's personality on externalizing behaviour. *European Journal of Personality, 17*(2), 95–117.

Pulkkinen, L., & Saastamoinen, M. (1986). Cross-cultural perspectives on youth violence. In S. J. Apter & A. P. Goldstein (Eds.), *Youth violence: Programs and prospects* (pp. 262–281). New York, NY: Pergamon Press.

Redding, S. (2013). Getting personal: The promise of personalized learning. In M. Murphy, S. Redding, & J. Twyman (Eds.), *Handbook on innovations in learning*. Philadelphia, PA.: Center on Innovations in Learning, Temple University; Charlotte, NC: Information Age Publishing.

Rothbart, M. K., Ahadi, S. A., & Hershey, K. L. (1994). Temperament and social behavior in childhood. *Merrill-Palmer Quarterly, 40*(1), 21–39.

Rothbart, M. K., & Bates, J. E. (2006). Temperament. In W. Damon & R. Lerner (Series Eds.), & N. Eisenberg (Vol. Ed.), *Handbook of child psychology*, Vol. 3. Social, emotional, and personality development (6th ed., pp. 99–166). New York, NY: Wiley.

Rothstein, J. (2014). *The great recession and its aftermath: What role for structural changes?* Paper presented at the Building Human Capitol and Economic Potential Conference: Institute for Research on Poverty, University of Wisconsin, Madison, WI.

Ruble, D. N., Martin, C., & Berenbaum, S. (2006). Gender development. In N. Eisenberg (Ed.), *Handbook of child psychology: Vol. 3, Personality and social development* (6th ed., pp. 858–932). New York, NY: Wiley.

Sarkisian, N., & Gerstel, N. (2004). Kin support among Blacks and Whites: Race and family organization. *American Sociological Review, 69*(6), 812–837.

Sheldon, B., Epstein, J. L., & Galindo, C. L. (2010). Not just numbers: Creating a partnership climate to improve math proficiency in schools. *Leadership and Policy in Schools, 9*(1), 27–48.

Steinberg, L., Lamborn, S. D., Dornbusch, S. M., & Darling, N. (1992). Impact of parenting practices on adolescent achievement: Authoritative parenting, school involvement, and encouragement to succeed. *Child Development, 63*(5), 1266–1281.

Steinberg, L., Mounts, N. S., Lamborn, S. D., & Dornbusch, S. M. (1991). Authoritative parenting and adolescent adjustment across varied ecological niches. *Journal of Research on Adolescence, 1*(1), 19–36.

Stoolmiller, M. (2001). Synergistic interaction of child manageability problems and parent-discipline tactics in predicting future growth in externalizing behavior for boys. *Developmental Psychology, 37*(6), 814–825.

Taylor, R. D. (1996). Kinship support, family management, and adolescent adjustment and competence in African-American families. *Developmental Psychology, 32*(4), 687–695.

Taylor, R. D. (2000). An examination of the association of African-American mothers' perceptions of their neighborhood with their parenting and adolescent adjustment. *Journal of Black Psychology, 26*(3), 267–287.

Taylor, R. D. (2011). Kin support and parenting practices among low income African American mothers: Moderating effects of mothers' psychological adjustment. *Journal of Black Psychology, 37*(1), 3–23.

Taylor, R. D., & Lopez, E. I. (2005). Family management practice, school achievement and problem behavior in African American adolescents: Mediating processes. *Journal of Applied Developmental Psychology, 26*(1), 39–49.

Taylor, R. D., & Roberts, D. (1995). Kinship support and parental and adolescent well being in economically disadvantaged African American families. *Child Development, 66*(6), 1585–1597.

Taylor, R. D., Seaton, E., & Dominguez, A. (2008). Kinship support, family relations, and psychological adjustment among low-income African American mothers and adolescents. *Journal of Research on Adolescence, 18*(1), 1–22.

Tenenbaum, H. R., & Leaper, C. (2003). Parent–child conversations about science: Socialization of gender inequities. *Developmental Psychology, 39*(1), 34–47.

Tiedemann, J. (2000). Parents' gender stereotypes and teachers' beliefs as predictors of children's concept of their mathematical ability in elementary school. *Journal of Educational Psychology, 92*(1), 144–151.

Turner, E. A., Chandler, M., & Heffer, R. W. (2009). The influence of parenting styles, achievement motivation, and self-efficacy on academic performance in college students. *Journal of College Student Development, 50*(3), 337–346.

U.S. Department of Education. (2010). *Transforming American education: Learning powered by technology.* Retrieved from http://tech.ed.gov/netp/learning-engage-and-empower/

Wachs, T. D. (1979). Proximal experience and early cognitive intellectual development: The physical environment. *Merrill-Palmer Quarterly, 25*(1), 3–42.

Walker, J. M. (2008). Looking at teacher practices through the lens of parenting style. *The Journal of Experimental Education, 76*(2), 218–240.

Wentzel, K. R., & Caldwell, K. (1997). Friendships, peer acceptance, and group membership: Relations to academic achievement in middle school. *Child Development, 68*(6), 1198–1209.

Personalizing Professional Development for Teachers

Catherine C. Schifter

Personalized professional development (PPD) takes the notion of individualized instruction for students and applies it to teachers. An assistant principal from a California school stated, "We all have different strengths and areas of potential growth" (Ullman, 2015, p. 19). PPD for teachers includes many facets, such as developing their skills to use multiple methods of teaching for each child's strengths and challenges, but also developing teachers' own professional knowledge and skills based on their own strengths and weaknesses.

The concept of professional development is a long, time-honored tradition. There are few jobs or professions today that do not need to update skills and/or knowledge. Whether you are a car mechanic, dentist, secretary, or statistician, new technologies and procedures are required to stay current.

With this trend comes scholarly reviews, studies, and theories for effective and valid professional development. The National Staff Development Council (now Learning Forward) published standards for staff development. The *Journal of Staff Development* (2001), out of the Learning Forward organization, provides a dedicated vehicle for publication of both scholarly research and opinion pieces to guide professional development practice across all fields. Books have been written to provide road maps for professional development (see Guskey, 2000; Joyce & Showers, 2002; among others). It is important to point out that research on professional development tends to be program and/or content specific, and atomistic in nature, making outcomes difficult to generalize.

> There are few jobs or professions today that do not need to update skills and/or knowledge.

Within education, the No Child Left Behind Act of 2001 (U.S. Department of Education, 2002) required highly qualified teachers in all grades for all subjects, but also required high-quality professional development to be available for all teachers. The Teaching Commission (2004) report titled "Teaching at Risk: A Call to Action" argued

Handbook on Personalized Learning for States, Districts, and Schools, pages 221–235

that "helping our teachers to succeed and enabling our children to learn is an investment in human potential, one that is essential to guaranteeing America's future freedom and prosperity" (p. 11). In order to meet these requirements, high-quality professional development, that meets the specific needs of each and every individual teacher, must be established as a priority for teachers.

This chapter provides a brief overview of the literature on professional development as it relates to education, but not an in-depth review due to the extensiveness of the literature; introduces the change theory within the realm of professional development (often missing from the literature); introduces two adult learning theories to support the self-directed approach of personalized PD; provides an in-depth example of personalized PD for teachers; and provides action principles for state, district, and local leaders around the concept of personalized PD for teachers.

Professional Development Literature Review

Griffin (1979) wrote, one requirement of a profession is that "members somehow continue to learn, to grow, to renew themselves, so that their interaction with ideas and with clients are reflective of the best knowledge and skill available to them" (p. 127). This concept has not diminished over the last 30 plus years. On the contrary, the growth in information, the explosion of access to information and data through the Internet, and Cloud computing make the notion of being on the cutting edge (depending on the discipline) difficult to maintain. While it is true that we have access to more and more information, having a thorough understanding of all that information, in order to say one is currently knowledgeable, is exponentially more difficult as the amount of information to which one has access grows. In some areas of study (e.g., games in education, medicine, physics, or computing), keeping up with the new information and trends can be a monumental challenge.

The majority of the literature speaks of professional development in many ways, providing practitioners with a myriad of ideas, but constantly stressing what is wrong with those efforts. Wood and Thompson (1980), in discussing guidelines for better staff development, suggested professional development consisted of a series of "[d]isjointed workshops and courses focus[ed] on information dissemination rather than stressing the use of information or appropriate practice in the classroom" (p. 374). The authors go on to state that most professional development programs were not part of an overall, well-planned approach for school staff. Ball and Cohen (1999) agreed with this depiction, adding that while districts spend lots of money on professional development in the United States annually, "most is spent on sessions and workshops that are often intellectually superficial and disconnected from deep issues of curriculum and learning, fragmented and non-cumulative" (p. 4). Wilson and Berne (1999) suggested that professional development for teachers tends to be scattered half-day or full-day events that are not well planned or coordinated over time, thus giving the appearance of being disconnected and/or serendipitous.

Many papers written in the last 35 years provided guidelines or advice to school districts on how professional development can be successful. Sparks (1994) posited three factors: (1) results-driven education using student outcomes as the focus; (2) systems thinking for seeing the big picture or sum of the parts, rather than individual pieces; and (3) constructivist, action research and reflective practice in the classroom with peer collaboration. These concepts were born out of the accountability movement that began in the mid-1980s, and while they are not considered novel in 2015, perhaps they were in 1994 given trends of that time.

As noted before, several authors have presented ideas of what makes for effective professional development (Abdal-Haqq, 1996; Richardson, 2003; Sparks, 1994, 2002). Concepts in common include:

- school-based and or school-wide and ongoing;
- collaborative in nature facilitating collegiality across and between teachers much like a community of scholars (see introduction of communities of practice below);
- focuses on student learning;
- recognizes teachers as professionals;
- constructivist in nature;
- supports teacher deeper understanding of both content and research-based approaches to teaching; and
- supported by administrators with funding and time to practice new skills.

Wilson and Berne (1999) conducted an analysis of the professional development literature across disciplines, such as mathematics, English, and science, and they explored three themes which they suggested crossed the literature. These were: communities of learners redefining practices; teacher learning activated for maximum effect; and adopting Lord's (1994) "critical colleagueship" (p. 194-195) with professional, critical discourse among peers.

Collaborative models, supported by Borko and Putnum (1998) and Perry, Watson, and Calder (1999), suggest "nurturing learning communities within which teachers try new ideas, reflect on outcomes, and co-construct knowledge about teaching and learning in the context of authentic activity" (Butler, Lauscher, Jarvis-Selinger, & Beckingham, 2004, p. 436). This collaborative community of practice (COP) resonates with the work of Lave & Wenger (1991) and that of Brown, Collins, and Duguid (1989) that puts learning as essential within a socially situated context. As noted by Butler and colleagues, the collaborative model includes common goals within the local school setting. While each teacher explored innovative teaching strategies for his or her classroom, it was through the collaborative dialogue where the teachers shared and co-constructed knowledge. Butler et al. (2004) continued by demonstrating how individual, self-regulated learning was not antithetical to COP frameworks. They noted, "...focusing on individual learning does not require divorcing the individual from context. Indeed, the potential of merging a COP framework and models of self-regulation is that the latter describes how individuals strategically adapt within environments to achieve authentic goals" (p. 439). The social collaboration supports self-regulated, individualized practices in ways that could not be attained otherwise. Sometimes working alone on a problem is not sufficient.

The idea of communities of learners came out of the work of Lave and Wenger (1991) on communities of practice. Subsequently, Wenger and Trayner (2015) defined communities of practice as "people who engage in a process of collective learning in a shared domain of human endeavor" (p. 1). From Wilson and Berne's perspective (1999), being in a community of learners gives teachers support within the classroom giving them a way to discuss action research ideas in a supportive and collaborative environment.

Professional development would not be just prepackaged and delivered, but activated for maximum effect using the community of learners for support. Lord's (1994) concept of critical colleagueship brings these two themes together to establish a peer-to-peer meaningful relationship. These ideas will come up again in this chapter.

Putnum and Borko (2000), working with situated cognition (which also comes out of the work of Brown, Collins, & Duguid, 1989; Lave & Wenger, 1991), argued that knowing and learning are "(a) situated in a particular physical and social context; (b) social in nature; and (c) distributed across the individual, other persons, and tools" (p. 4). As Schifter (2008) wrote, "Professional knowledge is not developed in a vacuum, but in a context relevant to the knowledge, organized and accessed in meaningful ways as relating to the classroom for teachers" (p. 45). Again, there is a connection across these different authors' perspectives: teachers working collaboratively with critical colleagues to support renewal and new learning, over time.

Since the enactment of the NCLB (U.S. Department of Education, 2002), teachers are held accountable for students' learning at proficiency levels across content and grades. Assuring continuing teachers have the knowledge and skills required becomes essential for all schools across all states. The need for effective professional development became imperative, and yet, change takes time. Both Sparks (1994) and Lauro (1995) noted that it can take up to five years for an innovation (i.e., change in practice) to be fully implemented. Collins (2001), in his study of successful companies, supported this concept when he stressed that suc-

> *Assuring continuing teachers have the knowledge and skills required becomes essential for all schools across all states.*

cessful innovation includes patience, along with persistently sustained support and effort over time. DuFour (2004) suggests this works in schools as well.

Sparks (2002) strongly suggested that effective PD meets the goals of the standards-based era. He gave a nod to change theory when he cited Michael Fullan (1991), who said "The greatest problem faced by school districts and schools is not resistance to innovation, but the fragmentation, overload, and incoherence resulting from the uncritical acceptance of too many different innovations" (p. 197). As I tell my own students, just because you know of an innovation does not mean you have to try to incorporate it, if it does not match or answer the problem you are trying to solve. Changing practice every year because of some new idea makes no sense because the teacher never has time to master the first innovation or to figure out whether an innovation worked or not.

In making his case for these practices, Sparks (2002) cited a number of studies looking at professional development initiatives. From *Does Professional Development Change Teaching Practice?: Results from a Three-Year Study* (U.S. Department of Education, 2000), a study of the federal Eisenhower professional development program, he noted that teachers who participated in what was termed "reform type" of professional development increased their use of new strategies in teaching science and math. The "reform type" of activities were described as teacher study groups; teacher collaboratives, networks, or committees; mentoring; internships; and resource centers—or activities best described as promoting active learning (p. 15).

Richardson (2003) suggested three reasons why research-based practices are not the norm today: it is expensive, it occurs over a long time period, and it is hard to support when the participants are allowed to make decisions regarding goals and outcomes. She suggested that it is much easier, and considered cost efficient, to offer one training for all. She further suggested the "closed classroom door" effect (p. 402) allowed teachers to assume autonomy precluding anyone telling them how to teach: "This classroom is unique and is therefore unlike any other classroom because of my uniqueness and my particular group of students" (p. 402). While the notion of teacher individuality/uniqueness pervades the U.S. system, since NCLB there was a call for teachers across grade levels to equally be responsible for all students' progress. Are the ideas of teacher autonomy and professional development antithetical? Not really, but the approach taken may make the difference in teacher buy-in and participation.

Hilda Borko (2004) skillfully mapped the terrain of educational professional development as having three actors/agents (teachers, the program itself, and facilitators), all within a unique context (school, district, community, etc.). Looking at the factors identified by Ball (1996) for how teachers learn, understanding how and why a particular professional development program impacts an individual teacher is a complex question to answer. Perhaps the answer is not merely in the literature but also, considering what we know about the "change processes," in schools as well as in adult learning theory.

A Few Models to Consider

The idea of individualized, or personalized, instruction for teachers is not new. Indeed, Frances Fuller suggested in 1970 that research supported individualized instruction for students and future teachers, thus providing the first evidence of thought toward teacher individualized professional development. In considering personalized learning for teachers, Fuller noted the importance of what she termed "the concerns model" (p. 30). Within the concerns model, Fuller posited the need to have "concerns" about students' needs, motives, abilities, and emotions in the forefront of thought for planning. If we consider the term 'students' broadly, then professional development should be personalized to concerns about each teacher's needs, motives, abilities, and emotions. Overall, these concerns revolved around the students in the teacher's classroom. Because each classroom has a unique community of students, which changes as students evolve from one year to the next, professional development that supports one teacher one year may or may not support the teacher next door or upstairs.

Clark and Hollingsworth (2002) developed an interconnected model of professional growth. The model "suggests that change occurs through the mediating processes of 'reflection' and 'enactment', in four distinct domains which encompass the teachers' world" (p. 950). This includes the personal domain of teacher knowledge, beliefs, and attitudes; the professional practice domain of experience developed over time; the domain of consequences, or outcomes in the age of assessment and testing; and the external domain which is outside the teacher's personal world (e.g., sources of information, support). They suggest that this model recognizes the idiosyncratic and individual nature of teacher professional growth, more so than other theories of teacher development.

In 2008, the International Academy of Education published the booklet *Teacher Professional Learning and Development* (Timperley, 2008) as part of their Educational Practices series. This booklet synthesized research on teacher professional development that "has been demonstrated to have a positive impact on student outcomes" (p. 6). There were 10 key principles for success presented, but behind these were four essential understandings:

- Notwithstanding the influence of factors such as socio-economic status, home, and community, student learning is strongly influenced by what and how teachers teach;

- Teaching is a complex activity;

- It is important to set up conditions that are responsive to the ways in which teachers learn; and

- Professional learning is strongly shaped by the context in which the teacher practices. (p. 6)

However, there was no reference to community of practice or learners. On the contrary, the emphasis was on context and how teachers learn, which is often ignored in the professional development literature. Deborah Ball (1996) suggested that how teachers learn should be considered when planning and developing professional development. She suggested several factors that impact teacher learning, which mirrored those listed above as essential for successful professional development overall, but also included prior beliefs and experiences, context of the school (inner city, rural, private or public education), competing demands on time, and reflective practice.

Richardson (2003) suggested an inquiry approach to professional development. Here the teachers determine their individual goals (which could be "concerns," a la Fuller, 1970) and perhaps collective goals, try out new practices, gather data along the way, and engage in collegial dialogue regarding what works or not using their evidence to support claims and discussion. As she noted, "[T]here are times when a collective sense of goals and instructional approaches is called for" (p. 402). This is especially true when a chosen curriculum crosses grades, thus causing teachers in all grades affected to have a need to work collaboratively. While this may sound like standardization, the reality is that teachers can work collaboratively while concentrating on their individual classroom needs.

Voogt and colleagues (2015) proposed a collaborative design. They suggested "that teacher professional development needs to be concerned with social aspects of learning, distributed across individuals and events, and directly meaningful to teachers' practice" (p. 260). They go on to suggest that formal professional development is not enough to consider, but also what happens within the classroom, COP in the school, and the school environments are important as well (see discussion before related to Borko & Putnam, 1998, and Perry et al., 1999). Voogt et al. suggested, through shared collaborative adaptation of curricula, teachers not only learn about new curricula and/or teaching methods, but also develop personal ownership for implementing within their classrooms.

Voogt et al. (2015) noted how, using a situated learning viewpoint, teachers were actively engaged in personalized learning for their own practices while collaborating with others in a COP that was meaningful for all (p. 261). This process capitalized on distributed knowledge and the collaborative nature of COPs. Here teachers identified and valued differing perspectives and interpretations, and negotiated toward collective growth. Teachers became personalized agents of change, yet collectively they could accomplish so much more.

How is self-directed, or individualized, learning manifested in the 21st century? Actually, there are more—and easier to access—opportunities than ever before. Ferriter and Provenzano (2015) describe how one teacher's use of a blog and a Twitter account established vehicles whereby he networked with over 30,000 followers/teachers on Twitter.

He established a social space through social media where teachers could explore teaching methods along with other teachers from across the country, not just in their school or community. This is an example of learning from others, sharing what works or not, discussing ideas, true collaborative dialogue – just not in real time. As they noted, "The relationship that develops between blog writers is symbiotic" (p.18). They challenge each other, give advice, all of which results in strong professional, albeit virtual, relationships. This process mirrors the concept of COP, but in a virtual environment. It also personalizes the learning space, which is powerful.

One last model needs to be included here. As chronicled in a *Philadelphia Inquirer* article, Graham (2015) presented the EdCamp "unconference" approach to professional development, which has gotten the attention of the Bill & Melinda Gates Foundation. She states, "A recent foundation report found that the $18 billion schools are spending annually on professional development 'is simply not working'" (p. A6). What makes EdCamp different is the design of the event. There are no fees and no predetermined sessions or topics. Teachers are asked to sign up to lead discussions about topics for which they believe they can serve as the "expert." Teachers then attend only those sessions that they see as appropriate for their needs. The structure allows teachers to become leaders in their fields and with others, to collaborate with like-minded professionals, and to come away with ideas and resources to implement changes in their classrooms. While the EdCamp idea is considered a collaborative professional development model, one can easily see the translation to the personalized construct where teachers bring their classroom needs and learn from each other. The concept of the EdCamp "unconference" spawned 225 EdCamps in 2014 held around the world. The most recent was EdCamp Ukraine in June 2015. The Gates Foundation has found the model so compelling that they are investing two million dollars.

The first question to ask is whether the term "professional development" captures the essence of what is being proposed through self-directed or individualized professional learning. If the idea is "deficit reduction," then "professional development" works. If, as proposed by Webster-Wright (2009), the concept is about continuous professional learning, then we should use that phrase and call it "continuous professional learning" (CPL). Or we should look again at the work of Clark and Hollingsworth (2002) to explore further their interconnected model of professional growth as it focuses on the individual teacher's development. While the EdCamp structure is intriguing, there is no evidence, as yet, on the impact of that model on individual classrooms.

Overall, the literature on professional development is mixed. There are myriads of papers presented at conferences, published in journals, and presented as roadmaps for successfully guiding teachers toward innovative curricula and/or teaching methods. And yet, experts continue to lament the discrepancies between research-based programs and those implemented traditionally in schools. Is the problem a lack of distribution of ideas, lack of funding in schools, or perhaps something else? We do not know the definitive answer to that question, but there are many examples of good program design to choose between.

Across the literature reviewed for this chapter, one idea runs throughout: teachers working collaboratively with critical colleagues while also pursuing self-directed learning to support renewal, new learning, over time. The operative terms are all related to active engagement in commonly held goals for the betterment of all students.

Change Theory Applied to Personalized PD

All professional development, or professional learning, or CPL, relate to changing practices. Again, there is a wealth of literature on change in education (see Fullan, 1982). But what is striking in reading the literature is the lack of consideration of how change occurs in organizations or within teachers.

Change does not happen easily nor in a vacuum. For teachers, change is particularly hard because it seems never ending. As Larry Cuban (1986) noted, "Constants amid change…" (p. 1). We can always count on changes in subject matter (e.g., standards, curriculum, pedagogical methods), equity among diverse learners, uses of student assessments, the social organization called "school," and the profession of teaching (Little, 1993). Every change or innovation brought into schools comes with good intentions. But with all the change comes skepticism, waiting for the next change or innovation to come through the door. Little's paper did not address personalized professional development (PPD); however, one could hypothesize PPD for teachers as a way to facilitate implementation of an innovation as it applies to each individual teacher, rather than thinking schoolwide.

> Change does not happen easily nor in a vacuum. For teachers, change is particularly hard because it seems never ending.

Rogers (2003), in his book *Diffusion of Innovations,* proposed that for an innovation (or change) to be accepted in a school or classroom, teachers must have knowledge of the innovation, have interest in exploring the innovation, be able to evaluate the innovation before trying it out, implement it in the classroom, and, finally, fully integrate and promote the innovation to others. As part of this process, Rogers suggested five criteria for an innovation (or change) that must be met. From the above stages, these five criteria would come into play with evaluating and trying out the innovation. The innovation must demonstrate relative advantage (e.g., Is the innovation considered to be better than what is currently used?), compatibility (e.g., Is the innovation well-matched with the culture of the classroom?), ease of use to implement and trialability (e.g., Can I test it out before adopting it fully in my classroom?) and observability in other teachers' classrooms where it has worked well. Each of these criteria can be applied to PPD for implementing change into an individual teacher's classroom.

Further, Rogers (1962) noted that "[t]he diffusion of innovations takes place within a social system" (p. 303). Looking at the five criteria above, the social aspect of schools comes through with peers demonstrating to peers what works, how it works, and why it works. The social organization of schools can be an asset for implementing change, or it can be the biggest hurtle to overcome. Personalized professional development comes into play with change theory as the most effective way to impact individual teacher's practices and classroom outcomes.

Lastly, in a review of a professional development program designed for the Philadelphia School District in partnership with IBM Corporation, I developed a lens for reviewing technology-oriented PPD, but suggest it resonated with the professional development literature (reviewed above) and the change literature (just presented). From studying the implementation of the Continuous Practice Improvement professional development program over a seven-year period, using change theories to guide the analysis, the outcome was a view of successful change through PPD—but only when *all* elements were successfully in place. Assuming that one starts with strong and useful professional development training (no matter the content), the principles were:

- Time to practice, develop interest and knowledge, evaluate usefulness for own classroom and students, try new skills with students, and to adopt or reject the innovation based on these opportunities;
- Effective, ongoing, post-training support in the classroom;
- Ongoing communication and a local social support system, including significant support from the principal and/or other influential school staff; and
- Changes in classroom structures, roles and behaviors, knowledge and understanding, and thus values.

As noted above, change is difficult, and for teachers, change is a constant in their lives from new curricula, new leadership, new students, and more. However, if change is managed according to what is known about how change happens, everyone involved will be satisfied. We know that change takes time. We know that change happens best if the participants feel and believe they are valued members of the community. We know that change happens best if there is transparent communication about goals, expectations, peer-to-peer collaborations, and outcomes. We cannot ignore the aspects of change processes as we consider how professional learning improves teachers' classroom practices. From these attributes we can speculate that, through PPD, change will more likely happen and be sustained over time.

Adult Learning Theory Applied to PPD

Malcolm Knowles (1968) adopted the term *andragogy* as a way of differentiating between how adults prefer to learn and how pre-adults are taught in K–12 environments, or *pedagogy*. While the term tends to only be used in organizational development arenas, the assumptions articulated by Knowles speak to the concept of PPD for teachers. Specifically, Knowles posited that, as we mature, we become more self-confident and move away from dependence on others to tell us what we need to know, to being self-directed and deciding what we want/need to know and why. Knowles said adults expect new knowledge to have an immediate impact on their lives, not to be used only in the future when it seems needed. Further, Knowles noted the most important motivation for adult learners was interest, examples being wanting a promotion, changing jobs, or being evaluated on job performance. PPD for teachers directly relates to self-directed learning with clear reasons for why skill/knowledge development is important for teachers (i.e., helping all children maximize their strengths and work on challenges).

McClusky's (1963) Theory of Margin presented a concept of adult learning as a dynamic process of continuous development over time requiring energy and resources for all aspects of daily life. The theory views motivation to learn (i.e., develop) as the relationship between how many resources (i.e., power) the learner has and the demands (i.e., load) that diminish motivation for learning. The power is defined as abilities, position, or allies which a person can muster in coping with the load. Load is then defined as the social and self-demands to maintain autonomy of life (McClusky, 1970). Thus, an appropriate "margin" is needed for the adult to be motivated to learn (i.e., more motivated with greater power/load ratio; less motivated by greater load/power ratio). Theory of Margin relates to PPD for teachers in that this approach gives the learner more power over their learning process and goals.

Teachers are adults, and thus consideration of how adults learn is an important aspect of both professional development as a whole, but PPD in particular. Consideration of the best aspects of self-directed learning, along with considering how to maximize learner resources (power) and minimize the impact of the demands (load), will be helpful in developing well-received and impactful professional development for teachers over time.

Example of PPD

In the mid-1990s, IBM Corporation's education division partnered with the School District of Philadelphia to help teachers incorporate computer technology into their classroom practices. The project was called Continuous Practice Improvement (CPI). The book *Infusing Technology into the Classroom: Continuous Practice Improvement* presents 57 out of nearly 200 kindergarten through eighth-grade teachers who participated in the CPI professional development program and the impact (or lack thereof) on daily classroom practices from three to seven years after graduating from the program. For over half of these teachers, the impact was found up to seven years post professional development.

CPI consisted of three formal, five-hour, Saturday, face-to-face training sessions where the teachers learned how to use such applications as email and concept mapping tools, along with how to search the Internet and more. They used and were given examples for using the applications with their grade-level students and curricula. In addition, they learned how to use a laptop, loaned to each teacher so they could practice skills and access district resources and the CPI website. For many of these teachers, this was their first contact with a computer. After the formal training, each teacher was paired with another teacher in the district who served as a mentor and expert example for infusing computers into classroom lessons and experiences. Every effort was made for the mentor teacher to teach the same or close grade level so the observations would resonate with the home classroom for the CPI teacher. A substitute teacher took the CPI teacher's class in order for her to spend three full days observing the mentor teacher, and an additional day while the CPI teacher reimagined her classroom and lessons to be able to truly infuse computers into her activities.

The one primary instructor for CPI was available for questions, troubleshooting problems, and classroom visits over the next three to six months. The CPI teacher also could contact their mentor teacher with whom she could share ideas, ask questions, and gain further support. In some schools, whole cohorts of grade-level teachers became CPI teachers together, thus giving them "in house" support. In fact, where there were more than one CPI teacher in a school, these teachers developed a community of practice around using computers in their classrooms and shared ideas and resources with each other as well as other teachers in the school.

CPI was a combination of whole-group (or cohort) basic instruction, with self-directed learning by each teacher based on his/her own classroom and students' needs. During the whole-group Saturday sessions, teachers were encouraged to bring their own experiences and expertise into the conversation. The level of technical/computer experience was broad, with some teachers needing to learn how to turn on their loaner laptop, while others were very familiar with email and Internet resources. What all had in common was a lack of knowledge for how to incorporate computer solutions into their daily classrooms.

Using the Clark and Hollingsworth (2002) model of interconnected professional growth, each of the four domains were addressed. Prior knowledge, beliefs, and attitudes were embraced and used as starting points for growth. The teachers were afforded time and support to develop a level of confidence through experiences as appropriate for their classrooms. This included learning that using student computer expertise was not shameful, but actually supported their teaching in meaningful ways, along with allowing student peer teaching to occur. Outcomes were important in discussions, as the school district implemented a common curriculum with regularly scheduled benchmark assessments, designed to match the competencies being addressed over a six-week period of instruction. Lastly, the CPI program was flexible enough to meet the needs of the ever-changing world of information access and computer technology. While CPI was initially built using the IBM computer, over time it moved to the Apple computer platform as the district standardized elementary classrooms with Apple technology. CPI attempted to minimize the operation system differences by focusing on the needs of each teacher and classroom rather than on the technology. Through this process, a model of PPD was established for each teacher and classroom.

As noted, each teacher used his or her new knowledge and skills to meet the needs of their own classroom. One example is June, who had taught third grade for over 30 years. When June came to the first CPI session, she was afraid of the laptop computer she was being loaned. When it did not do what she expected, she would say loudly that she had broken it. She felt very uncomfortable, but had another teacher from her school there with her, who gave her support. June made it through the formal PD sessions and the mentoring. When observed three months later, she showed me how she was entering her grades by computer, and her students showed me their projects for a social studies lesson on the United States. For classroom resources, June's classroom was hurting. Her world and U.S. maps were torn and could not be used. She had very few books in her classroom. Her social studies resources were three computers. She created individual folders for each child on the computer and a schedule for each to have appropriate time during the day to gather their information. Each child was assigned one of the states, and he or she was to research the state flag, motto, primary industries, major cities and parks, governor's name, and the like. Then each child made a poster about their state as they became the "expert" on that state, and they were asked to teach the other students what they learned (e.g., student peer teaching). The posters were posted around the room as resources for all. June said, "I would never have done this but for CPI! The examples, the homework, the other teachers all helped me get over my fears." In the end, June changed her practices because she had new knowledge and skills just for her students (power from Theory of Margin), and the resources to minimize the load (Schifter, 2008).

The success of the CPI program was demonstrated at the kindergarten through fourth-grade levels, while showing limited success in middle grades, mostly due to the demands of No Child Left Behind legislation (U.S. Department of Education, 2002), along with new curricular and testing requirements of the district. Lastly, CPI was an expensive program requiring finances for 15 hours on Saturdays (i.e., teacher professional development pay), mentor teacher time, substitute teachers pay, and technology resources (e.g., computers, software, printers, cameras).

This example of a PPD program combines the best aspects of good whole-group professional development with appropriate ways to personalize the skills and knowledge development for each teacher who participated in the CPI program. The most important aspect was that the teachers could observe other teachers modeling the concepts they learned in the formal training, could try them out in their own classroom with resources to support their efforts, and could then customize their classrooms as appropriate for their students' needs. This is an example of Clark and Hollingsworth's interconnected model of professional growth, and a successful example of PPD for teachers.

Action Principles for States, Districts, and Schools

From the above discussion, one concept came out over and over again, that of a community of practice (COP) of learners. Lave and Wenger (1991) posited the idea of a COP where one begins at the periphery of activities and knowledge, and over time slowly becomes a full member of the COP. In education, the members at the periphery are student teachers and novice teachers. As they learn their craft through experience in their classrooms, interacting with other teachers within their context of work (the school), they become more full-fledged members of the COP. It used to be that in order for a COP to exist, the members needed to be in close proximity (thus the notion of legitimate peripheral participation; Lave & Wenger, 1991). However, in the 21st century, social media provides opportunities for establishing COPs across cyberspace using such tools as Twitter, Google Groups, blogs, and more. These tools provide vehicles for teachers by which self-regulated, individualized learning can happen with or without the support of school leadership. These social media tools allow teachers to connect with peers, to collaborate across time and space, and to establish critical friendships that can support self-directed, individualized learning. They may or may not support common goals within a specific school, but to ignore the power of these tools would be unfortunate as they may provide opportunities that could not be afforded through traditional means.

Action Principles for States, Districts and Schools

Action Principles for States and Districts

  a. Provide administrators with sufficient resources (including funding) to provide high-quality professional development for teachers based on research-based outcomes.

  b. Provide assessment and accountability guidelines for measuring change in teacher effectiveness and/or practices over time.

  c. Provide assessment and accountability systems, or guidelines, to accurately measure the impact of professional development on students in terms of simple cognitive and complex cognitive learning.

  d. Encourage schools to promote communities of practice within and across grade levels and schools.

  e. Reward and/or recognize teachers who successfully develop individualized, self-directed professional development plans while taking advantage of the six secrets of change as outlined by Michael Fullan (2008).

  f. Reward and/or recognize schools/districts that support teacher professional learning over time, with clear guidelines demonstrating that time is a key to change in classroom practices.

Action Principles for Schools

a. Engage all teachers in planning for change, valuing peer-to-peer and individualized action-research activities.

b. Facilitate change by allowing sufficient time for teachers to explore innovations, share outcomes, provide feedback to each other, and thus make wise and appropriate change decisions.

c. Support high-quality professional development efforts at the whole-school, peer-to-peer, and individualized levels, capitalizing on the "concerns model" elements of needs, motives, abilities, and emotions of all teachers.

d. Use the six secrets of change presented by Fullan (2008) as a guide for ensuring (a) all teachers are valued, (b) all teachers are connected through common purpose and goals, (c) capacity building for all is a common goal, (d) collaboration and collegiality are encouraged for learning together, (e) transparency across all actions and planning is promoted to make change less threatening, and (f) all of these steps are taken together to result in systems learning, which means change happens.

References

Abdal-Haqq, I. (1996). *Making time for teacher professional development.* (Digest 95-4). Washington, DC: ERIC Clearinghouse of Teaching and Teacher Education. (ERIC #ED400259).

Ball, D. L. (1996). Teacher learning and the mathematics reforms: What we think we know and what we need to learn. *Phi Delta Kappa, 77*(7), 500–508.

Ball, D. L., & Cohen, D. K. (1999). Developing practice, developing practitioners: Toward a practice-based theory of professional education. In G. Sykes & L. Darling-Hammond (Eds.), *Teaching as the learning profession: Handbook of policy and practice* (pp.3–32). San Francisco, CA: Jossey-Bass.

Borko, H. (2004). Professional development and teacher learning: Mapping the terrain. *Educational Researcher, 33*(8), 3–15.

Borko, H., & Putnam, R. (1998). Professional development and reform-based teaching: Introduction to the theme issue. *Teaching and Teacher Education, 14*(1), 1–3.

Brown, J. S., Collins, A., & Duguid, P. (1989). Situated cognition and the culture of learning. *Educational Researcher, 18*(1), 32–42.

Butler, D. L., Lauscher, H. N., Jarvis-Selinger, S., & Beckingham, B. (2004). Collaboration and self-regulation in teacher's professional development. *Teaching and Teacher Education, 20*(5), 435–455.

Clark, D., & Hollingsworth, H. (2002). Elaborating a model of teacher professional growth. *Teaching and Teacher Education, 18*(8), 947–967.

Collins, J. (2001). *Good to great: Why some companies make the leap... and others don't.* New York, NY: Harper Business.

Cuban, L. (1986). *Teachers and machines: The classroom use of technology since 1920.* New York, NY: Teachers College Press.

DuFour, R. (2004). Leading edge: The best staff development is in the workplace, not in a workshop. *Journal of Staff Development, 25*(2). Retrieved from http://learningforward.org/docs/jsd-spring-2004/dufour252.pdf?sfvrsn=2

Ferriter, W. M., & Provenzano, N. (2015). Self-directed learning...for teachers. *Phi Delta Kappan, 95*(3), 16–21.

Fuller, F. F. (1970). *Personalized education for teachers: An introduction for teacher educators.* Washington, DC: ERIC Clearinghouse of Teaching and Teacher Education. (ERIC #ED048105). Retrieved from http://files.eric.ed.gov/fulltext/ED048105.pdf

Fullan, M. (1982). *The meaning of educational change.* New York, NY: Teachers College Press.

Fullan, M. (1991). *The new meaning of educational change.* New York, NY: Teachers College Press.

Fullan, M. (2008). *The six secrets of change: What the best leaders do to help their organizations survive and thrive.* San Francisco, CA: Jossey-Bass.

Graham, K. A. (2015, August 17). Boost for grassroots education: A teacher training camp started in Philadelphia went worldwide, and the Gates Foundation took notice. *The Philadelphia Inquirer,* pp. A1, A6.

Griffin, G. A. (1979). Guidelines for the evaluation of staff development programs. In A. Lieberman & L. Miller (Eds.). *Staff development: New demands, new realities, a new perspective* (pp. 126–143). New York, NY: Teachers College Press.

Guskey, T. R. (2000). *Evaluating professional development.* Thousand Oaks, CA: Corwin Press.

Joyce, B., & Showers, B. (2002). *Student achievement through staff development* (3rd ed.). Alexandria, VA: ASCD.

Knowles, M. S. (1968). Andragogy, not pedagogy. *Adult Leadership, 16*(10), 350–352, 386.

Lauro, D. R. (1995). Five approaches to professional development compared. *THE Journal Online.* Retrieved from https://thejournal.com/articles/1995/05/01/five-approaches-to-professional-development-compared.aspx

Lave, J., & Wenger, E. (1991). *Situated learning: Legitimate peripheral participation.* Cambridge UK: Cambridge University Press.

Little, J. W. (1993). Teachers' professional development in a climate of education reform. *Education Evaluation and Policy Analysis, 15*(2), 129–151.

Lord, B. (1994). Teachers' professional development: Critical colleagueship and the role of professional communities. In N. Cobb (Ed.), *The future of education: Perspectives on national standards in education* (pp. 175–204). New York, NY: College Entrance Examination Board.

McClusky, H. Y. (1963). The course of the adult life span. In I. Lorge, H. Y. McClusky, G. E. Jensen, & W. C. Hallenbeck (Eds.), *Psychology of adults* (pp. 10–19). Washington, DC: Adult Education Association.

McClusky, H. Y. (1970). A dynamic approach to participation in community development. *Journal of Community Development Society, 1*(1), 25–32.

National Staff Development Council. (2001). *Revised standards for staff development.* Oxford, OH: Author.

Perry, N. E., Walton, C., & Calder, K. (1999). Teachers developing assessments of early literacy: A community of practice project. *Teacher Education and Special Education, 22*(4), 218–233.

Putnam, R. T., & Borko, H. (2000). What do new views of knowledge and thinking have to say about research on teacher learning? *Educational Researcher, 29*(1), 4–15.

Richardson, V. (2003). The dilemmas of professional development: Why do so few staff development programs incorporate features that research has shown to be effective? *Phi Delta Kappan, 84*(5), 401–406.

Rogers, E. M. (1962, 2003). *Diffusion of innovations.* New York, NY: Basic Books.

Schifter, C. C. (2008). *Infusing technology into the classroom: Continuous practice improvement.* Hershey, PA: IGI Global.

Sparks, D. (1994). A paradigm shift in staff development. *Journal of Staff Development, 15*(4), 26–29. Washington, DC: ERIC Clearinghouse of Teaching and Teacher Education. (ERIC #EJ497009).

Sparks, D. (2002). *Designing powerful professional development for teachers and principals.* Oxford, OH: National Staff Development Council.

Teaching Commission. (2004). *Teaching at risk: A call to action.* Denver, CO: Author. Retrieved from https://www.ecu.edu/cs-educ/account/upload/Teaching%20At%20Risk.pdf

Timperley, H. (2008). *Teacher professional learning and development.* Geneva, Switzerland: International Academy of Education.

Ullman, E. (2015). Room for improvement: How districts are trying to integrate professional learning into the teacher evaluation process. *Tech & Learning, 35*(9), 18–22.

U.S. Department of Education. (2000). *Does professional development change teaching practice? Results from a three-year study*. Washington, DC: Author. (ERIC # ED455227). Retrieved from http://files.eric.ed.gov/fulltext/ED455227.pdf

U.S. Department of Education. (2002). *No Child Left Behind Act of 2001*, Pub. L. No. 107-11-0, 115 Stat. 1425.

Voogt, J., Laferrière, T., Breuleux, A., Itow, R. C., Hickey, D. T., & McKenney, S. (2015). Collaborative design as a form of professional development. *Instructional Science, 42*, 259–282. DOI 10.1007/s11251-014-9340-7

Webster-Wright, A. (2009). Reframing professional development through understanding authentic professional learning. *Review of Educational Research, 79*(2), 702–739.

Wenger, E., & Trayner, B. (2015). *Communities of practice: A brief introduction.* Grass Valley, CA: Wenger-Trayner. Retrieved from http://wenger-trayner.com/introduction-to-communities-of-practice/

Wilson, S. M., & Berne, J. (1999). Teacher learning and the acquisition of professional knowledge: An examination of research on contemporary professional development. *Review of Research in Education, 24*(1), 173–209.

Wood, F. H., & Thompson, S. R. (1980). Guidelines for better staff development. *Educational Leadership, 37*(5), 374–378.

V. Descriptive Studies of Specific Instructional Applications

Using Universal Design for Learning to Personalize an Evidence-Based Practice for Students With Disabilities

Sara Cothren Cook, Kavita Rao, and Bryan G. Cook

Personalized learning lies at the heart of special education. From the foundational work of Itard (Lane, 1976) and Farrell (1908–1909) to the Individualized Education Programs (IEPs) mandated by the Individuals with Disabilities Education Act, prominent elements of personalized education have been and continue to be guiding principles of special education. Personalized learning requires practitioners to use multiple modes of instruction in order to scaffold learning and enhance student motivation with the aim of improving educational outcomes (see Redding's chapter elsewhere in this volume) and includes (a) variation in time, pace, and place; (b) technological aids; (c) individualized and varied instruction with student engagement in design; (d) teacher–student–family relationships; and (e) personal competencies (i.e., cognitive, metacognitive, motivational, social/emotional). Consistent with special education, these core tenets of personalized learning focus on individualized and differentiated instruction that take into account student needs, preferences, and interests (Twyman, 2014).

Two contemporary educational initiatives, evidence-based practices and Universal Design for Learning (UDL), hold considerable promise for improving the educational experiences and outcomes of students. We propose that evidence-based practices and UDL can be applied to promote personalization of effective instruction for students with disabilities. In this chapter, we provide a brief overview and definition of evidence-based practices and UDL and describe how one teacher implements an evidence-based practice in her inclusive classroom, applying principles of UDL and personalized learning in order to support students with disabilities.

Spencer, Detrich, and Slocum (2012) defined evidence-based practice as "a decision-making process in which empirical evidence is one of several important influences" (p. 130). That is, instructional practices are implemented when they align with the best available research evidence, teachers' professional judgment, and clients' (e.g., learners and their families) values and contexts. Replacing generally ineffective practices that are sometimes used in special education (e.g., Burns & Ysseldyke, 2009) with

---

Handbook on Personalized Learning for States, Districts, and Schools, pages 239–247

"evidence-based practices" shown to be generally effective by bodies of high-quality, experimental research should result in generally improved learner outcomes (Cook, Smith, & Tankersley, 2012). Scholars have emphasized the importance of implementing evidence-based practices as they were designed, that is, with fidelity (Dulak & DuPre, 2008). If core elements of an evidence-based practice are not implemented as designed, then the practice may lose its effectiveness. However, emphasizing strict adherence to core elements of evidence-based practices in a way that does not account for unique learner characteristics, experiences, and preferences may be counterproductive and ineffective (Johnson & McMaster, 2013). To optimize learner outcomes, we recommend that special educators strike a balance between evidence-based practice and fidelity on one hand and personalization and adaptation on the other. UDL provides a means for balancing fidelity and personalization when engaging in evidence-based practice.

UDL is a framework for designing flexible instructional environments that reduces barriers to learning in the curriculum and increases cognitive access to instruction with the goal of developing expert learners (Meyer, Rose, & Gordon, 2013). Teachers can use the UDL framework during the lesson planning process to consider and proactively design instruction that addresses learner variability and personalizes learning. The three main principles of UDL are to provide multiple means of (a) representation, (b) action and expression, and (c) engagement. These three foundational principles are further defined by nine guidelines and 31 specific "checkpoints" that provide detailed guidance about how to apply UDL to instruction (National Center on Universal Design for Learning, 2014). Teachers can apply these guidelines to instructional goals, materials, methods, and assessments. By definition, UDL-based lessons provide multiple access points that can support a range of learners in a classroom while concurrently providing personalized choices and options for individual students.

Redding (2014) identified four personal competencies that are integral to personalized learning: (a) cognitive competency, (b) metacognitive competency, (c) motivational competency, and (d) social/emotional competency. Redding defined the term competency as "a general and evolving accumulation of related capabilities that facilitate learning and other forms of goal attainment" (p. 4). The intention of developing these competencies within the personalized learning framework is consistent with UDL's goal of developing expert learners. Both UDL and personalized learning ultimately focus on instructional strategies and the provision of supports that develop learner agency and mastery learning.

In this field report, we describe how one teacher uses an evidence-based practice in mathematics—the concrete–representational–abstract strategy (CRA)—and illustrate how she uses personal learning strategies and UDL guidelines to provide supports for learners with disabilities in the classroom. We highlight ways in which she uses strategies that vary the pace of learning, individualize curriculum, provide instructional choices that foster student engagement, make use of appropriate technology tools, and develop personal competencies in alignment with UDL guidelines and the personalized learning framework.

Concrete–Representational–Abstract: Instructional Strategies for an Inclusive Setting

Ms. B. is a math teacher at a public middle school in an urban school district. In the second quarter of the academic year, the seventh-grade math curriculum adopted by her district focuses on solving algebraic equations. Ms. B.'s fourth period inclusive math class is composed of 25 students, including six students receiving special education services. Three students have learning disabilities, two students have emotional/behavioral disabilities, and one student has been diagnosed with autism. To meet the needs of all the students in this inclusion setting, Ms. B. understands the importance of using evidence-based practices that are likely to improve academic outcomes and of applying UDL principles to her instruction to provide flexible options and choices for her students with and without disabilities.

Ms. B. has read the research on the CRA strategy and believes that it is an effective practice to use for her diverse students (see Witzel, 2005; Witzel, Mercer, & Miller, 2003; Witzel, Riccomini, & Schneider, 2008). The CRA strategy involves a sequence of three steps (Flores, 2010) that scaffolds support to achieve student mastery of abstract concepts. In the first phase, the teacher demonstrates the math skill or process with **concrete**, manipulative objects. In the second phase, the teacher uses **representational** objects (e.g., pictures, drawings) to replace the concrete manipulatives. In the final **abstract** phase, students use only numbers to complete mathematical tasks with a focus on developing fluency when problem solving. In all three phases, the teacher models strategies for the whole class followed by guided practice and then an opportunity for independent practice.

> The CRA strategy involves a sequence of three steps (Flores, 2010) that scaffolds support to achieve student mastery of abstract concepts.

Ms. B. knows that although CRA is evidence based and already aligns with UDL guidelines in many ways, she can provide additional supports for the special education students in her classroom. She plans her lessons with the goals of maintaining the key elements of the CRA strategy and integrating additional personalized supports to meet the needs of the individual students in her class in accordance with UDL guidelines. Table 1 shows how the core elements of the CRA strategy in addition to related personalized supports that Ms. B implements align with UDL guidelines and elements of the personalized learning framework.

Table 1. CRA Strategies, Personalized Learning Supports, and Universal Design for Learning Guidelines

Core CRA Supports and Related Personalized Learning Supports Implemented by Teacher	Alignment With UDL Guidelines and Personalized Learning Elements
Concrete and representational phases support • decoding of mathematical notation and symbols • understanding of abstract concepts across languages by providing alternatives to linguistic representation Related personalized learning supports implemented by teacher: • Pre-teaching activity clarifies vocabulary and symbols related to mathematical notation and symbols	UDL Guideline 2: Options for language, mathematical expressions, and symbols Personalized learning elements: individualized and varied instruction, cognitive and metacognitive personal competencies

Core CRA Supports and Related Personalized Learning Supports Implemented by Teacher	Alignment With UDL Guidelines and Personalized Learning Elements
All three CRA phases • guide information processing by providing alternative means to comprehend abstract information • provide progressive scaffolds that maximize transfer and generalization of knowledge and skills Related personalized learning supports implemented by teacher: • Flashcard activity provides reinforcement to all students while specifically supporting students with disabilities • Charts and mnemonics activate background knowledge and support transfer and generalization	UDL Guideline 1: Options for perception UDL Guideline 3: Options for comprehension Personalized learning elements: varied instructional strategies, cognitive and metacognitive personal competencies
CRA instructional process builds fluency by providing graduated levels of support for practicing problem solving in repeated and varied ways Related personalized learning supports implemented by teacher: • Teacher provides access to tools and assistive technology as appropriate (e.g., iPad apps, calculator); use of iPad apps helps minimize threats and distractions for student with autism • Resources such as organizational chart and mnemonics facilitate information management • Students are given options at various points (e.g., to work individually or in pairs, to use physical or digital tools) • Students can make choices about which CRA strategy to use when completing individual work in the abstract phase	UDL Guideline 4: Options for physical action UDL Guideline 5: Options for expression and communication UDL Guideline 6: Options for executive functions UDL Guideline 7: Options for recruiting interest Personalized learning elements: varied pace of instruction; instructional choice based on learning preferences and interest; cognitive, metacognitive, and motivational personal competencies
Working in pairs fosters collaboration between students, providing peer support for learning process Related personalized learning supports implemented by teacher: • Teacher determines how to pair students to optimally support students with disabilities • Process places emphasis on student mastery of concepts; students have opportunities to practice and get teacher feedback in independent phase	UDL Guideline 8: Options for sustaining effort and persistence UDL Guideline 9: Options for self-regulation Personalized learning elements: individualized and varied instruction, varied pacing, motivational and social/emotional personal competencies

Note: UDL Guidelines v 2.0 can be downloaded at http://www.udlcenter.org/aboutudl/udlguidelines
CRA = concrete–representational–abstract; UDL = Universal Design for Learning.

Personalized Learning: Preteaching Vocabulary

Ms. B. starts by implementing a learning support that students can benefit from before she employs specific CRA strategies. Realizing that many students, including those with learning disabilities, will benefit from revisiting key vocabulary related to this unit on solving algebraic equations, she preteaches vocabulary words (e.g., variable, equation, equal) using student-friendly language and symbols to help support understanding. To give students an opportunity to practice the vocabulary, she asks them to create flashcards and gives them the choice of practicing with a partner or individually. These practices are consistent with UDL guidelines on providing options for language and comprehension (UDL Guidelines 2 and 3) and providing students with choices (UDL Guideline 7). For the student with autism, who uses apps on a tablet device as part of his IEP, Ms. B. provides the option to create and use flashcards on an iPad. In this way, she addresses this student's needs by providing access to tools and assistive technologies (UDL Guideline 4) and minimizing threats and distractions (UDL Guideline 7). These personalized learning practices provide individualized supports, integrate instructional choices, utilize appropriate technology tools, and support the development of cognitive and metacognitive personal competencies.

Phase One: Concrete

For the first stage of the CRA process, Ms. B. uses algebra tiles as the concrete manipulative. She explicitly teaches all students (a) the values of each of the different tiles (e.g., square tiles represent 1, rectangular tiles represent the variable) and (b) what the colors of tiles represent (e.g., blue tiles represent adding, red tiles represent subtracting). She posts a visual chart on the board to provide students a guide for what each tile represents.

Whole-Class Modeling

To teach students how to solve algebraic problems using the algebra tiles, Ms. B. demonstrates the process and steps of solving the problems for the class. She creates a chart that has space to (a) write the algebraic equation, (b) place tiles on each side of the equal sign, and (c) write in the answer to the equation. She will use this chart in all three phases of the CRA strategy. Ms. B. also posts the steps to solving algebraic problems on the board as she visually demonstrates how to use the manipulatives to solve the equation. Using these resources, Ms. B. models the problem-solving process with several examples.

Guided Practice

Ms. B. provides guided practice with the manipulatives in two ways. First, she gives each student the organizational chart as described earlier and a set of his or her own algebra tiles and asks them to copy a problem from the board. She then calls on individual students to help her place the appropriate tiles on each side of the equation and use additional tiles to solve the equation. She provides several examples to the whole class to allow students to use the manipulatives with her guidance. Next, she places students into pairs and has them work together using the chart and manipulatives to solve additional problems. She monitors the classroom to check for understanding among the pairs of students.

Individual Practice

To ensure that each student understands how to solve algebraic equations individually, Ms. B. provides students with three additional problems to solve independently. She allows students a choice to use either the algebra tiles or a digital manipulatives app on the classroom iPads. Ms. B. provides each student with the organizational chart to support their problem solving. She uses this independent practice as a formative assessment to determine whether students are able to individually solve algebraic equations using concrete manipulatives and are ready to move on to the next phase.

Personalized Learning

Ms. B. integrates several UDL-related supports to personalize learning in the concrete phase. First, Ms. B. provides both visual and organizational charts as guides to help students remember the values of each of the algebra tiles and stay organized when solving each problem (UDL Guidelines 3 and 6). In addition, Ms. B. pairs students intentionally to ensure that the students with disabilities are with peers who will collaborate effectively and provide peer-learning supports (UDL Guideline 8). Providing a choice of using algebra tiles or the digital manipulatives app in the independent practice phase also provides a personalized learning support for specific students. The digital manipulatives provide access to tools and technologies (UDL Guideline 4), and the provision of choice helps to recruit student interest and foster motivation (UDL Guideline 7). These personalized learning practices provide students with choices that align with their interests and motivation, utilize technological tools as needed, and contribute to the development of cognitive, motivational, and social/emotional personal competencies.

> *These personalized learning practices provide students with choices that align with their interests and motivation...*

Phase 2: Representational

The representational phase of the CRA strategy provides a transitional step between the concrete and abstract levels (Flores, 2010). For the representational phase, Ms. B. replaces the concrete tiles with picture representations.

Whole-Class Modeling

Ms. B. begins by modeling how to solve algebraic equations with pictures, which act as a substitute for the manipulatives of the concrete phase. Ms. B. uses the organizational chart and colored pencils to solve problems using pictures of the algebra tiles. As part of modeling this process, Ms. B. explicitly describes how her pictures represent the concrete tiles that were used in the previous lesson.

Guided Practice

Ms. B. gives each student an organizational chart and colored pencils. Ms. B. writes a problem on the board and calls on individual students to help her draw the appropriate pictures on each side of the equation. To support some of the students with disabilities, who often struggle with keeping up with class notes, Ms. B. provides premade pictures for them to glue on their organizational chart during this guided practice. As they work through the problems, Ms. B. poses questions regarding the picture and color students are using when drawing and solving their equation; she monitors the students using premade pictures to make sure they are choosing the appropriate pictures to place on either side of the equation. She provides several examples to the whole class to reinforce the concepts. Next, she places students into pairs and has them work together using the chart and pictures to solve several more problems. She monitors the students to check for understanding.

Independent Practice

Ms. B. provides several problems for the students to solve on their own. She offers all students a choice to draw their pictures using either colored pencils or a program on computers. For students with learning disabilities, who tend to struggle with basic math computations, and for students with emotional/behavioral disabilities, who become frustrated working on multistep problems, Ms. B. provides the option of using a calculator to check their work while practicing independently. She uses this independent practice as a formative assessment to determine whether students are ready to move on to the abstract phase.

Transition to the Abstract Phase

Because transitioning students from the representational to the abstract phase can be challenging, Ms. B. decides to introduce students to the "CAP" mnemonic (Mercer, Jordan, & Miller, 1996). She shows students how the steps they have used to solve algebraic equations align with the CAP mnemonic and asks students to practice using it.

- C: Combine like terms on both sides of the equation.
- A: Ask yourself how you can get the variable on one side of the equation (e.g., undo all addition, subtraction, multiplication, and division).
- P: Put the value of the variable into the original equation to check your answer.

Personalized Learning

In the representational phase, Ms. B. provides many of the same personalized learning supports as the concrete phase (i.e., visual chart, organizational chart, purposeful student pairing). In addition, Ms. B. minimizes students' frustration by providing students the choice of using premade pictures during guided practice and the computer during independent practice. Both supports are consistent with UDL Guideline 4 to provide appropriate tools and assistive technologies. Using the calculator provides additional access to an assistive technology tool (UDL Guideline 4) and gives students the opportunity to gain fluency through practice (UDL Guideline 5) while reducing the frustration they may feel when checking problems manually. Ms. B. also introduces the mnemonic strategy to personalize learning and support students' transition from the representational to the abstract phase, helping students activate background knowledge and supporting transfer and generalization (UDL Guideline 3). These personalized learning practices vary pace of instruction, utilize technological tools to support specific students, and support the development of cognitive and metacognitive personal competencies.

Phase 3: Abstract

After ensuring students are able to use the CAP mnemonic to solve algebraic equations using pictures, Ms. B. is ready to transition her students to the abstract phase of algebraic problem solving.

Whole-Class Modeling

During this phase, Ms. B. uses the organizational sheet described in previous steps and models several problems on the board for students. Ms. B. uses a think-aloud process to model the CAP mnemonic when solving algebraic equations. In the abstract phase, Ms. B. replaces the pictures with numbers and shows how the same steps students used in the earlier concrete and representational phases can be used with problems in the abstract form.

Guided Practice

Ms. B. provides all students with a modified version of the organizational chart that includes the steps of solving the algebraic equation using the CAP mnemonic. She calls on students individually to help her solve problems on the board, practicing the steps with the abstract (numerical) representation. Ms. B. checks for understanding and provides feedback to students during guided practice.

Independent Practice

Ms. B. provides five problems to practice independently. For the students with disabilities, Ms. B. adds in an element of choice. She allows these students to select any of the three methods for solving the problems (concrete, representational, or abstract) with the guideline that at least two problems have to be solved using the abstract method. Students complete five problems on their own.

Personalized Learning

In the abstract phase, Ms. B. again provides some personalized learning supports used in earlier phases (i.e., organizational chart, mnemonic). The organizational chart, as used in the abstract phase, incorporates the CAP mnemonic, alleviating the need for students to refer back to the board for each step and providing them with a scaffold when solving problems abstractly. In addition, Ms. B. allows the students with disabilities to choose how they will solve the problems during the independent practice, giving them an option to use concrete or representation strategies. Students are motivated by having the opportunity to choose how they want to complete the problems (UDL Guideline 7) and are given varied ways to practice and reach mastery in this independent practice phase (UDL Guideline 8). These personalized learning practices vary pace of instruction, provide instructional choice based on learning preferences and interest, and support the development of cognitive, metacognitive, and motivational personal competencies.

Considerations for Personalized Learning and Evidence-Based Practices

The vignette in this chapter focuses on how one evidence-based practice in mathematics, the CRA strategy, can be used to improve academic outcomes for all students in an inclusive classroom and how UDL strategies can be used to personalize learning for students with disabilities. The UDL guidelines provide a menu of options that teachers can use as the vehicle for adapting evidence-based practice to create a more personalized curriculum and can be applied to any instructional strategy, intervention, or evidence-based practice. Although we believe that UDL guidelines represent a promising approach for beginning to personalize evidence-based practice, we recognize that other strategies, as discussed in the other chapters in this book, can and should be used to maximize the personalization and effectiveness of instruction for learners with disabilities.

References

Burns, M. K., & Ysseldyke, J. E. (2009). Reported prevalence of evidence-based instructional practices in special education. *Journal of Special Education, 43*(1), 3–11.

Cook, B. G., Smith, G. J., & Tankersley, M. (2012). Evidence-based practices in education. In K. R. Harris, S. Graham, & T. Urdan (Eds.), *APA educational psychology handbook* (Vol. 1, pp. 495–528). Washington, DC: American Psychological Association.

Durlak, J. A., & DuPre, E. P. (2008). Implementation matters: A review of research on the influence of implementation on program outcomes and the factors affecting implementation. *American Journal of Community Psychology, 41*(3–4), 327–350.

Farrell, E. K. (1908–1909). Special classes in the New York City schools. *Journal of Psycho-Aesthenics, 13*, 91–96.

Flores, M. M. (2010). Using the Concrete–Representational–Abstract Sequence to teach subtractions with regrouping to students at risk for failure. *Remedial and Special Education, 31*(3), 195–207.

Johnson, L. D., & McMaster, K. L. (2013). Adapting research-based practices with fidelity: Flexibility by design. In B. G. Cook, M. Tankersley, & T. J. Landrum (Eds.), *Advances in learning and behavioral disabilities* (Vol. 26, pp. 65–91). London, UK: Emerald.

Lane, H. (1976). *The wild boy of Aveyron.* Cambridge, MA: Harvard University Press.

Mercer, C., Jordan, L., & Miller, S. (1996). Constructivistic math instruction for diverse learners. *Learning Disabilities Research & Practice, 11*(3), 147–156.

Meyer, A., Rose, D. H., & Gordon, D. (2013). *Universal design for learning: Theory and practice.* Wakefield, MA: Center for Applied Special Technology. Retrieved from http://udltheorypractice.cast.org/login

National Center on Universal Design for Learning. (2014). *UDL guidelines—Version 2.0.* Retrieved from http://www.udlcenter.org/aboutudl/udlguidelines

Redding, S. (2013). *Through the student's eyes: A perspective on personalized learning.* Philadelphia, PA: Center on Innovations in Learning, Temple University. Retrieved from http://www.centeril.org/publications/2013_09_Through_the_Eyes.pdf

Redding, S. (2014). *Personal competencies in personalized learning.* Philadelphia, PA: Center on Innovations in Learning, Temple University. Retrieved from http://www.centeril.org/publications/Personalized_Learning.pdf

Spencer, T. D., Detrich, R., & Slocum, T. A. (2012). Evidence-based practice: A framework for making effective decisions. *Education and Treatment of Children, 35*, 127–151. Retrieved from http://muse.jhu.edu/journals/education_and_treatment_of_children/v035/35.2.spencer.pdf

Twyman, J. S. (2014). *Competency-based education: Supporting personalized learning.* Philadelphia, PA: Temple University Center on Innovations in Learning. Retrieved from http://www.centeril.org/connect/resources/Connect_CB_Education_Twyman-2014_11.12.pdf

Witzel, B. S. (2005). Using CRA to teach algebra to students with math difficulties in inclusive settings. *Learning Disabilities: A Contemporary Journal, 3*(2), 49–60.

Witzel, B. S., Mercer, C. D., & Miller, M. D. (2003). Teaching algebra to students with learning difficulties: An investigation of an explicit instruction model. *Learning Disabilities Research & Practice, 18*(2), 121–131.

Witzel, B. S., Riccomini, P. J., & Schneider, E. (2008). Implementing CRA with secondary students with learning disabilities in mathematics. *Intervention in School and Clinic, 43*(5), 270–276.

Next-Generation Teachers in Linguistically Diverse Classrooms

Tamara Sniad

Language learning is a lifelong process. Recently, at the age of 41, I learned about "transoms," or windows that sit above doors or larger windows, during a Victorian home tour. Around the same time, I began using "squish," which, according to the online *Urban Dictionary*, refers to a platonic crush. I acquired this term through a class discussion with undergraduate education majors about my fondness for my child's first grade teacher. Whether it is gaining technical language specific to a profession or field, such as "transom"; expanding uses of existing words and structures to new meanings, such as "squish"; or incorporating brand new words added to the language through technology, pop culture, or other languages, we are continuously developing as language users. Keeping this perspective is important while reading this chapter.

All Learners Are Language Learners; All Teachers Are Language Teachers

In all the content areas—science, math, history, physical education, and the arts— effective teachers recognize and appreciate the interconnectivity of content and language. Interacting with academic content and conveying understanding requires, but is not limited to, new vocabulary, specialized structures in written and spoken language, and awareness of appropriate language styles based on contexts. As Tan (2011) argues, when content area teachers see language teaching as the responsibility of others (i.e., the English language specialists), they fail to see or take advantage of rich, meaningful language learning opportunities in their classrooms. These moments can substantially improve not only the language development of English learners (ELs), but also their connections to the content and classroom community.

Language learning inherently is personal and varied. In linguistically diverse classrooms, teachers need to be prepared to adjust, adapt, challenge, and support based on what they know about their students' abilities, approaches to learning, and experiences. High-level English users need supports in growing in their knowledge and uses of technical language and academic structures. Students learning English as a second or third language, or emergent bilinguals (EBs; Garcia, 2009c), need personalized support to

Handbook on Personalized Learning for States, Districts, and Schools, pages 249–261

acquire the (basic) English language required to participate in class activities and content instruction (Garcia, 2009c).[1]

This chapter, therefore, is not about becoming an English language teaching specialist. Rather, it is about personalizing teaching to the English language needs, interests, and goals of all students in an academic program. This personalization, as Redding (2013) emphasizes, "ensues from the relationships among teachers and learners and the teacher's orchestration of multiple means for enhancing every aspect of each student's learning and development" (p. 6). The information in this chapter will equip teachers with background information on maximizing resources, differentiation strategies to maintain high academic standards, and techniques for promoting language acquisition in linguistically diverse classrooms.

Linguistic Diversity in U.S. Schools

The past 40 years have seen an unprecedented growth in the number of EBs enrolled in K–12 schools in the U.S. From 1980 to 2009, the number of EBs enrolled in K–12 schools rose 42% (Aud et al., 2011), making this group the fastest growing student population in the U.S. With more than 2.6 million school-age learners identified as EBs, the majority of teachers across the country likely have at least one EB in their classes. With this diversification of classrooms come new responsibilities and needs within schools, from increasing support staff for English language support and communications with families to preparing teachers for the challenges—and opportunities—this population of students brings to the mainstream classroom.

> *The past 40 years have seen an unprecedented growth in the number of EBs enrolled in K–12 schools in the U.S.*

Although the demand is well documented, schools and districts continue to struggle to meet these needs. Intentionally or not, many EBs are marginalized in their classes, relegated to the back or side of the room to "absorb" what they can. After years of not receiving the appropriate support, EBs fall increasingly behind their English-speaking peers. In 2013, fourth graders classified as EBs scored 39 points lower than their English-speaking peers (187 vs. 226) on a 500-point reading scale. The achievement gap widens to a 45-point difference among eighth graders. In math, fourth graders classified as EBs scored 25 points lower than their English-speaking peers, and eighth graders, the same year, had a 41-point gap (Kena et al., 2014). Ultimately, these trends lead to dropout rates almost twice that of native and fluent English speakers (Callahan, 2013) as well as lower employment opportunities.

Teacher Support and Preparation

To address a lack of consistency within and across states in the identification, progress tracking, and instruction of EBs, Wisconsin and Delaware partnered in 2002 to establish the World-Class Instructional Design and Assessment (WIDA) consortium and craft a set of standards. The group published resources, provided training, and advocated for additional states to join. Today 36 states plus the District of Columbia belong

---

[1] Garcia (2009c) convincingly argues, "Calling these children emergent bilinguals makes reference to a positive characteristic—not one of being limited or being learners, as LEPs and ELLs suggest" (p. 322). As such, the term emergent bilingual (EB) will be used in place of the more traditional English language learner (ELL), limited English proficient (LEP), or English learner (EL).

to the consortium effectively creating—or working toward—uniformity in terminology, assessment, and instructional targets. According to WIDA's website, from 2013 to 2014, ACCESS for EBs, the WIDA proficiency assessment, was administered by 33 state education agencies to 1,372,611 students.

Although more than half of the U.S. states are sharing testing and pedagogical materials related to EBs, there is less consistency in teacher preparation for teaching in the linguistically diverse classroom. According to a 2008 national survey of new teacher preparation programs, only four states require specific coursework related to second language acquisition in all of their certification programs. Seventeen states make some degree of reference to the special needs of EBs in their teacher certification standards. Another 17 states refer to "language" as an example of diversity in their general teacher certification standards (Ballantyne, Sanderman, & Levy, 2008). The limited attention in mainstream teacher training might be attributed to outdated assumptions that either teachers will not have these students in their classrooms or emergent bilinguals will be within the purview of a school's language (ESL) specialist. To the contrary, research shows that EB students are spending the majority of their time during the school day in mainstream classrooms with teachers unaccustomed and ill prepared to address the needs of students learning a second language alongside the content of their classes (Lopes-Murphy, 2012; Reeves, 2006; Walker, Shafer, & Liams, 2004).

One of the first states to require coursework that attends to EBs is Pennsylvania. The Pennsylvania Department of Education teacher preparation mandate includes "3 credits or 90 course hours addressing the academic needs and adaptations for ELL students" (Pennsylvania Department of Education, 2008, p. 48). The course or professional development requirements include foundational knowledge in language and language structures; processes of acquiring multiple language and literacy skills; distinctions among academic and social language; social, cultural, and learning style influences on language acquisition processes; bias in instruction, assessments, and materials; and cross-cultural interaction competencies.

As the coordinator and field placement supervisor for this required course in a Pennsylvania public university teacher education program, I have collaborated with other Teachers of English to Speakers of Other Languages (TESOL) faculty and instructors for the past several years to design and deliver a course that meets these state specifications. What follows in this chapter are the "headlines" from this work. Specifically, what is offered here is a condensed, accessible synopsis of research-based strategies and approaches most effective for K–12 educators seeking to personalize instruction for EBs in their content areas.

Closely connected to personalized learning, the perspective presented in this chapter is grounded in the ecological approach to language and learning which views language as a multifarious and complex system and language learning as a powerful, creative, and individual process (Kramsch & Whiteside, 2008). Ecology, by definition, is comprehensive, dynamic and interactive, and situated (Garner & Borg, 2005). In contrast to cognitive theories, which consider language learning a relatively uniform process, the ecological approach looks holistically at the learner and learning context. Interactions among learners and their peers, teachers, and texts have long been accepted as contributors to language learning, especially when they provide opportunities for negotiation for meaning (see Moss & Ross-Feldman, 2003). Expanding on this concept, the ecological perspective also appreciates the nuanced contexts in which these activities take place as either source or resource for learning. As van Lier (2011) writes, "at the micro level of the classroom, a focus on ecological processes can awaken in the students (and teachers) a spirit of inquiry and reflection and a philosophy of seeing and hearing for yourself, thinking for yourself, speaking with your own voice, and acting jointly within your community" (p. 99).

The following sections of this chapter offer strategies and rationales for personalized learning for EBs in the content areas, including personalized (English) language learning trajectories and strategies for broadening students' awareness, skills, and knowledge of (English) language forms and uses needed for school success.

Personalized Learning Environments in Linguistically Diverse Classrooms

At the onset of each semester, I am inevitably asked some variation of, "How can I teach them [math/science/literature/history]? They don't know a word of English, and I don't speak their language." Such statements are typically followed by critiques of school structures and limitations of resources to create isolated, specialized programs. Undoubtedly, some of the greatest hurdles to educating EBs in an inclusive environment are fears, insecurities, biases, and assumptions of the school and classroom leaders. Low teacher expectations, consciously or not, are transmitted through teachers' classroom talk (Kendall, 1983; Straehler-Pohl et al., 2014) and, even when attempting to comfort students for low performance, can discourage students (Rattan, Good, & Dweck, 2012).

Not only do teachers' attitudes toward EBs in their classes potentially shape their behaviors, those attitudes can also impact the attitudes of students toward themselves and one another. If the teachers consider the instruction of EBs in their classes as extraneous work, see EBs as not "real" members of their classes, as unable to contribute productively to the classes, or as pity cases, so will the students in the class, including the EBs themselves. Before planning, preparing, and delivering instruction, teachers must reflect honestly and completely on the environment they are creating for their students. The more positive teachers' attitudes and behaviors are toward these students, the more welcoming, inclusive, and effective the classroom will be for them.

Use Table 1 to reflect candidly on your own attitudes about learners of English, their families, and communities.

Table 1. Inventory of Attitudes and Perceptions

Having EBs takes away from English-dominant students.	Having EBs enriches the learning of my English-dominant students
I'm frustrated these students are part of my class.	I'm excited these students are part of my class.
There is no way for me to communicate with them.	I can communicate using images, gestures, facial expression, and so on.
The EBs in my class are really the ESL specialist's students.	The EBs in my class are my students.
Until they are proficient in English, these students will not be able to do content area work.	EBs need differentiation; some know more about the content than my English-dominant students do.

Note: EB = emergent bilinguals; ESL = English as a second language.

Overtly Value Bilingualism

Respond to students' comments—or preemptively comment regularly—"It's so amazing to know two or more languages!" Talk about your own experiences using, learning, or trying to learn another language. Ask questions about your EBs' first languages and display interest. Have them share experiences with what Garcia (2009a) calls *translanguaging*, or how they navigate the use of multiple languages. Beyond code switching, translanguaging is "the act performed by bilinguals of accessing different linguistic features or various modes...to maximize communicative potential" (Garcia, 2009b, p. 140).

As they communicate, language users draw on all their linguistic resources, whether it is using a word or phrase in one language when an equivalent does not exist—or is not known—in another, or stylizing language for emphasis, humor, or in-group marking. In addition to social and communicative benefits, translanguaging has been associated with advanced cognition, executive function, and problem solving.

Personalize the Classroom

Avoid the token or generic cultural decorations. Rather, have all students bring in something or create something that represents *them*, not their "culture" to decorate your room. As new students arrive, they can add to the environment as a step toward being part of the class community. When you have multiple classes of students in the same room, dedicate different spaces to each.

Draw on Students' Resources

Conceptualizing your students as resources will not only enhance the relevancy of your lessons but will also provide opportunities to value and build a dynamic and respectful community. Two concepts contribute to this recommendation, (a) funds of knowledge, or perspectives and (cultural) knowledge acquired in the home (Moll, Amanti, Neff, & Gonzalez, 1992), and (b) funds of identity, or lived experiences that contribute to a child's worldview and sense of self (Esteban-Guitart & Moll, 2014). Make concerted efforts to learn about your students' talents, personal and family experiences, and background knowledge related to academic learning and life outside of school. When you show that you want to know more about your EBs, particularly as you are making efforts to communicate using adjusted language and gestures, you will set an example for students and contribute to the relationships needed for personalized teaching and learning.

Prepare to Help Students Communicate Their Immediate Needs

A newcomer with very limited English proficiency could arrive in your class any day. Make sure you are ready. Have on hand a way these students can communicate their basic needs, such as picture cards. If a student has to go to the bathroom or is worried she does not know where one is, how to get permission to go, and so on, that student will likely not be thinking about much else. Show students how to hold up a picture card or how to get your attention.

Make Peer Support a Norm

Provide opportunities for classmates to help each other out—but do not rely on them. EBs with higher English proficiency are not in your class to translate for you and EBs with lower English proficiency. They are certainly a resource, but they should not be your sole means of communicating with the learners. Interpreting is considered a highly stress-provoking activity, requiring "a superb command of both the source language and the target language, immaculate memory retention, and quick information retrieval from the memory vault" (Po-Chi & Craigie, 2013, p. 1035). Although building these skills can be beneficial, this can also monopolize a student's time and energy otherwise spent on academics. Rather, use and teach all of your students how to use gestures, adjusted speech, and visuals to aid communication. Include English monolingual students in the "buddy" pool and make the position a reward or honor. In other words, avoid rewarding students for helping out other students; make being a helper the reward itself.

Personalizing Content Instruction in the Linguistically Diverse Classroom

To be equitable and attainable by all learners, clearly articulated subject-related goals need to be rooted in skills that are not dependent on high levels of language to perform. Teachers miss opportunities to personalize learning when they write objectives that EBs cannot achieve, not because the EBs cannot or would not be able to do the content work, but because the content work is deeply embedded or dependent on students' abilities to use English beyond their current proficiency level (see WIDA, n.d.).

> Because subject content and language are so intertwined, teachers may question if and how the EBs in their classes could do the work.

Because subject content and language are so intertwined, teachers may question if and how the EBs in their classes could do the work. As a result, they might (a) lower their expectations for students, (b) change the work so that students are not working toward the same goals, or (c) give up and not try. The recommendations in this section encourage teachers to personalize modes and means to facilitate learning, maintain high academic standards for all students, and authentically assess students on their skills and knowledge.

Craft Content Objectives Achievable by All Students

As teachers work to craft clear, attainable, and measurable objectives, they must be mindful of learning goals that can only be met with certain language skills and knowledge. Specifically, objectives that require learners to "describe," "explain," "list," or "name" set expectations for language use that may well exceed the proficiency level of EBs in the class (see WIDA, n.d.). In no way does this suggest the language use targets be removed altogether from the lesson. Rather, under the umbrella term "learning goals," we need to distinguish between two types of objectives: (a) content objectives, or those that focus on the physical skill or cognitive work of the subject, which are consistent for all learners (see Table 2 for appropriate verbs), and (b) language objectives, or those that focus on the language needed to participate in the class activities or communicate content knowledge or ability. This latter set of objectives is varied, or personalized, based on the language proficiency needs, levels, and abilities of the learners.

Table 2. Measurable Action Verbs to Create English Language Learner–Inclusive Content Objectives*

Math	Science	Social Studies & History	Art, Music, & Drama	English Language Arts	Physical Education
Calculate	Record	Locate	Critique	Contrast	Manipulate
Draw	Compare	Distinguish	Perform	Sequence	Record
Identify	Predict	Analyze	Compose	Generalize	Climb
Count	Apply	Compare	Harmonize	Question	Swim
Group	Calibrate	Criticize	Display	Reconstruct	Bat
Convert	Demonstrate	Defend	Whistle	Synthesize	Pitch
Estimate	Insert	Formulate	Tap	Design	Skip
Sequence	Operate	Map	Hum	Predict	Swing
Measure	Report	Appraise	Assemble	Systematize	Predict
Solve	Conduct	Conclude	Recreate	Arrange	Measure
Operate	Dissect	Deduce	Originate	Organize	Skate
Diagram	Prepare	Evaluate	Create	Sort	Stretch
Compare	Weigh	Contrast	Illustrate	Record	Race
Predict	Convert	Induce	Produce	Represent	Clock

*The list is not exhaustive, nor are the verbs limited to the content area columns.

For example, a math objective might read, "Solve a two-digit multiplication problem and describe the process." Although this objective does meet the criteria of being measurable and clear, the language demands of the second part of the objective may well make it unattainable for EB students. Another way to look at this objective is that it contains two sets of skills—the cognitive skill of solving the math problem and the (English) oral language skills to be able to describe the process. An objective like this is best crafted as two objectives: "Solve a two-digit multiplication problem" (content objective) and "Describe, list, or name the process of solving a two-digit multiplication problem" (language objective).

Communicate Your Content in Accessible Ways

The term "input" in the field of language teaching and learning refers to language to which learners are exposed, either written or spoken. It is what they hear and see around them in the target language. It is not necessarily what they can understand or use. "Comprehensible input," a term introduced to the field by Krashen (1982), is a subset of general language input and refers specifically to what is accessible to learners. Factors that help make input comprehensible include the use of images, signs, gestures, repetition, and simpler vocabulary and grammar structure. These concepts apply to printed materials as well as oral communication. Use all of these as you guide students in content area instruction. Specifically, as you interact with EBs, personalizing their learning, point to the board or book, gesture, model, and repeat what you are saying a few times, and, when possible, use more common language to define academic terms. Provide images alongside language. Use videos and other forms of multimedia to facilitate their understanding.

Differentiate Assignments Based on Language Development Needs

The type of product or performance you request of students as part of your assessments must align with their language proficiency level, contribute to their language and academic development, and allow you to see their progress toward the content objective.

Avoid just making the assignment easier by reducing the quantity of work. In a survey conducted by Reeves (2006), teachers cited equity, or perceived equity, as a concern with modifying materials for EBs. Reeves suggests this comes from a lack of training or preparation in the types of modifications needed for language learners. Appropriate, fair instruction for EBs is neither overly simplified nor unmodified (Gebhard, 2003). "To increase equity for English language learners, schools must provide the support that these students need to engage in challenging, content-based learning tasks" (p. 35). The modifications need to be related to language levels. If the content of the class or product of an assignment requires levels of language beyond the students' current levels, teachers must make adjustments to the *language demands* to improve access.

To personalize modifications based on language needs, consider all the different ways we communicate. We demonstrate or perform, illustrate, create or build, write, speak, gesture, and so on. Just as teachers should engage in these various means to share concepts and interact with EBs, the students can and should use these as well to communicate their thoughts, emotions, and needs. To best align what you ask of students with the students' abilities, consider Table 3.

Table 3. Language Demands of Communicative Actions

Communicative Actions (by Emergent Bilinguals)	**Language Demands (on Emergent Bilinguals)**
Pointing, gesturing, modeling, performing (nonverbal or limited verbal), illustrating, creating, using manipulatives	Receptive oral language skills (listening and understanding oral directions) Receptive literacy skills (reading written directions)
Speaking: naming, describing, arguing, retelling, suggesting, asking, presenting, persuading (verbal), expressing opinion, joking, directing, introducing, explaining, defining	Receptive oral or literacy skills *plus* Productive oral language skills (pronunciation, vocabulary, structure, social appropriateness)
Writing: noting, creating (a story, script, essay), composing, addressing, texting, emailing, inscribing, formulating, authoring, rewriting, recording, editing, drafting, summarizing	Receptive oral or literacy skills *plus* Productive written language skills (spelling, writing conventions, structure, genre)

For example, suppose a science lesson requires students to differentiate between items that can and cannot be recycled. Students at lower levels can be asked to sort or point to items that fit categories. The language goal will be for students to respond with gestures to the oral prompts "can recycle" and "cannot recycle." Mid- and high-level English users can be asked to name or describe orally which items fit the categories or, given appropriate literacy skills, they can be asked to label as well. The concept remains consistent across groups, but the language levels are personalized to the students' English language abilities. Other possible modifications might include pairing students to collaborate on assignments; providing language supports, such as a word bank or dictionary; or providing additional time for completion.

Last, when focusing on the content of a class and even when developing second language literacy skills, teachers may also include use of first language materials. Contrary to the belief that language learners should be compelled to exclusively use the second language to gain mastery, research has highlighted the importance of continued first language use in developing second language literacy (Cummins, 1981b; Wong Fillmore, 1991; see also Krashen, 2003).

Personalizing (English) Language Development in Linguistically Diverse Classrooms

Remember, all learners are language learners, and all teachers are language teachers. Effective teachers make targeted language usage part of instructional planning for high-level EBs and native speakers as well as students with lower proficiency. As described in the introduction, the choices and attention paid to classroom language usage must be personalized to what students already know and can do as well as their language goals, needs, and interests.

Because language learning critically relies on access and input, teachers must consider not only their expectations for learners' language production or responses to language (i.e., listening and reading skills), but also, ecologically speaking, their contextualized and meaningful use of targeted language forms throughout their lessons. The recommendations in this section encourage teachers to create realistic expectations for their students as well as themselves; maintain focus on language targets; and, at the same time, remain open and flexible to language change, unexpected outcomes, and opportunities to learn alongside their students.

Language and Instructional Plans

Determine what language is needed to participate in your instructional plan. You may have key terms or phrases or there may be specific language structures students need to understand to participate in the learning activities or that you will want your students to use in some part of the lesson. Some of these targets relate to academic language, or what Cummins (1979, 1981b) refers to as cognitive academic language proficiency (CALP). This includes content specific vocabulary and grammatical structures normed for academic and professional settings. Examples are using terms *equation*, *expression*, *variable*, *term*, *coefficient*, and *equality* when describing one-step linear equations and solutions (algebra) or including relative clauses in a descriptive writing activity. (See later discussion for how to personalize these language targets.)

Other language needs may be more casual or social, or what Cummins (1979, 1981b) calls basic interpersonal communicative skills (BICS). Gibbons (1991) uses the term "playground language," language that "enables children to make friends, join in games, and take part in a variety of day-to-day activities that develop and maintain social contacts" (p. 3). In the classroom, BICS (or playground language) is used in group work negotiations, making requests, and relationship building. The BICS targets that teachers can set might be very scripted, such as asking, "Can I play?" when joining a game or using basic terms to reference classroom items, family members, and social activities. Others goals might be more rule driven, such as using appropriate pronouns in speech or writing or subject–verb agreement (e.g., I am, she is, they are). Although proficiency in all aspects of BICS may be the goal, effective teachers personalize the targets for language gains based on the student's current ability and the immediate needs of the lesson.

Note: Because language learners have greater access and more frequent interactions using BICS, learners tend to acquire BICS at a quicker rate than CALP—3 to 5 years versus 5 to 7 years (Cummins, 1981a). It is important for teachers to keep this in mind and avoid assumptions about students' academic language knowledge and skills based on observations of the students' use of BICS in social settings.

Plan Language Targets Based on (Individual) Language Proficiencies

Relevant, targeted language usage for teachers and students should be part of every lesson. Typically, teachers do include language learning and usage expectations in their plans. They have vocabulary lists, key phrases, and expectations for writing and speaking structures consistent with norms of specific academic areas. However, these targets are often buried or implied in rubrics or in the "content" objectives. To be clear on how students can meet the goals of participating in lessons and demonstrating what they have learned, teachers need to isolate the language targets and explicitly set personalized, realistic, language learning targets for their students.

Keep the Focus on Meaning

Teachers often wonder when, how, and how often they should correct students' language errors. There is no straightforward answer to this. Errors are part of the language learning process and often signal progress in language acquisition. Early in language learning, EBs acquire "chunks" of language. As they gain new knowledge or awareness of grammatical forms and rules, they explore when and how to apply these rules across contexts. For example, learners lower on the WIDA scale might produce utterances such as, "I bought lunch." As they move up on the scale, they might start saying, "I buyed lunch." This error suggests that the learner has noticed a pattern of adding "-ed" to indicate past tense and is overgeneralizing the rule as he sorts out when it applies and when it does not.

Studies on feedback suggest that students have to be ready in their developmental stage to receive corrective feedback. Also, learner preferences in the types and frequency in which they receive corrective feedback play roles in their responses to the feedback offered (Borg, 2003; Grotjahn, 1991). When there is a mismatch in feedback type and preference, learners may be less likely to notice or accept the feedback. Other research studies suggest that regardless of learners' stated preferences, some forms of feedback are better than nothing (McDonough, 2007), and opportunities for learners to be exposed repeatedly to correct forms after errors contribute to their language development even if it is not aligned with learners' stated preferences (Leeman, 2003; Lyster & Izquierdo, 2009). Ultimately, whether through direct or indirect feedback or through personalized daily interactions, with enough exposure to the target forms (i.e., the "bought" example) or opportunities to self-correct, learners will likely improve accuracy.

Promote Talk as Part of Learning for All Students

Although some theories of second language learning regard output, or language produced by learners, as being relatively unnecessary to the language learning process (Krashen, 1994), others have argued that learners' production of language plays a critical role. As learners actively participate in meaningful communication, they test hypotheses about language rules, get feedback on whether or not they can be understood, request more accessible input from speakers, and modify their own output to better match targets. All of these social usages of language contribute to learners' language development (Gass, 1997; Long, 1996; Pica, 1994; Swain, 2000). Recently, these activities, which not only involve production of language but also meaning making and the transforming of thinking into artifactual form, have been referred to as "languaging" (Swain, 2006).

To facilitate languaging, cluster desks and tables and design activities to encourage students to talk. Set an expectation that all students have strengths—in language, academics, social interaction, and creativity—that benefit the group. Also, throughout your class, mix up the grouping of students according to activity goals and students' strengths and needs. At times, each of your groups will need a strong writer, artist, and orator in a group. At other times, you will group students based on math abilities. Others might be based on interests, with dancers in one group and team sports participants in another. Each time you group, be aware and explicit about your expectations for inclusion and participation.

Conclusion

Linguistically diverse classrooms offer teachers and students—whether mono- or multilingual—rich opportunities to expand worldviews; deepen understandings of culture, norms, and identity; and collaboratively develop language and academic skills and knowledge. The strategies presented here support these efforts as well as suggest (new) ways to view and maximize classroom instruction and participation among all participants. By regarding every individual in the learning environment as a language learner and teacher; setting clear, attainable learning goals; valuing contributions of students; and personalizing the process and targets, teachers will not only create a context conducive for academic success but will also contribute to each student's empowered sense of self and belonging.

References

Aud, S., Hussar, W., Kena, G., Bianco, K., Frohlich, L., Kemp, J., & Tahan, K. (2011). *The condition of education 2011* (NCES 2011-033). U.S. Department of Education, National Center for Education Statistics. Washington, DC: U.S. Government Printing Office. Retrieved from https://nces.ed.gov/pubs2011/2011033.pdf

Ballantyne, K. G., Sanderman, A. R., & Levy, J. (2008). *Educating English language learners: Building teacher capacity*. Washington, DC: National Clearinghouse for English Language Acquisition.

Borg, S. (2003). Teacher cognition in language teaching: A review of research on what teachers think, know, believe, and do. *Language Teaching, 36*(1), 81–109.

Callahan, R. M. (2013). *The English learner dropout dilemma: Multiple risks and multiple resources*. Santa Barbara, CA: University of California, California Dropout Research Project.

Cummins, J. (1979). Cognitive/academic language proficiency, linguistic interdependence, the optimum age question, and some other matters. *Working Papers on Bilingualism, 19*, 121–129.

Cummins, J. (1981a). Age on arrival and immigrant second language learning in Canada. A reassessment. *Applied Linguistics, 2*, 132–149.

Cummins, J. (1981b). The role of primary language development in promoting educational success for language minority students. In California State Department of Education (Ed.), *Schooling and language minority students: A theoretical framework* (pp. 3–49). Los Angeles, CA: Evaluation, Dissemination, and Assessment Center, California State University.

Esteban-Guitart, M., & Moll, L. C. (2014). Lived experience, funds of identity, and education. *Culture & Psychology, 20*(1), 70–81.

Garcia, O. (2009a). *Bilingual education in the 21st century: A global perspective*. Malden, MA: Wiley-Blackwell.

Garcia, O. (2009b). Education, multilingualism, and translanguaging in the 21st century. In T. Skutnabb-Kangas, R. Phillipson, A. Mohanty, & M. Panda (Eds.), *Multilingual education and social justice* (pp. 128-145). Tonawanda, NY: Multilingual Matters.

Garcia, O. (2009c). Emergent bilinguals and TESOL: What's in a name? *TESOL Quarterly, 43,* 322–326.

Garner, M., & Borg, E. (2005). An ecological perspective on content-based instruction. *Journal of English for Academic Purposes, 4,* 119–134.

Gass, S. M. (1997). *Input, interaction, and the second language learner*. Mahwah, NJ: Lawrence Erlbaum Associates.

Gebhard, M. (2003). Getting past "See spot run." *Educational Leadership, 60*(4), 35–39.

Gibbons, P. (2002). *Scaffolding language, scaffolding learning: Teaching second language learners in the mainstream classroom*. Portsmouth, NH: Heinemann.

Grotjahn, R. (1991). The research programme: Subjective theories. *Studies in Second Language Acquisition, 13*(2), 187–214.

Kena, G., Aud, S., Johnson, F., Wang, X., Zhang, J., Rathbun, A.,...Kristapovich, P. (2014). *The condition of education 2014* (NCES 2014-083). Washington, DC: U.S. Department of Education, National Center for Education Statistics.

Kendall, F. E. (1983). *Diversity in the classroom: A multicultural approach to the education of young children*. New York, NY: Teachers College Press, Columbia University.

Kramsch, C., & Whiteside, A. (2008). Language ecology in multilingual settings. Towards a theory of symbolic competence. *Applied Linguistics, 29*(4), 645.

Krashen, S. D. (1982). *Principles and practice in second language acquisition*. Oxford, England: Pergamon Press.

Krashen, S. (1994). The input hypothesis and its rivals. In N. Ellis (Ed.), *Implicit and explicit learning of languages* (pp. 45–77). London, UK: Academic Press.

Krashen, S. D. (2003). *Explorations in language acquisition*. Portsmouth, NH: Heinemann.

Leeman, J. (2003). Recasts and L2 development: Beyond negative evidence. *Studies in Second Language Acquisition, 25*(1), 37–63.

Long, M. H. (1996). The role of linguistic environment in second language acquisition. In W. Ritchie, & T. K. Bhatia (Eds.), *Handbook of second language acquisition* (pp. 413–468). San Diego, CA: Academic Press.

Lopes-Murphy, S. (2012). Universal design for learning: Preparing secondary education teachers in training to increase academic accessibility of high school English learners. *The Clearing House, 85*(6), 226–230.

Lyster, R., & Izquierdo, J. (2009). Prompts versus recasts in dyadic interaction. *Language Learning, 59*(2), 453–498.

McDonough, K. (2007). Interactional feedback and the emergence of simple past activity verbs in L2 English. In A. Mackey (Ed.), *Conversational interaction in second language acquisition: A collection of empirical studies* (pp. 323–338). Oxford, UK: Oxford University Press.

Moll, L. C., Amanti, C., Neff, D., & Gonzalez, N. (1992). Funds of knowledge for teaching: Using a qualitative approach to connect homes and classrooms. *Theory into Practice, 31*(2), 132.

Moss, D., & Ross-Feldman, L. (2003). *Second language acquisition in adults: From research to practice*. Washington, DC: National Center for ESL Literacy Education.

Pennsylvania Department of Education. (2008). *The framework for special education grades pre k–8 & 7–12 program guidelines*. Harrisburg, PA: Author.

Pica, T. (1994). Questions from the language classroom: Research perspectives. *TESOL Quarterly, 28*, 49–79.

Po-Chi, K., & Craigie, P. (2013). Evaluating student interpreters' stress and coping strategies. *Social Behavior & Personality, 41*(6), 1035–1043.

Rattan, A., Good, C., & Dweck, C. S. (2012). "It's ok—Not everyone can be good at math": Instructors with an entity theory comfort (and demotivate) students. *Journal of Experimental Social Psychology, 48*(3), 731–737.

Redding, S. (2013). *Through the student's eyes: A perspective on personalized learning*. Philadelphia, PA: Center on Innovations in Learning, Temple University. Retrieved from http://www.centeril.org/publications/2013_09_Through_the_Eyes.pdf

Reeves, J. R. (2006). Secondary teacher attitudes toward including English language learners in mainstream classrooms. *Journal of Educational Research, 99*(3), 131–142.

Straehler-Pohl, H., Fernández, S., Gellert, U., & Figueiras, L. (2014). School mathematics registers in a context of low academic expectations. *Educational Studies in Mathematics, 85*(2), 175–199.

Swain, M. (2000). The output hypothesis and beyond: Mediating acquisition through collaborative dialogue. In J. P. Lantolf (Ed.), *Sociocultural theory and second language learning* (pp. 97–114). Oxford, UK: Oxford University Press.

Swain, M. (2006). Languaging, agency, and collaboration in advanced second language proficiency. In H. Byrnes (Ed.), *Advanced language learning: The contribution of Halliday and Vygotsky* (pp. 95–108). New York, NY: Continuum.

Tan, M. (2011). Mathematics and science teachers' beliefs and practices regarding the teaching of language in content learning. *Language Teaching Research, 15*(3), 325–342.

van Lier, L. (2011). Research in and around the language classroom: Qualitative and quantitative approaches. Introduction to the Supplementary Issue. *Modern Language Journal, 95*, Supplement s1, 1–3.

Walker, A., Shafer, J., & Liams, M. (2004). Not in my classroom: Teacher attitudes towards English language learners in the mainstream classroom. *Journal of Research and Practice, 2*(1), 130–160.

WIDA. (n.d.). *Standards and Instruction*. Retrieved from https://www.wida.us/standards/

Wong Fillmore, L. (1991). When learning a second language means losing the first. *Early Childhood Research Quarterly, 6*, 323–346.

On Personalized Learning in the Context of Common Core Literacy Standards: A Sociocultural Perspective

Francis J. Sullivan, Jr.

In his article on the potential of personalized learning and the conflicts that need to be negotiated for it to achieve that potential, Redding (2013) reminds us of its long lineage, emerging from the "educational philosophy from the Progressive Era, especially John Dewey's (1915, 1998) emphasis on experiential, child-centered learning; social learning; expansion of the curriculum; and preparation for a changing world" (p. 121). While ensuing research may have tempered some of its progressive ideals, at least within Anglo-American schooling, Redding shows how its current revitalization as "personalized learning" retains the core concepts that have animated it from the beginning: "Personalization ensues from the relationships among teachers and learners and the teacher's orchestration of multiple means for enhancing every aspect of each student's learning and development" (p. 126).

The 2009 Common Core State Standards (CCSS) for literacy in the content areas poses fundamental challenges to the continued development of student-centered approaches to learning that Redding calls for. Though the new CCSS do expand literacy instruction into all content areas, not just in English, they narrow the scope of that expansion by emphasizing the role of "informational" texts that analyze, interpret, or evaluate over "narrative" texts that simply tell a story and by the application of a kind of "close reading" based on text-dependent questioning that treats meaning as residing entirely within the written text (National Governors Association & Council of Chief State School Officers, 2009). These shifts strike at the core of personalized learning, objectifying and depersonalizing readers' experience of texts. That is, the emphasis on close, supposedly objective, reading creates a false dichotomy between text meaning and the lived experience that students bring to their reading of that text. In doing so, these shifts radically devalue students' use of affect and emotion in their responses to texts. Further, in calling for teachers to abandon "scaffolding" strategies that prepare students for reading and guide their development of reading strategies in favor of students' unmediated encounters with texts, these shifts risk undermining students' developing self-efficacy and their social relationships with their teachers as caring guides.

Handbook on Personalized Learning for States, Districts, and Schools, pages 263–272

The keystone of the CCSS for literacy framework is the tripartite concept of complexity. The first two components of complexity focus on features and qualities of texts. The "quantitative" component builds on traditional notions of readability—polysyllabic vocabulary and sentence length—to add in the element of "rarity" of vocabulary built into the Lexile measure. The "qualitative" component is comprised of text qualities—layout, levels of meaning, structure, language conventions, and background knowledge—whose complexity can be determined only through human judgment. The third, and according to the CCSS crucial, component is the "reader/task" relationship. This component combines those elements that a reader brings—in particular, motivation—with the level of cognitive and metacognitive activity required to accomplish the learning task as set by the teacher (Ciardiello, 2012). Schools have allowed standards to fall, the authors of CCSS insist, first, by the inclusion of too many "simple" narrative texts in the curriculum and, second, by the adoption of instructional practices that encourage learners to substitute their personal reactions for close analysis of textual features and qualities key to understanding an author's intended meaning. It is the announced aim of CCSS to raise this bar, using the concept of complexity to clearly define the rigor of both texts and tasks. It is the aim of the new assessments to evaluate whether students, teachers, and schools are clearing the bar set by CCSS (National Governors Association & Council of Chief State School Officers, n.d.a, n.d.b).

> It is the announced aim of CCSS to raise this bar, using the concept of complexity to clearly define the rigor of both texts and tasks.

This curricular shift in emphasis—away from narrative texts to "informational" genres—is mirrored in a second shift—away from personal response to reading and toward an emphasis on "the text itself," as the authors make clear in their revised criteria:

> The standards and these criteria sharpen the focus on the close connection between comprehension of text and acquisition of knowledge. While the link between comprehension and knowledge in reading science and history texts is clear, the same principle applies to all reading. The criteria make plain that developing students' prowess at drawing knowledge from the text itself is the point of reading; reading well means gaining the maximum insight or knowledge possible from each source. Student knowledge drawn from the text is demonstrated when the student uses evidence from the text to support a claim about the text. Hence evidence and knowledge link directly to the text. (Coleman & Pimentel, 2012, p. 1)

The chief instructional strategy so far identified has been to advocate a kind of decontextualized "close reading" of texts, to be guided by the teacher relying almost entirely on "text dependent" questioning (Coleman & Pimentel, 2012), completely abandoning the kinds of evidence-based, student-centered reading strategies that research has shown to be effective in scaffolding student engagement with texts over the last 30 years (Anderson & Pearson, 1984; Hinchman & Sheridan-Thomas, 2008). Smith, Appleman, and Wilhelm (2014), who have harshly criticized this text-dependent approach as a kind of "Zombie New Criticism," note pointedly that there is absolutely no empirical evidence for its effectiveness. If anything, the evidence points to its ineffectiveness—its inability to engage students in attending closely to a text; to develop ways of reading a text deeply that can transfer readily to other texts and genres; to do this reading within contexts that are, in fact, meaningful to learners; and, most significantly, to foster a critical literacy in which readers learn how to identify and challenge the assumptions and claims of the texts that they are reading (Smith et al., 2014).

Notable in these shifts is that, while the pendulum may have swung from subjective stories to objective informational texts and from personal response to impersonal close reading, the shifts retain the same dichotomies about literacy and learning that can be traced back at least as far as Dewey's work in the 1920s. Objective is pitted against subjective, personal against impersonal. What we need is a literacy and learning framework that actually incorporates these tensions as resources we can use. Though less well known within education, sociocultural frameworks for discourse analysis offer a far more robust perspective to support the kind of careful, thoughtful engagement with texts that the CCSS claim to want from students but do little to promote. Proponents of sociocultural frameworks, with roots deep in anthropology, linguistics, and sociology, have developed remarkably effective methods for explaining how people actually use literacy in real-world contexts, methods that have been adapted for use in classroom contexts in the United States, Great Britain, Australia, and the Far East. I have found these frameworks to be quite powerful in my own research on teaching and learning as well as in curriculum development in schools, college, and the workplace (Sullivan, 1995, 1997a, 1997b; Sullivan & Baren, 1997; Sullivan, Lyon, Lebofsky, Wells, & Goldblatt, 1997). For the last five years, I have been reshaping my own courses—and my teaching as well—so that they embody the pedagogical principles that I have distilled from my scholarly work in and with these frameworks. In what follows, I first explain the framework, contrasting it with that implicit in the CCSS notion of "complexity," and then outline those principles at the core of my curriculum development work, in particular with preservice secondary teachers in the secondary education content areas, illustrating how those principles function in the courses that I teach.

Studying Literacy "in the Wild"

Though sociocultural perspectives on literacy do not use the term "complexity" explicitly, they nevertheless redefine it radically by refocusing our attention on the dynamics of the situation in which literate activity takes place. Such perspectives always connect language use to the social contexts in which it is being used and to the multiple—sometimes conflicting—ways of making sense of reality that those contexts may demand. Gee (1999) puts it this way:

> Language, in fact, serves a great many functions, and "giving and getting information," yes, even in our new "Information Age," is but one, and by no means the only one. If I had to single out a primary function of language, it would be, not one, but the following two: to scaffold the performance of social activities (whether play or work or both), and to scaffold social affiliations within cultures and social groups and institutions. (p. 1)

From a sociocultural perspective, the meanings of text and context are co-created. In "the real world," our use of language doesn't distinguish between the ideas that we are explaining and the way that our phrasing of those ideas represents our social identities—our "affiliations," as Gee (1999) puts it. Rather, we use language to accomplish goals, but always as a particular kind of person within a particular social context.

How does this occur? Briefly, elements of the social context name the "rules of the game." They constrain both the kinds of social activity in which we are supposed to engage *and* whom we are supposed to represent, or be affiliated with, in the activity. They may even constrain the goals themselves. At the same time, the ways that we respond to those constraints in order to achieve our goals and represent our affiliations make use of these rules, which may even include violating or ignoring the rules. It is in that sense that we talk about language use as being a cooperative activity.

For example, suppose that a local news show is doing "people in the street" interviews on the topic of whether people prefer city or country living. The interviewer walks up to someone, asks, "Which do you prefer, city or country?" and puts the microphone out for the person to speak. Speaker A replies, "*I prefer* the city." Speaker B says, "*My preference* is the city." What difference does the way each answered make to the social meaning of what each of them said? At one level, it would seem to make no difference. Both have "said" that they want to live in the same kind of surroundings. That information is the same. But a closer look, the kind that a sociocultural perspective allows, reveals important differences about each speaker's relationship to that information and the kind of person represented in that way of speaking.

Speaker A's phrasing would be considered "direct," meaning that the grammatical structure of the statement is congruent with the idea being stated. The verb states the "action," the subject identifies the "agent" of the action, the object the "goal." This sentence represents a speaker who "says what he means and means what he says," one who values definite, concrete statements and opinions. The phrasing of this reply is like a miniature narrative, telling the story of the speaker's experience.

Speaker B's phrasing contrasts with the above in significant ways. It would be considered "indirect"; its grammatical structure is incongruent with the ideas being presented. In this version, the action is no longer stated by the verb; that action is now the grammatical subject, transformed through the process of "nominalization." This transformation "objectifies" (Kuipers & Viechnicki, 2008) the action as a kind of conceptual object, making it available for discussion as if it were an actual thing. In short, objectification distances the speaker from both the experience being discussed and also from the speaker's audience. Rather than narrating an experience, this way of speaking is a reflection on experience; note how the verb states, not an action, but an equivalence between "my preference" and "the city," which itself is now defined as the speaker's "preference." In contrast to Speaker A's phrasing, this phrasing represents the speaker as a kind of person who values reflection as a means to come to considered conclusions.

These may seem small changes, in an imagined example, but they have dramatic consequences for schooling. The psychologized, "reflective" style above has been shown to characterize the responses of high-performing adolescents (Gee, 2000). In fact, the distinction between "direct" and "indirect" ways of making meaning is a well-established phenomenon, with research extending over the last 50 years (Bernstein, 2000). Often referred to as "codes" (Delpit, 1986; Halliday & Webster, 2009), these ways of making meaning are not intrinsically unequal; rather, they draw upon different "cultural models" used to construct meaning out of one's experience of the world, models that Gee (2005) labels "everyday" and "specialized" (pp. 42–43). Direct codes rely on "common sense" reasoning and concrete experience to construct explanations of reality. Specialized codes rely on the kinds of counterintuitive reasoning developed in academic and professional fields. Not surprisingly, these correspond roughly to ways of making meaning valued in schools and those less valued ways used in out-of-school activities, and they correspond with the distinction between "narrative" and "informational" texts in the CCSS.

One implication of this distinction for understanding the dynamics of teaching and learning is that, too often, student responses to teacher questions are evaluated simply as correct or incorrect when, in reality, students are using codes (i.e., cultural models) other than the one that the teacher wants them to use in the classroom situation. For instance, in a science class, when children are asked, "How far does light from a candle travel?" many, including adolescents, respond in terms of how much space a light illuminates. Obviously, this is not an acceptable answer from the perspective or cultural model used in physics. Yet, anyone operating from the cultural model that we use in our everyday lives might give the same answer as these youth, not because we are ignorant of physics, but because the situated meaning of light typically concerns illumination, "the range through which an observer can see visible effects of light" (Gee, 1999, pp. 44–45). If we want to know what size lightbulb we need to use in a large room, that's exactly the problem we need to pose. Students responding in unacceptable ways need to learn that there are other cultural models for understanding light, frameworks that distinguish between such things as illumination and light itself. Doing otherwise is like calling Newton ignorant for saying that the shortest route between two points is a straight line because that definition doesn't take into account the principle of relativity.

> If we want to know what size lightbulb we need to use in a large room, that's exactly the problem we need to pose.

Using literacy to evaluate the competence of individuals this way is not just an element of schooling. It occurs also in the workplace. In my work developing a literacy curriculum for entry-level IRS tax examiners, this element was at its heart. Top management insisted that the examiners, who possessed only a high-school degree or GED, were functionally illiterate, unable to read or write simple messages. Though errors were not uncommon among these examiners, it remained the case that most of their work was completed accurately. Still, management ordered that all memos inviting examiners to apply for our program must contain the word "deficiencies" to label the focus of the program. It also demanded that we develop a proficiency examination, which anyone enrolled in our program must pass or be fired.[1]

The problem, as my interviews with tax examiners revealed, was not that they needed support for making decisions about the vast majority of cases that came across their desks, which were straightforward and thus easy for them to process. Rather, they needed to be able to distinguish reliably between those cases and others that were complex or problematic, to determine the nature of the problem, and to use the relevant procedures to make the appropriate response. To accomplish this, they needed to be able to interpret and apply the official manual, called an IRM. This manual outlines the precise procedures examiners should follow for each regulation in the tax code, defining all its concepts and specifying the exact steps to take and the specific contingencies that would require alternatives to resolve the issue. In other words, it represented the work of examiners as reasoning one's way through a potentially complex tax situation that might arise with any new case an examiner was assigned. Examiners avoided these manuals whenever possible. In the words of one, referring to the IRM, "I know what it says; I just don't know what it means."

---

[1] Because our contract did not include such a test, we were able to refuse this demand.

The literacy activity in which these examiners engaged, then, was more like that of biologists or botanists, sorting phenomena into the correct categories even as they searched for one case that did not fit easily into any of the established categories. The curriculum I developed began by introducing examiners to the problem through a simulation in which they had to define a common animal, in this case a bird, in such a way that the definition would distinguish all birds from non-birds. Examiners then had to apply their definitions to a set of images of increasing complexity, ending with one of an apteryx—a wingless bird with hairy feathers that lays its eggs in the sand. Calling this animal a bird is about as counterintuitive as it gets, unless you are an ornithologist, for whom it makes perfect sense. As a result, examiners began to see their work and themselves in a new context, one in which they were engaged in a complex endeavor that required an equally complex manual to address. Subsequent lessons immersed examiners in examinations of actual cases of increasing complexity while interpreting and applying procedures from the manuals correctly and appropriately. Examiners who completed the program improved substantively in their work as measured by our assessments and, more importantly, as judged by their supervisors.

Thinking of literacy as a sociocultural phenomenon thus enables us to take learners' cultural models seriously, as a resource rather than a deficit. It reminds us that all cultural models are limited to the situational contexts out of which they emerged and to the purposes that motivated them. Broadly speaking, this work allows us to identify not only the patterns underlying adolescents' speaking, writing, and reading, but also the logic of their responses to texts. Instead of simply attributing differences in learners' speech or writing to ignorance or misunderstanding of the rules of "Standard" English, we can instead make use of the knowledge and skills learners bring to using language to achieve their goals and establish their social identities. In fact, work on the use of various vernaculars in the speech and writing of working-class and racial minority youth have been used as a basis for student inquiry into those patterns, the contrasts between those patterns and those of "Standard" English, and the situations in which each pattern is—and is not—effective (Baker, 2002; Baugh, 1987; Brown, 2009). Other studies on out-of-school literacies, such as "tagging" and online social media, have been used to scaffold student engagement with in-school, academic literacies (Alvermann, 2010; Finders, 1996; Lee, 2004; Moje, 2000).

Discourse Analysis as Pedagogical Tool: Principles and Practices

From a sociocultural perspective, then, "complexity" is best understood, not as a feature of texts or of reader/task relationships, but as a product of the entire activity in which we are engaged, whether in or out of the classroom. The more authentic the activity, the deeper the understanding that results. Moreover, a sociocultural perspective demands that we treat development not as a linear progression nor even as a spiral, but as dialectic. Learners develop through struggle with multiple and conflicting perspectives and—even more important—situated identities. It is their reshaping of these perspectives and identities that constitutes development. Finally, it requires teachers to see themselves and their work differently, to consider the cultural models that support work in their field in the light of students' everyday practices through which they construct meaning, so that those differences can be used to scaffold student learning in the relevant discipline. In the remainder of my discussion, I want to elaborate how each of these principles has enabled me to design innovative classroom practices that can support students' development of discipline-specific literacies.

Principle I: Authenticity

Real means real. The course that I teach, Literacy and Differentiation in the Content Areas, Grades 7–12, relies heavily on the curriculum development work of Wiggins and McTighe and on Tomlinson's work on differentiation (Tomlinson & McTighe, 2006). Theirs is not, strictly speaking, a sociocultural approach, but it does offer a flexible platform on which I can scaffold student learning. The advantage that this sociocultural perspective provides is to guide my development of activities and assessments that address actual problems that learners will face as student teachers and in the profession. To that end, the course is organized around the essential questions, "What is complexity?" and "How can I design curriculum and instruction that enables all my students to develop deep understandings of big ideas in my field in the context of high-stakes testing?" In the authentic performance assessment that is the culminating course task, learners must address these questions in the context of a presentation to the principal, teachers, and students at The LINC, a new public high school in Philadelphia. This is, in fact, an actual school, which requires teacher applicants to construct a unit of instruction using the Understanding by Design framework. The school also represents a "bet" by the School District of Philadelphia that a comprehensive high school based on project-based and inquiry-oriented learning principles can meet the new demands of CCSS.

Developing control of a professional discourse is about learning to affiliate oneself with the knowledge, beliefs, values, and commitments central to it. It is about learning to construct "who I am" in this situation. The situational context of this assessment thus immerses learners in a very real situation, one in which there are serious consequences, in which professional expertise is necessary, yet one in which no one has the final answer. In a very real sense, my students must successfully affiliate themselves with that professional community even as they argue for the efficacy—and the limits—of this approach to teaching and learning.

Principle II: Social Identity and Development

Development is dialectical, not linear. We tend to think of development as additive. Using existing schema, we add new knowledge to it, and thus progress to the next level. The more I have worked from a sociocultural perspective, the better I have come to understand development as the product of conflicts and contradictions with which we are struggling, conflicts that are more associated with our attempts to come to terms with the situated identity we are in the process of acquiring versus the situated identity we have now. This conflict is very real with those that I teach. The very phrase "preservice teachers" captures the conflict. Having almost completed their preparation, increasingly involved in classrooms working with students and teachers, and soon to be given responsibility for an entire roster of classes for a whole semester, they nevertheless still identify themselves as students, with the knowledge, beliefs, values, and commitments of a discourse that they have mastered over their 16 years of schooling.

The questions and assessments described above thus challenge students to reframe themselves as professionals with real expertise that they can use with authority. At the beginning of the semester, class discussion on curriculum and instruction has a quite conflicted nature. As my students wrestle with the implications of committing themselves to the kind of curriculum design and instructional practice that I have outlined here, they become increasingly concerned about the responsibilities that they are placing on themselves. Not yet able to speak authoritatively as teachers, they begin to question and even reject these instructional practices which they now call "idealized" and "impractical" in "the real world" or with "those students." This, however, is a necessary step in their development. My role at this point is to encourage their questioning and to guide them in examining these concerns. I do this chiefly by acknowledging their anxieties about what might happen, while reminding them that the authors whom they are reading are or have been teachers themselves, that the practices we are considering have been used with all kinds of students in all kinds of schools, and, finally, by inviting them to think of this as something they will put into practice over multiple years, not in a single marking period.

Principle III: Teaching and Assessing

The teacher leads from behind. I have been quite surprised as I have come to realize how much this sociocultural perspective demands of me as the teacher. It is much more labor intensive than my former courses were. It is one thing to design curriculum along sociocultural lines. It is essentially a conceptual project. However, it is quite different to actually put this perspective into practice, especially in the ways that I respond to my students' writing throughout the semester and how I evaluate their final performance assessment. Modules in the course immerse students in increasingly complex activities in which they must adapt and apply the big ideas taught. Each module leads up to a report on implementing that big idea in an instructional routine, together with an explanation of their reasoning in constructing the routine as they did. Each report receives extensive marginal responses from me in addition to a grade. The reports may be revised, but all the reports must be included—and discussed as evidence—in the final performance assessment.

From a sociocultural perspective, my formative assessment of their reports focuses on their changing social identities. Who is speaking in the piece? Whom does he represent? By what authority does she ground her reasoning? Even though the final performance task is mainly summative, I can still use similar questions to guide my evaluation of it. How successfully has the writer affiliated him- or herself with the professional expertise of the education community? Overall, this strategy seems quite effective, if I judge by students' actual revisions to their work and the quality of their final task. Many of them even thank me for the depth of the responses they receive, even though much of it critiques the substance of their explanations. I believe that they appreciate the fact that a professor is taking them seriously, treating them more like colleagues than like students.

References

Alvermann, D. E. (2010). *Adolescents' online literacies: Connecting classrooms, digital media, and popular culture.* New York, NY: Peter Lang.

Anderson, R. C., & Pearson, P. D. (1984). A schema-theoretic view of basic processes in reading. In P. D. Pearson, R. Barr, & M. L. Kamil (Eds.), *Handbook of reading research* (pp. 255–291). New York, NY: Longman.

Baker, J. (2002). Tri-lingualism. In L. Delpit & J. K. Dowdy (Eds.), *The skin that we speak: Thoughts on language and culture in the classroom* (pp. 49–62). New York, NY: New Press.

Baugh, J. (1987). Research currents: The situational dimension of linguistic power in social context. *Language Arts, 64*(2), 234–240.

Bernstein, B. (2000). *Pedagogy, symbolic control, and identity: Theory, research, critique* (Rev. ed.). Oxford, England: Rowman & Littlefield.

Brown, D. W. (2009). *In other words: Lessons on grammar, code-switching, and academic writing.* Portsmouth, NH: Heinemann.

Ciardiello, A. V. (2012). Did you ask a good Common Core question today? The cognitive and metacognitive dimensions of enhanced inquiry skills. *Reading Today, 30*(3), 14–16.

Coleman, D., & Pimentel, S. (2012). *Revised publishers' criteria for the Common Core State Standards in English language arts and literacy, Grades 3–12.* Retrieved from http://www.corestandards.org/assets/Publishers_Criteria_for_3-12.pdf

Delpit, L. (1986). Skills and other dilemmas of a Black educator. *Harvard Educational Review, 56*(4), 379–386.

Finders, M. J. (1996). "Just Girls": Literacy and allegiance in junior high school. *Written Communication, 13*(1), 93–129. Retrieved from http://doi.org/10.1177/0741088396013001005

Gee, J. P. (1999). *An introduction to discourse analysis: Theory and method.* New York, NY: Routledge.

Gee, J. P. (2000). Teenagers in new times: A new literacy studies perspective. *Journal of Adolescent & Adult Literacy, 43*(5), 412–420.

Gee, J. P. (2005). *An introduction to discourse analysis: Theory and method* (2nd ed.). London, England: Routledge.

Halliday, M. A. K., & Webster, J. J. (2009). *Language and education: Volume 9.* London, England: Continuum.

Hinchman, K. A., & Sheridan-Thomas, H. K. (2008). *Best practices in adolescent literacy instruction. Solving problems in the teaching of literacy.* New York, NY: Guilford Press.

Kuipers, J., & Viechnicki, G. B. (2008). Special issue on objectification and the inscription of knowledge in science classrooms. *Linguistics and Education, 19*(3), 203–205. Retrieved from http://doi.org/10.1016/j.linged.2008.06.005

Lee, C. D. (2004). Literacy in the academic disciplines and the needs of adolescent struggling readers. *Voices in Urban Education, 3*, 14–25. Retrieved from http://www.achievementseminars.com/seminar_series_2005_2006/readings/Lee_Literacy_in_the_Academic_Disciplines_2004.pdf

Moje, E. B. (2000). "To be part of the story": The literacy practices of gangsta adolescents. *Teachers College Record, 102*(3), 651–690.

National Governors Association & Council of Chief State School Officers. (n.d.a.). *Common Core State Standards for English language arts & literacy in history/social studies, science, and technical subjects.* Washington, DC: Authors. Retrieved from http://www.corestandards.org/ELA-Literacy/

National Governors Association & Council of Chief State School Officers. (n.d.b.). *Key shifts in English language arts.* Washington, DC: Authors. Retrieved from http://www.corestandards.org/other-resources/key-shifts-in-english-language-arts/

National Governors Association & Council of Chief State School Officers. (2009). *Common Core State Standards initiative.* Washington, DC: Authors. Retrieved from http://www.corestandards.org

Redding, S. (2013). Getting personal: The promise of personalized learning. In M. Murphy, S. Redding, & J. Twyman (Eds.), *Handbook on innovations in learning* (pp. 113–129). Charlotte, NC: Information Age Publishing. Retrieved from http://www.centeril.org/handbook/

Smith, M. W., Appleman, D., & Wilhelm, J. D. (2014). *Uncommon core: Where the authors of the standards go wrong about instruction–and how you can get it right.* Thousand Oaks, CA: Corwin Press.

Sullivan, F. J. (1995). Critical theory and systemic linguistics: Textualizing the contact zone. *JAC: A Journal of Composition Theory, 15*(3), 411–434.

Sullivan, F. J. (1997a). Calling writers' bluffs: The social production of writing ability in university placement-testing. *Assessing Writing, 4*(1), 53–81.

Sullivan, F. J. (1997b). Dysfunctional workers, functional texts: The transformation of work in institutional procedure manuals. *Written Communication, 14*(3), 313–359. Retrieved from http://doi.org/10.1177/0741088397014003002

Sullivan, F. J., & Baren, R. (1997). Simulating the workplace in an engineering technology course: A rhetorical model. *Journal of Engineering Education, 86*(3), 279–284.

Sullivan, F. J., Lyon, A., Lebofsky, D., Wells, S., & Goldblatt, E. (1997). Student needs and strong composition: The dialectics of writing program reform. *College Composition and Communication, 48*(3), 372–391. Retrieved from http://doi.org/10.2307/358404

Tomlinson, C. A., & McTighe, J. (2006). *Integrating differentiated instruction & understanding by design: Connecting content and kids*. Alexandria, VA: ASCD.

Social Studies and Personalized Learning: Emerging Promising Practices From the Field

Christine Woyshner

At first glance, the central goals of social studies appear to be at odds with personalized learning. Although personalized learning approaches stress differentiation and student autonomy, social studies emphasizes helping young people become "citizens of a culturally diverse, democratic society in an interdependent world" (National Council for the Social Studies [NCSS], 2010, p. 3; Redding, 2014a, 2014c). In this chapter, I begin with the premise that—contrary to what may appear at first glance—the objectives in social studies do relate closely to the goals of personalized learning. I begin by defining social studies and personalized learning, demonstrating how their core ideals and best practices align. Then I show ways that social studies can be taught to meet the aims of personalized learning through a discussion of emerging promising practices. Ultimately, the learning goals of social studies and the aims of personalization overlap significantly to support the learning and development of diverse students in becoming engaged citizens in a democracy.

Social studies has suffered from lack of definitional clarity since it was created as a content area in the early twentieth century. Originally developed as a social-skills curriculum for African Americans and American Indians at Hampton Institute, social studies became an integrative field of study in the 1910s, after it was redesigned by educational theorists to serve progressive educational ends. This iteration of social studies focused on developing a relevant curriculum that would cultivate active citizens in local communities. Today, the NCSS defines social studies as the "integrated study of the social sciences and humanities to promote civic competence" (NCSS, 2010, p. 3). The central goals of the social studies are threefold: to support the common good; to adopt common and multiple perspectives; and to apply knowledge, skills, and values to civic action (NCSS, 1994).

The content of social studies includes various disciplines in the social sciences, not the least of which is history. History focuses on origins, continuity, and changes over time, and teaching it well necessarily involves using primary sources. Teaching history also

Handbook on Personalized Learning for States, Districts, and Schools, pages 273–284
Copyright © 2016 by Information Age Publishing

means helping students understand the historical roots of events and occurrences, helping them locate themselves in time, and helping them understand what life was like in the past. Learning history not only involves helping students develop content knowledge, it also entails developing critical skills, such as interpreting primary sources and determining chronology of events; also, it includes developing empathy for historical actors in appropriate instances. Ultimately, the learning of history should result in citizens taking informed action (Barton & Levstik, 2004). Geography, another discipline in social studies, emphasizes location and movement, and political science explores people and institutions as they relate to creating a common good. Economics, sociology, anthropology, and psychology each are a part of the broader subject area of social studies, although the degree to which each of these disciplines is taught before the college level varies by state, type of school (e.g., public, private), and locality. Nonetheless, each of these seven social sciences comprises the integrated course of study called social studies.

Personalized learning refers to differentiating the curriculum to address different learning preferences and needs. Even though personalized learning as an approach involves the coordination of an entire school community, at the classroom level it is defined as "a sociocultural authorization of individual freedom, community interactivity, and flexibility of time and space" (Deed et al., 2014, p. 67). Student choice is a central tenet of personalized learning, although it does not mean that teachers abdicate their roles. Student choice, according to scholars on this topic, is a means by which children become more engaged and invested in their education (Prain et al., 2013). Also, it is important that teachers and school districts maintain a consistent, high-level curriculum that is balanced and representative of all people, despite the emphasis on student choice. As Moje (2007) points out, a socially just curriculum (which is at the heart of social studies) needs to provide access to a quality curriculum for all students, and "this implies necessary productive constraint on both the content and appropriate teaching and learning methods of the curriculum" (p. 3).

> *Student choice is a central tenet of personalized learning, although it does not mean that teachers abdicate their roles.*

Relevant to my purposes in this chapter are Redding's (2014b) four integral components of adopting a personalized approach in the classroom: *choice* for students in their selection of topics, greater *access* to learning resources, greater *control* for students over their learning environment and learning strategies, and frequent *feedback* on students' work. In this chapter, I discuss how emerging promising practices can be taught in social studies to support each of these four essentials of personalized learning. In the discussion that follows, it will be evident that they overlap to an extent; however, I discuss each in turn to highlight the key features of each. In order to do so, I begin with the understanding that the curriculum and instruction are organized along the principles of backwards design, also called Teaching for Understanding or Universal Design for Learning.

According to Prain et al. (2013), backwards design is a recent development in educational theory, and its application dovetails with the principles of personalized learning. Backwards design is compatible with personalization because it "provides the structure to support flexibility in teaching and assessing, to honor the integrity of content while respecting the individuality of learners" (McTighe & Brown, 2005, p. 242; see also Blythe, 1998). Moreover, the key features of universal or backwards design incorporate the same four key components of personalization outlined above: student choice, greater access to learning resources, greater student control over learning environment and strategies, and frequent feedback.

In discussing emerging promising practices in relation to these four integral components of personalization, it must be noted that the social studies curriculum has ample opportunities for personalization, and teachers who embrace a project-based approach may already incorporate some of the elements of personalization. For instance, it is not unusual for social studies teachers to assign the following individual projects which incorporate the four essential components:

- sociology or geography: students develop their own society or nation
- civics: students select a community improvement project, plan it, and execute it to the fullest extent possible
- economics: students develop their own model economy
- history: students research a topic or theme, such as migration, and complete an independent research project

Projects such as these occur across the K–12 spectrum and in each of the content areas of social studies. My discussion below will add further details on how personalization can be accomplished in social studies through a hypothetical case that elaborates on Redding's four integral components of personalization.

Student Choice

Student choice is one of the central tenets of differentiation and personalized learning, and it is an important element of backwards design. Choice can be exercised by students in three ways. First, students can have choice in terms of content, or what they should know and be able to do. Choice in content also speaks to the materials used by students to support their understanding. Second, choice can be reflected in processes or in the activities that help students make sense of what they are learning. Finally, choice can be exercised in terms of the products students produce, which serve as the evidence of learning (Jackson & Davis, 2000).

Teachers who employ a backwards design approach typically allow students to choose topics, activities, and resources in social studies that enable them to draw on their family backgrounds, cultures, learning tendencies, and personal interests. There are many opportunities for student choice in the social studies curriculum because the content is so expansive. This expansiveness greatly facilitates personalization; it enables students to choose topics that interest them, and in turn enables teachers to focus on depth of understanding through students' own selection of topics, strategies, and activities.

Teaching with broad themes and/or essential questions allows for personalization, but as mentioned above, it is important to remember that teachers do not entirely give up authority or guidance in the classroom (Deed et al., 2014). So, in terms of choice of topic or resources, personalization can be accomplished by teachers offering students a selection of subjects within or under a broader theme or topic in social studies. (I will discuss choice of resources below, along with greater selection of resources). For our example, the theme is movement or migrations of people. Students have three weeks to select a group of people in United States history that moved from one place to another, whether forced or voluntary. They are to research the reasons and/or conditions around their moving and to prepare a series of products that scaffold, or lead to, a culminating activity that demonstrates their understanding of the reasons for moving, experiences, and how the move changed their lives and the communities they left and joined. Then, the teacher can guide them in developing individual goal statements that align with the district curricular goals. Each student is to choose one theme or episode which speaks to his or her interests or background. For example, one student could choose to study the forced relocation of the American Indian nations as a result of the Indian Removal Act of 1830. Another could choose to study the trans-Atlantic slave trade from the 16th to 19th centuries. Still another student might choose voluntary immigration of people, from southern and eastern Europe to the United States at the turn of the 20th century. For the purposes of showcasing emerging promising practices, I will focus on an episode of the voluntary movement of people: the Great Migration of African Americans in the early 20th century.

The Great Migration of African Americans from the southern United States was, according to historian Nicholas Lemann (1991), "one of the largest and most rapid mass internal movements of people in history" (p. 6). Between the First World War and 1970, 6.5 million African Americans moved to the North and Midwest, the bulk of which took place from 1916 to 1930. The rapid increase in migration north was in large part due to the damage done by the boll weevil, a beetle that feeds on cotton buds and flowers, which devastated the southern cotton crop in the early 20th century. As a result, a large part of the agricultural opportunities for African Americans disappeared. However, historians agree that a major pull factor encouraged migration: the prospect of job opportunities in northern industries, such as steel manufacturing.

Teachers can use the familiar activity of creating an idea web to work with students in further narrowing a topic, which can help them develop goals, locate resources, identify activities, and determine products. This activity helps teachers guide students in identifying topics, themes, examples, individuals, as well as what might be of interest to students through multiple connections to their lives (Blythe, 1998). Students can work

Figure 1. Idea Web to Develop Topics and Projects for Student Choice

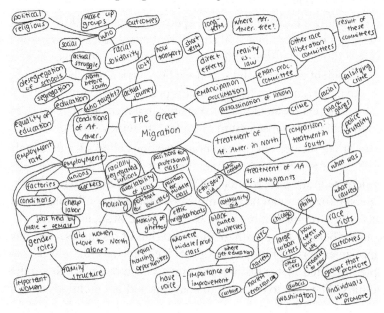

together in groups or pairs to develop idea webs around the theme of movement or can work individually followed by sharing with their peers what they've written. As one can see from an example of a concept web in Figure 1, our exemplary but fictional 10th-grade student, Arthur, came up with many varied topics to explore related to the Great Migration. He listed treatment, racial solidarity, outcomes, large urban cities (such as Chicago, New York, and Philadelphia), family structure, and gender roles. Not all of these topics are covered in the traditional course materials, textbooks, and curriculum guides. This is why personalization is important: It allows for students to make meaning of the curriculum by studying topics interesting to them. Our student then identifies a couple of essential questions to guide his learning. First, he wonders why great numbers of African Americans wanted to migrate north and what they hoped to gain. Then, he asks how migrants changed and what they experienced once they relocated to northern urban areas. Following identification of areas of a particular theme to study, teachers can personalize learning by guiding students to a wide variety of resources.

Greater Access to Learning Resources

The second integral component to assuming a personalized approach according to Redding (2014b) is greater access to learning resources. The most traditional and widely used resource in teaching social studies is the textbook, and research has shown that teachers depend almost exclusively on it at the expense of integrating other learning materials (Ross, 2006). Therefore, in the context of social studies, greater access to learning resources refers to teachers broadening the types of materials they use and make available to students in their classrooms, and it means letting and/or helping students choose items that they can relate to and that help them meet their goals. Many types of resources can be used to support personalizing instruction, including primary sources—great numbers of which are digitized and available on the web— as well as books, films, artwork, literature, and artifacts. In personalization, the teacher can help

> *This is why personalization is important: It allows for students to make meaning of the curriculum by studying topics interesting to them.*

students locate resources from among this wide variety of what is available. Moreover, by including visual and auditory resources—such as images, artwork, and videos—students who struggle with reading or who are English language learners have a broader array of accessible resources to support their learning, rather than relying solely on having to decode sophisticated text. Furthermore, images can teach powerful lessons to a diverse range of students about identity and representation (Schocker & Woyshner, 2012; Woyshner, 2006).

In our example of emerging promising practices, the teacher works with each student to develop essential questions for their study of movement and migrations. She may put students in groups to brainstorm together or use a blended learning approach, in which students are given time to peruse digital resources to learn about their particular focus and/or address their questions. Arthur has chosen to learn about the Great Migration and has determined the essential questions of his study:

- Why did the migrants want to move north?
- What was the experience like for them?

He is very much drawn to visual media and art. So, while participating in a blended learning activity in which he has the freedom to go online and search for resources, Arthur finds an image related to his topic. He shows it to his teacher, who recognizes the image as one in a series of sixty panels by the artist Jacob Lawrence; she then directs Arthur's attention to the rest of Lawrence's series. Called "The Migration Series," Lawrence's murals, because of the artist's extensive historical research, have been described as "a complex account of social history that accounts for the individual agency of African American migrants as well as the forbidding social, economic, and ideological structures that shaped the world in which they acted" (Capozzola, 2006, p. 293). Arthur selects two of the sixty captioned panels, "The Recruitment of Migrants" and "The Journey Begins," from the website for the New York Public Library's Schomburg Center for Research in Black Culture (http://www.inmotionaame.org/migrations/landing.cfm?migration=8), which he finds through a further Internet search.

Given that a variety of resources in personalization in social studies is important, the teacher can help the student locate text-rich primary and secondary sources to help Arthur learn about the period and events being studied. Two important resources for this topic found by the teacher are Christopher Capozzola's brief and accessible article about Lawrence's murals and a 1989 doctoral dissertation which has transcriptions of oral histories of many African American migrants to Philadelphia. The teacher culls excerpts from the dissertation which are related to the Lawrence panels Arthur chose. Other visual media, including interactive maps and historical photographs, are identified by Arthur in his exploration of the Great Migration. Our student studying the Great Migration is able to read excerpts from Nicholas Lemann's 1991 history of the event, as well as first-hand accounts, or oral histories, located in Charles A. Hardy's dissertation (1989). The Appendix identifies selected websites where students and teachers can locate a breadth of resources to personalize learning. This list is just a beginning; there are many other sites with which teachers are familiar that they can share with students.

> *Student control over the learning environment and learning strategies is a key component of personalization.*

Student Control Over Learning Environment and Learning Strategies

Student control over the learning environment and learning strategies is a key component of personalization. Personalizing the learning environment entails rethinking the classroom as a community space, which could involve, for example, arrangements and features that support blended learning or that adopt an open classroom structure (Deed et al., 2014). Likewise, personalized learning strategies can include establishing reflexive opportunities between teacher and students and students with other students to support and promote choice and decision making, "pervasive use of technology" to determine a learning path, and problem solving through "collective intelligence" (Deed et al., 2014, p. 67). In personalization, students have opportunities to discuss different approaches to learning, to find multiple solutions to problems, and to develop their independent problem-solving skills.

As this discussion of emerging promising practices of personalization in social studies unfolds, it is important to remember that this approach to teaching and learning is based, like many other best practices, on an inquiry model. Therefore, it is not a linear process, but an iterative one. However, for the purposes of discussion, in this chapter I address each one of the four integral components of personalization in turn, while I acknowledge that the process for teachers will be much more complex and circular (see Woyshner, 2010). A further complication is that personalization necessarily involves varying time, place, and pace, in which "each learner demonstrates competency, regardless of the amount of time demonstration of that competency may take" (Twyman, 2014, p. 3). So, to recap, we have our study of migrations, or movement of people, forced and unforced; from within that broad subject, students have chosen their own focused topic to research and, based on that research, create a product. The teacher structures time for the students to work together to problem solve and share ideas, drawing on the collective intelligence of the group. In this hypothetical class of students who have chosen various topics, we are following Arthur as he works with the teacher to learn about the Great Migration. He has written two essential questions and begun to identify resources for learning.

Our student has already brainstormed his concept web and drafted essential questions, both of which he shared with classmates and received feedback. He located digital resources readily found online that speak to his interests in art and visual media. Arthur decides he is going to use art to convey his learning about the Great Migration, and he pairs the two panels with two oral histories that help him understand what it was like to travel north and what life was like for the migrants once they relocated. He presents these juxtapositions to the class for feedback. As Arthur continues his research project, he spends additional time looking at art, reading the oral histories of migrants to Philadelphia, reading excerpts from Lemann's *The Promised Land* (1991) that his teacher helps him select, and locating other resources such as digital maps, historical photographs, and census data, all available online.

Like the rest of the students in this class, Arthur continues to work with his teacher to select learning strategies that best serve his interests, learning preferences, and cultural background. The teacher notes that he prefers to work alone, read materials at his own pace, and incorporate art or creative expression in his assignments. Working at his own pace, Arthur makes use of a variety of learning strategies to produce various artifacts—such as the juxtaposition referred to above—that reflect his emerging understanding of this topic. Table 1 below shows the main activities that Arthur takes on and how he works with other students as he follows his own path at his own pace.

Table 1. Personalized Learning Path in Migrations Unit

Activity or direction for personalization	Who chose it	Arthur's role	Collective intelligence
Concept web	Teacher	Creates his own web of the Great Migration	Shared with other students to see if they had any other terms to add; did the same for other students

Activity or direction for personalization	Who chose it	Arthur's role	Collective intelligence
Research on Great Migration to locate primary sources (on-going throughout the unit of study)	Arthur	Looks online for sources; finds Schomburg website and locates information about the Great Migration and the Lawrence panels	Compared notes with other students in terms of good websites to use and selection of appropriate and interesting primary sources
Further research on Great Migration to support student	Teacher	Locates Capozzola article and Hardy dissertation	Teacher gives Capozzola article to student to read and culls excerpts for and with student to use
Decision to focus on artwork and Philadelphia migrants	Arthur	Looks online and locates historical neighborhood maps at the Urban Archives at Temple University	n/a
Letter to folks back home	Teacher	Writes letter from migrant moving to Philadelphia from the South about his experiences	Uploads letters to blog on migrations; reads other students' posts
Graphic organizer	Arthur	Organizes what he finds into graphic organizer that included institutions, events, housing, and organizations	Shares with other students to fill in gaps

Activity or direction for personalization	Who chose it	Arthur's role	Collective intelligence
Poster that tells the story of migration north that uses art to express feelings and ideas	Arthur	Creates a juxtaposition of text and image to show what he has learned so far and to provoke thought in other students	Shares with other students to see what questions they raise
Story of his community's history of migration presented as an exhibit at the local library	Arthur	Interviews community and family members in his Philadelphia neighborhood; conducts online research and finds historical photographs	Works with other students to develop interview protocol and to analyze data

These learning activities draw on Arthur's strengths and interests and help him work toward the essential questions he has written as they meet the objectives of his teacher and the district curriculum standards for history. In the next section I discuss the fourth essential component, frequent feedback, in relation to the activities outlined in Table 1.

Frequent Feedback

Frequent feedback in order to improve student understanding is one of the hallmarks of personalized learning and Universal Design for Learning as discussed above. Frequent feedback has two components: make the criteria for success explicit to students; and students get continual feedback on their efforts from the teacher, other students, and themselves through reflection (Blythe, 1998). Personalization thereby relies on "relational agency" in which teachers co-regulate different tasks for students, such as planning, goal setting, feedback, and reflection. Likewise, students help one another through group learning, peer discussion, coaching, peer assessment, and monitoring of performance (Prain et al., 2013).

The activities chosen by the students with teacher guidance and oversight meet the various needs, backgrounds, and interests of students in order to personalize learning. In our chart above, the various activities Arthur and the other students undertake reside in this web of relational agency. Throughout the three-week course of study, Arthur makes choices about what to study, what resources to select, and what activities to carry out. Even though the teacher has selected three weeks as the duration of this period of study, Arthur may take more or less time, depending on how he progresses. He worked with his peers for feedback and ideas to answer his essential questions, and he, in turn, helps them with their explorations. As the students work, they note themes across migrations, such as the challenges different populations faced in terms of employment, use of native language, and remaking the communities into which they moved. The teacher continually reminds students about the timeline, meets with individuals and groups to make sure they are on track, and gives mini-lectures to the whole class about particular historical events that contextualize their individual projects. She also monitors the blog and other class assignments. Therefore, frequent feedback throughout the three-week project, rather than at the end, ensures that all students are progressing adequately and getting guidance at important junctures, rather than after the work has been done. This approach not only supports the pillars of personalization, it models community building and interdependence, which are important lessons in social studies.

Conclusion

As social studies scholars claim, "Our democratic republic will not sustain unless students are aware of their changing cultural and physical environments; know the past; read, write, and think deeply; and act in ways that promote the common good" (NCSS, 2014, p. 5). These important goals are aligned with the personalized learning approach outlined in this discussion of emerging promising practices of personalization. In this chapter, I presented a hypothetical case to highlight emerging promising practices in social studies in a personalized learning framework. By attending to four essential components of personalized learning outlined by Redding (2014b)—student choice in selection of topics, greater access to learning resources, students having greater control over the learning environment and learning strategies, and frequent feedback—teachers will be able to teach diverse students and vary instruction according to time, pace, and place. As scholars who research personalization have asserted, "Teachers need the expertise, time, resources, and teamwork to develop a flexible curriculum that is adequately structured in content, learning tasks, and adaptable classroom practices to engage all learners and address contrasting learner needs" (Prain et al., 2013, p. 660). Such an approach supports the tenets of personalized learning and the goals of social studies.

References

Barton, K. C., & Levstik, L. S. (2004). *Teaching history for the common good.* Mahwah, NJ: Erlbaum.

Blythe, T. (1998). *The teaching for understanding guide.* San Francisco, CA: Jossey-Bass.

Capozzola, C. (2006). Jacob Lawrence: Historian. *Rethinking History: The Journal of Theory and Practice, 10*(2), 291–295.

Deed, C., Cox, P., Dorman, J., Edwards, D., Farrelly, C., Keeffe, M....Yager, Z. (2014). Personalised learning in the open classroom: The mutuality of teacher and student agency. *International Journal of Pedagogies and Learning, 9*(1), 66–75.

Hardy, C. A. (1989). *Race and opportunity: Black Philadelphia during the era of the great migration, 1916–1930* (Unpublished doctoral dissertation). Temple University, Philadelphia, PA.

Jackson, A., & Davis, G. (2000). *Turning points 2000: Educating adolescents in the twenty-first century.* New York, NY: Teachers College Press.

Lemann, N. (1991). *The promised land: The great Black migration and how it changed America.* New York, NY: A. A. Knopf.

McTighe, J., & Brown, J. (2005). Differentiated instruction and educational standards: Is détente possible? *Theory into Practice, 44*(3), 234–244.

Moje, E. (2007). Developing socially just subject-matter instruction: A review of the literature on disciplinary literacy learning. *Review of Research in Education, 31*(1), 1–44.

National Council for the Social Studies. (1994). *Expectations of excellence: Curriculum standards for social studies.* Washington, DC: Author.

National Council for the Social Studies. (2010). *National curriculum standards for social studies*. Washington, DC: Author.

National Council for the Social Studies. (2014). *The college, career, and civic life (C3) framework for social studies standards: Guidance for enhancing the rigor of K–12 civics, economics, geography, and history*. Washington, DC: Author.

Prain, V., Cox, P., Deed, C., Dorman, J., Edwards, D., Farrelly, C....Yager, Z. (2013). Personalised learning: Lessons to be learnt. *British Educational Research Journal, 39*(4), 654–676.

Redding, S. (2014a). *Personal competencies: A conceptual framework*. Philadelphia, PA: Temple University, Center on Innovations in Learning. Retrieved from http://www.centeril.org

Redding, S. (2014b). *Personal competencies in personalized learning*. Philadelphia, PA: Temple University, Center on Innovations in Learning. Retrieved from http://www.centeril.org

Redding, S. (2014c). *The something other: Personal competencies for learning and life*. Philadelphia, PA: Temple University, Center on Innovations in Learning. Retrieved from http://www.centeril.org

Ross, E. W. (Ed.). (2006). *The social studies curriculum: Purposes, problems, and possibilities* (3rd ed.). Albany, NY: State University of New York Press.

Schocker, J., & Woyshner, C. (2012). Representing African American women in U.S. history textbooks. *The Social Studies, 104*(1), 23–31.

Twyman, J. S. (2014). *Competency-based education: Supporting personalized learning. Connect: Making learning personal*. Retrieved from http://www.centeril.org/connect/resources/Connect_CB_Education_Twyman-2014_11.12.pdf

Woyshner, C. (2006). Picturing women: Gender, images, and representation in social studies. *Social Education, 70*(6), 358–362.

Woyshner, C. (2010). Inquiry teaching with primary source documents: An iterative approach. *Social Studies Research and Practice, 5*(3), 36–45.

Appendix

Resources for Teaching About the Great Migration

Greenfield, E., & Gilchrist, J. S. (2011). *The Great Migration: Journey to the North*. New York, NY: Amistad.

Lemann, N. (1991). *The promised land: The great Black migration and how it changed America*. New York, NY: A. A. Knopf.

New York Public Library, Schomburg Center for Research in Black Culture. (n.d.) Retrieved from http://www.inmotionaame.org/migrations/landing.cfm?migration=8

Washington, J. (1993). *The quest for equality*. New York, NY: World Press.

Selected Resources That Support Personalized Learning in the Social Studies

- 270 to Win: A nonpartisan geopolitical site containing electoral maps of every presidential election. http://www.270towin.com

- Historical Society of Pennsylvania: Archives and website have many rich resources and lessons for teachers, with an emphasis on U.S. history and immigration. http://www.hsp.org

- Library of Congress: The largest collection of online resources, this site has extensive lessons and teaching suggestions for educators. http://www.loc.govNational Model United Nations: Students role-play as diplomats, researching and presenting resolutions. http://www.nmun.org

- National Archives and Records Administration: Also a large and important repository, the National Archives online has many important resources for educators. http://www.nara.gov

- National Budget Simulation: Students serve as economic advisors to the U.S. president. http://www.econedlink.org
- Stanford History Education Group: For assessment and teaching with primary sources. http://sheg.stanford.edu
- Teaching History: For resources and K–12 teaching ideas; has ideas on teaching with new technologies. http://www.teachinghistory.org
- Zinn Education Project: For resources and teaching students more complex, engaging, and accurate U.S. history; open to the various needs of diverse students. http://zinnedproject.org/

About the Authors

Ryan Baker, Ph.D., is an associate professor of cognitive studies at Teachers College, Columbia University. He earned his Ph.D. in human–computer interaction from Carnegie Mellon University. Baker was previously assistant professor of psychology and the learning sciences at Worcester Polytechnic Institute, and he served as the first technical director of the Pittsburgh Science of Learning Center DataShop, the largest public repository for data on the interaction between learners and educational software. He is currently serving as the founding president of the International Educational Data Mining Society, and as associate editor of the *Journal of Educational Data Mining*. He has taught two massive online open courses on the subject to a combined audience of over 70,000. His research combines educational data mining and quantitative field observation methods in order to better understand how students respond to educational software, and how these responses impact their learning. He studies these issues within intelligent tutors, simulations, multi-user virtual environments, and educational games.

Andrea Beesley, Ph.D., has over 15 years of experience in managing large research projects, proposal development, program evaluation, quantitative research (experimental and quasi-experimental designs), qualitative research, instrument development, study recruitment, and instructional design, in education and health. She focuses particularly on teacher quality, motivation, STEM education, and classroom assessment. Beesley led the Institute of Education Sciences grant Learning to Use Formative Assessment with the Assessment Work Sample Method upon which her chapter is based. In addition, Beesley led the external evaluation of the STeLLA Professional Development: Scaling for Effectiveness project, a National Science Foundation scale-up grant. Other recent experience includes a randomized, controlled trial of a professional development program in mathematics classroom assessment, an implementation study of math remediation in high schools in Tennessee, a social return on investment study of Georgia's Race to the Top STEM initiatives, the development of a survey of motivation and engagement in Expeditionary Learning Schools, and the national evaluation of the Comprehensive Technical Assistance Centers. A former senior director of research at McREL International, she is a senior research associate at IMPAQ International. She holds a Ph.D. in instructional psychology and technology from the University of Oklahoma.

Tedra Fazendeiro Clark, Ph.D., is a managing researcher at McREL International. She has ten years of experience in cognitive science research and more than six years of experience in applied education research. Since 2007, she has worked for McREL to improve K–12 education through research focused on school climate, classroom instructional practices, formative assessment, and teacher professional development. Her main responsibilities include research design, instrument development, data collection, SAS programming for data management, statistical analysis (including psychometric analysis, hierarchical linear modeling, and longitudinal growth modeling), research synthesis, and dissemination. Recently, Clark led the data management and analysis efforts for two cluster randomized trials funded by the Institute of Education Sciences (IES). She is a co-principal investigator of an IES-funded project to develop and evaluate a teacher professional development program in formative assessment. Prior to joining McREL, she was a graduate research assistant in the Department of Psychology at the University of Denver, where she facilitated NIH- and NSF-sponsored research on cognition and learning. She also served as an adjunct instructor of research methods, neuroscience, human cognition, and social psychology. She holds a doctorate in experimental psychology from the University of Denver.

Bryan G. Cook, Ph.D., is currently professor of special education at the University of Hawaii at Manoa in Honolulu, HI. He received his Ph.D. in special education from the University of California at Santa Barbara in 1997; Cook's primary scholarly focus is evidence-based practices in special education. He chaired the Council for Exceptional Children's (CEC's) Workgroup on Evidence-Based Practices, which developed CEC's Standards for Evidence-Based Practices in Special Education. In addition to publishing and presenting widely on evidence-based practices in special education, he has co-guest edited a number of special issues of scholarly journals on the topic, including two issues of *Exceptional Children,* two issues of *Intervention in School and Clinic,* and one issue of the *Journal of Special Education.* He also co-edited, with Melody Tankersley, *Research-based Practices in Special Education,* a four-volume text. Cook is past-president of CEC's Division for Research, chair of the Research Committee for CEC's Division for Learning Disabilities, chair of CEC's Interdivisional Research Group, and co-editor of the journal *Behavioral Disorders* (the research journal of CEC's Council for Children with Behavioral Disorders).

Sara Cook, Ph.D., received her degree in exceptionalities from the University of Hawaii at Manoa (UHM) in Honolulu, HI, in 2014 and is currently an assistant professor in the special education department at UHM. Cook is a former special education teacher who has taught language arts and mathematics in inclusive secondary settings. Cook's research interests include identifying evidence-based practices (EBPs) for students with high incidence disabilities, methods of supporting students with disabilities in inclusive classrooms via co-teaching and integration of EBPs, and performance assessments for preservice special education teachers. She conducted a pilot study of the initial set of quality indicators and standards for determining EBPs in special education proposed by Council for Exceptional Children's (CEC's) Workgroup on EBPs. Findings from this initial study (i.e., inter-rater reliability, qualitative feedback) were used in finalizing the CEC (2014) Standards for Evidence-Based Practices in Special Education. Cook has presented widely on EBPs in special education and has published on the topic in outlets such as the *Journal of Special Education* and *Teaching Exceptional Children.* She has also provided consultation and professional development in the areas of co-teaching, inclusion, and EBPs at elementary and high schools.

Allison Crean Davis, Ph.D., is a senior advisor to Bellwether Education Partners, focusing on issues related to evaluation and planning, predictive analytics, extended learning opportunities, and Native American education. Davis is co-founder of New Legacy Partnerships, LLC, a consulting firm working with schools, districts, state education agencies, nonprofits, and foundations to harness research and organization-specific evidence throughout the planning, execution, and evaluation phases of their work. Davis acts as coordinator for evaluation at the Center on Innovations in Learning at Temple University and has provided evaluation and planning support for several summer learning initiatives, including those funded by the Wallace Foundation and The John T. Gorman Foundation. She is a founder and vice-chair of the board of directors at Baxter Academy for Technology and Science, Maine's first charter high school. Davis has served as external advisor to the Bureau of Indian Education and guided that organization in the design and implementation of a system of support for schools across 23 states. In addition to providing evaluation services, she has done extensive work building the capacity of organizations to evaluate their own efforts for continuous improvement, including state education agencies, districts, schools, and foundation grantees.

Kathleen Dempsey, M.Ed., is a client solutions directing consultant at McREL International. She is a co-principal investigator on the IES Goal 3 grant, Learning to Use Formative Assessment in Mathematics with the Assessment Work Sample Method, and a co-principal investigator on a Task 2 IES grant studying the efficacy of a pre-algebra supplemental program in rural Mississippi schools. She is a coauthor of *Common Core Standards for High School Mathematics: A Quick-Start Guide* and *Common Core Standards for Middle School Mathematics: A Quick-Start Guide,* published by McREL and ASCD. She has managed staff and resources for large projects, including her work as the director for the North Central Comprehensive Center. Dempsey has more than 30 years of experience as a teacher and administrator at all levels of the K–12 spectrum, and has served as an adjunct instructor at the university level for prospective elementary mathematics teachers. She holds a master's degree in educational supervision from The College of William and Mary and endorsements in mathematics-Algebra I, gifted education, and middle school education. Before coming to McREL, she served as the secondary mathematics coordinator for Virginia Beach City Public Schools in Virginia Beach, Virginia.

Patricia A. Edwards, Ph.D., is a professor of language and literacy in the department of teacher education and a senior university outreach fellow at Michigan State University. She is a nationally and internationally recognized expert in parent involvement; home, school, and community partnerships; multicultural literacy; early literacy; and family/intergenerational literacy, especially among poor and minority children. She received the Outstanding Teacher Educator Award from the Michigan Reading Association, the Jerry Johns Outstanding Teacher Educator in Reading Award from the International Reading Association (now the International Literacy Association), the Albert J. Kingston Award from the Literacy Research Association, and the Edward B. Fry Book Award from the Literacy Research Association. She was elected to the IRA (now ILA) Reading Hall of Fame in 2012. She served as a member of the IRA Board of Directors as the first African American president of the Literacy Research Association (formerly the National Reading Conference), and as president of the International Reading Association. Edwards has authored, coauthored, and/or edited seven books on family, community, and literacy/equity issues and written articles and chapters on the same topics. She has consulted with school districts throughout the U.S., as well as a variety of agencies/organizations outside the U.S. about the importance of developing family, school, and community partnerships.

Azeb Gebre is a doctoral candidate at Temple University. In Ronald D. Taylor's adolescent adjustment lab, she has examined the role of positive and negative extended family relations on adolescents' social, emotional, and academic adjustment. In her ongoing research, she focuses on understanding the role and function of social support systems in adolescents' adjustment. In particular, she builds upon the traditional social support framework by investigating the influence of extended family relations and online social networking behaviors on college adjustment. Her research focuses on individual and institutional-level factors that predict poor student adjustment and retention. Further, she is committed to understanding the individual characteristics that may affect how students engage with social networking sites, the risk and protective factors associated with social media use, and its impact on socioemotional development. She earned her B.A. in psychology and neuroscience and behavior and her M.A. in psychology from Wesleyan University. At Temple, Gebre has taught undergraduate and graduate introductory statistics courses and labs.

Erin McNamara Horvat, Ph.D., is professor in the School of Education at Drexel University in Philadelphia, PA. Her research agenda has explored how race and class shape access throughout the educational pipeline, focusing especially on the role of social and cultural capital in shaping families' interactions with schools, often drawing on Bourdieu's theoretical framework. She has been motivated by a desire to understand how interactions between individual and structural forces shape educational outcomes and life chances, including explorations of how race and class affect school and college experiences, college access, and high school dropout and reentry. Her current work is focused on the groundbreaking and visionary civic engagement.com efforts being undertaken by Drexel University in the West Philadelphia area in which it resides, and is aimed at developing institutional capacity to improve academic outcomes and life chances for neighborhood residents. She co-edited (with Carla O'Connor) *Beyond Acting White: Reframing the Debate on Black Student Achievement,* and authored *Doing Qualitative Research,* published by Teachers College Press. Her work has been funded by the Spencer Foundation and the Ford Foundation.

William Jeynes, Ph.D., is a senior fellow from the Witherspoon Institute in Princeton, NJ, and a professor of education at California State University, Long Beach. He has graduate degrees from Harvard University and the University of Chicago. He graduated first in his class from Harvard University. He has about 145 academic publications, including 12 books. His articles have appeared in journals by Columbia University, Harvard University, the University of Chicago, Cambridge University, Notre Dame University, the London School of Economics, and other prestigious academic journals. He is a well-known public speaker and researcher on various expressions of private education, including homeschooling. He has spoken at the White House, the U.S. Department of Justice, the U.S. Department of Education, the U.S. Department of Health and Human Services, members of Congress, and Harvard, Cambridge, Oxford, Columbia, and many other well-known universities. He has spoken for and interacted with both George W. Bush and Barack Obama. He has been interviewed or quoted by most of the nation's leading newspapers and news networks, and his work is frequently cited and quoted. Jeynes wrote the most frequently cited article in the nearly 50-year histories of two major academic journals. He received the Distinguished Scholar Award from the California State Senate, the California State Assembly, and his present university.

Karl M. Kapp, Ed.D., is a professor of instructional technology at Bloomsburg University in Bloomsburg, PA. He teaches several game design and gamification classes. He serves as the director of Bloomsburg's Institute for Interactive Technologies which works with organizations to create interactive instruction including games and simulations. He has authored six books, including *The Gamification of Learning and Instruction* and its accompanying how-to book, *The Gamification of Learning and Instruction Fieldbook.* Kapp's work explores the research, theoretical foundations, and application of effective game-based learning. He is quoted in several volumes of Jeannie Novak's *Game Development Essentials* series and is author of the Lynda.com course *Gamification of Learning.* Karl has served as a co-principle investigator on two National Science Foundation (NSF) grants related to games and simulations, and serves as an external evaluator on a third game-related NSF grant. He is co-founder of the educational game company 2Klearn-ing.com which creates a combination of video-game and hands-on STEM curriculum for middle school students. In 2007, Kapp was named one of the top 20 most influential training professionals as voted by Training Industry, Inc. He has been a TEDx speaker, an award winning instructor, and an international speaker on the convergence of games, learning, and technology. He blogs at http://karlkapp.com/kapp-notes/

T. V. Joe Layng, Ph.D., cofounded Headsprout, located in Seattle, WA, and served as the company's senior scientist, where he was the chief architect of Headsprout Early Reading and Headsprout Reading Comprehension online programs. Headsprout was eventually acquired by the Cambium Learning Group. Previous to Headsprout, Layng served as director of academic support and dean of public agency and special training programs at Malcolm X College in Chicago, where he developed the award-winning Personalized Curriculum Institute. While in Chicago, he served as a member of several task forces for the Chicago Public Schools, including the High School Redesign Task Force, and served as co-chair of the High School Curriculum and Instruction Redesign Task Force. He has over 35 years of experience in the learning sciences. As an undergraduate student at Western Illinois University, he founded the Centre for Innovative Design and Programmed Instruction. Layng holds a Ph.D. in behavioral science (biopsychology) from the University of Chicago. While at the university, he performed basic research and developed some of the key elements of what has become known as generative instruction. He is now a partner in Generategy, LLC, which provides educational software applications for mobile devices. He serves on the board of trustees for the Cambridge Center for Behavioral Studies, TCS Education System, the Chicago School for Professional Psychology, and Pacific Oaks College.

Karen L. Mahon, Ed.D., is the president and founder of Balefire Labs, an online educational app review service that focuses on evaluating the instructional quality and usability of mobile apps for grades preK–12. She is an educational psychologist and instructional designer with more than 15 years' experience in education technology. Prior to founding Balefire Labs, she was global senior manager of learning sciences at Mimio Interactive Teaching Technologies, where she established Mimio's global content strategy and instructional philosophy. Other previous appointments have included principal investigator and research scientist at Praxis, Inc., a Waltham, Massachusetts, education technology startup that produced instructional software for children with severe and profound intellectual disabilities; research assistant professor at the University of Kansas, Parsons Research Center; and positive behavior support specialist at the Autism Training Center at Marshall University. In all of these roles, she has consulted with numerous schools and conducted countless teacher trainings. Mahon is also on the advisory board for the Cambridge Center for Behavioral Studies, and the scientific advisory board for the Center on Innovations in Learning at Temple University. She received her Ed.D. and M.A. in educational psychology from West Virginia University; her product management certificate from the University of California, Berkeley, Haas School of Business; and her B.A. in psychology from the University of California, San Diego.

Marilyn Murphy, Ed.D., is the director of the Center on Innovations in Learning (CIL). She has served as the interim executive director of the Institute for Schools and Society, the research branch of the Temple University College of Education. Previously, Murphy was the assistant director for communications at the Center on Innovation and

Improvement (CII) and the codirector of the Laboratory for Student Success, the mid-Atlantic Regional Educational Laboratory at Temple University. She received her doctorate in education from Temple University in curriculum, instruction, and technology in education. Her research interests include communication processes, engagement theory, learning theory, and the use of metaphor by children and adults. She has made frequent presentations and contributions to numerous educational publications, including chapters in the CII volumes *Handbook on Strengthening the Statewide System of Support*, the *Handbook on Effective Implementation of School Improvement Grants*, the *Handbook on Family and Community Engagement*, and the *Handbook on Innovations in Learning*.

Kavita Rao, Ph.D., received her doctorate in education from the University of Hawaii at Manoa (UHM) and is currently an associate professor of special education at the UHM College of Education. Her primary scholarly focus is on universal design for learning (UDL) and instructional/assistive technologies that support inclusive learning environments. As part of her research, she also examines issues of equity and access for culturally and linguistically diverse students. As a member of the Center for Applied Special Technology UDL Professional Learning Cadre, Rao conducts UDL implementation trainings for school districts nationally and internationally. She has published numerous articles and book chapters on the topics of technology-based instructional strategies for diverse students, UDL implementation, and online learning in leading journals in the field, including *Remedial and Special Education*, *Phi Delta Kappan*, *Journal of Special Education Technology*, and *Teaching Exceptional Children*. She works with university faculty and pre- and in-service teachers in Asia and the U.S.-affiliated Pacific Islands on various curriculum development, school improvement, and technology integration initiatives.

Sam Redding, Ed.D., is the senior learning specialist of the Center on Innovations in Learning (CIL). Since 1984, Redding has served as the executive director of the Academic Development Institute (ADI) and from 2005 to 2011 as director of the Center on Innovation & Improvement. He headed the development of Indistar, a web-based school improvement technology, and Indicators in Action, web-based tutorials for online professional development for educators. Redding is a former high school teacher and college dean and vice president. He received the Those Who Excel Award from the Illinois State Board of Education, the Ben Hubbard Leadership Award from Illinois State University, and the Ernie Wing Award for Excellence in Evidence-Based Education from the California-based Wing Institute. He has been executive editor of the *School Community Journal* since 1991 and was a senior research associate of the Laboratory for Student Success at Temple University from 1995 to 2005, where he led the Lab's work on comprehensive school reform. He has edited four books on family–school relationships, authored a book on school improvement and personalized learning, edited books on statewide systems of support and school turnaround, and written articles and chapters in the areas of school management, school improvement, and factors affecting school learning. Redding has recently published on "personal competencies" as propellants of learning. He has consulted with more than 30 SEAs on their systems for school improvement.

Catherine Schifter, Ph.D., is an associate professor in psychological, organizational and leadership studies in the College of Education at Temple University and a Carnegie Scholar. In her time at Temple, she has been director of the online learning program, the founding director of the Temple Teaching and Learning Center, and department chair in the College of Education. Her research has focused on professional development and technology integration in education, with recent interest in using game-based design to assess understanding of science inquiry. In addition to publishing numerous articles, she sole authored *Infusing Technology into the Classroom: Continuous Practice Improvement*, and co-edited *New Media in Education: Beyond Constructivism*. Schifter's work, whether at the School of Dental Medicine at the University of Pennsylvania or in the College of Education at Temple University, has focused on the impact of new media, or technologies, in supporting teaching and learning at the individual level.

Tamara Sniad, Ph.D., is an assistant professor of teaching English as a second language (TESOL) with the College of Education at Temple University. Sniad's 20 years of experience in TESOL and urban education includes administrative and teacher development work in Camden, NJ; college access programming; national training for out-of-school education; and university teacher preparation. She has conducted research on classroom discourse in work force readiness education as well as in-service and preservice teacher professional development. As a College of Education faculty member at Rowan University for two years and now at Temple, Sniad has taught courses on diversity and equity in education, linguistics, second language acquisition, and language teaching methodology. This array of educational contexts, research, and teaching experiences informs Sniad's perspectives on pedagogy and equity in the classroom and has shaped her current work preparing K–12 teachers to support English language learners in content area classrooms. Sniad is a recipient of the Temple College of Education Owlie Award for Innovative Teaching. She has published in the *Journal of Pragmatics* and *Academic Exchange Quarterly* and presented at over 30 national and state conferences.

Melinda Sota, Ph.D., is an instructional designer with special interests in designing K–12 educational technology products and the role of formative evaluation in the design process. She received her Ph.D. in instructional systems from Florida State University and engaged in educational research as an Institute of Education Sciences postdoctoral fellow at the University of Oregon's Center on Teaching and Learning. From 2007 to 2012, she served as a lead instructional designer at Headsprout and Mimio, where she codesigned several iPad, online, and interactive whiteboard programs for teaching music, science, and reading, including Headsprout *Reading Comprehension*, which was awarded the Software and Information Industry Association's CODiE award for best online instructional solution. She has written articles and book chapters on reading comprehension, differentiated instruction, response to intervention, and research-based practices, and presented on a number of topics related to instructional design and education.

Frank Sullivan, Ph.D., is an associate professor of language and literacy in the College of Education at Temple University. Until last year, when he stepped down, he was program coordinator for secondary education. In his career at Temple, his research has consistently emerged from his professional work in program development across the university and with professional organizations. As director of basic writing, he was asked to revamp the university's policies and procedures on writing assessment. Studies emerging from that work received a Phi Delta Kappa award from the University of Pennsylvania and a Promising Research Award from the National Council of Teachers of English. The founding director of the Temple University Writing Center, Sullivan developed support programs for undergraduate and graduate students in all of its schools and colleges. He developed professional development seminars for faculty teaching discipline-based writing courses, which resulted in several publications, including one on simulating the workplace in an engineering design course. His leadership of an institution-wide redesign of the university writing program also resulted in a national publication. Prior to this work, Sullivan taught in Philadelphia public schools. At Temple, he has maintained his relationship with the schools, designing professional development programs in literacy for teachers. At Temple he now teaches courses on literacy and language arts.

Ronald D. Taylor, Ph.D., is an associate professor in the Department of Psychology at Temple University. Taylor graduated with a B.A. in developmental psychology from the University of California, Santa Barbara. He received his doctoral degree from the University of Michigan in developmental psychology and then joined the faculty in the Department of Psychology at Temple University in 1987. In addition to his position in the Department of Psychology, Taylor has been affiliated with the Center for Research in Human Development and Education (CRHDE), where he served as a senior research associate. He was also a senior research associate at the Laboratory for Student Success at Temple University. Taylor's work has focused on factors associated with the social and emotional adjustment of ethnic minority adolescents. His work has examined family relations, including parent styles and parenting practices and the links to African American adolescents' psychological well-being. Taylor's work has also focused on family social support networks and their links to parent and adolescent psychological well-being. In his work, Taylor has been especially interested in assessing potential mediating and moderating processes linking family and kinship relations with adolescents' social adjustment. Taylor has also served as assistant director of the CRHDE and director of the developmental psychology area in the Department of Psychology.

Anne Tweed, M.S., is the director of STEM Learning with McREL International in Denver. She holds a bachelor's degree in biology from Colorado College and a master's in botany from the University of Minnesota. Her work at McREL includes educational research, curriculum development, and professional development related to STEM teaching and learning. She is a co-principal investigator on an NSF NanoTeach project and on an IES formative assessment project. Her ongoing professional development workshops feature effective science, engineering, and math instruction; designing effective STEM lessons; developing Next Generation Science Standards lessons; and implementing formative assessment. A 30-year veteran classroom teacher, she also served as a past president of the National Science Teachers Association from 2004–2005. She has published many articles; authored and coauthored several books, such as *Designing Effective Science Instruction: What Works in Science Classrooms*; and given more than 300 presentations and workshops at state, national, and international conferences. Most recently, she coauthored with Susan Koba the second edition of *Hard-to-Teach Biology Concepts: A Framework to Deepen Student Understanding*, which incorporates the Next Generation Science Standards.

Janet S. Twyman, Ph.D., BCBA, is the director of innovation and technology for the Center on Innovations in Learning. A career educator, Twyman has been a preschool and elementary school teacher, a principal and school administrator, and a university professor. She has worked directly improving the personalization of learning via the engineering of self-paced learning with typically developing students, preschoolers with intellectual disabilities, adolescents with emotional and behavioral problems, learners with autism spectrum disorders, college students, and adult learners. For over a decade, she has worked at the forefront of merging evidence-based educational methods with new and emerging technologies, including selecting technologies that incorporate adaptive instructional systems to support personalized learning. As a vice president at Headsprout, she led the design, development, and dissemination of the company's Internet-based reading programs and oversaw their implementation in over 1,500 public and private schools. These programs featured built-in, data-based decision-making, and real-time, individualized use of data to inform instruction. In 2007–2008 she served as president of the Association for Behavior Analysis International. Currently an associate professor of pediatrics at the University of Massachusetts Medical School, Twyman's work involves building meaningful instructional technology programs for use with all learners.

Christine Woyshner, Ed.D., is professor of education at Temple University, where she coordinates the social studies certification program and serves as chair of the Teaching and Learning Department. She has written extensively on social studies education and curriculum, with a particular emphasis on diversifying the K–12 curriculum. Woyshner earned her doctorate at Harvard University's Graduate School of Education. In addition to publishing numerous articles and book chapters, she is author or co-editor of *Minding Women: Reshaping the Educational Realm*; *Social Education in the Twentieth Century: Curriculum and Context for Citizenship*; *The Educational Work of Women's Organizations, 1890–1960*; *The National PTA, Race, and Civic Engagement, 1897–1970*; *Histories of Social Studies and Race, 1865–2000*; and *Leaders in Social Education: Intellectual Self-Portraits*.